## You Can Use the Stars to Improve Your Sex Life

"One of the most popular misconceptions about astrology is that after you've had your horoscope drawn up, you just sit back and wait for it all to happen. On the contrary, your horoscope is merely a map or outline of your potential; it is up to you to seize upon your opportunities and gifts and make the most of them to overcome your negative aspects.

"What this book is designed to do is indicate pathways and offer guidelines which will help you to better understand yourself and those with whom you may have liaisons in the present or future as well as enable you to get a better grasp on your love and sex nature...."

—From *Astrology for Lovers*

**ASTROLOGY FOR LOVERS**
is an original
*Pocket Book* edition.

# Astrology for Lovers

by
## Jeanne Rejaunier

with
## Lu Ann Horstman

"who to love...and how to love them"

with
## Rhymes by Mother Goose

PUBLISHED BY POCKET BOOKS NEW YORK

The charts appearing on pages 70-110, 114-116, 143-151, 154-157, 160-162, 165-166, and 169 are reprinted from **Write Your Own Horoscope**, by Joseph F. Goodavage, copyright, ©, 1968, by Joseph F. Goodavage, Member of The Society of Magazine Writers. Reprinted by permission of The New American Library, Inc., New York.

Portions of "A City Kind of Love" (copyright, ©, 1970, by Gail Sheehy) appearing on pages 13-14 are taken from **New York** Magazine, February 16, 1970.

**ASTROLOGY FOR LOVERS**

POCKET BOOK edition published October, 1971

Standard Book Number: 671-78047-6.

Printed in the U.S.A.

# Astrology for Lovers

*Twinkle Twinkle, Little Star*
*How I wonder what you are!*
*Up above the world so high,*
*Like a diamond in the sky.*

# Sex, the Life Force

*We are all in the dumps*
*For Diamonds are trumps;*
*The kittens are gone to St. Paul's!*
*The babies are bit,*
*The moon's in a fit,*
*And the Houses are built without walls.*

This book is about astrology and your sex life. First of all, we hope you have one—a sex life, that is. Everyone is born with a horoscope. The other has never been a birthright. If you find yourself one of the unfortunates who has been denied this basic pleasure, maybe this book can be of some benefit to you. If you are already in the groove with someone, maybe we can help you stay in there. Or should you be one of those unlucky ones who've ended up there with the wrong person—chances are in that case it's more of a rut than a groove—maybe we'll be able to help you out, too.

To begin with, let's discuss sex. It's one of the most talked about subjects around today. That probably says more about the basic American attitude toward it than a book ever could. It may also have to do with the fact that whether or not we have a sex life, we all have a sex drive. Of course not everyone expresses it in the same manner. Some sublimate it, others exaggerate it, and there are those who repress it all together. Some are given to license and perversion. It would seem today the world is in a state of confusion on this subject, the likes of which many cannot remember witnessing over the past decades. All this can be explained astrologically, as can the "sex revolution" and the new emphasis on "anything goes" with the consequent deviation and aberration of all sorts cropping into the forefront everywhere.

3

Even the Supreme Court has trouble in accurately defining obscenity. Who, then, can be the judge of what is "aberrant behavior"? Perhaps we could say that when an unusual desire gets out of control and there is a constant demand for its fulfillment plaguing one's psyche, when one sacrifices one's own personal needs, or when one is driven to any activity that diminishes his innate dignity as a human being or is demeaning to another person, his behavior is aberrant. And as far as "normal" or desirable sexual behavior is concerned, it seems no one has ever come up with a rule more applicable than Aristotle's old golden mean or "the happy medium" as it is often called today, as apropos now as it ever was in the glorious days of Greece; blessed are the few who have attained it.

There seems to be little doubt in anyone's mind that no one single person had more to do with shaping twentieth-century thinking and actual behavior in this area than Sigmund Freud. We're just now getting around to separating the wheat from the chaff in a lot of his concepts and theories. Freud saw man as centered in sex, never giving much credit to the possibility that man possessed a "soul" or "spirit" as did his disciple and sometime colleague, Carl Jung, who, incidentally, became quite involved in astrology himself. Freud emphasized sex, above all, in the physical sense, how it grows out of an instinctive biological need and reflects organic pressures and the need to release these tensions in the orgasm. He used the word "libido" as applied to the energy of this need. Sex, in the most basic physical sense, then, is a need conditioned by chemical changes, its physical aim being the discharge of tension, its fulfillment characterized by release. This need exists in different proportions in different individuals, and can readily be identified in one's astrological chart.

But, alas, there is far more to sex than Freud suspected, much more than a chemical itch and tension. Sex is the union of polarities, of the electric current of the male and the magnetic current of the female.

Then, as if things weren't bad enough already for Western folk, Kinsey had to come along with his startling statistics on the amount of women who had never experienced orgasm. The men, of course, did not share this problem nor were they aware that concentrating sex pleasure locally and genitally only brings temporary alleviation of tension. This attitude culminated finally in the American *Playboy*-oriented male whose sex drive has become like a monkey on his back, driving him on an endless, frantic quest to discharge his energy as often as and wherever possible, only to find himself in a vicious circle of the perpetuation of his own guilt, frustration and sex hang-ups, hating himself after each futile, slipshod, hasty conquest. (But not nearly as much as the woman does.)

Alas, there is far more to sex than an orgasm, far more. The creative power of love depends on current and control, vibration and energy levels, and the underlying concealed unconscious. Sex intensity is the Life Force. When each unit of the polarity meets head-on dead center, an illuminating experience is the result. A great power is released in its totality; all atoms of the body and spirit are sparked and generated, not just the genitals. In lower sex the resulting spark is not felt by the whole organism, but is experienced only in part, due to the inability of the person or persons involved to experience totality. The couple involved in higher sex provide a conduit for cosmic force flowing through them on the earth plane, a tremendous power radiating from them, polarizing the surrounding atmosphere.

Sex is creative energy, the same energy which inspires artists and the great Saints and Masters. This energy begins as an impulse at the root of the spinal column—or Kundalini as it is called in Indian philosophy, the tree of life or serpent power. In Tibet today the Masters still choose disciples to initiate into Tantra Yoga, the Yoga of sex. Through proper principles, some of which will be explained and illustrated later on in the book, man can achieve sex potency enabling him to extend the ecstasy of orgasm for an hour or more, rather than just the few brief seconds he now achieves.

"Slow down," the popular rock song warns. "You move too fast. . . ."

If more American women would develop their Kundalini power, their men would never stray. If more American men would develop their Kundalini power, women would be their eager recipients. Now doesn't this sound like a better formula for America's sex life than a quickie in the back of a '39 Chevy? A flash of thigh from a *Playboy* bunny? A skin flick or a "squash" on the subway during rush hour?

Of course, no one wants to take his or her time with a

partner who turns out to be in any way undesirable. In that case, one would just as soon get it over with. Living as we do so much today on the surface and adhering to the importance of externals, mistakes in choices of sex and love partners are often caused by the criteria of our judgment. Astrology can act as a wonderful guide in this respect, helping us to know ourselves better as well as others, and to activate wiser choices, where sex harmony and love will find a ground from which to develop.

However, with the alarming increase in the divorce rate in this country,* it is hard to imagine that all of these well-meaning couples were badly aspected astrologically. More likely, many of them, well suited to each other in the beginning, grew apart as tension, irritation and even hostility and impotence set in because of shortcomings in their sex relations. In many cases, long after their cessation of attempts at having sex, the spiritual love of the two people still persists. In a Victorian morality, the pattern of marriage deterioration is often thus: it is usually the woman who, after having had her children, finds the sex act which she always considered somewhat repugnant, now unnecessary, and kicks her husband out of bed and sometimes even out of the bedroom. This often causes him to get out of the house, either altogether, or at least during those times when he is driven to fulfill himself through extramarital activities. In this case, both partners suffer untold physical and spiritual deprivation although it is the man who is most conscious of it; yet one cannot entirely blame the woman as she is obviously the victim of her puritanical upbringing and more than likely also of a husband whose similar background hang-ups prevent him from becoming open and free enough in the sex area to ever be more than a clumsy, inept lover, completely incapable of helping an uptight wife overcome her problems and fears.

Wrought during the beginning of this century we see around us a generation of lonely men who inhabit bars where they seek out a temporary sex partner, and often a new mate, while their wife usually remains without, her sex drive having been repressed for so long she barely recognizes that

* Forty-one percent of all marriages in America end in divorce (or one out of three) and statisticians claim that if this unprecedented rate of increase continues, the ratio in ten years will be 1:1. One divorce for every marriage! We won't stand a chance!

she has one. While the men are attending services at the corner pub, their women form asexual circles often centered around the church, where they sublimate their loneliness and frustration into a kind of pious, self-righteous way of life they consider "holy." It is ironic that what they seek they are actually running from; for sex, when it transcends sensation, can open up vistas of ecstasy where there is a higher awareness which can be likened to mystical states. For many ordinary people who never have the time or opportunity to pursue such teachings as metaphysics, mysticism and the art of meditation, the greatest single opportunity of achieving a high level of consciousness is available in proper understanding and functioning of sex. Nothing else brings us so near the limit of human possibility beyond which lies the unknown. *La petite mort,* the French say, and this is apropos, approaching the eternal love-death enigma.

These days we hear a lot of talk about vibrations. "I didn't dig his vibrations," or "She has good vibes." In astrology it is not just the planets themselves that affect us but their vibrations. Actually all of life is vibration and it is only appropriate that at the dawning of the age of Aquarius* we would be more conscious of the metaphysical dimension of our environment; and a relief it is, having just come out of an era that was overly concerned with technology, physics and chemistry. From out of the vibrations the many creatures manifest, each with his own specific frequency or rate. We all tend to gravitate toward those with like vibrations to our own, and there we feel most comfortable, in that one special place where we most belong. There, with that particular one whose vibration frequency is most complementary to our own is the closest we'll ever come to finding a "home" here in this mundane, earthly plane. Have you found yours yet? If not, read on. If so, read on anyway.

Our degree of vibration and frequency determines our sex need and even who our children will be. At the time of conception a certain vibratory rate is set up, determined by the frequencies of the two people involved, their degree of caring and love for each other and for their potential child being conceived at that moment. The vibration rate of the child can be neither above nor below, only equal to that rate

---

* Some astrologers say we're already in it; others say it won't be here until we're well into the twenty-first century.

of vibration and intensity of the parents' energy field when the child is conceived. Here is another place where astrology can be helpful—as a guideline in the consideration and comparison of all the aspects of the astrological chart, in order to reveal the sexual compatibility and harmony potential of two individuals. Studies have found that where this is taken into careful consideration beforehand, marriages are much more likely to be lasting and harmonious, in the higher sex that occurs and prevails as a result.

When wrong combinations are mated and a woman has a positive reaction to a man who reacts negatively to her, lower sex results, as well as pathological quarreling, irritation and even fighting on a physical level. We're sure you've been around these couples; if you're within their vibratory range at a restaurant or other public place, you may want to get up and leave, the friction is so great and the pervading atmosphere so unpleasant. You can sometimes hear them arguing a block away. These ill-matched types get together because of external reasons and circumstances and improper knowledge of their vibratory rate and astrological influences.

In the case of union of positive types, they're a joy to be with, emanating love and mutual goodwill to each other and everyone else who is fortunate enough to be around them. Always trusting of each other, they are as if magnetized together by an irresistible force from within, which distance or all of the prying, often envious and even jealous humanity around (who said "all the world loves a lover"?) * cannot alter or affect, so strong is their vibratory response to each other and their ESP type love communication. In sex they do not have to rely on manipulative techniques, they are so strongly drawn to each other by seeming forces greater than themselves, and nothing can ever part them or come between their inward relationship or prevent them from fulfilling each other sexually and spiritually. This is the kind of high attraction and relationship that lends itself to that lengthy, fulfilled lovemaking encounter we were talking about earlier, not just those disgusting quickies in the car. It seems to be that meeting of the missing half; the union with the "soulmate" that Plato spoke of in his *Symposium*.

---

* Look what happened to Romeo and Juliet! Hamlet and Ophelia! Bonnie and Clyde!

Here is where your spiritual development is important, in making sure that your partner is one who is desirable and attractive. The stronger and more evolved you are, the more likely you will attract an intellectually and emotionally appealing person, and the greater will be your recognition, understanding, preparedness and appreciation for each other. In finding this person, affinities, vibrations and your degree of development reach the subconscious of the other party. Thus, even on an unconscious level, you are aware of each other, all of which carries over into a conscious recognition of the particular personality who is here to help you further your destiny, development and fulfillment on a soul level.

There is really no choice in the matter, when looking at it from a metaphysical standpoint, only the inexorable, impersonal laws to which we are all subject, just as on the physical level "water reaches its own level." When you look at your love partner, you're seeing yourself, your inner state and the exact stage you're at in your development. You may look at that person disgustedly and say, "What am *I* doing with such a creep! I wish he'd drop dead!" or "Imagine a person like me, wasted on someone as stupid as she!" What you are unwilling to accept then is that he or she is the one exactly suited to the awakening at this particular moment of certain soul qualities necessary for the evolution of your Divine Expression. The mere fact that you *cannot* or *do not* leave this person and seek a new partner is indicative of this. And it will be only when you have gained soul qualities above and beyond your current status that you will be given the strength to step out of this position and enter into a higher, more appealing one.

There is no escaping the truth but there are those who avoid confronting and admitting it through various means, one of which is the sloughing off of one's mate as someone who is merely an instrument for sexual gratification. The people guilty of this often categorize other areas of their lives similarly. So and so is for sex, so and so is for social encounters, so and so is for intellectual stimulation and so forth, all the time revealing the obvious lack of integration in their own personalities. Today both men and women will refer to someone as "a good lay and nothing else." In thinking it is possible to cheapen and "use" others to fulfill a biological need, isn't it obvious how degrading it is to both parties? Too many people today are involved in erotic love alone. This is all that those prowling married people are after in their eternal, frantic quest—a few cheap thrills—instead of dealing with their own partners' needs. Don't you sometimes yearn to tell all those lying cheats who come up to you with a tale of woe to "get lost"? "Go home and stoke your own home fires instead of trying to start another one that you won't be able to keep lit!"

Nature has offered man in erotic love the opportunity for transcendence. Unfortunately in our modern society we find too many who seek sex for its own sake, exploiting it, advertising it, selling it and, with the exception of the military industrial complex, practically the whole economy is built around it. Somebody must have misunderstood! We didn't say "sell" love, not war"! Of course, this attitude can't help rub off onto us, making it a constant challenge to our own inner battle for honesty and true love.

Today there is a trend on the part of the young to try to remove the puritanical hang-ups our society has always believed in and perpetuated in every possible way, primarily the fallacy that the subject of sex was dirty.* War and murder have always been clean and acceptable, fit for the front page of *The New York Times,* whereas sex in print was something for which pornographers were jailed. In emphasizing their point that nothing is dirty about sex, save what is in the beholder's mind, the kids often lead the pornographers in a race to use every four letter word in the English language openly and repeatedly in classrooms, underground papers and movies, on records, and even in television interviews. Of course, if you think the things the kids are saying are bad, you should open your eyes to the world they have to live in! And so what started out as an intellectually based and spiritually motivated protest has deteriorated into a state where the "hard core" people have taken over, flooding the newsstands with tabloids that would make such an enthusiast of the four letter word as Lenny Bruce turn over in his grave. The obscenity and language revolution has reached such vast proportions that Ralph Ginzburg, who still has some obscenity case proceedings pending, says he is offended by what he

---

* The youth-sex revolution is further discussed in the section on Pluto.

sees in the pornographic bookstores and on the newsstands. "I am carnal and sold under sin," said St. Paul in Romans VII, Verses 14 and 15, "for that which I do I allow not: for that I would, that I do not: but what I hate, that I do." I guess we've all felt that way at some time or other, haven't we? Christian doctrine and teachings can in many cases be considered one of the greatest sources of the great confusion that abounds everywhere in Western culture. In Verse 18 Paul goes on to say, "For I know that in me (that is, in my flesh) dwelleth no good thing."

It is pretty discouraging, especially when we're trying to alleviate sex guilt and when our doctors tell us sex is necessary for our health and full expression of life; without it there is a decline in the body mechanism and a decrease in powers causing the organism to work to less than its fullest efficiency. Hippocrates himself said sex is necessary to the circulation, and any sort of abstinence in this area can upset the normal balance and cause illness. So it seems that to deny sex, to block the flow of this life force, is unnatural, and can be as sinful as overindulgence, except in the case of highly developed religious people for whom the very desire has been transcended in their spiritual sublimation and transmutation. Furthermore, those people who seek to suppress anything dealing openly with sex, who endanger young people by blowing their minds with prudery and the unwholesome attitude that sex is dirty, are just as harmful to society as those who go out of their way to portray sex in the most unattractive, perverted ways.

Caught in a world that seems polarized by extremes of permissiveness and puritanism, what are those of us who do not fall into either category to do? Those of us who are earnestly and open-mindedly seeking some kind of a code by which we can conduct ourselves and deal maturely and courageously with this consciousness expanding, transcendent experience, one approaching the Dionysian ecstasy Nietzsche describes in the *Birth of Tragedy*, followed by reverence, reflection and beatitude similar to Nietzsche's Apollonian quality. But what is it about these subtle states of consciousness and ecstasy of union that makes man prefer to cop out with some cheap, noninvolved erotic thrills? Why, when an act of higher love offers the possibility of shedding off all earthly reality, when the pure energy of love can be poured from every cell of the body into the fingertips, toes, the entire body of another, stirring, merging, invigorating and giving a renewed current of life and spirit to each partner; why is man afraid to accept this state that transcends words; why is he afraid of growth, change, and the unfamiliar, fearful of the unknown and the beyond to which sex is so irrevocably linked; why in his cowardice does he choose to "pass out of love's threshing floor, into the seasonless world, where you shall laugh, but not all of your laughter, and weep, but not all of your tears"?

André Breton has said, "Hardly anyone dares to face with open eyes the great delight of love," a quote which leaves room on the part of the authors to reflect on just what we're doing entering into this sacred area where even angels fear to tread, where only the pornographer rushes in and then obviously feels comfortable enough to stay with his dirty pen and ink, and capitalize.

Oh, they talk with great gusto and bravado about their conquests, the ones who seek to temporalize sex. The cool generation likes to verbalize each instant of its lovemaking in a vain attempt to perpetuate its actuality, and maybe their own. Perhaps this is why we've become such a civilization of talkers, in the hope that the hearing of our own voices will reassure us of our existence. And then when it's over, the rapping doesn't stop yet, because he or she tells his or her buddies how great it was, further minimizing the act. All of this, to avoid the passage of time, and the necessity of growth and change, and in many cases to laugh off an inner sadness and lack of fulfillment that pervades so many today. Dr. Wilhelm Reich observed that those who actually have the capacity to become truly involved in and to appreciate and enjoy sex do not (cannot) continue their "game level" conversation during lovemaking, some are unable to speak at all, except to utter phrases or words of love, adoration and tenderness. The ones who rap constantly don't know it, but they're incapable of full sexual surrender, according to Reich, one of the greatest bio-sex experts of this century.

With these people, sex is a game, a point of surface communication or contact with others, too easily explored, too easily exploited, too easily dispensed with and then too easily forgotten. (We're not worried about offending any of these people with all of our various put-downs, because they're probably not reading this book anyway. To them, sex is never a problem—they *THINK* they know where it's at. Besides, they're usually so insensate, it's impossible to insult any of them).

Warren Beatty, one of the most attractive, sought-after actors in Hollywood did not speak on their behalf in a recent interview when he said: "My overall feeling is that too little time is spent discovering the ability to get to know one person and to live with one person and the productivity that can come out of—the happiness that can come out of—simply living a life with someone else. There's a tremendous anti-romantic trend that might be an escape from the enormous amount of work it takes to live unselfishly with one person. . . . I mean, a person is just given every way *not* to need or to understand another person. It's very, very easy to avoid a relationship now. It's so easy to get a divorce. It's so easy not to get pregnant. It's so easy to do this, do that, to move in, move out. I mean *life* is a lot easier. I think the ease with which we move in and out of responsibilities makes a person resistant to the rough going in any relationship, whether it's a friendship or a romance or a business relationship, or whatever."

Gail Sheehy in discussing the new morality and love in New York City says, "The average family unit in New York is occupied by 1.2 people. If it weren't for economics, whole town might be a singles resort. But! The heart is a lonely apartment hunter. Hyphenated names. This is not love but economics.

"Just how many young couples are joined in a Greenthal lease rather than a marriage license is impossible to say. But rental agents notice the increase. 'The couple usually says they are going to be married, and we write down on the application *wife to be*. We really don't care,' says Green at Greenthal."

Miss Sheehy says that much of the intimate love New Yorkers share is exchanged outside of the city. "On weekend farms in wonderful podunk towns, in carriage houses being restored, hideaways in the Caribbean—anywhere off the compulsory entertainment track—New Yorkers can be found searching for a place to love and breathe.

"But most people live in Manhattan because they are in love with power. They exchange the kind of love displayed in *Women's Wear Daily* and this week's fashionable night spot. Beyond the urban pressures of time, space, absence of nature and the insane cost of real estate, New York has its own speciality in love-slaying."

And hasn't it long been known that New York sets the pace for the rest of the country? Maybe we can take heart in the fact that Miss Sheehy refers to this as only the "visible" love in the city.

"New York hides a surprising number of long-term devoted couples. They work at invisibility. At the end of the glaringly public work day, they meet for dinner in a favorite Hungarian restaurant. They keep the name to themselves and take home a doggie bag to the apartment they are building from its retaining walls out, a home seen only by real friends."

But there are still those of us who have not found and are still looking for the satisfaction and security of that one lover with whom we can bask in the glory of our love and rest in the blessing that we are no longer alone. We are not about to settle for the philosophy *Playboy* tries to sell us, the kind that breeds the unfulfillment and lack of character Beatty was talking about. Nor do we feel that sex is vile or shameful or require that it be sanctified as a sacrament. We find it naturally sacred in itself, and our need for it genuine, stimulated by our plight of aloneness and the need to find psychic ful fillment.

And so until that time we find someone whose attitude similar to our own, someone who brings to a sexual relationship the necessary ingredients of respect, responsibility, the capacity for concern and caring, we go on in our search for our own advancement and development, fulfilling and working out whatever Karma has sent us here (which is most likely where we will meet our soulmate anyway) and we delve into all of the ancient, esoteric teachings and metaphysics, looking for the answer, the key to the understanding of ourselves and the world around us, our destiny and romantic fulfillment. We don't limit ourselves to the modern poets, philosophers, scientists and psychologists, but we reach out to such age-old studies as that of the stars and their effect upon us. As did Cleopatra, Queen Elizabeth, and many before us we reach back in time to the city of Babylon in Mesopotamia, the source of the study known as . . .

# *Astrology,* the Life Science

*O that I was where I would be,*
*Then would I be where I am not;*
*But where I am I must be,*
*And where I would be I can not.*

Want to be the life of the next get-together you attend? Before you arrive, memorize a bit of data on each of the twelve Sun Signs,* let the word get around that you're an astrology buff and just wait for someone to start the onslaught of inquiries as to the horoscope of each of the guests. After you've given them their basic character analyses, proceed to tell each of the seekers after truth a lot of good things that are coming up for them. Such tidbits are readily available in the daily newspaper, little gems like, "TAURUS: Move with enthusiasm to take care of those tasks you've been procrastinating about for the past couple of weeks." What Taurus, or any other sign for that matter, doesn't have something he's neglected to do, even if it's just to return some overdue library books? "LIBRA: You will have pleasant encounters while traveling this month on a journey by either rail or water." What's to stop this from meaning the commute you take every day by subway or the Staten Island Ferry? If the forecast for Capricorn should happen to read, "Don't despair over that large assembly you lock horns with in the A.M. You have the perseverance to overcome this resistance and prevail," Nixon reading the *Washington Post* over his early morning cup of coffee anticipates rougher than usual opposition on a bill he's trying to pass through the Senate; and an exterminator from Brooklyn, born New

* These are listed on page 28.

17

Year's Eve during the Depression, loads his truck with more than the usual amount of DDT for an encounter with pestilence more resilient than he'd hoped for that morning. On and on go the generalizations, until one of the greatest of all life sciences is reduced to one of the most popular parlor game/ego trips of our time. Nor does it end there. Years later when you run into one of these acquaintances on the street or at the unemployment office he will open with, "I'm John so-and-so . . . remember . . . the Cancer from the party. Have you found out anything new about my sign? How are things for us Moon children this year?"

We call on an expert if we need brain surgery and even when the car breaks down we wouldn't dream of going to the corner bookstore and picking up a volume on automotive engineering. Yet if a paperback on astrology doesn't pinpoint all of our idiosyncrasies or the morning tabloid tells us to ". . . beware of troublesome irritations with spouse . . ." and we're in a state of confirmed bachelorhood, we see fit to debunk the whole science. What those guilty of such conclusions fail to take into consideration is that it is impossible to generalize and hit the nail on the head. There are only twelve Zodiacal signs and surely more people than that in the world; therefore one's Sun Sign can't possibly offer more than the sketchiest outline of general life expression, even ugh in your observations of the many analyses you ha read of your particular sign, you might have found much that was applicable. Naturally, being the most powerful planetary body affecting us—so strong it holds the earth in orbit, gives heat and light that make plant, animal and human life possible on our earth—the Sun's placement in our chart does warrant a lot of recognition but still this does not mean it exerts the greatest influence over us. It is the arrangement of all of the planets and various factors that determine one's full astrological makeup, often modifying the influence of the Sun Sign to the point where it might even be overshadowed by a stronger Ascendant or Moon Sign. When you look at your horoscope, you're seeing a wheel of time that represents your individual life expression; thus when a competent astrologer does a chart, he or she requires specific data as to time and place of birth so that the information contained therein is exact and complete. This, then, is known as the natal chart, the importance of which we have records dating back to the third century in the tablets of Joshua ben Levi, where Rabbi Hanina says to his pupils: "Go to the son of Levi and tell him that the fate of a person is not decided by the constellations of the day but by those of the *hour*."

One of the most popular misconceptions about astrology is that after you've had your horoscope drawn up, you just sit back and wait for it all to happen. On the contrary, your horoscope is merely a map or outline of your potential; it is up to you to seize upon your opportunities and gifts and make the most of them to overcome your negative aspects. Quite the opposite of developing a fatalistic attitude, your astrological consultation should leave you with even greater determination to become the master of your destiny, once familiar with a clear picture of the benefits and liabilities with which you've come into this life. This is where a responsible, talented astrologer will come in handy and you'll have to use your own wit and contacts in seeking one out as it is impossible for us to recommend any. Correct and constructive interpretation of a chart is as much a gift as it is a method, as astrology is as much an art as it is a science. Much as in the field of medicine where a doctor's knowledge of the body and its function does not guarantee his ability to come up with the proper diagnosis every time, so can an astrologer, regardless of his knowledge of the layout of the heavens and skill in the technique of plotting one's relationship to them, give you a bum steer.

Planets can be benefic and malefic. This is true of the natal chart, the plan we are given at birth, as it is of the solar return, or chart which is progressed with each year. As the planets move in their orbits, certain forces and vibrations are unleashed and set in motion which influence both our personal life and the world at large. Astrology is a very deep study and to fully understand the influence of all the various aspects, angles and vibrations acting upon us is a practice requiring years of application. Charlatans and frauds run rampant in this field as in any other, of course. Perhaps it will be on the recommendation of a trusted friend or associate that you will meet your greatest success in finding the astrologer whose services will be helpful to you instead of detrimental.

A yardstick one might use to help discern the validity of a reader's ability is whether or not the astrologer in question is predisposed toward predicting trends in one's life and propensities one has toward certain talents and behavior rather than actual names, dates, places and events. That such divination is possible and commonly revealed through the vast resources available overhead, there is no doubt. However, much of this prognostication can also be attributed to the psychic ability of the person interpreting the chart. We suggest the science of astrology per se is more realistically utilized if one employs it for the study of cycles, harmonious and discordant times and places to pursue an objective, and for the revelation of directions affairs are more likely to take with the most profitable results. Timing is one of the most important elements in success of any kind, be it planting, harvesting, building, marrying, speaking up, keeping quiet or whatever. When we get into harmony with our universal pattern through the study of our relationship to it, we find that things begin to fall into place at the proper time, as if by magic, and all of the questions of prophecy we once had are answered.

Another determining factor as to the quality of an astrologer's instrumentation of the science is his point of view toward the many squares, retrogrades and other configurations which can mean struggle, thwarting of purpose and barriers to success. Many people are dismayed when they learn they have these things in their chart, but actually such challeng can be beneficial. While it is true that an unevolved soul respond negatively to adverse planetary vibration, history full of Abraham Lincoln and Horatio Alger stories. Our country was built on the foundation of underprivileged people from the most humble beginnings fighting against innumerable odds to make great their destinies and that of their country, as well.

Over and over again the charts of great people demonstrate their ability to overcome. Therefore it should be the task of every reputable astrologer to point out that the obstacles one encounters in his horoscope and ultimately in his experiences can be his greatest blessing, if he looks upon life as a learning and refining process, a testing ground where the chaff is being sifted out from the wheat or worthwhile substance in his soul and personality. So whether we wake up and find ourselves on the wrong side of the bed or the tracks, we do have the ability to accomplish our destiny and should set out to attain our goal no matter what the circumstances. The true sport, then, is to defy the stars, and the purpose of studying the chart is to better familiarize oneself with the enemy, odds or whatever we prefer to call it. Astrology can help us to fulfill the well-known prayer by Reinhold Niebuhr: "O God, grant us the serenity to accept what cannot be changed, courage to change what should be changed and the wisdom to distinguish the one from the other."

Do not be the resigned or passive person who uses astrology as a cop-out, who sits back and says, "It's my Karma. You see, I have all these squares in my chart. That's why I'm such a square." Remember, the stars impel, they do not compel. Shakespeare was into mysticism and his plays contain many astrological and occult allusions, yet he knew that the effects of the stars upon the flood tides of humanity and on the individual were not inextricable. "The fault, dear Brutus, is not in our stars, but in ourselves, that we are underlings."

What this book is designed to do, then, is indicate pathways and offer guidelines which will help you to better understand yourself and those with whom you may have liaisons in the present or future, as well as enable you to get a better grasp on your love and sex nature which may be a hidden quality or quantity about which you've previously known very little. It's possible you have had erroneous notions about yourself and have been mischanneling your energies and wasting your sexual prowess instead of utilizing it to your advantage. The chapter on Tantra Yoga should be most helpful in getting yourself "together."

Every person is two-faceted in that he has an outer and inner nature. If these two natures are in harmony, chances are you're a fairly well-adjusted person; you express what you feel and your desires are fulfilled and actualized. But should your outer and inner natures not be in harmony with one another, you may have strange desires you don't quite understand; in your attempts to fulfill them you are left frustrated; you never meet the right person; your affairs end disastrously and all you ever find yourself turning on to are freaky scenes. Your problem could be any number of afflictions, all determinable in your astrological chart.

For instance, one prominent playboy of our acquaintance, a Pisces, has his medicine chest stuffed with amyl nitrate, a drug commonly used in the treatment of heart patients, as he

feels unable to perform sexually without the boost it gives
his libido. His warped psyche can best be viewed through his
astrological chart, fraught with oppositions and those lower
aspects which manifest themselves as weakness and negativity,
as well as in his statement: "I will never love a woman. Man
is a beast and should act out his animal nature. Love is
weakness. Tenderness is weakness. To be masculine is to be
bestial in every sense of the word."

All types of sexual expression, from the highest to the
lowest, are readable in the chart, and astrology is now becoming part and parcel of many a shrink's treatment. It was
the well-known psychiatrist Carl Jung who said, "We are
born at a given moment, in a given place and, like vintage
years of wine, we have the qualities of the year and the
season in which we are born." He often would have a patient's
chart drawn up as the first step in his orientation and inves-
tigation of his patient's basic makeup, and kept an astrologer
as a member of his staff for this, so aware was he of the
numerous parallels between a man's psychological nature and
hang-ups, and his horoscope.

Interest in astrology has endured since time immemorial,
and while its current rebirth of interest in the United States
deals for the most part in vague generalities the science itself
does not. It has remained pretty much the same since the
dawn of history when it was discovered by the Babylonian
priests, only changing enough to update itself and incorporate
into its system any new astral discoveries as they occur. In
spite of astrology's having kept company with such distin-
guished men as Copernicus, Galileo, Sir Isaac Newton, Nostra-
damus—who used it some five hundred years ago to predict
the discovery of America, the atomic bomb and Napoleon's
birth and rise to power—and its more recent recognition by
Dr. Carl Jung, the Western press has never been overly kind
to it. The *Encyclopaedia Britannica* ends its general descrip-
tion/put-down of astrology by condescending: "Scholarship,
in its concern with the history of ideas, shows how easily
genuine elements of knowledge can combine with illusory
notions to form grandiose systems of thought in which the
mind is content to dwell for a time." Whew! . . . a sentence
which could hardly hold together under the rigors of the
scientific scrutiny of which its authors claim to be the pro-
ponents. (Well, folks, at least we're giving you both sides of

the picture.) They go on to say, "As a popular pastime or superstition, however, astrology still engages the attention of civilized people." Not only do they call us *civilized,* they call us *people!*

Still, cultures exist where without the blessing of the stars houses are not built, marriages do not take place, business transactions are not carried out, ceremonies are not fixed and the dead are not buried, for there are days that are favorable and unfavorable for each of these occasions. Recently in India the wedding of Nepal's crown prince took place at three A.M. At one point in the proceedings, the royal astrologer took over, abruptly halting a huge procession for three quarters of an hour until the time was auspicious for it to proceed on schedule.

As we pointed out before, most astrology books of necessity are superficial. However, in this book we are attempting to give you a rounder than usual portrait of yourself with particular emphasis on the sex nature. Bear in mind though that astrology is a lifetime study. Beyond the solar system to which the earth belongs are many other systems, galaxies and nebulae. All of life is interrelated and the effect of any cause set in motion is reverberated throughout infinity. "Are not two sparrows sold for a farthing? and one of them shall not on the ground without your Father. But the very hairs on ur head are all numbered," Matthew states in Chapter X, erse 29 of the New Testament. The synthesis of other solar systems in relation to our own astrologically necessitates not only years of esoteric study but also setting up additional charts. One Los Angeles astrologer of our acquaintance, Roberta Wilson, who has been studying and teaching astrology for about sixty of her eighty-some-odd years now, tells us a good ninety hours are needed to do a fuller, more detailed "cosmic chart" such as those put out by herself and the rest of the staff of the Los Angeles College of Astrology.

Roberta, in addition to employing the planets, houses, their rulers and the various other aspects ordinarily used in astrology, finds it helpful in doing her charts to place the nodes and "planets X & Y" as well as the "KSY factor," the Lilith and the fixed stars. Believe it or not, from your fixed stars, Roberta will tell you whether or not you'll "have a peaceful end and a good-looking corpse."

But assuming you readers are at present a good distance

from this fate, let's proceed further into cosmic sex and how it can be your present realization. Yes, astrology can help you to understand your sex nature better and thus bring about greater fulfillment of your libido. Once you have recognized and are able to examine your own pattern, it is just a matter of looking at the facts squarely and deciding where to go from there.

Urban living and our vast technological resources have succeeded to a great degree in isolating us from nature and our innate harmony with its rhythms. Now ecologists are fast making us aware that if we don't get back to these fundamental truths and once again align ourselves with the laws of nature, we may face serious pollution problems, a worldwide food shortage, and other disasters resulting from an imbalance of the Divine Scheme. And so it is in our personal lives, too, that we must learn to meditate upon and delve into the mysteries and truths connected with our beings; the new perspective gained through the ancient art of astrology and the interpretation of these truths in the light of our own lives can increase our serenity and understanding.

To a great extent the world is afflicted with a form of apathy, a spiritual lethargy and a feeling of hopelessness. Few people understand their true place in the scheme of things. Astrology can also help us to conquer our fear of life, our fear of meaninglessness, for it can teach us that there is indeed a great purpose for each and every one of our being here, that every person has been placed alongside us for a reason and no meetings in life are chance or accidental. Many opportunities are given to us which are left unsuspected and unrecognized and therefore unfulfilled. That is why it is important to look at one's horoscope as a road-map rather than the outline of a tour that has been preplanned to the last inch. Yes, there are certain predestined goals on the map that we are bound to hit—but how we reach them, the paths we take, is left strictly to our own choice and free will. We can travel at whatever pace we choose, detour if we like, or even waste many years sidetracked in the boggy marshes of misspent time and energy; maybe we won't get there at all this trip. But whatever worthwhile fruits we are able to reap from this life—or, should it be the other way, the ravages of our wasted, wanton years—will determine our Karma for next time round. An astrologer

# You, the Life Expressers

| Your Birth Date | Your Sun Sign | Ruling Planet | Pictograph | Symbol | Element | Part of Body |
|---|---|---|---|---|---|---|
| March 21—April 20 | ARIES | MARS | ♈ | RAM | FIRE | Head |
| April 21—May 21 | TAURUS | VENUS | ♉ | BULL | EARTH | Throat |
| May 22—June 21 | GEMINI | MERCURY | ♊ | TWINS | AIR | Chest, arms & hands |
| June 22—July 23 | CANCER | MOON | ♋ | CRAB | WATER | Stomach & Breasts |
| July 24—August 23 | LEO | SUN | ♌ | LION | FIRE | Heart & Back |
| August 24—September 23 | VIRGO | MERCURY | ♍ | VIRGIN | EARTH | Intestines |
| September 24—October 23 | LIBRA | VENUS | ♎ | SCALES | AIR | Kidneys |
| October 24—November 22 | SCORPIO | MARS & PLUTO | ♏ | SCORPION | WATER | Sex Organs |
| November 23—December 21 | SAGITTARIUS | JUPITER | ♐ | ARCHER | FIRE | Hips & Thighs |
| December 22—January 20 | CAPRICORN | SATURN | ♑ | SEA GOAT | EARTH | Knees |
| January 21—February 19 | AQUARIUS | URANUS | ♒ | WATER BEARER | AIR | Calves & Ankles |
| February 20—March 20 | PISCES | NEPTUNE | ♓ | FISHES | WATER | Feet |

*As I walked by myself*
*And talked by myself*
*   Myself said unto me,*
*Look to thyself*
*Take care of thyself*
*   For nobody cares for thee.*

*I answered myself*
*And said to myself*
*   In the self-same repartee*
*Look to thyself*
*Or not to thyself*
*   The self-same thing will be.*

## ARIES

You are dynamic, quick, original, energetic, an innovator, the way-shower, blessed with an overwhelming amount of drive and enthusiasm and a passion for adventure, the unknown and even the dangerous. You are not only first in the Zodiac, but first in most enterprises as well. You often pave the way for other more conservative and tenacious signs to follow and fulfill your prophetic aims.

In love, as in all of your other endeavors, you are honest and direct, and have been known to plunge headlong into affairs impulsively and heedlessly, no matter what the consequences; should they be disastrous (and they often are) with equal resilience you just pick up the pieces and start all over again with the same amount of enthusiasm, spontaneously and completely, as you are virtually incapable of a halfway commitment.

In your love habits you are more likely to shun conventions and restrictions than other signs and are sometimes given to impulsive generosity, often to a fault, and can be quite grandiose in your romantic gestures. You are an extrovert who likes a partner who flatters you and keeps you interested by imaginative lovemaking. You are curious and sometimes even attracted to the bizarre. The trick is not to *get* you, but to *keep* you, as you are not naturally drawn to fidelity but can be driven there if you realize the price of losing the partner would be greater than the thrill you are seeking. Aries is a strong sign, and you like to stay on top of your partner. For the females of this sign, the boudoir is a much less offensive place to display this natural aggression than at dinner or at a cocktail party.

When negatively aspected, you can be reckless, indiscriminate, headstrong, audacious, too self-willed, intolerant, impatient, incapable of foresight as to the consequences of your actions and prone to thrust yourself into challenges that are above your head, where you end up cheated and taken advantage of. You will deem yourself honest, but it will be only according to your own self-centered standards. In love affairs you will become bored, and the ardent enthusiasm and impulse with which you entered the involvement will only be equaled by the suddenness with which you will become temperamental and impatient once restlessness and discontent set in.

Those of you on a higher plane are some of the most popular, sought-after sex partners in the Zodiac, with your great charm and irresistible smiles. You perhaps need more mistakes than the average person before you end up with your feet placed firmly on the ground, but once you do you are capable of maintaining a constant, exciting relationship with the opposite sex, chock full of thrills, especially in the sexual area.

## Famous People Born Under The Sign of Aries

Bette Davis, Joan Crawford, Hayley Mills, Hugh O'Brian, Lily Pons, Charles Evans Hughes, Jack Webb, Arturo Toscanini, Johann Sebastian Bach, Pearl Bailey, Gregory Peck, Doris Day, Leopold Stokowski, Alec Guinness, Gloria Swanson, Claudia Cardinale, Julie Christie, Simone Signoret, Jeanne Rejaunier, Warren Beatty, Marlon Brando, Elizabeth Montgomery, Debbie Reynolds, Jane Powell, James Garner, Tennessee Williams, Omar Sharif, Peter Ustinov, John Gavin, Paul Verlaine, Sergei Rachmaninoff, Anatole France, J. P. Morgan, Henry Clay, Arnold Toynbee, Charles Baudelaire, George Arliss, Harry Houdini, William Wordsworth.

## TAURUS

You are an earthy, determined person with a natural, unself-conscious approach toward the opposite sex. You are not the impatient type, nor do you rush into things in life, sex included, yet you are a most loving and devoted sex partner with strong, sensual appetites. You are constant in your affections, conservative, traditional, practical, sometimes materialistic; basically even-tempered (at times even appearing to be lethargic); you can be aroused to quick, sudden passion or anger. You are possessive and sometimes materialistic with an attraction for beauty and the aesthetic, especially in your physical surroundings, and often like to maintain a lavish place for your lovemaking, and indulge in a high style of living. Your home is important to you, often well-appointed, and a showcase for your large collection of books, records, plaques, trophies, antiques and so forth that you are known to amass.

Your approach and reaction to the opposite sex are apt to be slow but strong, and once involved you are more the "one-love" person than the type who is tempted to want sex with a variety of people. You are not overly demonstrative about your emotions, nor are you one to toss about lightly a phrase of endearment.

You lesser evolved Taureans often tend toward excesses in sex, food, drink, spending, and can be even brutal and primitive. With your sometimes sybaritic nature and living habits, you may become jaded after having run the gamut of every possible kind of sexual experience and, once satiated, become suddenly alienated and cold toward your partner. In these natives, constancy becomes downright stubborn "bull-headedness" and you are incapable of change unless you make up your own mind to do so.

Well-aspected Taureans have great magnetism, a soothing, calming presence and especially fine speaking voices, as Taurus rules the throat. Many of the world's great singers are born under this sign. Warmhearted, straightforward, natural, loyal and compassionate, you have a talent for making friends, and once you make one you never give him up. You need good friends, ones who know you well, because sometimes your sensitivity remains hidden behind the facade of a tenacious plodding creature who is content with just a day to day routine. Yet you can be a very amorous and sensual sex partner with the right person and under the right circumstances, which you will often go to great lengths to create. The music, the wines, the colored lights, all the atmosphere and setting will be carefully planned and laid out for the occasion. With your slow, deliberate nature and bent toward hedonism, nothing is too elaborate or grandiose in your lengthy, sensual and often theatrical romantic foreplay. But when you are finished, the curtain can ring down as abruptly as it does at any Broadway opening, with nary a curtain call from the snoring, out-cold Taurus. You had better make sure your partner is equally down-to-earth about the whole matter or at least understands your matter-of-factness. A sensitive Pisces or Cancer or even a probing Aquarius or Libra could find himself or herself out in the cold, left in the lurch, so to speak, if they mistook your supine bliss for lack of caring.

When involved in a permanent relationship you sometimes get bogged down and out of touch with the outside world, letting it all go on around you, as you retire into a hobbit-like kind of domestic security. You should try to cultivate a more flexible nature as you are more likely to just adapt to situations than to really change. Therefore you're more likely to stay even in a bad marriage, and seek sex elsewhere if necessary, rather than rocking the boat with a divorce, while always maintaining a harmonious "happily-married" facade for the outside world. However, if you choose well and find the right partner this very same constancy in your nature can be a most desirable benefit to an enduring relationship.

## Famous People Born Under The Sign of Taurus

Audrey Hepburn, Barbra Streisand, Candice Bergen, Margot Fonteyn, Ann-Margret, Patrice Munsel, Sandy Dennis, Sandra Dee, Ella Fitzgerald, Shirley MacLaine, Catherine the Great, Glenn Ford, Salvador Dali, Perry Como, Zubin Mehta, Albert Finney, Robert Morse, James Mason, John Stuart Mill, Ellen Glasgow, James Buchanan, Irving Berlin, James M. Barrie, Joe Louis, Johannes Brahms, Horace Mann, John Audubon, Sigmund Freud, Richard D'Oyly Carte, James F. Byrnes, Sir Thomas Beecham, Marshal Henri Pétain of France, Marchese Marconi.

# GEMINI

You are the most unpredictable, curious, incongruous, misunderstood, dichotomous enigma in the whole Zodiac, the ideal mate for anyone who prefers the clever, entertaining, challenging, multi-faceted type over a dull, unstimulating bore, which you can often make even a halfway interesting person look like. Cerebral and intellectual, your first approach toward sex is often from a mental standpoint, whereby you can get turned on by just the thought of someone. When you do, you're enthusiastic, free, open and expressive in your lovemaking. You're quite easily aroused physically but it may take some doing (or undoing) to get to you emotionally. You know how to get to your partner though, possessing just the right inventive and experimental touch, using all your guile to get him or her to love you, but you are not so apt to love him or her in return. Expressing Gemini's lower tendencies, you could stoop to being a tease, using your detached, emotionless lovemaking coupled with your charm and keen imagination as cruel weapons with which you are able to prey upon the weaker, more emotional signs such as Pisces and Cancer.

Ideal in your attitude toward love, you may wend your way through quite a number of sexual encounters, looking for that perfect mate. The search is often justified, however, as it takes quite an exceptional person with an inordinate ability for change and adaptability to keep a Gemini native interested. You're not easy to live with. What incenses others amuses a Gemini. You have an excess of nervous energy, and with your dual nature constantly pulling you in two directions, you usually keep lots of irons in the fire and may have several occupations. You are often accused of being fickle, which may be the case, but it is hard for a person as driven as you are to stick with anything for very long. "If you haven't tried it, don't knock it" could be the classic motto of the Gemini, to the point where you may find yourself indulging in various forms of sexual perversion because of your natural inquisitiveness and lack of adherence to any kind of a standard. Because you remain unembarrassed by your unnatural behavior and can rationalize so well, you can delude yourself into maintaining a childlike innocence no matter how degenerate you become. You do not like to accept responsibility and your adeptness at fantasy can make you one of the biggest and best liars in the Zodiac.

You are quick, and anyone who thinks he is going to spend time playing games with you had better think twice, for chances are you'll have been in and out of several amours by the time he or she makes a decision. You zigzag and hopscotch around as if life were a game of Chinese checkers, and although you're not crazy about the restrictions of family life, your sometimes childlike naïveté makes you one of the most popular in the Zodiac with the young. You like to fantasize a lot, more likely about making love than war, because you're definitely the nonviolent type.

With you, Gemini, it's really just a matter of finding that person who fills your "ideal" and most of the stipulations will be on a mental level. You need someone who "understands" you, someone who is as open-minded as you are, and will be tolerant of your mercurial need for constant exploration and new adventure, one who will never restrict you and God forbid they should ever start to nag you! Even if you are guilty of their alleged accusations! Specific as your requirements in love partners may be, if you can once find them it's just a matter of keeping your dream of them intact, and you should be able to maintain an enduring, if erratic, relationship with them.

## Famous People Born Under The Sign of Gemini

Carroll Baker, Marilyn Monroe, Barbara Parkins, Dana Wynter, Joan Collins, Rosalind Russell, Isadora Duncan, Prince Rainier, Bob Hope, Tony Curtis, John Wayne, Pat Boone, Sir Laurence Olivier, Sir Arthur Conan Doyle, Queen Victoria, Ralph Waldo Emerson, Harriet Beecher Stowe, Robert Schumann, William B. Yeats, Jimmy Walker, Jacques Offenbach, Richard Strauss, Edvard Grieg, Thomas Mann, Walt Whitman, Brigham Young.

## CANCER

Because you cherish the home and family as no other sign you are sometimes known as the great mothers of the Zodiac (the men as well as women), usually associating sex with marriage and preferring such activity within the framework of matrimony. Affected by the moon more than any other, you are emotional, sensitive, romantic, changeable, restless, and often prone toward great melancholy and brooding. The soft inner body of your vulnerability is protected and sometimes hidden away inside a hard outer shell. If your lover insults you or criticizes you (which you hate more than anything else) you withdraw into that shell until he or she or someone else with convincing sincerity and perhaps a maternal compassion coaxes you out again, feeding your ego, quelling your self-doubt, and persuading you beyond a shadow of a doubt that you are wanted and loved.

It is important for you to avoid possessiveness and "smother-love" as you do not ever like to let go of loved ones, possessions or even memories, and despite the fact that you are moody and changeable, you resist and fear any great change. With your deep, sensitive emotions you are capable of becoming among the most satisfying of lovers in the Zodiac if you can somehow manage to let go, knowing that as you do, you only increase the depth and magnitude of the true love that returns to you. Still, it takes a partner with a great capacity for giving and receiving love to help you overcome the anxiety and insecurity that make natives of your sign such incessant clingers.

Casual affairs are not where you find the greatest heights of your amours, but within the proper circumstances you can make a passionate and devoted lover, emotional and quite uninhibited, although your reserve and conservative nature will only permit this under the most discriminate conditions. You are extremely loyal once committed, fantastic around the house, sensible and thrifty, and perhaps even a gourmet cook. You're more prone to make your worst decisions and let your imagination get away from you during the full moon. Curb your tendency to live in a dream world; try to force yourself to move around more and not dig those roots so deeply.

## Famous People Born Under The Sign of Cancer

Henry Ward Beecher, Ernest Hemingway, Stephen Vincent Benét, Edgar Degas, Mary Baker Eddy, William Thackeray, Josiah Wedgwood, John Quincy Adams, Elias Howe, Emperor Maximilian of Mexico, Phineas T. Barnum, James Whistler, Nelson Eddy, Jean-Jacques Rousseau, Lord Mountbatten, Ginger Rogers, Barbara Stanwyck, Leslie Caron, Eleanor Parker, Olivia de Havilland, Susan Hayward, Anne Baxter, Janet Leigh, Natalie Wood, Luci Johnson Nugent, Lena Horne, Gina Lollobrigida, Polly Bergen, Diahann Carroll, Yul Brynner, Red Skelton, Gower Champion, Van Cliburn.

## LEO

With your great personal charm and physical magnetism, you make acquaintances, friends and lovers readily and are often lavish and generous in your romantic gestures toward the opposite sex, sometimes even ostentatious. The Sun being at its greatest strength in Leo makes you dramatic in your actions, yet you somehow manage to remain amazingly conventional. With your great pride and self-respect, unless you find precisely the right mate, one who can match your ardor, enthusiasm and passion, you are in danger of completely taking command of both your partner and the relationship, to the point of becoming a ruthless bully and an insufferable bore. This excessive strength and bombastity is one of the reasons Leos are generally unfortunate when it comes to the matrimonial scene.

Self-sufficient, you are a born leader who, in spite of being impulsive and restless, is quite capable of choosing a goal and pursuing it. You have a tendency to be idealistic about your loved one, putting him or her on a pedestal, and glamorizing people and situations way out of proportion. With your strong domineering personality it is hard for you to recognize people for what they are, individuals in their own right. Your bent for self-delusion may cause you to overrate your own talents and abilities. On the other hand, your authority, style, optimism and good looks can cause you to become quite successful and make a sudden fortune which you may, through your lack of good judgment, lose as quickly as you acquire it.

You are a romantic and a dreamer who makes his desires come true; a good friend, though one who is hard to get really close to; and a person some people may regard as slightly eccentric the way you're always going out of your way to find a challenge, and keep trying again and again.

Your shortcomings can be conceit, vanity, insensitivity, an inclination to egotistically resent and defy authority. You're impatient and have the tendency to be a blowhard, compensating for your inadequacies with a lot of fast talk (without being above telling lies to impress a prospective lover); you're also frequently guilty of obliviousness to other people's existence or problems as well as the inability to see them other than in relation to yourself and as merely an extension of yourself. Sometimes one would think you'd misread your horoscope, interpreting yourself as being the sun with everyone orbiting around you, rather than your being ruled by the sun. The hang-up from which you yourself suffer the most is your indiscriminate generosity and trust, gullibility, and your refusal to face plain and obvious facts. This short-sightedness often makes you the victim of more beguiling, subtle creatures who succeed in duping you socially, economically or emotionally. Therefore it behooves you, in your hurried eagerness and impetuosity, to pay more attention to facts and to not ignore important details that can prevent you from being "taken for a ride."

Your excessive showmanship may gain you the reputation of being the flamboyant, exotic or even philandering type, putting off those more reserved, undemonstrative ones who would be the ideal complement for you. Total and generous in your emotional responses, giving with your whole heart—unless your partner should happen to downgrade you in some way, dampening your Leo-pride and enthusiasm—once you find that special person who equals your warmth and outgoingness and is not put off by all the pomp and ceremony you sometimes revel in, you can be a steadfast, uncomplicated, devoted and exciting lover.

### Famous People Born Under The Sign of Leo

Dolores del Rio, Jill St. John, Maureen O'Hara, Arlene Dahl, Yves St. Laurent, Peter O'Toole, Robert Mitchum, Ralph Bunche, George Hamilton, Mike Douglas, Lucille Ball, Edgar Lee Masters, Herman Melville, Simón Bolívar, Hilaire Belloc, George Bernard Shaw, Ernie Pyle, Alexandre Dumas *père*, Booth Tarkington, Henry Ford, Guy de Maupassant, Alfred Tennyson, Cecil B. De Mille, John Galsworthy, Ethel Barrymore, Benjamin Harrison, Claude Debussy.

## VIRGO

In the emotional realm, you are often considered a difficult person to stir, one who does not respond with ecstasy and surrender in any but the most unusual of cases, when the partner is gifted enough to bring out great response. Many have compared you to a piece of metal which is hard to ignite, but once it does, it burns with a white heat and takes a long time to cool down.

Your attitude toward sex is practical and realistic rather than romantic or emotional and you are known to have very few love affairs as you are not one of the experimenters of the Zodiac. Another thing that stands in the way of your getting involved is your fastidious, sometimes critical nature, and your endless quest for perfection and unattainable ideals. Neat and discriminating, you are the thinkers and reasoners of the Zodiac but sometimes you strive for such rigid ethical standards that you end up being prudish and puritanical, and when you inflict these inhibitions on others, they end up backfiring, leaving you with feelings of guilt and sexual repression. You may also have unrealistic standards of personal hygiene (which more often than not you fail to live up to yourself), an aversion to being touched or fussed over, and inner fears of becoming physically infected, all qualities which are not conducive to "grooving" with people, especially the opposite sex.

Though extremely articulate, you may be shy about openly displaying your emotions, and when you aren't preoccupied with analyzing and dissecting, you can be quite a witty, interesting person. Cooperative, kind, patient and persevering as a marriage partner, you are capable of keeping a relationship alive and flourishing for a much longer time than other types. You have a strong sense of duty and responsibility, provide well for your loved ones, are capable of making great sacrifices, but sometimes you will hold onto the purse strings until you are frugal and even stingy. Careful and systematic in the way you go about selecting a love partner, you are not given to thoughtless and haphazard affairs, but once committed you use your practical understanding and intelligence in methodically discovering just what pleases your mate and utilize that knowledge for your mutual pleasure. You like to make love in an atmosphere where order, cleanliness, good books, music and attractive surroundings prevail. The painstaking person who has the endurance to pursue and conquer you will find you constant, one of the least changeable of all the signs. Once kindled, your love has an enduring, true quality and you can be one of the most rewarding partners in the Zodiac.

## Famous People Born Under The Sign of Virgo

Bret Harte, Theodore Dreiser, Walter Reuther, General de Lafayette, J. Pierpont Morgan II, Leo Tolstoy, Carl Van Doren, H. L. Mencken, Walter Reed, Margaret Sanger, Samuel Johnson, Upton Sinclair, H. G. Wells, Ingrid Bergman, Sophia Loren, Lauren Bacall, Greta Garbo, Raquel Welch, Anne Bancroft, Kitty Carlisle, Carol Lawrence, Claudette Colbert, Rosemary Harris, Rossano Brazzi, Van Johnson, Cliff Robertson, Maurice Chevalier, Sean Connery, Roddy MacDowell, Alan Jay Lerner.

## LIBRA

You respond readily to admiration, affection, praise and sometimes flattery. You are flexible, artistic, good-natured, refined, persuasive, gracious, subtle, aesthetic, kind to your love partner, cheerful and optimistic. A charming and gracious host or hostess, you are blessed with a great desire to please, innate diplomacy and an inborn sense of justice and balance. You like to lavish affection and devotion on your sex partner, demonstration of love being an essential element in your affairs of the heart. Fine surroundings, a lovely and artistically planned home, lovely clothes and tasteful design all turn you on. Although you usually display a sunny disposition, you are not likely to be taken advantage of and for anyone who tries to push you too far, an extremely strong will is revealed underneath your rather gentle surface. Never overly dramatic or boisterous in the way you go about things, you nevertheless always get your way. You abound in Venus-endowed artistic ability which you may channel into any one of many arts, such as interior decoration, architecture, fashion, needlework, painting or music. Although you are capable of working long hours at a stretch without tiring, your sense of beauty and desire for perfection can make you too meticulous and may also cause you to spend way too much money.

In your love affairs, your passion for beauty and need to see loveliness in everything can become so acute that it may thwart your attitude toward the physical aspects of sex, causing you to view it as an animalistic act. You are so terribly romantic, you will sometimes fall in love with love itself, ignoring the fact that somewhere hidden within its foundation is that strong, enigmatic, sometimes overwhelming but always necessary urge, the sex drive.

You desire harmony at all costs, and sometimes in your efforts to gain it you are guilty of vacillation, procrastination, hypocrisy and even deliberate lies. You must also take care that in your attempt to rationalize everything you don't end up living in a world of make-believe and that your need to avoid unpleasantness doesn't make you end up looking at everything through rose-colored glasses. Your sign is more prone toward delusion than any other in the Zodiac, long periods of which could throw off the delicate balance your "Scales" require, plunging you into depression and in extreme cases even violence. A more frequent than usual rate of nervous breakdowns occurs among Libra natives. You should also guard against your craving for beauty and love becoming a lust for luxury and attention, making you proud, superficial and prone toward shallow displays of lavish affection and ostentation. Libras can make a career out of gracious living like no others, and your extreme finesse with the opposite sex may lead you into becoming an incorrig... flirt. With all the ability in which you pride yourself at making your mate the unrivaled object of your attention and devotion, very often, despite your great desire to please, you are unaware of what is going on right under your own nose, completely without the intuitive, empathetic nature desired by your love partner.

However, when well-balanced and mated with that special person who appeals to your idea of romance, you are one of the most charming, exciting, cooperative, romantic and imaginative lovers in the Zodiac, capable of just about always saying and doing the right thing at the right time.

### Famous People Born Under The Sign of Libra

Franz Liszt, Samuel Taylor Coleridge, Giuseppe Verdi, Friedrich Nietzsche, Eugene O'Neill, George Gershwin, Brigitte Bardot, Julie Andrews, Deborah Kerr, Rita Hayworth, Joan Fontaine, Angie Dickinson, Helen Hayes, Inger Stevens, Melina Mercouri, Greer Garson, Juliette Prowse, Glynis

Johns, Diane Cilento, Angela Lansbury, Jean Arthur, Arlene Francis, Pamela Tiffin, Eleanora Duse, Yves Montand, George Peppard, Charlton Heston, Anthony Newley.


## SCORPIO

The most highly sexed sign in the Zodiac, you literally cannot live without love. This rarely poses a problem for you, who with your bold spirit and vibrant, strong personality know just how to dress, walk, speak and act in the ....est of manners, often having to fend off admirers. Your sign rules the genitals, making you the most sex-conscious of all the signs, often driven through sex to solve the riddle of life and harnessing your excessive sex energy to satisfy your deep-seated curiosity about life, the life force, its inner workings and secrets.

Dynamic, passionate and capable of strong likes and dislikes, you possess powerful personal desires and are anything but wishy-washy in the way you pursue your goals and your loved one. You're capable of making quick decisions, are always ready to go to bed—even at the spur of the moment—and if not completely fulfilled by just one partner, will not be averse to sleeping with several at the same time. You are prone toward excesses of liquor and drugs as well as sensuality, and like to live life at a high key, trying to make every moment as exciting as possible, but if your debauchery gets out of hand it can wreck both your health and spirit.

Strong willed, sometimes to the point of being domineering, you despise weakness in others, especially in your sex partner. And in extreme cases you are capable of deliberate cruelty, perverting your sex drive into brutality, degeneracy and depraved acts. Because of your imaginative, uninhibited approach toward sex you appeal to less adventurous types who feel they want to "live dangerously" and sometimes you exploit and make them victims of your capability for total lust and sexual aberration. Because you sometimes tend to be coarsely opportunistic, you rarely get through life without making enemies; the heights of which you are capable in love are only equaled by the depths of your hatreds which are never forgotten. You may also become alienated from others through your uncontrolled jealousy, especially in ro-

mantic matters, your vicious temper or the malicious gossip
in which you sometimes indulge. Anyone who gets on your
wrong side had better watch it, because once you turn on a
person, like your namesake, the Scorpion, you hit hard, are
extremely vindictive and will resort to any means for retalia-
tion.

You possess great intellectual curiosity and creative talent,
like avant-garde, nonconformist people, are prone to think of
yourself as a rebel and are happiest when busy, traveling and
moving about. Sometimes proud to the point of being ar-
rogant, you are decisive, positive, self-motivated, have a great
sense of privacy and even secrecy, are sometimes shy with
strangers, often psychic and a mysterious person who keeps
his own counsel. There are no greater extremes of people
found anywhere in the Zodiac than under your sign, those
who epitomize higher spiritual values and use their magnetic
attraction for constructive purposes such as Billy Graham, or
for evil and destruction such as Charles Manson.

With your great intuitive powers, you are often able to
recognize your future marriage partner at first sight, take marriage seriously (if your partner satisfies you sexually), and
love a large family. With passion as your keynote, you are a
resourceful marriage partner, capable of deep love and sexual
response.

## Famous People Born Under The Sign of Scorpio

Norman Thomas, Sarah Bernhardt, Admiral Richard Byrd,
Theodore Roosevelt, James Boswell, John Keats, John Adams,
Sholem Asch, James K. Polk, Will Rogers, Robert Louis
Stevenson, Michael Arlen, President James Garfield, Jean
Shrimpton, Katharine Hepburn, Virna Lisi, Jean Seberg, Grace
Kelly, Joanna Pettet, Oskar Werner, Rock Hudson, Billy
Graham, Richard Burton, Pablo Picasso.

## SAGITTARIUS

Your positive, optimistic enthusiasm for the celebration
of life makes you an ideal companion and a delight to be
around, with never a dull moment. Even when things are

tough for you, and they frequently are, you manage to maintain a pleasant, unruffled facade, doing your best to let it all roll off, never burdening those around you with the difficulties you are going through. Democratic, direct, forthright and friendly, you take a genuine interest in people's problems, get along well with others and have the knack of making them get along with each other when you're around. With your adeptness for sparkling conversation on such a wide variety of subjects, you're in great demand socially and thrive on this constant whirl of activity. Large in spirit as well as in stature, you're a great lover of the outdoors, move quickly and have excellent coordination, revel in travel and freedom, are excellent with horses and animals generally.

You have a healthy sense of humor and are a warm, easygoing, trustful person, a straight shooter who finds it difficult to be deceitful or even evasive. You can spot a liar a mile off. Your health is robust, you're energetic, graceful, a free-roamer whose restlessness makes it difficult to buckle down and establish a definite goal. Adventurous, you're a seeker of truth, born under the sign of the sage, one who is never satisfied until you get the answer. You're a conscientious and untiring worker who hates to take orders, likes to run the business, and although you're vibrant and clever, you can benefit by developing a more cooperative nature.

In the areas of romance, love and sex, many of the very qualities that are so desirable in your casual relationships become the detriments that make it difficult for you to establish and maintain any lengthy period of intimacy with the opposite sex. Your down-to-earth honesty and common sense approach when applied to love affairs can destroy powerful emotions and your frank outspokenness is often the enemy of the aura of mystique enshrouding any romantic interlude, making it intriguing, alluring and appealing to the partner. Not one of the world's great experimenters in the bedroom, you prefer sex be kept on a conservative, conventional level, deeming all the other accoutrements in which connoisseurs of erotica indulge unnecessary, superfluous and even distasteful. You do not care to discuss sex with others, often shun the subject altogether, and sometimes react prudishly to people who don't. You also dislike being tied down or limited in any way. The restrictions intrinsic to a close relationship often chafe on your need for the free, open approach to life, leaving you angry and misunderstood when your partner mistakes your guileless, direct approach to people for brazenness or flirtation. It is hard for you to be patient and when you cannot have something *now* you are apt to lose your temper, becoming so angry as to lash out at anything in sight, throwing ashtrays and kicking furniture.

As we said, there is never a dull moment with a Sagittarius around and if you can find a partner who is up to the activity and excitement you always seem to generate, who prefers golf, tennis, large political or social gatherings, as well as skiing and horseback riding to intimate, romantic moments, and who is ready to accept the truth at all costs, even about how well she does or doesn't look in the morning, or how well he does or doesn't make love, you'd better hang onto him or her because you may never find another.

### Famous People Born Under The Sign of Sagittarius

Thomas Cook, Zachary Taylor, Franklin Pierce, George Santayana, John Milton, John Greenleaf Whittier, Heinrich Heine, Douglas Fairbanks Jr., Thomas Carlyle, Benjamin Disraeli, Martin Van Buren, Diego Rivera, Fiorello La Guardia, Heywood Broun, Louisa May Alcott, Jane Fonda, Mary Martin, Lee Remick, Betty Grable, Dina Merrill, Kirk Douglas, Agnes Moorehead, Karim Aga Khan, Dick Van Dyke, Efrem Zimbalist Jr., Frank Sinatra, Joe DiMaggio, Noel Coward, Andy Williams.

## CAPRICORN

Charm without frivolity, sex appeal without vulgarity, neat but not gaudy—they're always saying things like that about Capricorns. However, it is true that although sex is important to you, it is never so important that you will risk losing out on any of the things you really want because of it. With your ambitious, practical nature, rarely demonstrative of your inner feelings, you often gain the reputation for being cold, which is not the case at all. Your icy facade is just a protective defense you would sometimes hide behind, rather than reveal your powerful and sometimes desperate need for love, affection and approval, and you'll take the chance of ending up spurned, rejected and hurt. You are conventional and prefer love and sex within marriage, and also because it is within that framework that you are most likely to get the things you want out of life. You're traditional, conservative and socially conscious, and although you are willing to satisfy your more lustful desires with a voluptuous common type, you'll be quite careful and even snobbish in picking yourself a permanent mate, preferably someone who can enhance your position and material gains. You have good control of your emotions and aren't likely to allow yourself to become too deeply involved with someone unless you really love him or her; you won't waste your time in a relationship that is going nowhere.

The women born under this sign are sometimes magnificent calculators and manipulators, who with their strong sense of the value of money can stretch a dollar and usually limit their romantic interest to someone who is likely to be successful and able to provide well for them. Not adverse to working with competely raw material if nothing else is available, and provided the man has a modicum of potential and is someone worth learning to love, she will groom him and with her particular ability to create the drive for advancement in a man, she is just likely to end up with a winner. It has often been said that behind every successful man is a Capricorn woman. We'll leave it up to you to decide whether that applies to Macbeth too.

Often self-conscious, and overly concerned with what others think of you, you abhor criticism and in many cases are reluctant to admit it when you are wrong. Unforgiving when wronged, it has been said "Once you cross a Capricorn, you can cross him off your list." (Of good friends, that is.) He may remain coolly friendly and aloof after that, but nothing more. The tenacious, patient masters of your own destiny, you are farsighted, can wait it out in a business deal, and are capable of making great sacrifices to reach a chosen goal. It is often said that Capricorns are born old and grow younger through the years; as children you're usually too practical and intelligent for your contemporaries and spend large amounts of time either alone or with older, more mature people.

Once you are able to let go of your fears and anxieties with someone you feel you can trust and love, you can be one of the most passionate lovers in the Zodiac. You are capable of maintaining a secure, warm, if not conventional home and will hang on in marriage, through thick and thin, but should avoid being too protective, stiff, strict and dominating with your children. For anyone who is geared toward your particular peculiarities, you'll make a highly successful mate and a stimulating sex partner as well.

### Famous People Born Under The Sign of Capricorn

Louis Pasteur, Sir Henry Bessemer, Daniel Webster, Benjamin Franklin, Ludwig van Beethoven, Sir Isaac Newton, John Singer Sargent, Henry Miller, Henri Matisse, Rudyard Kipling, Andrew Johnson, Admiral George Dewey, Robert Nathan, Marlene Dietrich, Faye Dunaway, Loretta Young, Barbara Rush, Ava Gardner, Mary Tyler Moore, Danny Kaye, Robert Stack, Rod Taylor, Jack Jones, Laurence Harvey, Sandy Koufax, Cary Grant, Steve Allen, Yvette Mimieux, Lu Ann Horstman, Janis Joplin, Elvis Presley.

## AQUARIUS

Charming, exciting and completely unpredictable, you are one of the most original, inventive, complex and unique people in the Zodiac, a true humanitarian who loves freedom and independence. You always find time to concern yourself with the well-being of those around you; you are spontaneous, gregarious, outgoing, extroverted, have many interests and no problem in expressing yourself. You're an intuitive dreamer who is analytical and extremely perceptive. You are likely to be involved in the arts, philosophy, science, and the humanities, concerning yourself with advances in civilization, discoveries and new inventions.

You desire romance, tenderness and a gentle touch in your love life. You are highly idealistic and if you don't find exactly what you're looking for in a sex partner you're liable to go on sublimating your sex energy into one of your many interests until you do. You're often generous to a fault with your emotions, having a tendency to "lose your cool," as they say, playing every card in your hand, and then after "blowing your scene" with a soul-baring outburst, you pull the same thing again in your next relationship, repeating your mistake.

You like to be surrounded with people and will often belong to many clubs and organizations, especially those geared toward the benefit of mankind. You like to involve yourself in others' lives and have a keen perception about what makes them tick, an ability to understand their motivations, problems, foibles and dreams; but very often you offer your help when it is not required or sought after. When you make up your mind about something, only you can change it, and you often do—unexpectedly. You are a free soul, who gives little thought to others' opinions, and you are loyal, ardent, outspoken and honest.

Kindness, appreciation and understanding from your loved one are essential if you are to maintain your good nature and sense of well-being. Should you feel you are being overlooked or unjustly criticized you can explode in anger and say tactless, uncalled for things. If you are concentrating on something, you couldn't care less about sex or your partner at that moment and you're often guilty of becoming so absorbed in your activities and interest in the outside world that you neglect and become oblivious to those around you. At such times you may also become careless, slovenly and absentminded about your dress, your personal self, your environment and the details of your day to day duties. Ruled by the volatile planet Uranus, your life is full of change, revolution and upheaval. This often requires a great deal of freedom for movement on your part, so you had best avoid relationships in which you are possessed, dominated, dictated to or ordered around. Because you're so prone toward seeing things on a broad, overall scale, and often find yourself neglecting your own problems in the interest of the majority, you are often a lonely person. While you appear to be impersonal, your deepest need is for love and companionship and when you find this, you can be a passionate as well as compassionate lover and marriage partner.

## Famous People Born Under The Sign of Aquarius

Mia Farrow, Vanessa Redgrave, Zsa Zsa and Eva Gabor, Donna Reed, Kim Novak, Eartha Kitt, Suzanne Pleshette, Hildegarde, Claire Bloom, Garry Moore, Paul Newman, Jimmy Durante, Jack Benny, Clark Gable, Wendell Willkie, Horace Greeley, Charles A. Lindbergh, John Barrymore, Charles Darwin, Charles Dickens, Fritz Kreisler, Thomas A. Edison, John Ruskin, Sir Henry Irving, William McKinley, Lewis Carroll, Robert Burns, Edouard Manet.

## PISCES

Your symbol of two fishes swimming in opposite directions illustrates the two opposite forces at work within you but it can also denote the duality of types born under the sign of Pisces—positive and negative. The former are alluring, ethereal, mysterious, romantic, sensuous, kind, mystical, poetic, benevolent, amiable, pleasant, sociable, cheerful, sincere, sensitive, responsive, intuitive, psychic and a host of other superlatives; while the latter are whining, sniveling, highly emotional, ill-tempered, surly, deceiving, intemperate, wishywashy, liars, the "dustbin of the Zodiac" as they are known by so many astrologers. The two characterizations that fall under your sign are such paradoxes there could almost be two entirely separate descriptions written for each of them. Yet, it is these very same positive qualities that when distorted and twisted ultimately become your most negative attributes. For example, when all of Pisces' good qualities such as deep sensitivity, sympathy and the ability to understand and identify with human suffering are not channeled into useful activities for the benefit of others (often because they are completely centered upon himself), the native becomes maudlin, melodramatic, morbid, ineffectual, self-pitying and self-indulgent. This is just as love itself, when not given and expressed outward, but rather turned back upon the self, becomes self-centeredness, jealousy and even hatred.

As the last sign in the Zodiac, you are essentially all that there is, the sum and totality of all the characteristics of all the signs in varying degrees. Your life is one long search after the absolute essence of truth, and in so doing you assimilate and absorb people and events like a sponge; if you happen to be a strong Pisces, in control of your destiny and emotions, this will be beneficial in your life and put to use in your creative endeavor. Many of the world's finest poets, musicians, composers, writers and artists who were able to interpret these experiences—even pain and heartbreak—romantically and sensitively into art-forms, were born under your sign.

However, if you are weakly aspected and lacking strength of direction in your encounters you will extract the most unpleasant, unsavory and undesirable that life has to offer. In the name of your search for spiritual enlightenment you will indulge in infidelity, drug addiction, promiscuity, all of the vices imaginable, and if you can find a dominant lover, courtesan or pimp who makes immoral, sadistic demands on you, you will gladly submit to his or her will, using this as the ultimate cop-out—"He (or she) forced me to do it."

Nobody ever forces anybody to do anything, Pisces, and if for once and for all you'd accept the responsibility for your own destiny you'd be a lot better off! But as far as you're concerned, this gets you off the hook and you can continue your game, warped and self-destructive though it may be, without accepting the slightest accountability for your plight; you enjoy your martyrdom, and bask in the sadistic thrill you get out of making those around you acutely aware of and even guilty because of the pain and misery you have gotten yourself into. For anyone whose ego needs a clinging, dependent sex partner to cater to him, a weak Pisces can be ideal, so great is his need for love and emotional security, but he may soon begin to grate on a person's nerves with his nostalgia, melancholia and bouts with psychosomatic ill health, anything to get him attention and reassurance that he's still wanted.

You strong, self-sufficient Pisces (and there are some around) are romantic, considerate, sensitive, and devoted to your loved ones, using every effort in your power to please and be pleasing. You are sensuous, tasteful, artistic, capable of making love a completely absorbing and even transcendental experience, with your mystical and spiritual approach toward sex. You have the right touch, the right feel, the right words. You do everything intuitively and in tune to just the right moment so that you fuse and merge with your lover making sex an enthralling, totally overwhelming and unbelievable experience.

Because you are so much happier married than single, need love so much more than any other sign and have so much to give, it is important that you find just the person who can understand and cope with your sometimes insatiable needs. When you do, you can be one of the most gratifying, sympathetic partners for whom anyone could wish.

### Famous People Born Under The Sign of Pisces

Kate Greenaway. Henrik Ibsen, Gabriele d'Annunzio, James Madison, Andrew Jackson, Elizabeth Barrett Browning, Isaac Watts, Anaïs Nin, Elizabeth Taylor, Ursula Andress, Auguste Renoir, Merle Oberon, George Handel, Frédéric Chopin, Lynn Redgrave, Jennifer Jones, Samantha Eggar, Joanne Woodward, Michele Morgan, Linda Byrd Robb, Sidney Poitier, Rudolf Nureyev, Rex Harrison, Jerry Lewis, David Niven, Cyd Charisse, Diane Baker, Paula Prentiss, Liza Minelli, Johnny Cash, June Carter Cash, Luther Burbank, Henry Wadsworth Longfellow, Oliver Wendell Holmes, Samuel Pepys, Jackie Gleason, Dinah Shore, Lawrence Welk, Enrico Caruso, Mary Garden.

# Really Getting Heavy
## into It . . .

*Rowley Powley, pudding and pie,*
*Kissed the girls and made them cry;*
*When the girls began to cry,*
*Rowley Powley runs away.*

The complexities involved in drawing up one's chart and reading one's horoscope are far too vast to cover in this one chapter but we would like to give you a basic idea of how this is done. This knowledge will be invaluable should you decide to consult a professional astrologer, and also beneficial if you prefer to go no further than to employ our simplified system of tables following this chapter to create for yourself a general astrological portrait.

Before we can begin a chart, we must know the place of the subject's birth and the exact time, as near to the minute as possible, which is first converted into True Local Time and then to Sidereal Time or star time in order that we can employ the ephemerides or timetables of the planets' places or positions for any day of any given year. These and many other volumes that explain the exact delineation of the horoscope are available at your nearby astrological bookstore or if you consult a professional all of this will be taken care of for you. For purposes of this book you need only have the time given on your record of birth to check against each of our tables. When no accurate time of birth is available the astrologer casts a sunrise chart, one that assumes you were born between four and six A.M., the hour of sunrise. Otherwise an astrologer can find out the time of your birth through a process called "rectification" but this is quite time-consuming and therefore costly. Next we must figure out the birth place in exact degrees of latitude and longitude. This in-

formation is also provided in reference books or will be
taken care of by your astrologer.

On the following page you will find a 360° circle or wheel,
divided into twelve sections of 30° each, with a circle in the
center. This symbolic map of the heavens is used to show
the positions of the signs of the Zodiac in relation to the sun,
moon and various planets at a particular moment in time.
To employ absolutely correct usage, the map that is erected
and delineated from the information available is the *chart*
and the interpretation of your character and destiny drawn
from this is the *horoscope*. As time passed and the positions
of planets change, this same basic chart can be progressed
again and again to determine an updated reading of your
horoscope.

In order to better envision this wheel as a map of the
heavens, consider the circle in the center as the Earth and
the line going across the middle the Vernal Equinox or,
as it is known in astrological terms, 0-Aries, the point of
0° from which we always begin. As you can see from
the diagram, the directions are reversed from those on a
geographical map—with North on the bottom and so forth,
thus explaining why it is at this point, 0°, where the
sign rising on the *Eastern* horizon at the time of birth is
recorded. All planets falling under this line are below the
horizon. At the left of the wheel lies the Descendant, above
the Midheaven and below the Nadir, in case you ever
wondered what Henry Miller was talking about when he
used the following to describe the poet Rimbaud: "It was an
affliction which poisoned him both at the Zenith and Nadir
of his being." So it is around this center "earth" that we
place the planets, in the exact position they were at the time
of your birth to find out what effect they had on who you
are, astrologically speaking, and as we progress them we are
able to determine how they are influencing you at this very
moment. Thus is the intent and purpose of astrology.

Each of the sections of the circle can be considered as
inches on a ruler, for we are basically dealing with the
measurement of time, starting from 0 o'clock and progressing
the full twenty-four hours instead of stopping and starting
over again at twelve o'clock, as there is no A.M. or P.M. in
Sidereal Time. The sections are named beginning with Aries,
Taurus, Gemini and so on to Pisces as well as identified by

NAME_____

TIME OF BIRTH_____

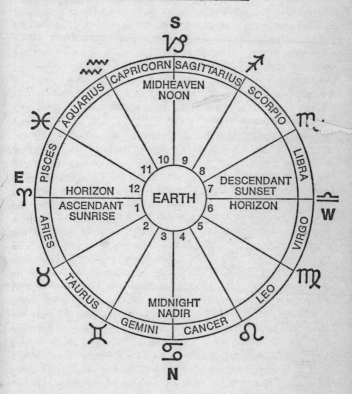

each respective astrological symbol. If you want to make up your own horoscope using the system contained in this book, check your time of birth against each of the tables following this chapter to determine where your ascendant, the moon and each of the planets were at the time of your birth. (We've already covered the sun earlier.) In case you didn't recognize them, the symbol for each of the planets and luminaries precedes the sections describing the significance of their placement in any particular sign of the Zodiac so you can draw them into the proper section of the wheel where they were found at the time of your birth. For instance if your sun was in Taurus, place a ♉ in the Taurus section of the wheel; if you had Aquarius rising place a ♒ near the cendant and so on. After completing all of the planets and ading their affect in that particular placement, you probably h ve some idea why you seem, look, act and love the way you do, and also can see how your basic nature is altered considerably by the influence of planets other than the sun. When you have an astrologer set up your wheel, you will see numerous other ways in which planetary configurations known as "aspects" determine even greater complexities and subtleties of your individual nature. We will go into some of these in a moment but first we'd like to explain briefly how after you have found the placements of each of your planets you can proceed to synthesize this information. For example, suppose your Sun Sign is Virgo—you've always read that Virgos are traditionally neat, clean, chaste, pristine, cool, and often indifferent about sex, yet you yourself did not completely fit this pattern as you're also sexy, passionate, sometimes haphazard and a bit messy. Perhaps through the tables you found out it was because you have your ascendant or moon in Cancer or Pisces, which could alter your nature considerably. Or maybe you're a cool, controlled Capricorn who occasionally goes off the deep end, drifting and day-dreaming for weeks on end. Could one of the other planets strongly influencing you be in Gemini or Aquarius? Or maybe you were one of those who fit their Sun Sign perfectly, and found out it's because that particular influence is fortified by an ascendant or moon placed similarly. This is the tricky, but also the fun and involved, part of reading a horoscope, cross-referencing all of the aspects against each other. This is something that only the most talented and informed of astrologers can really explore in depth, along with making predictions of possible future opportunities and events. In the following we will attempt to give you an idea of some of the numerous considerations that make up a complete reading, covering as much territory as we are able to within the obvious restrictions of a book of this nature.

The 30° sections of the wheel are also known as houses, numbering from one to twelve counterclockwise and starting at the ascendant, named thus because the various gods for whom many positions of the Zodiac were named were so personified in ancient times they were actually known to have lived in "houses." Each of the houses represents the following areas of one's life:

FIRST HOUSE: Physical body, the self, appearance, ego, your approach to the world and people.

SECOND HOUSE: Finances, possessions and security.

THIRD HOUSE: Education, communication, trips, acquaintances, relatives.

FOURTH HOUSE: Old age, the home, the father, what you inherit from your parents, beginnings and endings.

FIFTH HOUSE: Love, children, entertainment, recreation.

SIXTH HOUSE: Illness, health, domesticity, servants and inferiors, small animals, work, efficiency.

SEVENTH HOUSE: Business partners, associations, other people, marriage partner, public reaction, unity with others.

EIGHTH HOUSE: Sex expression, death, legacies, insurance, self-sacrifice.

NINTH HOUSE: The law, religion, long journeys, foreign travel, publications, new horizons.

TENTH HOUSE: The profession, fame, honor, social status, material possessions, the mother.

ELEVENTH HOUSE: Friends, groups, hopes and wishes, identification with objectives.

TWELFTH HOUSE: Foundation, subconscious, institutions, secret enemies, large animals, escapism, self-undoing.

In determining the influence of the various factors we will want to consider the twelve signs as fields of potential energy and influence which act upon the houses. All twelve signs will appear in your chart but you may not have a planet in each sign or house; also some of them may appear on the cusp or the lines separating the houses of your wheel, but this is another important factor in the interpretation of a chart. What further do we need to know about the houses? There are three kinds, angular, succedent and cadent. Where your planets fall in these houses is a further determinant of your character. For instance, planets falling in angular houses tend toward inspiring the native with action and increased activity, as well as mobility, while succedent houses give fixity of purpose and provide stability and added willpower. Cadent houses, on the other hand, bring adaptability, communication of ideas and the ability to get along well and project oneself to others.

Another thing the astrologer looks for in a chart is whether your planets fall in cardinal, fixed or mutable signs. Cardinal signs are Aries, Cancer, Libra and Capricorn. They tend toward making the nat*  active, restless, and aid in his accomplishment, somewhat the same as the angular houses do. Fixed signs, similar to cadent houses, give more will-power; these signs are Taurus, Leo, Scorpio and Aquarius. The mutable signs, Gemini, Virgo, Sagittarius and Pisces, like the succedent houses, bring adaptability, communication of ideas and a greater tendency toward thought.

The angles between planets also affect us. Some angles are harmonious and others not so harmonious. Angular distances are called aspects. (An aspect is also the linking together of any two planetary forces.) An angle can open doors or shut them, so such an aspect in a chart is of prime importance. These aspects are as follows:

180 degrees—Opposition
120 degrees—Trine
90 degrees—Square
60 degrees—Sextile
45 degrees—Semi-Square
30 degrees—Semi-Sextile
150 degrees—Inconjunct

Anything within 8° is known as a conjunction. Each of these angles represents a particular type of force of influence in the native's life experience. Oppositions, as we mentioned in an earlier chapter, make for struggle for mastery of warring forces often at odds with each other. Oppositions can also be beneficial, can be very positive, can bring things to fruition and are not necessarily only a negative aspect, depending upon other placements and one's personal reaction. Squares can mean the thwarting of purpose, barriers to success; semi-squares have the same effect but to a lesser degree; trines bring harmony and ease of conditions, facility in obtaining things in life with smooth sailing and little effort required to get by. A sextile can bring good benefits but effort is often required. A semi-sextile is similar but once again to a lesser degree.

As the planets proceed in their courses our aspects change, often for the better but sometimes for the worse, too. This is why sometimes everything seems to be going smoothly, with things working out the way we want them to, and then other times nothing goes right. Under good aspect of Mars we can be fortunate in our contacts with others. Adverse aspects of Saturn can create melancholy and depression; positive aspects can bring patience and endurance. Good Neptunian aspects can encourage our understanding of the inner mysteries of life. Mercury is often the message bearer and whether the news is good or bad depends on our aspect to that particular planet. Knowing these things beforehand can cause us to prepare for negative aspects, thus saving ourselves any amount of anguish and frustration. Many suicides could probably have been prevented had the persons involved been aware their condition was only due to a temporary planetary configuration.

Another factor to weigh in a chart is whether or not the planet is in retrograde. This would limit its action, some of the power having been lost, meaning you don't receive the full benefit of the planet. It can also cause restriction. Many geniuses and leaders have charts with retrogrades, necessitating their having to overcome obstacles. We must also consider the planetary dignitaries. When a planet is in its strongest position in the Zodiac, it is "in domicile." It is in its own ruler, its own sign. This planet will exert a stronger influence on the life, just as a planet in an angular house will, for example. Here is a list of the signs and their planetary rulers.

Aries—Mars                Libra—Venus
Taurus—Venus              Scorpio—Mars & Pluto
Gemini—Mercury           Sagittarius—Jupiter
Cancer—Moon              Capricorn—Saturn
Leo—Sun                     Aquarius—Uranus & Saturn
Virgo—Mercury            Pisces—Neptune

When a planet is in what is considered to be its second strongest position it is said to be in "Exaltation."

Sun is exalted in Aries
Moon is exalted in Taurus
Mercury is exalted in Virgo and/ r Gemini
Venus is exalted in Pisces
Mars is exalted in Capricorn
Jupiter is exalted in Cancer
Uranus is exalted in Scorpio
Saturn is exalted in Libra
Neptune is exalted in Leo
Uranus is exalted in Sagittarius or Capricorn
Pluto is exalted in Aquarius

We must also examine the detriments in a chart. A planet in a sign exactly opposite to the one it rules is said to be in "Detriment." There is considerable loss of power here.

Libra and Taurus are the detriment of Mars
Scorpio and Aries are the detriment of Venus
Sagittarius and Pisces are the detriment of Mercury
Capricorn is the detriment of the Moon
Aquarius is the detriment of the Sun
Gemini is the detriment of Jupiter
Leo and Cancer are the detriment of Saturn
Leo is the detriment of Uranus
Virgo is the detriment of Neptune
Libra and Taurus are the detriment of Pluto

In weighing the chart, another thing we must consider is the elements. All signs are either fire, earth, air or water signs.

We must ask ourselves how many planets in the chart fall in each of these categories, this being an added determinant to character. The elements of fire (Aries, Leo, Sagittarius) tend to give an added sense of self, a strong ego, enthusiasm, individuality, a magnetic personality and the ability to be forward-thinking. The earth signs (Taurus, Virgo and Capricorn) give added stability, dependability and discrimination and are practical, conservative, well-organized and serious. The air signs (Gemini, Libra and Aquarius) bring added thought and intelligence, an ability to meet people effectively, as well as adaptability, inventiveness and intellect, while the water signs (Cancer, Scorpio and Pisces) add the element of emotion, psychic ability, introspection, spirituality and soul development.

We must also ask, how many planets do we have above the horizon and how many are below? Above the horizon planets tend to bring early success, while below the horizon they give more endurance. We must also discern how many degrees into each sign the planets are placed, as well as examine the nodes and interceptions. We must find out the house rulers, the cusp rulers and the dispositor of the chart. An even vaster amount of detail than ever imagined awaits us on our embarking into the interpretation of a horoscope.

Astrology is also laden with symbols. The circle means infinity, the triangle will, wisdom and activity, the vertical line signifies spirit, the horizontal line matter and the cross the blending of the spiritual and the material. Each symbol for the planets and signs has a deep esoteric meaning; the symbol for Aries is the descent of the life force into the brain and head of man; and so it goes, on and on, with each of these symbols taking on a greater meaning, the more you meditate upon them. For a richer understanding of the whole study you will want to work on this dimension of the mind until these symbols take root in your subconscious.

As no two fingerprints are exactly alike, neither are any two horoscopes the same, and you now probably have a better idea of the many factors that go into making this statement true. But, alas! The stars merely indicate! And the horoscope is a pattern, a map, and its aspects only show up your tendencies and abilities, not definite attainments or events. It's up to *you* to put all of this into gear for yourself. Man's will is always free. The raw materials, potential and the general outline for life's pattern are detailed in the horoscope. From there on it's up to the individual.

Bon Voyage!

And on to discovery of further subtleties of your love and sex nature.

*Luna, every woman's friend*
*To me thy goodness condescend,*
*Let this night in visions see*
*Emblems of my destiny.*

Because the moon governs all that is receptive in your nature, it has much to do with your responses sexually and emotionally, as well as with your instincts, imagination, and desires. The moon discloses your subconscious mind, all that is contained there, all that you have been in the past and all that you are now. It is one of the most powerful planets affecting your love nature, and compatibility is best where your moon is in the same sign as your partner's sun, or vice versa.

MOON IN ARIES: This makes you restless, unpredictable, impatient, impractical, determined, impetuous, temperamental, impulsive, affectionate; this is most favorable for new beginnings and new adventures, and when intrigued and stimulated by this sense of newness, your love and sex life should be at their best. When the moon enters into Aries, watch it! You will have extra power and your sex drive will be at its strongest. Beware of feeling discontent, restless and of an inclination to seek change irrationally, before actually weighing all sides of the issue carefully. You also tend toward having a bad temper and an irritable disposition and may be extremely touchy at this time. You are often more turned on by "the chase" part of an encounter and then bore easily when things start to quiet down. You consider your prospective lovers prey to be hunted down, and often have many brief but intense affairs.

MOON IN TAURUS: You are practical, fond of luxury, travel, first-class accommodations, you love to entertain and do everything up brown. You are romantic and love expensive presents. Your approach to sex is marked by devotion and perseverance, sensuousness and sentimentality. Be careful that you're not fooled by outer appearances. You have a strong tendency to let your emotions get the best of your clear thinking, refusing to face facts even when they're spelled out for you. You females usually will better yourselves status-wise and financially as well through your marriage choice. You people are aspected with a natural and sensual quality.

MOON IN GEMINI: You are dual-natured, prone to gossip and flirt a lot, incautious, heedless, clever, interesting, always seeking out the spotlight. This is not the best placement for one's moon, as you are often too much the intellectual type, more interested in business and your profession than romance. You're also not as serious about your amours as you might be, thus making it difficult for the ones with whom you're involved. Try not to be so changeable, and subdue your tendency to split whenever the mood hits you.

MOON IN CANCER: You are a wonderful homemaker, devoted to the hearth, children and the home. A fine home and family are your true goals in life. You are faithful, sentimental and devoted. You expect life to run its course like a romantic fairy tale, and you are often quite conventional in your views. This can be the most favorable position for romance provided everything else is in good order planet-wise. You're sensitive, affectionate and have a keen intuition as to your partner's needs and are able to minister to his wants. Giving and devoted, you're emotional in your attitude toward love and sex. You're crazy for affection and crave those "little extras" your loved one bestows upon you. Take care that your possessive traits don't get out of hand. You're an appealing self-sacrificing lover but sometimes a little over-emotional and unpredictable depending on the changing phases of the moon.

MOON IN LEO: Domineering, jealous, commanding, in control, you can be generous and self-sacrificing but are often attracted to weaklings who you lead around by the nose. You are romantic, passionate and usually accomplish all that you set out to do. You have high ideals, are straight and conventional in your attitude toward sex and are usually quite successful romantically. Though your standards are high, watch out that you don't fall prey to such lesser tendencies as unnecessary pride, inexcusable conceit and vaingloriousness as well as a bit of pettiness. Beware when you're out for revenge, because you're a real freak and could hurt someone.

MOON IN VIRGO: It is difficult for you to give of yourself, as you are cold, sober, grave and even sexless, all aspects which do not lend themselves toward love and romance. You're often picky, critical, hard to please, too exacting and fussy and pristine in love matters. You make a good housekeeper, though, are dutiful and neat. But what good is that after midnight on a cold winter night? You do better out in society where you're tactful, discreet, and seem to have an inherent sense of what is right and what is wrong. But then who cares?

MOON IN LIBRA: You have strongly romantic inclinations and desires. You are forever seeking love and sex satisfaction, be it from a small flirtation to a great affair. You may find your marriage doesn't live up to your expectations but if at first you don't succeed you'll try again and again with subsequent marriages, affairs, divorces and remarriages. This is most favorably aspected, generally speaking, from the romantic standpoint as you can be a rapacious and voracious sex partner, but watch that you don't become overindulgent. Although you have an innate refinement about you, you sometimes lack a certain backbone that is desirable. You engage in love affairs discreetly, always displaying good taste but sometimes you're apt to circumvent situations, frustratingly so. You've an air of secrecy about you, will often be unfaithful, crave everything about love as an erotic adventure; but you must curtail your tendency toward promiscuity.

MOON IN SCORPIO: Demanding, obsessive, driving, intense, you have a great sex drive and can suffer from both the remorse of your excesses as well as from deprivation of a sexual outlet. You receive pleasure in sex but feel great guilt. You have endurance, intuition and strength of character although you're highly emotional and often a sensualist. If this is carried too far, your degeneracy, debauchery, wantonness, lasciviousness and so forth can endanger your health. On the other hand, if your incurable sexual curiosity is channeled into a search for the secrets of life contained in mutuality you may find that longed-for enlightenment that can never come through just physical sex alone.

MOON IN SAGITTARIUS: You are not domestic nor overly eager to settle down. You like your freedom and are independent and desirous of being on an equal footing with anyone you should link up with romantically. You are very adventurous and seek thrills and experiences, being involved in games and sports, anywhere you can sparkle and glow with all the activity in which you're engrossed. You like to spend money and make sure your life is in a constant state of flux, giving and receiving, a whirl of excitement. This lunation usually means you meet love's challenges with enthusiasm and think of it all as great sport. You'll probably land one of the most desirable partners around.

MOON IN CAPRICORN: You have a strong drive to succeed and are determined, ambitious and competitive, but this placement is not so hot in the love-romance area. You can be icy as January, cold as December, and not above exploiting and using others for your own self-gain. You're more likely to find yourself a workable situation—a convenient, profitable arrangement—than a romance, as you're so resourceful and success-bound. Be careful that you don't become too isolated in your "ivory tower."

MOON IN AQUARIUS: There's a lot of warmth here, combined with selflessness and a certain amount of stability. You're easy to get along with, friendly, and with your broad-minded outlook you make a wonderful love partner, but you're not terribly domestic. Try not to overdo it emotionally because when you delve in without any safeguard or restraint you're a real drag.

MOON IN PISCES: You love the home because it provides you with the stability and permanence you need and you make an affectionate, warm partner, devoted in marriage. Watch that dual thing you have, though, the characteristic which makes you restless and bored sometimes, wanting to dump your whole scene overboard. There's always that groping quality for personal fulfillment within yourself which tempts you to become a wanderer in search of something it's quite conclusive you're not going to find. While you're daydreaming about setting forth on your destiny, you're clinging to the home fires for dear life. Better hang onto the latter.

# HOW TO FIND THE PLACEMENT OF THE MOON AT THE TIME OF YOUR BIRTH

## 1890

| JAN. | FEB. | MAR. | APR. | MAY | JUNE | JULY | AUG. | SEPT. | OCT. | NOV. | DEC. |
|---|---|---|---|---|---|---|---|---|---|---|---|
| 2♊ | 1♋ | 2♌ | 1♍ | 1♎ | 2♐ | 1♑ | 2♓ | 2♉ | 2♊ | 1♋ | 1♌ |
| 4♋ | 3♌ | 5♍ | 4♎ | 3♏ | 4♑ | 3♒ | 4♈ | 5♊ | 4♋ | 3♌ | 3♍ |
| 7♌ | 6♍ | 7♎ | 6♏ | 6♐ | 6♒ | 5♓ | 6♉ | 7♋ | 7♌ | 6♍ | 6♎ |
| 9♍ | 8♎ | 10♏ | 8♐ | 8♑ | 8♓ | 7♈ | 8♊ | 10♌ | 9♍ | 8♎ | 8♏ |
| 12♎ | 10♏ | 12♐ | 10♑ | 10♒ | 10♈ | 10♉ | 11♋ | 12♍ | 12♎ | 11♏ | 10♐ |
| 14♏ | 13♐ | 14♑ | 12♒ | 12♓ | 12♉ | 12♊ | 13♌ | 15♎ | 14♏ | 13♐ | 12♑ |
| 16♐ | 15♑ | 16♒ | 15♓ | 14♈ | 15♊ | 14♋ | 16♍ | 17♏ | 16♐ | 15♑ | 14♒ |
| 18♑ | 17♒ | 18♓ | 17♈ | 16♉ | 17♋ | 17♌ | 18♎ | 19♐ | 19♑ | 17♒ | 16♓ |
| 20♒ | 19♓ | 20♈ | 19♉ | 19♊ | 20♌ | 20♍ | 21♏ | 22♑ | 21♒ | 19♓ | 19♈ |
| 22♓ | 21♈ | 23♉ | 21♊ | 21♋ | 22♍ | 22♎ | 23♐ | 24♒ | 23♓ | 21♈ | 21♉ |
| 24♈ | 23♉ | 25♊ | 24♋ | 23♌ | 25♎ | 24♏ | 25♑ | 26♓ | 25♈ | 24♉ | 23♊ |
| 27♉ | 25♊ | 27♋ | 26♌ | 26♍ | 27♏ | 27♐ | 27♒ | 28♈ | 27♉ | 26♊ | 25♋ |
| 29♊ | 28♋ | 30♌ | 29♍ | 28♎ | 29♐ | 29♑ | 29♓ | 30♉ | 29♊ | 28♋ | 28♌ |
|  |  |  |  | 31♏ |  | 31♒ | 31♈ |  |  |  | 30♍ |

## 1891

| JAN. | FEB. | MAR. | APR. | MAY | JUNE | JULY | AUG. | SEPT. | OCT. | NOV. | DEC. |
|---|---|---|---|---|---|---|---|---|---|---|---|
| 2♎ | 1♏ | 2♐ | 1♑ | 2♓ | 1♈ | 2♊ | 1♋ | 2♍ | 2♎ | 1♏ | 3♑ |
| 4♏ | 3♐ | 5♑ | 3♒ | 4♈ | 3♉ | 5♋ | 3♌ | 4♎ | 4♏ | 3♐ | 5♒ |
| 7♐ | 5♑ | 7♒ | 5♓ | 7♉ | 5♊ | 7♌ | 6♍ | 7♏ | 7♐ | 5♑ | 7♓ |
| 9♑ | 7♒ | 9♓ | 7♈ | 9♊ | 7♋ | 9♍ | 8♎ | 9♐ | 9♑ | 7♒ | 8♈ |
| 11♒ | 9♓ | 11♈ | 9♉ | 11♋ | 10♌ | 12♎ | 11♏ | 12♑ | 11♒ | 9♓ | 11♉ |
| 13♓ | 11♈ | 13♉ | 11♊ | 14♌ | 12♍ | 14♏ | 13♐ | 14♒ | 13♓ | 11♈ | 13♊ |
| 15♈ | 13♉ | 15♊ | 14♋ | 16♍ | 15♎ | 17♐ | 15♑ | 16♓ | 15♈ | 14♉ | 16♋ |
| 17♉ | 16♊ | 17♋ | 16♌ | 18♎ | 17♏ | 19♑ | 18♒ | 18♈ | 17♉ | 16♊ | 18♌ |
| 19♊ | 18♋ | 20♌ | 18♍ | 21♏ | 19♐ | 21♒ | 20♓ | 20♉ | 20♊ | 18♋ | 20♍ |
| 22♋ | 20♌ | 22♍ | 21♎ | 23♐ | 22♑ | 23♓ | 22♈ | 22♊ | 22♋ | 20♌ | 23♎ |
| 24♌ | 23♍ | 25♎ | 23♏ | 25♑ | 24♒ | 25♈ | 24♉ | 24♋ | 24♌ | 23♍ | 25♏ |
| 27♍ | 25♎ | 27♏ | 26♐ | 28♒ | 26♓ | 27♉ | 26♊ | 27♌ | 26♍ | 25♎ | 28♐ |
| 29♎ | 28♏ | 30♐ | 28♑ | 30♓ | 28♈ | 30♊ | 28♋ | 29♍ | 29♎ | 28♏ | 30♑ |
|  |  |  | 30♒ |  | 30♉ |  | 30♌ |  |  | 30♐ |  |

| Key: | Aries | Taurus | Gemini | Cancer | Leo | Virgo |
|---|---|---|---|---|---|---|
|  | ♈ | ♉ | ♊ | ♋ | ♌ | ♍ |

70

## 1892

| JAN. | FEB. | MAR. | APR. | MAY | JUNE | JULY | AUG. | SEPT. | OCT. | NOV. | DEC. |
|---|---|---|---|---|---|---|---|---|---|---|---|
| 1♒ | 2♈ | 2♉ | 1♊ | 2♌ | 1♍ | 1♎ | 2♐ | 1♑ | 1♒ | 1♈ | 1♉ |
| 3♓ | 4♉ | 4♊ | 3♋ | 5♍ | 3♎ | 3♏ | 5♑ | 3♒ | 3♓ | 3♉ | 3♊ |
| 5♈ | 6♊ | 6♋ | 5♌ | 7♎ | 6♏ | 6♐ | 7♒ | 5♓ | 5♈ | 5♊ | 5♋ |
| 8♉ | 8♋ | 9♌ | 7♍ | 10♏ | 8♐ | 8♑ | 9♓ | 7♈ | 7♉ | 7♋ | 7♌ |
| 10♊ | 10♌ | 11♍ | 10♎ | 12♐ | 11♑ | 10♒ | 11♈ | 9♉ | 9♊ | 9♌ | 9♍ |
| 12♋ | 13♍ | 14♎ | 12♏ | 15♑ | 13♒ | 13♓ | 13♉ | 12♊ | 11♋ | 12♍ | 11♎ |
| 14♌ | 15♎ | 16♏ | 15♐ | 17♒ | 15♓ | 15♈ | 15♊ | 14♋ | 13♌ | 14♎ | 14♏ |
| 17♍ | 18♏ | 19♐ | 17♑ | 19♓ | 18♈ | 17♉ | 17♋ | 16♌ | 15♍ | 17♏ | 17♐ |
| 19♎ | 20♐ | 21♑ | 20♒ | 21♈ | 20♉ | 19♊ | 20♌ | 18♍ | 18♎ | 19♐ | 19♑ |
| 22♏ | 23♑ | 23♒ | 22♓ | 23♉ | 22♊ | 21♋ | 22♍ | 21♎ | 20♏ | 22♑ | 21♒ |
| 24♐ | 25♒ | 25♓ | 24♈ | 25♊ | 24♋ | 23♌ | 24♎ | 23♏ | 23♐ | 24♒ | 24♓ |
| 26♑ | 27♓ | 28♈ | 26♉ | 27♋ | 26♌ | 26♍ | 27♏ | 26♐ | 26♑ | 27♓ | 26♈ |
| 29♒ | 29♈ | 29♉ | 28♊ | 30♌ | 28♍ | 28♎ | 29♐ | 28♑ | 28♒ | 29♈ | 28♉ |
| 31♓ |  |  | 30♋ |  |  | 31♏ |  |  | 30♓ |  | 30♊ |

## 1893

| JAN. | FEB. | MAR. | APR. | MAY | JUNE | JULY | AUG. | SEPT. | OCT. | NOV. | DEC. |
|---|---|---|---|---|---|---|---|---|---|---|---|
| 1♋ | 2♍ | 1♍ | 2♏ | 2♐ | 1♑ | 1♒ | 2♈ | 2♊ | 1♋ | 2♍ | 2♎ |
| 3♌ | 4♎ | 4♎ | 5♐ | 5♑ | 3♒ | 3♓ | 4♉ | 4♋ | 4♌ | 4♎ | 4♏ |
| 5♍ | 7♏ | 6♏ | 7♑ | 7♒ | 6♓ | 5♈ | 6♊ | 6♌ | 6♍ | 7♏ | 6♐ |
| 8♎ | 9♐ | 8♐ | 10♒ | 9♓ | 8♈ | 8♉ | 8♋ | 8♍ | 8♎ | 9♐ | 9♑ |
| 10♏ | 12♑ | 11♑ | 12♓ | 12♈ | 10♉ | 10♊ | 10♌ | 11♎ | 10♏ | 12♐ | 11♒ |
| 13♐ | 14♒ | 13♒ | 14♈ | 14♉ | 12♊ | 12♋ | 12♍ | 13♐ | 13♑ | 14♒ | 14♓ |
| 15♑ | 16♓ | 16♓ | 16♉ | 16♊ | 14♋ | 14♌ | 14♎ | 15♑ | 15♒ | 17♓ | 16♈ |
| 18♒ | 18♈ | 18♈ | 18♊ | 18♋ | 16♌ | 16♍ | 17♏ | 18♒ | 18♓ | 19♈ | 19♉ |
| 20♓ | 21♉ | 20♉ | 20♋ | 20♌ | 18♍ | 18♎ | 19♐ | 21♓ | 20♈ | 21♉ | 21♊ |
| 22♈ | 23♊ | 22♊ | 22♌ | 22♍ | 21♎ | 20♏ | 22♑ | 23♈ | 23♉ | 23♊ | 23♋ |
| 24♉ | 25♋ | 24♋ | 25♍ | 24♎ | 23♏ | 23♐ | 24♒ | 25♉ | 25♊ | 25♋ | 25♌ |
| 26♊ | 27♌ | 26♌ | 27♎ | 27♏ | 26♐ | 25♑ | 27♓ | 27♊ | 27♋ | 27♌ | 27♍ |
| 29♋ |  | 29♍ | 30♏ | 29♐ | 28♑ | 28♒ | 29♈ | 29♋ | 29♌ | 29♍ | 29♎ |
| 31♌ |  | 31♎ |  |  |  | 30♓ | 31♉ |  | 31♍ |  | 31♏ |

| Libra | Scorpio | Sagittarius | Capricorn | Aquarius | Pisces |
|---|---|---|---|---|---|
| ♎ | ♏ | ♐ | ♑ | ♒ | ♓ |

## 1894

| JAN. | FEB. | MAR. | APR. | MAY | JUNE | JULY | AUG. | SEPT. | OCT. | NOV. | DEC. |
|---|---|---|---|---|---|---|---|---|---|---|---|
| 3♐ | 1♑ | 1♑ | 2♓ | 2♈ | 3♊ | 2♋ | 2♍ | 1♎ | 3♐ | 2♑ | 1♒ |
| 5♑ | 4♒ | 3♒ | 4♈ | 4♉ | 5♋ | 4♌ | 4♎ | 3♏ | 5♑ | 4♒ | 4♓ |
| 8♒ | 6♓ | 6♓ | 6♉ | 6♊ | 7♌ | 6♍ | 7♏ | 5♐ | 8♒ | 7♓ | 6♈ |
| 10♓ | 9♈ | 8♈ | 9♊ | 8♋ | 9♍ | 8♎ | 9♐ | 8♑ | 10♓ | 9♈ | 9♉ |
| 13♈ | 11♉ | 10♉ | 11♋ | 10♌ | 11♎ | 10♏ | 12♑ | 10♒ | 13♈ | 11♉ | 11♊ |
| 15♉ | 13♊ | 13♊ | 13♌ | 12♍ | 13♏ | 13♐ | 14♒ | 13♓ | 15♉ | 13♊ | 13♋ |
| 17♊ | 15♋ | 15♋ | 15♍ | 15♎ | 16♐ | 15♑ | 17♓ | 15♈ | 17♊ | 16♋ | 15♌ |
| 19♋ | 17♌ | 17♌ | 17♎ | 17♏ | 18♑ | 18♒ | 19♈ | 18♉ | 19♋ | 18♌ | 17♍ |
| 21♌ | 19♍ | 19♍ | 20♏ | 19♐ | 21♒ | 20♓ | 21♉ | 20♊ | 21♌ | 20♍ | 19♎ |
| 23♍ | 22♎ | 21♎ | 22♐ | 22♑ | 23♓ | 23♈ | 24♊ | 22♋ | 24♍ | 22♎ | 21♏ |
| 25♎ | 24♏ | 23♏ | 24♑ | 24♒ | 26♈ | 25♉ | 26♋ | 24♌ | 26♎ | 24♏ | 24♐ |
| 27♏ | 26♐ | 26♐ | 27♒ | 27♓ | 28♉ | 27♊ | 28♌ | 26♍ | 28♏ | 26♐ | 26♑ |
| 30♐ |  | 28♑ | 29♓ | 29♈ | 30♊ | 29♋ | 30♍ | 28♎ | 30♐ | 29♑ | 29♒ |
|  |  | 31♒ |  | 31♉ |  | 31♌ |  | 30♏ |  |  | 31♓ |

## 1895

| JAN. | FEB. | MAR. | APR. | MAY | JUNE | JULY | AUG. | SEPT. | OCT. | NOV. | DEC. |
|---|---|---|---|---|---|---|---|---|---|---|---|
| 3♈ | 1♉ | 1♉ | 1♋ | 1♌ | 1♎ | 1♏ | 2♑ | 3♓ | 3♈ | 1♉ | 1♊ |
| 5♉ | 4♊ | 3♊ | 4♌ | 3♍ | 3♏ | 3♐ | 4♒ | 5♈ | 5♉ | 4♊ | 3♋ |
| 7♊ | 6♋ | 5♋ | 6♍ | 5♎ | 6♐ | 5♑ | 7♓ | 8♉ | 7♊ | 6♋ | 5♌ |
| 9♋ | 8♌ | 7♌ | 8♎ | 7♏ | 8♑ | 8♒ | 9♈ | 10♊ | 10♋ | 8♌ | 8♍ |
| 11♌ | 10♍ | 9♍ | 10♏ | 9♐ | 10♒ | 10♓ | 12♉ | 13♋ | 12♌ | 10♍ | 10♎ |
| 13♍ | 12♎ | 11♎ | 12♐ | 12♑ | 13♓ | 13♈ | 14♊ | 15♌ | 14♍ | 12♎ | 12♏ |
| 15♎ | 14♏ | 13♏ | 14♑ | 14♒ | 15♈ | 15♉ | 16♋ | 17♍ | 16♎ | 15♏ | 14♐ |
| 18♏ | 16♐ | 16♐ | 17♒ | 17♓ | 18♉ | 18♊ | 18♌ | 19♎ | 18♏ | 17♐ | 16♑ |
| 20♐ | 19♑ | 18♑ | 19♓ | 19♈ | 20♊ | 20♋ | 20♍ | 21♏ | 20♐ | 19♑ | 19♒ |
| 22♑ | 21♒ | 20♒ | 22♈ | 22♉ | 22♋ | 22♌ | 22♎ | 23♐ | 22♑ | 21♒ | 21♓ |
| 25♒ | 24♓ | 23♓ | 24♉ | 24♊ | 24♌ | 24♍ | 24♏ | 25♑ | 25♒ | 24♓ | 24♈ |
| 27♓ | 26♈ | 25♈ | 26♊ | 26♋ | 26♍ | 26♎ | 26♐ | 28♒ | 27♓ | 26♈ | 26♉ |
| 30♈ |  | 28♉ | 29♋ | 28♌ | 28♎ | 28♏ | 28♑ | 30♓ | 30♈ | 29♉ | 28♊ |
|  |  | 30♊ |  | 30♍ |  | 30♐ | 31♒ |  |  |  | 31♋ |

| *Key:* | Aries | Taurus | Gemini | Cancer | Leo | Virgo |
|---|---|---|---|---|---|---|
|  | ♈ | ♉ | ♊ | ♋ | ♌ | ♍ |

## 1896

| JAN. | FEB. | MAR. | APR. | MAY | JUNE | JULY | AUG. | SEPT. | OCT. | NOV. | DEC. |
|---|---|---|---|---|---|---|---|---|---|---|---|
| 2♌ | 2♎ | 1♎ | 1♐ | 1♑ | 2♓ | 2♈ | 3♊ | 2♋ | 1♌ | 2♎ | 1♏ |
| 4♍ | 4♏ | 3♏ | 3♑ | 3♒ | 4♈ | 4♉ | 5♋ | 4♌ | 3♍ | 4♏ | 3♐ |
| 6♎ | 6♐ | 5♐ | 6♒ | 5♓ | 7♉ | 7♊ | 7♌ | 6♍ | 5♎ | 6♐ | 5♑ |
| 8♏ | 9♑ | 7♑ | 8♓ | 8♈ | 9♊ | 9♋ | 10♍ | 8♎ | 7♏ | 8♑ | 8♒ |
| 10♐ | 11♒ | 9♒ | 11♈ | 10♉ | 12♋ | 11♌ | 12♎ | 10♏ | 9♐ | 10♒ | 10♓ |
| 13♑ | 14♓ | 12♓ | 13♉ | 13♊ | 14♌ | 13♍ | 14♏ | 12♐ | 12♑ | 13♓ | 12♈ |
| 15♒ | 16♈ | 14♈ | 16♊ | 15♋ | 16♍ | 15♎ | 16♐ | 14♑ | 14♒ | 15♈ | 15♉ |
| 17♓ | 19♉ | 17♉ | 18♋ | 18♌ | 18♎ | 17♏ | 18♑ | 17♒ | 16♓ | 18♉ | 17♊ |
| 20♈ | 21♊ | 19♊ | 20♌ | 20♍ | 20♏ | 20♐ | 20♒ | 19♓ | 19♈ | 20♊ | 20♋ |
| 22♉ | 23♋ | 22♋ | 23♍ | 22♎ | 22♐ | 22♑ | 23♓ | 22♈ | 21♉ | 22♋ | 22♌ |
| 25♊ | 26♌ | 24♌ | 25♎ | 24♏ | 24♑ | 24♒ | 25♈ | 24♉ | 24♊ | 25♌ | 24♍ |
| 27♋ | 28♍ | 26♍ | 27♏ | 26♐ | 27♒ | 26♓ | 28♉ | 27♊ | 26♋ | 27♍ | 27♎ |
| 29♌ | | 28♎ | 29♐ | 28♑ | 29♓ | 29♈ | 30♊ | 29♋ | | 29♎ | 29♏ |
| 31♏ | | 30♏ | | 30♒ | | 31♉ | | | | 31♍ | 31♐ |

## 1897

| JAN. | FEB. | MAR. | APR. | MAY | JUNE | JULY | AUG. | SEPT. | OCT. | NOV. | DEC. |
|---|---|---|---|---|---|---|---|---|---|---|---|
| 2♑ | 3♓ | 2♓ | 1♈ | 3♊ | 2♋ | 1♌ | 2♎ | 1♏ | 2♑ | 3♓ | 2♈ |
| 4♒ | 5♈ | 4♈ | 3♉ | 5♋ | 4♌ | 4♍ | 4♏ | 3♐ | 4♒ | 5♈ | 5♉ |
| 6♓ | 8♉ | 7♉ | 6♊ | 8♌ | 6♍ | 6♎ | 6♐ | 5♑ | 6♓ | 7♉ | 7♊ |
| 9♈ | 10♊ | 9♊ | 8♋ | 10♍ | 9♎ | 8♏ | 9♑ | 7♒ | 9♈ | 10♊ | 10♋ |
| 11♉ | 12♋ | 12♋ | 11♌ | 12♎ | 11♏ | 10♐ | 11♒ | 9♓ | 11♉ | 13♋ | 12♌ |
| 14♊ | 15♌ | 14♌ | 13♍ | 14♏ | 13♐ | 12♑ | 13♓ | 11♈ | 14♊ | 15♌ | 15♍ |
| 16♋ | 17♍ | 16♍ | 15♎ | 16♐ | 15♑ | 14♒ | 15♈ | 14♉ | 16♋ | 17♍ | 17♎ |
| 18♌ | 19♎ | 18♎ | 17♏ | 18♑ | 17♒ | 16♓ | 18♉ | 16♊ | 19♌ | 20♎ | 19♏ |
| 21♍ | 21♏ | 20♏ | 19♐ | 20♒ | 19♓ | 19♈ | 20♊ | 19♋ | 21♍ | 22♏ | 21♐ |
| 23♎ | 23♐ | 23♐ | 21♑ | 23♓ | 21♈ | 21♉ | 23♋ | 21♌ | 23♎ | 24♐ | 23♑ |
| 25♏ | 25♑ | 25♑ | 23♒ | 25♈ | 24♉ | 24♊ | 25♌ | 24♍ | 25♏ | 26♑ | 25♒ |
| 27♐ | 28♒ | 27♒ | 25♓ | 28♉ | 26♊ | 26♋ | 27♍ | 26♎ | 27♐ | 28♒ | 27♓ |
| 29♑ | | 29♓ | 28♈ | 30♊ | 29♋ | 29♌ | 29♎ | 28♏ | 29♑ | 30♓ | 30♈ |
| 31♒ | | 30♉ | | | | 31♍ | | 30♐ | 31♒ | | |

| Libra | Scorpio | Sagittarius | Capricorn | Aquarius | Pisces |
|---|---|---|---|---|---|
| ♎ | ♏ | ♐ | ♑ | ♒ | ♓ |

## 1898

| JAN. | FEB. | MAR. | APR. | MAY | JUNE | JULY | AUG. | SEPT. | OCT. | NOV. | DEC. |
|---|---|---|---|---|---|---|---|---|---|---|---|
| 1♉ | 2♋ | 1♋ | 1♌ | 3♎ | 1♏ | 1♐ | 1♒ | 2♈ | 1♉ | 2♋ | 2♌ |
| 3♊ | 5♌ | 4♌ | 3♍ | 5♏ | 3♐ | 3♑ | 3♓ | 4♉ | 4♊ | 5♌ | 5♍ |
| 6♋ | 7♍ | 7♍ | 5♎ | 7♐ | 5♑ | 5♒ | 5♈ | 6♊ | 6♋ | 7♍ | 7♎ |
| 9♌ | 9♎ | 9♎ | 7♏ | 9♑ | 7♒ | 7♓ | 7♉ | 9♋ | 9♌ | 10♎ | 9♏ |
| 11♍ | 12♏ | 11♏ | 9♐ | 11♒ | 9♓ | 9♈ | 10♊ | 11♌ | 11♍ | 12♏ | 12♐ |
| 13♎ | 14♐ | 13♐ | 11♑ | 13♓ | 11♈ | 11♉ | 12♋ | 14♍ | 13♎ | 14♐ | 14♑ |
| 15♏ | 16♑ | 15♑ | 14♒ | 15♈ | 14♉ | 14♊ | 15♌ | 16♎ | 16♏ | 16♑ | 16♒ |
| 18♐ | 18♒ | 17♒ | 16♓ | 18♉ | 16♊ | 16♋ | 17♍ | 18♏ | 18♐ | 18♒ | 18♓ |
| 20♑ | 20♓ | 20♓ | 18♈ | 20♊ | 19♋ | 19♌ | 20♎ | 20♐ | 20♑ | 20♓ | 20♈ |
| 22♒ | 22♈ | 22♈ | 20♉ | 23♋ | 21♌ | 21♍ | 22♏ | 23♑ | 22♒ | 23♈ | 22♉ |
| 24♓ | 25♉ | 24♉ | 23♊ | 25♌ | 24♍ | 24♎ | 24♐ | 25♒ | 24♓ | 25♉ | 24♊ |
| 26♈ | 27♊ | 26♊ | 25♋ | 28♍ | 26♎ | 26♏ | 26♑ | 27♓ | 26♈ | 27♊ | 27♋ |
| 28♉ | 29♋ | 29♋ | 28♌ | 30♎ | 29♏ | 28♐ | 28♒ | 29♈ | 29♉ | 30♋ | 29♌ |
| 31♊ | | 30♍ | 30♍ | | | 30♑ | 30♓ | | 31♊ | | |

## 1899

| JAN. | FEB. | MAR. | APR. | MAY | JUNE | JULY | AUG. | SEPT. | OCT. | NOV. | DEC. |
|---|---|---|---|---|---|---|---|---|---|---|---|
| 1♍ | 2♏ | 1♏ | 2♑ | 1♒ | 2♈ | 1♉ | 2♋ | 1♌ | 1♍ | 2♏ | 2♐ |
| 3♎ | 4♐ | 4♐ | 4♒ | 4♓ | 4♉ | 4♊ | 5♌ | 4♍ | 3♎ | 4♐ | 4♑ |
| 6♏ | 6♑ | 6♑ | 6♓ | 6♈ | 6♊ | 6♋ | 7♍ | 6♎ | 6♏ | 7♑ | 6♒ |
| 8♐ | 8♒ | 8♒ | 8♈ | 8♉ | 9♋ | 9♌ | 10♎ | 8♏ | 8♐ | 9♒ | 8♓ |
| 10♑ | 10♓ | 10♓ | 10♉ | 10♊ | 11♌ | 11♍ | 12♏ | 11♐ | 10♑ | 11♓ | 10♈ |
| 12♒ | 12♈ | 12♈ | 13♊ | 12♋ | 14♍ | 14♎ | 15♐ | 13♑ | 13♒ | 13♈ | 12♉ |
| 14♓ | 15♉ | 14♉ | 15♋ | 15♌ | 16♎ | 16♏ | 17♑ | 15♒ | 15♓ | 15♉ | 15♊ |
| 16♈ | 17♊ | 16♊ | 18♌ | 18♍ | 19♏ | 18♐ | 19♒ | 17♓ | 17♈ | 17♊ | 17♋ |
| 18♉ | 19♋ | 19♋ | 20♍ | 20♎ | 21♐ | 20♑ | 21♓ | 19♈ | 19♉ | 20♋ | 19♌ |
| 21♊ | 22♌ | 21♌ | 23♎ | 22♏ | 23♑ | 22♒ | 23♈ | 21♉ | 21♊ | 22♌ | 22♍ |
| 23♋ | 23♍ | 24♍ | 25♏ | 24♐ | 25♒ | 24♓ | 25♉ | 24♊ | 23♋ | 25♍ | 24♎ |
| 26♌ | 27♎ | 26♎ | 27♐ | 27♑ | 27♓ | 26♈ | 27♊ | 26♋ | 26♌ | 27♎ | 27♏ |
| 28♍ | | 29♏ | 29♑ | 29♒ | 29♈ | 29♉ | 30♋ | 28♌ | 29♍ | 29♏ | 29♐ |
| 31♎ | | 31♐ | | 31♓ | | 31♊ | | | 31♎ | | 31♑ |

*Key:*   Aries   Taurus   Gemini   Cancer   Leo   Virgo

♈          ♉          ♊          ♋          ♌          ♍

## 1900

| JAN. | FEB. | MAR. | APR. | MAY | JUNE | JULY | AUG. | SEPT. | OCT. | NOV. | DEC. |
|---|---|---|---|---|---|---|---|---|---|---|---|
| 2♒ | 1♓ | 2♈ | 1♉ | 2♋ | 1♌ | 1♍ | 2♏ | 1♐ | 1♑ | 1♓ | 1♈ |
| 4♓ | 3♈ | 4♉ | 3♊ | 5♌ | 4♍ | 3♎ | 5♐ | 3♑ | 3♒ | 4♈ | 3♉ |
| 6♈ | 5♉ | 6♊ | 5♋ | 7♍ | 6♎ | 6♏ | 7♑ | 6♒ | 5♓ | 6♉ | 5♊ |
| 9♉ | 7♊ | 8♋ | 7♌ | 10♎ | 9♏ | 8♐ | 9♒ | 8♓ | 7♈ | 8♊ | 7♋ |
| 11♊ | 9♋ | 11♌ | 10♍ | 12♏ | 11♐ | 11♑ | 11♓ | 10♈ | 9♉ | 10♋ | 9♌ |
| 13♋ | 12♌ | 14♍ | 12♎ | 15♐ | 13♑ | 13♒ | 13♈ | 12♉ | 11♊ | 12♌ | 11♍ |
| 16♌ | 14♍ | 16♎ | 15♏ | 17♑ | 15♒ | 15♓ | 15♉ | 14♊ | 13♋ | 14♍ | 14♎ |
| 18♍ | 17♎ | 19♏ | 17♐ | 19♒ | 18♓ | 17♈ | 17♊ | 16♋ | 16♌ | 17♎ | 17♏ |
| 21♎ | 19♏ | 21♐ | 20♑ | 21♓ | 20♈ | 19♉ | 20♋ | 18♌ | 18♍ | 19♏ | 19♐ |
| 23♏ | 22♐ | 23♑ | 22♒ | 23♈ | 22♉ | 21♊ | 22♌ | 21♍ | 21♎ | 22♐ | 22♑ |
| 26♐ | 24♑ | 26♒ | 24♓ | 26♉ | 24♊ | 23♋ | 25♍ | 23♎ | 23♏ | 24♑ | 24♒ |
| 28♑ | 26♒ | 28♓ | 26♈ | 28♊ | 26♋ | 26♌ | 27♎ | 26♏ | 26♐ | 27♒ | 26♓ |
| 30♒ | 28♓ | 30♈ | 28♉ | 30♋ | 29♌ | 28♍ | 30♏ | 28♐ | 28♑ | 29♓ | 28♈ |
|  |  |  | 30♊ |  |  | 31♎ |  |  | 30♒ |  | 30♉ |

## 1901

| JAN. | FEB. | MAR. | APR. | MAY | JUNE | JULY | AUG. | SEPT. | OCT. | NOV. | DEC. |
|---|---|---|---|---|---|---|---|---|---|---|---|
| 1♊ | 2♌ | 1♌ | 2♎ | 2♏ | 1♐ | 1♑ | 2♓ | 2♉ | 1♊ | 2♌ | 2♍ |
| 3♋ | 4♍ | 4♍ | 5♏ | 5♐ | 3♑ | 3♒ | 4♈ | 4♊ | 4♋ | 4♍ | 4♎ |
| 6♌ | 7♎ | 6♎ | 7♐ | 7♑ | 6♒ | 5♓ | 6♉ | 6♋ | 6♌ | 7♎ | 7♏ |
| 8♍ | 9♏ | 9♏ | 10♑ | 10♒ | 8♓ | 7♈ | 8♊ | 9♌ | 8♍ | 9♏ | 9♐ |
| 11♎ | 12♐ | 11♐ | 12♒ | 12♓ | 10♈ | 10♉ | 10♋ | 11♍ | 11♎ | 12♐ | 12♑ |
| 13♏ | 14♑ | 14♑ | 14♓ | 14♈ | 12♉ | 12♊ | 12♌ | 13♎ | 13♏ | 14♑ | 14♒ |
| 16♐ | 16♒ | 16♒ | 17♈ | 16♉ | 14♊ | 14♋ | 15♍ | 16♏ | 16♐ | 17♒ | 16♓ |
| 18♑ | 19♓ | 18♓ | 19♉ | 18♊ | 16♋ | 16♌ | 17♎ | 18♐ | 18♑ | 19♓ | 19♈ |
| 20♒ | 21♈ | 20♈ | 21♊ | 20♋ | 18♌ | 18♍ | 19♏ | 21♑ | 21♒ | 21♈ | 21♉ |
| 22♓ | 23♉ | 22♉ | 23♋ | 22♌ | 21♍ | 21♎ | 22♐ | 23♒ | 23♓ | 23♉ | 23♊ |
| 24♈ | 25♊ | 24♊ | 25♌ | 24♍ | 23♎ | 23♏ | 24♑ | 25♓ | 25♈ | 25♊ | 25♋ |
| 26♉ | 27♋ | 26♋ | 27♍ | 27♎ | 26♏ | 26♐ | 27♒ | 27♈ | 27♉ | 27♋ | 27♌ |
| 29♊ |  | 29♌ | 30♎ | 29♏ | 28♐ | 28♑ | 29♓ | 29♉ | 29♊ | 29♌ | 29♍ |
| 31♋ |  | 31♍ |  |  |  | 30♒ | 31♈ |  | 31♋ |  | 31♎ |

| Libra | Scorpio | Sagittarius | Capricorn | Aquarius | Pisces |
|---|---|---|---|---|---|
| ♎ | ♏ | ♐ | ♑ | ♒ | ♓ |

## 1902

| JAN. | FEB. | MAR. | APR. | MAY | JUNE | JULY | AUG. | SEPT. | OCT. | NOV. | DEC. |
|---|---|---|---|---|---|---|---|---|---|---|---|
| 3♏ | 2♐ | 1♐ | 2♒ | 2♓ | 1♈ | 2♊ | 1♋ | 1♍ | 1♎ | 2♐ | 2♑ |
| 5♐ | 4♑ | 4♑ | 5♓ | 4♈ | 3♉ | 4♋ | 3♌ | 3♎ | 3♏ | 4♑ | 4♒ |
| 8♑ | 7♒ | 6♒ | 7♈ | 6♉ | 5♊ | 6♌ | 5♍ | 6♏ | 5♐ | 7♒ | 7♓ |
| 10♒ | 9♓ | 8♓ | 9♉ | 8♊ | 7♋ | 8♍ | 7♎ | 8♐ | 8♑ | 9♓ | 9♈ |
| 13♓ | 11♈ | 10♈ | 11♊ | 10♋ | 9♌ | 11♎ | 9♏ | 11♑ | 10♒ | 12♈ | 11♉ |
| 15♈ | 13♉ | 13♉ | 13♋ | 12♌ | 11♍ | 13♏ | 14♐ | 13♒ | 13♓ | 14♉ | 13♊ |
| 17♉ | 15♊ | 15♊ | 15♌ | 15♍ | 13♎ | 15♐ | 17♑ | 15♓ | 15♈ | 16♊ | 15♋ |
| 19♊ | 18♋ | 17♋ | 17♍ | 17♎ | 16♏ | 18♑ | 19♒ | 18♈ | 17♉ | 18♋ | 17♌ |
| 21♋ | 20♌ | 19♌ | 20♎ | 19♏ | 18♐ | 20♒ | 21♓ | 20♉ | 19♊ | 20♌ | 19♍ |
| 23♌ | 22♍ | 21♍ | 22♏ | 22♐ | 21♑ | 23♓ | 24♈ | 22♊ | 21♋ | 22♍ | 21♎ |
| 25♍ | 24♎ | 23♎ | 25♐ | 24♑ | 23♒ | 25♈ | 26♉ | 24♋ | 23♌ | 24♎ | 24♏ |
| 28♎ | 27♏ | 26♏ | 27♑ | 27♒ | 26♓ | 27♉ | 28♊ | 26♌ | 26♍ | 27♏ | 26♐ |
| 30♏ |  | 28♐ | 29♒ | 29♓ | 28♈ | 30♊ | 30♋ | 28♍ | 28♎ | 29♐ | 29♑ |
|  |  | 31♑ |  |  | 30♉ |  |  |  |  |  | 31♒ |

## 1903

| JAN. | FEB. | MAR. | APR. | MAY | JUNE | JULY | AUG. | SEPT. | OCT. | NOV. | DEC. |
|---|---|---|---|---|---|---|---|---|---|---|---|
| 3♓ | 1♈ | 1♈ | 1♊ | 1♋ | 1♍ | 1♎ | 2♐ | 3♒ | 3♓ | 2♈ | 1♉ |
| 5♈ | 4♉ | 3♉ | 4♋ | 3♌ | 3♎ | 3♏ | 4♑ | 5♓ | 5♈ | 4♉ | 3♊ |
| 8♉ | 6♊ | 5♊ | 6♌ | 5♍ | 6♏ | 5♐ | 7♒ | 8♈ | 8♉ | 6♊ | 6♋ |
| 10♊ | 8♋ | 7♋ | 8♍ | 7♎ | 8♐ | 8♑ | 9♓ | 10♉ | 10♊ | 8♋ | 8♌ |
| 12♋ | 10♌ | 9♌ | 10♎ | 10♏ | 11♑ | 10♒ | 12♈ | 13♊ | 12♋ | 10♌ | 10♍ |
| 14♌ | 12♍ | 11♍ | 12♏ | 12♐ | 13♒ | 13♓ | 14♉ | 15♋ | 14♌ | 12♍ | 12♎ |
| 16♍ | 14♎ | 14♎ | 15♐ | 14♑ | 16♓ | 15♈ | 16♊ | 17♌ | 16♍ | 15♎ | 14♏ |
| 18♎ | 16♏ | 16♏ | 17♑ | 17♒ | 18♈ | 18♉ | 18♋ | 19♍ | 18♎ | 17♏ | 16♐ |
| 20♏ | 19♐ | 18♐ | 20♒ | 19♓ | 20♉ | 20♊ | 20♌ | 21♎ | 20♏ | 19♐ | 19♑ |
| 23♐ | 21♑ | 21♑ | 22♓ | 22♈ | 23♊ | 22♋ | 22♍ | 23♏ | 23♐ | 21♑ | 21♒ |
| 25♑ | 24♒ | 23♒ | 24♈ | 24♉ | 25♋ | 24♌ | 25♎ | 25♐ | 25♑ | 24♒ | 24♓ |
| 28♒ | 26♓ | 26♓ | 27♉ | 26♊ | 27♌ | 26♍ | 27♏ | 28♑ | 28♒ | 26♓ | 26♈ |
| 30♓ |  | 28♈ | 29♊ | 28♋ | 29♍ | 28♎ | 29♐ | 30♒ | 30♓ | 29♈ | 28♉ |
|  |  | 30♉ |  | 30♌ |  | 30♏ | 31♑ |  |  |  | 31♊ |

| Key: | Aries | Taurus | Gemini | Cancer | Leo | Virgo |
|---|---|---|---|---|---|---|
|  | ♈ | ♉ | ♊ | ♋ | ♌ | ♍ |

## 1904

| JAN. | FEB. | MAR. | APR. | MAY | JUNE | JULY | AUG. | SEPT. | OCT. | NOV. | DEC. |
|---|---|---|---|---|---|---|---|---|---|---|---|
| 2♋ | 2♍ | 1♍ | 1♏ | 1♐ | 2♒ | 2♓ | 1♈ | 2♊ | 1♋ | 2♍ | 1♎ |
| 4♌ | 4♎ | 3♎ | 4♐ | 3♑ | 4♓ | 4♈ | 3♉ | 4♋ | 4♌ | 4♎ | 4♏ |
| 6♍ | 7♏ | 5♏ | 6♑ | 6♒ | 7♈ | 7♉ | 6♊ | 6♌ | 6♍ | 6♏ | 6♐ |
| 8♎ | 9♐ | 7♐ | 8♒ | 8♓ | 9♉ | 9♊ | 8♋ | 8♍ | 8♎ | 8♐ | 8♑ |
| 10♏ | 11♑ | 10♑ | 11♓ | 11♈ | 12♊ | 11♋ | 10♌ | 10♎ | 10♏ | 10♑ | 10♒ |
| 13♐ | 14♒ | 12♒ | 13♈ | 13♉ | 14♋ | 13♌ | 12♍ | 12♏ | 12♐ | 13♒ | 13♓ |
| 15♑ | 16♓ | 15♓ | 16♉ | 15♊ | 16♌ | 15♍ | 14♎ | 14♐ | 14♑ | 15♓ | 15♈ |
| 17♒ | 19♈ | 17♈ | 18♊ | 18♋ | 18♍ | 17♎ | 16♏ | 17♑ | 16♒ | 18♈ | 18♉ |
| 20♓ | 21♉ | 20♉ | 20♋ | 20♌ | 20♎ | 19♏ | 18♐ | 19♒ | 19♓ | 20♉ | 20♊ |
| 23♈ | 24♊ | 22♊ | 23♌ | 22♍ | 22♏ | 22♐ | 20♑ | 22♓ | 21♈ | 23♊ | 22♋ |
| 25♉ | 26♋ | 24♋ | 25♍ | 24♎ | 25♐ | 24♑ | 23♒ | 24♈ | 24♉ | 25♋ | 24♌ |
| 27♊ | 28♌ | 26♌ | 27♎ | 26♏ | 27♑ | 27♒ | 25♓ | 27♉ | 26♊ | 27♌ | 26♍ |
| 29♋ | | 28♍ | 29♏ | 28♐ | 29♒ | 29♓ | 28♈ | 29♊ | 29♋ | 29♍ | 29♎ |
| 31♌ | | 30♎ | | 31♑ | | 31♈ | | | 31♌ | | 31♏ |

## 1905

| JAN. | FEB. | MAR. | APR. | MAY | JUNE | JULY | AUG. | SEPT. | OCT. | NOV. | DEC. |
|---|---|---|---|---|---|---|---|---|---|---|---|
| 2♐ | 3♒ | 2♒ | 1♓ | 1♈ | 2♊ | 1♋ | 2♍ | 1♎ | 2♐ | 1♑ | 2♓ |
| 4♑ | 5♓ | 4♓ | 3♈ | 3♉ | 4♋ | 4♌ | 4♎ | 4♏ | 4♑ | 3♒ | 5♈ |
| 6♒ | 8♈ | 7♈ | 6♉ | 6♊ | 6♌ | 6♍ | 6♏ | 6♐ | 6♒ | 5♓ | 7♉ |
| 9♓ | 10♉ | 10♉ | 8♊ | 8♋ | 9♍ | 8♎ | 9♐ | 8♑ | 9♓ | 8♈ | 10♊ |
| 11♈ | 13♊ | 12♊ | 11♋ | 10♌ | 11♎ | 10♏ | 11♑ | 10♒ | 11♈ | 10♉ | 12♋ |
| 14♉ | 15♋ | 14♋ | 13♌ | 12♍ | 13♏ | 12♐ | 13♒ | 13♓ | 14♉ | 13♊ | 15♌ |
| 16♊ | 17♌ | 17♌ | 15♍ | 15♎ | 15♐ | 14♑ | 15♓ | 15♈ | 16♊ | 15♋ | 17♍ |
| 19♋ | 19♍ | 19♍ | 17♎ | 17♏ | 17♑ | 17♒ | 18♈ | 17♉ | 19♋ | 17♌ | 19♎ |
| 21♌ | 21♎ | 21♎ | 19♏ | 19♐ | 19♒ | 19♓ | 20♉ | 19♊ | 21♌ | 20♍ | 21♏ |
| 23♍ | 23♏ | 23♏ | 21♐ | 21♑ | 22♓ | 21♈ | 22♊ | 22♋ | 23♍ | 22♎ | 23♐ |
| 25♎ | 25♐ | 25♐ | 23♑ | 23♒ | 24♈ | 24♉ | 24♋ | 24♌ | 25♎ | 24♏ | 25♑ |
| 27♏ | 28♑ | 27♑ | 26♒ | 25♓ | 27♉ | 26♊ | 26♌ | 26♍ | 27♏ | 26♐ | 28♒ |
| 29♐ | | 29♒ | 28♓ | 27♈ | 29♊ | 29♋ | 28♍ | 28♎ | 29♐ | 28♑ | 30♓ |
| 31♑ | | 31♓ | | 30♉ | | 31♌ | 30♎ | 30♏ | 31♑ | 30♒ | |

| Libra | Scorpio | Sagittarius | Capricorn | Aquarius | Pisces |
|---|---|---|---|---|---|
| ♎ | ♏ | ♐ | ♑ | ♒ | ♓ |

## 1906

| JAN. | FEB. | MAR. | APR. | MAY | JUNE | JULY | AUG. | SEPT. | OCT. | NOV. | DEC. |
|---|---|---|---|---|---|---|---|---|---|---|---|
| 1♈ | 3♊ | 2♊ | 1♋ | 3♍ | 1♎ | 1♏ | 1♑ | 2♓ | 1♈ | 3♊ | 2♋ |
| 4♉ | 5♋ | 4♋ | 3♌ | 5♎ | 3♏ | 3♐ | 3♒ | 4♈ | 4♉ | 5♋ | 5♌ |
| 6♊ | 7♌ | 7♌ | 5♍ | 7♏ | 5♐ | 5♑ | 5♓ | 6♉ | 6♊ | 8♌ | 7♍ |
| 9♋ | 10♍ | 9♍ | 8♎ | 9♐ | 7♑ | 7♒ | 8♈ | 9♊ | 9♋ | 10♍ | 10♎ |
| 11♌ | 12♎ | 11♎ | 10♏ | 11♑ | 9♒ | 9♓ | 10♉ | 11♋ | 11♌ | 12♎ | 12♏ |
| 13♍ | 14♏ | 13♏ | 12♐ | 13♒ | 12♓ | 11♈ | 13♊ | 14♌ | 14♍ | 14♏ | 14♐ |
| 15♎ | 16♐ | 15♐ | 14♑ | 15♓ | 14♈ | 14♉ | 15♋ | 16♍ | 16♎ | 16♐ | 16♑ |
| 18♏ | 18♑ | 17♑ | 16♒ | 18♈ | 16♉ | 16♊ | 18♌ | 18♎ | 18♏ | 18♑ | 18♒ |
| 20♐ | 20♒ | 20♒ | 18♓ | 20♉ | 19♊ | 19♋ | 20♍ | 20♏ | 20♐ | 20♒ | 20♓ |
| 22♑ | 23♓ | 22♓ | 20♈ | 23♊ | 21♋ | 21♌ | 22♎ | 23♐ | 22♑ | 23♓ | 22♈ |
| 24♒ | 25♈ | 24♈ | 23♉ | 25♋ | 24♌ | 24♍ | 24♏ | 25♑ | 24♒ | 25♈ | 25♉ |
| 26♓ | 27♉ | 27♉ | 25♊ | 28♌ | 26♍ | 26♎ | 26♐ | 27♒ | 26♓ | 27♉ | 27♊ |
| 29♈ | | 29♊ | 28♋ | 30♍ | 29♎ | 28♏ | 28♑ | 29♓ | 29♈ | 30♊ | 30♋ |
| 31♉ | | | 30♌ | | | 30♐ | 31♒ | | 31♉ | | |

## 1907

| JAN. | FEB. | MAR. | APR. | MAY | JUNE | JULY | AUG. | SEPT. | OCT. | NOV. | DEC. |
|---|---|---|---|---|---|---|---|---|---|---|---|
| 1♌ | 2♎ | 1♎ | 2♐ | 1♑ | 2♓ | 1♈ | 2♊ | 1♋ | 1♌ | 2♎ | 2♏ |
| 4♍ | 4♏ | 4♏ | 4♑ | 3♒ | 4♈ | 4♉ | 5♋ | 4♌ | 4♍ | 5♏ | 4♐ |
| 6♎ | 7♐ | 6♐ | 6♒ | 6♓ | 6♉ | 6♊ | 7♌ | 6♍ | 6♎ | 7♐ | 6♑ |
| 8♏ | 9♑ | 8♑ | 8♓ | 8♈ | 9♊ | 9♋ | 10♍ | 9♎ | 8♏ | 9♑ | 8♒ |
| 10♐ | 11♒ | 10♒ | 11♈ | 10♉ | 11♋ | 11♌ | 12♎ | 11♏ | 10♐ | 11♒ | 10♓ |
| 12♑ | 13♓ | 12♓ | 13♉ | 13♊ | 14♌ | 14♍ | 15♏ | 13♐ | 13♑ | 13♓ | 12♈ |
| 14♒ | 15♈ | 14♈ | 15♊ | 15♋ | 16♍ | 16♎ | 17♐ | 15♑ | 15♒ | 15♈ | 15♉ |
| 16♓ | 17♉ | 17♉ | 18♋ | 18♌ | 19♎ | 18♏ | 19♑ | 17♒ | 17♓ | 17♉ | 17♊ |
| 18♈ | 20♊ | 19♊ | 20♌ | 20♍ | 21♏ | 21♐ | 21♒ | 19♓ | 19♈ | 20♊ | 20♋ |
| 21♉ | 22♋ | 22♋ | 23♍ | 23♎ | 23♐ | 23♑ | 23♓ | 22♈ | 21♉ | 22♋ | 22♌ |
| 23♊ | 25♌ | 24♌ | 25♎ | 25♏ | 25♑ | 25♒ | 25♈ | 24♉ | 23♊ | 25♌ | 25♍ |
| 26♋ | 27♍ | 26♍ | 27♏ | 27♐ | 27♒ | 27♓ | 27♉ | 26♊ | 26♋ | 27♍ | 27♎ |
| 28♌ | | 29♎ | 29♐ | 29♑ | 29♓ | 29♈ | 30♊ | 29♋ | 28♌ | 30♎ | 29♏ |
| 31♍ | | 31♏ | | 31♒ | | 31♉ | | | 31♍ | | |

| Key: | Aries | Taurus | Gemini | Cancer | Leo | Virgo |
|---|---|---|---|---|---|---|
| | ♈ | ♉ | ♊ | ♋ | ♌ | ♍ |

## 1908

| JAN. | FEB. | MAR. | APR. | MAY | JUNE | JULY | AUG. | SEPT. | OCT. | NOV. | DEC. |
|---|---|---|---|---|---|---|---|---|---|---|---|
| 1♐ | 1♒ | 2♓ | 2♉ | 2♊ | 3♌ | 3♍ | 1♎ | 3♐ | 2♑ | 3♓ | 2♈ |
| 3♑ | 3♓ | 4♈ | 4♉ | 4♋ | 5♍ | 5♎ | 4♏ | 5♑ | 4♒ | 5♈ | 4♉ |
| 5♒ | 5♈ | 6♉ | 7♋ | 7♌ | 8♎ | 8♏ | 6♐ | 7♒ | 6♓ | 7♉ | 6♊ |
| 7♓ | 7♉ | 8♊ | 9♌ | 9♍ | 10♏ | 10♐ | 8♑ | 9♓ | 8♈ | 9♊ | 9♋ |
| 9♈ | 10♊ | 10♋ | 11♎ | 11♏ | 12♐ | 12♑ | 10♒ | 11♈ | 10♉ | 11♋ | 11♌ |
| 11♉ | 12♋ | 13♌ | 14♏ | 14♏ | 15♑ | 14♒ | 12♓ | 13♉ | 12♊ | 14♌ | 13♍ |
| 13♊ | 15♌ | 15♍ | 16♏ | 16♐ | 17♒ | 16♓ | 14♈ | 15♊ | 15♋ | 16♍ | 16♎ |
| 16♋ | 17♍ | 18♎ | 19♐ | 18♑ | 19♓ | 18♈ | 16♉ | 17♋ | 17♌ | 19♎ | 18♏ |
| 18♌ | 20♎ | 20♏ | 21♑ | 20♒ | 21♈ | 20♉ | 19♊ | 20♌ | 20♍ | 21♍ | 21♐ |
| 21♍ | 22♏ | 22♐ | 23♒ | 22♓ | 23♉ | 22♊ | 21♋ | 22♍ | 22♎ | 23♐ | 23♑ |
| 23♎ | 24♐ | 25♑ | 25♓ | 25♈ | 25♊ | 25♋ | 24♌ | 25♎ | 25♏ | 26♑ | 25♒ |
| 26♏ | 26♑ | 27♒ | 27♈ | 27♉ | 28♋ | 27♌ | 26♍ | 27♏ | 27♐ | 28♒ | 27♓ |
| 28♐ | 29♒ | 29♓ | 29♉ | 29♊ | 30♌ | 30♍ | 29♎ | 30♐ | 29♑ | 30♓ | 29♈ |
| 30♑ | | 31♈ | | 31♋ | | | 31♏ | | 31♑ | | 31♉ |

## 1909

| JAN. | FEB. | MAR. | APR. | MAY | JUNE | JULY | AUG. | SEPT. | OCT. | NOV. | DEC. |
|---|---|---|---|---|---|---|---|---|---|---|---|
| 3♊ | 1♋ | 3♌ | 2♍ | 1♎ | 3♐ | 2♑ | 1♒ | 1♈ | 1♉ | 1♋ | 1♌ |
| 5♋ | 4♌ | 5♍ | 4♎ | 4♏ | 5♑ | 4♒ | 3♓ | 3♉ | 3♊ | 3♌ | 3♍ |
| 7♌ | 6♍ | 8♎ | 7♏ | 6♐ | 7♒ | 6♓ | 5♈ | 5♊ | 5♋ | 6♍ | 6♎ |
| 10♍ | 9♎ | 10♏ | 9♐ | 9♑ | 9♓ | 9♈ | 7♉ | 8♋ | 7♌ | 8♎ | 8♏ |
| 12♎ | 11♏ | 13♐ | 11♑ | 11♒ | 11♈ | 11♉ | 9♊ | 10♌ | 10♍ | 11♏ | 11♐ |
| 15♏ | 13♐ | 15♑ | 14♒ | 13♓ | 13♉ | 13♊ | 11♋ | 12♍ | 12♎ | 13♐ | 13♑ |
| 17♐ | 16♑ | 17♒ | 16♓ | 15♈ | 16♊ | 15♋ | 14♌ | 15♎ | 15♏ | 16♑ | 15♒ |
| 19♑ | 18♒ | 19♓ | 18♈ | 17♉ | 18♋ | 17♌ | 16♍ | 17♏ | 17♐ | 18♒ | 18♓ |
| 21♒ | 20♓ | 21♈ | 20♉ | 19♊ | 20♌ | 20♍ | 19♎ | 20♐ | 20♑ | 20♒ | 20♈ |
| 23♓ | 22♈ | 23♉ | 22♊ | 21♋ | 22♍ | 22♎ | 21♏ | 22♑ | 22♒ | 23♈ | 22♉ |
| 25♈ | 24♉ | 25♊ | 24♋ | 24♌ | 25♎ | 25♏ | 24♐ | 25♒ | 24♓ | 25♉ | 24♊ |
| 28♉ | 26♊ | 28♋ | 26♌ | 26♍ | 27♏ | 27♐ | 26♑ | 27♓ | 26♈ | 27♊ | 26♋ |
| 30♊ | 28♋ | 30♌ | 29♍ | 29♎ | 30♐ | 30♑ | 28♒ | 29♈ | 28♉ | 29♋ | 28♌ |
| | | | | 31♏ | | | 30♓ | | 30♊ | | 31♍ |

| Libra | Scorpio | Sagittarius | Capricorn | Aquarius | Pisces |
|---|---|---|---|---|---|
| ♎ | ♏ | ♐ | ♑ | ♒ | ♓ |

## 1910

| JAN. | FEB. | MAR. | APR. | MAY | JUNE | JULY | AUG. | SEPT. | OCT. | NOV. | DEC. |
|---|---|---|---|---|---|---|---|---|---|---|---|
| 2♎ | 1♏ | 3♐ | 2♑ | 1♒ | 2♈ | 1♉ | 2♋ | 2♍ | 2♎ | 1♏ | 1♐ |
| 5♏ | 3♐ | 5♑ | 4♒ | 3♓ | 4♉ | 3♊ | 4♌ | 5♎ | 5♏ | 3♐ | 3♑ |
| 7♐ | 6♑ | 8♒ | 6♓ | 6♈ | 6♊ | 5♋ | 6♍ | 7♏ | 7♐ | 6♑ | 6♒ |
| 9♑ | 8♒ | 10♓ | 8♈ | 8♉ | 8♋ | 8♌ | 8♎ | 10♐ | 10♑ | 8♒ | 8♓ |
| 12♒ | 10♓ | 12♈ | 10♉ | 10♊ | 10♌ | 10♍ | 11♏ | 12♑ | 12♒ | 11♓ | 10♈ |
| 14♓ | 12♈ | 14♉ | 12♊ | 12♋ | 12♍ | 12♎ | 13♐ | 15♒ | 14♓ | 13♈ | 12♉ |
| 16♈ | 14♉ | 16♊ | 14♋ | 14♌ | 15♎ | 15♏ | 16♐ | 17♓ | 16♈ | 15♉ | 14♊ |
| 18♉ | 16♊ | 18♋ | 16♌ | 16♍ | 17♏ | 17♐ | 18♒ | 19♈ | 18♉ | 17♊ | 16♋ |
| 20♊ | 19♋ | 20♌ | 19♍ | 18♎ | 20♐ | 20♑ | 21♓ | 21♉ | 20♊ | 19♋ | 18♌ |
| 22♋ | 21♌ | 23♍ | 21♎ | 21♏ | 22♑ | 22♒ | 23♈ | 23♊ | 23♋ | 21♌ | 20♍ |
| 25♌ | 23♍ | 25♎ | 24♏ | 24♐ | 25♒ | 24♓ | 25♉ | 25♋ | 25♌ | 23♍ | 23♎ |
| 27♍ | 26♎ | 28♏ | 26♐ | 26♑ | 27♓ | 26♈ | 27♊ | 27♌ | 27♍ | 26♎ | 25♏ |
| 29♎ | 28♏ | 30♐ | 29♑ | 28♒ | 29♈ | 29♉ | 29♋ | 30♍ | 29♎ | 28♏ | 28♐ |
|  |  |  |  | 31♓ |  | 31♊ | 31♌ |  |  |  | 30♑ |

## 1911

| JAN. | FEB. | MAR. | APR. | MAY | JUNE | JULY | AUG. | SEPT. | OCT. | NOV. | DEC. |
|---|---|---|---|---|---|---|---|---|---|---|---|
| 2♒ | 3♈ | 2♈ | 1♉ | 2♋ | 3♍ | 2♎ | 1♏ | 2♑ | 2♒ | 1♓ | 3♉ |
| 4♓ | 5♉ | 4♉ | 3♊ | 4♌ | 5♎ | 4♏ | 3♐ | 5♒ | 4♓ | 3♈ | 5♊ |
| 6♈ | 7♊ | 6♊ | 5♋ | 6♍ | 7♏ | 7♐ | 6♑ | 7♓ | 7♈ | 5♉ | 7♋ |
| 9♉ | 9♋ | 8♋ | 7♌ | 9♎ | 10♐ | 10♑ | 8♒ | 9♈ | 9♉ | 7♊ | 9♌ |
| 11♊ | 11♌ | 11♌ | 9♍ | 11♏ | 12♑ | 12♒ | 11♓ | 12♉ | 11♊ | 9♋ | 11♍ |
| 13♋ | 13♍ | 13♍ | 11♎ | 13♐ | 15♒ | 14♓ | 13♈ | 14♊ | 13♋ | 11♌ | 13♎ |
| 15♌ | 16♎ | 15♎ | 14♏ | 16♑ | 17♓ | 17♈ | 15♉ | 16♋ | 15♌ | 14♍ | 15♏ |
| 17♍ | 18♏ | 17♏ | 16♐ | 19♒ | 20♈ | 19♉ | 17♊ | 18♌ | 17♍ | 16♎ | 18♐ |
| 19♎ | 21♐ | 20♐ | 19♑ | 21♓ | 22♉ | 21♊ | 20♋ | 20♍ | 20♎ | 18♏ | 20♑ |
| 22♏ | 23♑ | 22♑ | 21♒ | 23♈ | 24♊ | 23♋ | 22♌ | 22♎ | 22♏ | 21♐ | 23♒ |
| 24♐ | 26♒ | 25♒ | 24♓ | 25♉ | 26♋ | 25♌ | 24♍ | 25♏ | 24♐ | 23♑ | 25♓ |
| 27♑ | 28♓ | 27♓ | 26♈ | 27♊ | 28♌ | 27♍ | 26♎ | 27♐ | 27♑ | 26♒ | 28♈ |
| 29♒ |  | 29♈ | 28♉ | 29♋ | 30♍ | 29♎ | 28♏ | 29♑ | 29♒ | 28♓ | 30♉ |
| 31♓ |  |  | 30♊ | 31♌ |  | 31♏ |  |  |  | 30♈ |  |

| Key: | Aries | Taurus | Gemini | Cancer | Leo | Virgo |
|---|---|---|---|---|---|---|
|  | ♈ | ♉ | ♊ | ♋ | ♌ | ♍ |

## 1912

| JAN. | FEB. | MAR. | APR. | MAY | JUNE | JULY | AUG. | SEPT. | OCT. | NOV. | DEC. |
|---|---|---|---|---|---|---|---|---|---|---|---|
| 1♊ | 2♌ | 2♍ | 1♎ | 2♐ | 1♑ | 1♒ | 2♈ | 1♉ | 3♋ | 1♌ | 2♎ |
| 3♋ | 4♍ | 4♎ | 3♏ | 5♑ | 4♒ | 3♓ | 5♉ | 3♊ | 5♌ | 3♍ | 5♏ |
| 5♌ | 6♎ | 6♏ | 5♐ | 7♒ | 6♓ | 6♈ | 7♊ | 5♋ | 7♍ | 5♎ | 7♐ |
| 7♍ | 8♏ | 9♐ | 8♑ | 10♓ | 9♈ | 8♉ | 9♋ | 7♌ | 9♎ | 7♏ | 9♑ |
| 9♎ | 10♐ | 11♑ | 10♒ | 12♈ | 11♉ | 11♊ | 11♌ | 9♍ | 11♏ | 10♐ | 12♒ |
| 12♏ | 13♑ | 14♒ | 13♓ | 15♉ | 13♊ | 13♋ | 13♍ | 11♎ | 13♐ | 12♑ | 14♓ |
| 14♐ | 15♒ | 16♓ | 15♈ | 17♊ | 15♋ | 15♌ | 15♎ | 14♏ | 16♑ | 14♒ | 17♈ |
| 17♑ | 18♓ | 19♈ | 17♉ | 19♋ | 17♌ | 17♍ | 17♏ | 16♐ | 18♒ | 17♓ | 19♉ |
| 19♒ | 20♈ | 21♉ | 19♊ | 21♌ | 19♍ | 19♎ | 19♐ | 18♑ | 21♓ | 19♈ | 21♊ |
| 22♓ | 23♉ | 23♊ | 21♋ | 23♍ | 21♎ | 21♏ | 22♑ | 21♒ | 23♈ | 22♉ | 24♋ |
| 24♈ | 25♊ | 25♋ | 24♌ | 25♎ | 24♏ | 23♐ | 24♒ | 23♓ | 25♉ | 24♊ | 26♌ |
| 26♉ | 27♋ | 27♌ | 26♍ | 27♏ | 26♐ | 26♑ | 27♓ | 26♈ | 28♊ | 26♋ | 28♍ |
| 29♊ | 29♌ | 29♍ | 28♎ | 30♐ | 28♑ | 28♒ | 29♈ | 28♉ | 30♋ | 28♌ | 30♎ |
| 31♋ |  |  | 30♏ |  |  | 31♓ |  | 30♊ |  | 30♍ |  |

## 1913

| JAN. | FEB. | MAR. | APR. | MAY | JUNE | JULY | AUG. | SEPT. | OCT. | NOV. | DEC. |
|---|---|---|---|---|---|---|---|---|---|---|---|
| 1♏ | 2♑ | 1♑ | 2♓ | 2♈ | 1♉ | 1♊ | 1♌ | 2♎ | 1♏ | 2♑ | 2♒ |
| 3♐ | 4♒ | 4♒ | 5♈ | 5♉ | 3♊ | 3♋ | 3♍ | 4♏ | 3♐ | 4♒ | 4♓ |
| 6♑ | 7♓ | 6♓ | 7♉ | 7♊ | 6♋ | 5♌ | 5♎ | 6♐ | 6♑ | 7♓ | 7♈ |
| 8♒ | 9♈ | 9♈ | 10♊ | 9♋ | 8♌ | 7♍ | 8♏ | 8♑ | 8♒ | 9♈ | 9♉ |
| 11♓ | 12♉ | 11♉ | 12♋ | 11♌ | 10♍ | 9♎ | 10♐ | 11♒ | 10♓ | 12♉ | 12♊ |
| 13♈ | 14♊ | 13♊ | 14♌ | 14♍ | 12♎ | 11♏ | 12♑ | 13♓ | 13♈ | 14♊ | 14♋ |
| 16♉ | 16♋ | 16♋ | 16♍ | 16♎ | 14♏ | 13♐ | 14♒ | 16♈ | 15♉ | 17♋ | 16♌ |
| 18♊ | 18♌ | 18♌ | 18♎ | 18♏ | 16♐ | 16♑ | 17♓ | 18♉ | 18♊ | 19♌ | 18♍ |
| 20♋ | 20♍ | 20♍ | 20♏ | 20♐ | 18♑ | 18♒ | 19♈ | 21♊ | 20♋ | 21♍ | 20♎ |
| 22♌ | 22♎ | 22♎ | 23♐ | 22♑ | 21♒ | 21♓ | 22♉ | 23♋ | 23♌ | 23♎ | 22♏ |
| 24♍ | 25♏ | 24♏ | 25♑ | 24♒ | 23♓ | 23♈ | 24♊ | 25♌ | 25♍ | 25♏ | 25♐ |
| 26♎ | 27♐ | 26♐ | 27♒ | 27♓ | 26♈ | 26♉ | 27♋ | 27♍ | 27♎ | 27♐ | 27♑ |
| 28♏ |  | 28♑ | 30♓ | 30♈ | 28♉ | 28♊ | 29♌ | 29♎ | 29♏ | 29♑ | 29♒ |
| 30♐ |  | 31♒ |  |  | 30♊ | 30♋ | 31♍ |  | 31♐ |  | 31♓ |

| Libra | Scorpio | Sagittarius | Capricorn | Aquarius | Pisces |
|---|---|---|---|---|---|
| ♎ | ♏ | ♐ | ♑ | ♒ | ♓ |

## 1914

| JAN. | FEB. | MAR. | APR. | MAY | JUNE | JULY | AUG. | SEPT. | OCT. | NOV. | DEC. |
|---|---|---|---|---|---|---|---|---|---|---|---|
| 3♈ | 2♉ | 1♉ | 2♋ | 2♌ | 2♎ | 2♏ | 2♑ | 1♒ | 3♈ | 2♉ | 1♊ |
| 5♉ | 4♊ | 4♊ | 5♌ | 4♍ | 5♏ | 4♐ | 5♒ | 3♓ | 5♉ | 4♊ | 4♋ |
| 8♊ | 7♋ | 6♋ | 7♍ | 6♎ | 7♐ | 6♑ | 7♓ | 6♈ | 8♊ | 7♋ | 6♌ |
| 10♋ | 9♌ | 8♌ | 9♎ | 8♏ | 9♑ | 8♒ | 9♈ | 8♉ | 10♋ | 9♌ | 9♍ |
| 12♌ | 11♍ | 10♍ | 11♏ | 10♐ | 11♒ | 11♓ | 12♉ | 11♊ | 13♌ | 11♍ | 11♎ |
| 14♍ | 13♎ | 12♎ | 13♐ | 12♑ | 13♓ | 13♈ | 14♊ | 13♋ | 15♍ | 14♎ | 13♏ |
| 17♎ | 15♏ | 14♏ | 15♑ | 14♒ | 16♈ | 15♉ | 17♋ | 15♌ | 17♎ | 16♏ | 15♐ |
| 19♏ | 17♐ | 16♐ | 17♒ | 17♓ | 18♉ | 18♊ | 19♌ | 18♍ | 19♏ | 18♐ | 17♑ |
| 21♐ | 19♑ | 19♑ | 20♓ | 19♈ | 21♊ | 20♋ | 21♍ | 20♎ | 21♐ | 20♑ | 19♒ |
| 23♑ | 22♒ | 21♒ | 22♈ | 22♉ | 23♋ | 23♌ | 23♎ | 23♏ | 23♑ | 22♒ | 21♓ |
| 25♒ | 24♓ | 23♓ | 25♉ | 24♊ | 25♌ | 25♍ | 25♏ | 24♐ | 25♒ | 24♓ | 24♈ |
| 28♓ | 27♈ | 26♈ | 27♊ | 27♋ | 28♍ | 27♎ | 27♐ | 26♑ | 28♓ | 26♈ | 26♉ |
| 30♈ |  | 28♉ | 30♋ | 29♌ | 30♎ | 29♏ | 30♑ | 28♒ | 30♈ | 29♉ | 29♊ |
|  |  | 31♊ |  | 31♍ |  | 31♐ |  | 30♓ |  |  | 31♋ |

## 1915

| JAN. | FEB. | MAR. | APR. | MAY | JUNE | JULY | AUG. | SEPT. | OCT. | NOV. | DEC. |
|---|---|---|---|---|---|---|---|---|---|---|---|
| 3♌ | 1♍ | 1♍ | 1♏ | 1♐ | 1♒ | 1♓ | 2♉ | 3♋ | 3♌ | 2♍ | 1♎ |
| 5♍ | 3♎ | 3♎ | 3♐ | 3♑ | 4♓ | 3♈ | 4♊ | 5♌ | 5♍ | 4♎ | 3♏ |
| 7♎ | 5♏ | 5♏ | 5♑ | 5♒ | 6♈ | 5♉ | 7♋ | 7♍ | 7♎ | 6♏ | 5♐ |
| 9♏ | 8♐ | 7♐ | 7♒ | 7♓ | 8♉ | 8♊ | 9♌ | 10♎ | 9♏ | 8♐ | 7♑ |
| 11♐ | 10♑ | 9♑ | 10♓ | 9♈ | 11♊ | 10♋ | 11♍ | 12♏ | 12♐ | 11♑ | 9♒ |
| 13♑ | 12♒ | 11♒ | 12♈ | 12♉ | 13♋ | 13♌ | 14♎ | 14♐ | 14♑ | 13♒ | 11♓ |
| 16♒ | 14♓ | 13♓ | 15♉ | 14♊ | 16♌ | 15♍ | 16♏ | 16♑ | 16♒ | 15♓ | 14♈ |
| 18♓ | 16♈ | 16♈ | 17♊ | 17♋ | 18♍ | 17♎ | 18♐ | 18♒ | 18♓ | 17♈ | 16♉ |
| 20♈ | 19♉ | 18♉ | 20♋ | 19♌ | 20♎ | 19♏ | 20♑ | 21♓ | 20♈ | 19♉ | 19♊ |
| 23♉ | 21♊ | 21♊ | 22♌ | 22♍ | 22♏ | 22♐ | 22♒ | 23♈ | 23♉ | 21♊ | 21♋ |
| 25♊ | 24♋ | 23♋ | 24♍ | 24♎ | 24♐ | 24♑ | 24♓ | 25♉ | 25♊ | 24♋ | 24♌ |
| 28♋ | 26♌ | 26♌ | 27♎ | 26♏ | 26♑ | 26♒ | 27♈ | 28♊ | 28♋ | 26♌ | 26♍ |
| 30♌ |  | 28♍ | 29♏ | 28♐ | 28♒ | 28♓ | 29♉ | 30♋ | 30♌ | 29♍ | 29♎ |
|  |  | 30♎ |  | 30♑ | 30♓ | 31♈ | 31♊ |  |  |  | 31♏ |

| *Key:* | Aries | Taurus | Gemini | Cancer | Leo | Virgo |
|---|---|---|---|---|---|---|
|  | ♈ | ♉ | ♊ | ♋ | ♌ | ♍ |

## 1916

| JAN. | FEB. | MAR. | APR. | MAY | JUNE | JULY | AUG. | SEPT. | OCT. | NOV. | DEC. |
|---|---|---|---|---|---|---|---|---|---|---|---|
| 2♐ | 2♒ | 1♒ | 1♈ | 1♉ | 2♋ | 2♌ | 1♍ | 2♏ | 1♐ | 2♒ | 1♓ |
| 4♑ | 4♓ | 3♓ | 4♉ | 3♊ | 5♌ | 4♍ | 3♎ | 4♐ | 3♑ | 4♓ | 3♈ |
| 6♒ | 6♈ | 5♈ | 6♊ | 6♋ | 7♍ | 7♎ | 5♏ | 6♑ | 5♒ | 6♈ | 5♉ |
| 8♓ | 9♉ | 7♉ | 8♋ | 8♌ | 9♎ | 9♏ | 8♐ | 8♒ | 7♓ | 8♉ | 8♊ |
| 10♈ | 11♊ | 10♊ | 11♌ | 11♍ | 12♏ | 11♐ | 10♑ | 10♓ | 10♈ | 10♊ | 10♋ |
| 12♉ | 14♋ | 12♋ | 13♍ | 13♎ | 14♐ | 13♑ | 12♒ | 12♈ | 12♉ | 13♋ | 13♌ |
| 15♊ | 16♌ | 15♌ | 16♎ | 15♏ | 16♑ | 15♒ | 14♓ | 14♉ | 14♊ | 15♌ | 15♍ |
| 17♋ | 19♍ | 17♍ | 18♏ | 17♐ | 18♒ | 17♓ | 16♈ | 17♊ | 16♋ | 18♍ | 18♎ |
| 20♌ | 21♎ | 19♎ | 20♐ | 19♑ | 20♓ | 19♈ | 18♉ | 19♋ | 19♌ | 20♎ | 20♏ |
| 22♍ | 23♏ | 22♏ | 22♑ | 21♒ | 22♈ | 22♉ | 20♊ | 22♌ | 21♍ | 23♏ | 22♐ |
| 25♎ | 25♐ | 24♐ | 24♒ | 24♓ | 24♉ | 24♊ | 23♋ | 24♍ | 24♎ | 25♐ | 24♑ |
| 27♏ | 28♑ | 26♑ | 26♓ | 26♈ | 27♊ | 26♋ | 25♌ | 27♎ | 26♏ | 27♑ | 26♒ |
| 29♐ |  | 28♒ | 29♈ | 28♉ | 29♋ | 29♌ | 28♍ | 29♏ | 28♐ | 29♒ | 28♓ |
| 31♑ |  | 30♓ |  | 30♊ |  |  | 30♎ |  | 30♑ |  | 30♈ |

## 1917

| JAN. | FEB. | MAR. | APR. | MAY | JUNE | JULY | AUG. | SEPT. | OCT. | NOV. | DEC. |
|---|---|---|---|---|---|---|---|---|---|---|---|
| 2♉ | 3♋ | 2♋ | 1♌ | 1♍ | 2♏ | 1♐ | 2♒ | 2♈ | 2♉ | 3♋ | 2♌ |
| 4♊ | 5♌ | 4♌ | 3♍ | 3♎ | 4♐ | 4♑ | 4♓ | 4♉ | 4♊ | 5♌ | 5♍ |
| 6♋ | 8♍ | 7♍ | 6♎ | 5♏ | 6♑ | 6♒ | 6♈ | 7♊ | 6♋ | 8♍ | 7♎ |
| 9♌ | 10♎ | 9♎ | 8♏ | 8♐ | 8♒ | 8♓ | 8♉ | 9♋ | 9♌ | 10♎ | 10♏ |
| 11♍ | 13♏ | 12♏ | 10♐ | 10♑ | 10♓ | 10♈ | 10♊ | 11♌ | 11♍ | 13♏ | 12♐ |
| 14♎ | 15♐ | 14♐ | 13♑ | 12♒ | 12♈ | 12♉ | 13♋ | 14♍ | 14♎ | 15♐ | 14♑ |
| 16♏ | 17♑ | 16♑ | 15♒ | 14♓ | 15♉ | 14♊ | 15♌ | 17♎ | 16♏ | 17♑ | 17♒ |
| 19♐ | 19♒ | 18♒ | 17♓ | 16♈ | 17♊ | 16♋ | 18♍ | 19♏ | 19♐ | 19♒ | 19♓ |
| 21♑ | 21♓ | 21♓ | 19♈ | 18♉ | 19♋ | 19♌ | 20♎ | 21♐ | 21♑ | 23♓ | 21♈ |
| 23♒ | 23♈ | 23♈ | 21♉ | 21♊ | 22♌ | 21♍ | 23♏ | 24♑ | 23♒ | 24♈ | 23♉ |
| 25♓ | 25♉ | 25♉ | 23♊ | 23♋ | 24♍ | 24♎ | 25♐ | 26♒ | 25♓ | 26♉ | 25♊ |
| 27♈ | 27♊ | 27♊ | 26♋ | 25♌ | 27♎ | 26♏ | 27♑ | 28♓ | 27♈ | 28♊ | 27♋ |
| 29♉ |  | 29♋ | 28♌ | 28♍ | 29♏ | 29♐ | 29♒ | 30♈ | 29♉ | 30♋ | 30♌ |
| 31♊ |  |  |  | 30♎ |  | 31♑ | 31♓ |  | 31♊ |  |  |

| Libra | Scorpio | Sagittarius | Capricorn | Aquarius | Pisces |
|---|---|---|---|---|---|
| ♎ | ♏ | ♐ | ♑ | ♒ | ♓ |

## 1918

| JAN. | FEB. | MAR. | APR. | MAY | JUNE | JULY | AUG. | SEPT. | OCT. | NOV. | DEC. |
|---|---|---|---|---|---|---|---|---|---|---|---|
| 1♍ | 3♏ | 2♏ | 1♐ | 3♒ | 1♓ | 2♉ | 1♊ | 2♌ | 1♍ | 2♏ | 2♐ |
| 4♎ | 5♐ | 4♐ | 3♑ | 5♓ | 3♈ | 5♊ | 3♋ | 4♍ | 4♎ | 5♐ | 5♑ |
| 6♏ | 7♑ | 7♑ | 5♒ | 7♈ | 5♉ | 7♋ | 5♌ | 6♎ | 6♏ | 7♑ | 7♒ |
| 9♐ | 9♒ | 9♒ | 7♓ | 9♉ | 7♊ | 9♌ | 8♍ | 9♏ | 9♐ | 10♒ | 9♓ |
| 11♑ | 11♓ | 11♓ | 9♈ | 11♊ | 9♋ | 11♍ | 10♎ | 11♐ | 11♑ | 12♓ | 11♈ |
| 13♒ | 13♈ | 13♈ | 11♉ | 13♋ | 12♌ | 14♎ | 13♏ | 14♑ | 14♒ | 14♈ | 14♉ |
| 15♓ | 15♉ | 15♉ | 13♊ | 15♌ | 14♍ | 16♏ | 15♐ | 16♒ | 16♓ | 16♉ | 16♊ |
| 17♈ | 18♊ | 17♊ | 16♋ | 18♍ | 17♎ | 19♐ | 18♑ | 18♓ | 18♈ | 18♊ | 18♋ |
| 19♉ | 20♋ | 19♋ | 18♌ | 20♎ | 19♏ | 21♑ | 20♒ | 20♈ | 20♉ | 20♋ | 20♌ |
| 21♊ | 22♌ | 22♌ | 20♍ | 23♏ | 21♐ | 23♒ | 22♓ | 22♉ | 22♊ | 22♌ | 22♍ |
| 24♋ | 25♍ | 24♍ | 23♎ | 25♐ | 24♑ | 25♓ | 24♈ | 24♊ | 24♋ | 25♍ | 25♎ |
| 26♌ | 27♎ | 27♎ | 25♏ | 27♑ | 26♒ | 27♈ | 26♉ | 26♋ | 26♌ | 27♎ | 27♏ |
| 29♍ | | 29♏ | 28♐ | 28♒ | 28♓ | 30♉ | 28♊ | 29♋ | 28♍ | 30♏ | 30♐ |
| 31♎ | | | 30♑ | 30♓ | 30♈ | | 30♋ | | 31♎ | | |

## 1919

| JAN. | FEB. | MAR. | APR. | MAY | JUNE | JULY | AUG. | SEPT. | OCT. | NOV. | DEC. |
|---|---|---|---|---|---|---|---|---|---|---|---|
| 1♑ | 2♓ | 1♓ | 2♉ | 1♊ | 2♌ | 1♍ | 2♏ | 1♐ | 1♑ | 2♓ | 2♈ |
| 3♒ | 4♈ | 3♈ | 4♊ | 3♋ | 4♍ | 4♎ | 5♐ | 4♑ | 4♒ | 4♈ | 4♉ |
| 6♓ | 6♉ | 5♉ | 6♋ | 5♌ | 6♎ | 6♏ | 7♑ | 6♒ | 6♓ | 7♉ | 6♊ |
| 8♈ | 8♊ | 7♊ | 8♌ | 8♍ | 9♏ | 9♐ | 10♒ | 8♓ | 8♈ | 9♊ | 8♋ |
| 10♉ | 10♋ | 10♋ | 10♍ | 10♎ | 11♐ | 11♑ | 12♓ | 11♈ | 10♉ | 11♋ | 10♌ |
| 12♊ | 13♌ | 12♌ | 13♎ | 13♏ | 14♑ | 14♒ | 14♈ | 13♉ | 12♊ | 13♌ | 12♍ |
| 14♋ | 15♍ | 14♍ | 15♏ | 15♐ | 16♒ | 16♓ | 16♉ | 15♊ | 14♋ | 15♍ | 14♎ |
| 16♌ | 17♎ | 17♎ | 18♐ | 18♑ | 18♓ | 18♈ | 19♊ | 17♋ | 17♌ | 17♎ | 17♏ |
| 18♍ | 20♏ | 19♏ | 20♑ | 20♒ | 21♈ | 20♉ | 21♋ | 19♌ | 19♍ | 20♏ | 19♐ |
| 21♎ | 22♐ | 22♐ | 23♒ | 22♓ | 23♉ | 22♊ | 23♌ | 21♍ | 21♎ | 22♐ | 22♑ |
| 23♏ | 25♑ | 24♑ | 25♓ | 25♈ | 25♊ | 24♋ | 25♍ | 24♎ | 23♏ | 25♑ | 24♒ |
| 26♐ | 27♒ | 26♒ | 27♈ | 27♉ | 27♋ | 27♌ | 27♎ | 26♏ | 26♐ | 27♒ | 27♓ |
| 28♑ | | 28♓ | 29♉ | 29♊ | 29♌ | 29♍ | 29♏ | 28♐ | 28♑ | 30♓ | 29♈ |
| 31♒ | | 31♈ | | 31♋ | | 31♎ | | | 31♒ | | 31♉ |

| Key: | Aries | Taurus | Gemini | Cancer | Leo | Virgo |
|---|---|---|---|---|---|---|
| | ♈ | ♉ | ♊ | ♋ | ♌ | ♍ |

## 1920

| JAN. | FEB. | MAR. | APR. | MAY | JUNE | JULY | AUG. | SEPT. | OCT. | NOV. | DEC. |
|---|---|---|---|---|---|---|---|---|---|---|---|
| 2♊ | 1♋ | 1♌ | 2♎ | 2♏ | 3♑ | 3♒ | 1♓ | 2♉ | 2♊ | 2♌ | 1♍ |
| 4♋ | 3♌ | 3♍ | 4♏ | 4♐ | 5♒ | 5♓ | 4♈ | 4♊ | 4♋ | 4♍ | 4♎ |
| 6♌ | 5♍ | 6♎ | 7♐ | 7♑ | 8♓ | 7♈ | 6♉ | 7♋ | 6♌ | 6♎ | 6♏ |
| 9♍ | 7♎ | 8♏ | 9♑ | 9♒ | 10♈ | 10♉ | 8♊ | 9♌ | 8♍ | 9♏ | 8♐ |
| 11♎ | 10♏ | 10♐ | 12♒ | 12♓ | 12♉ | 12♊ | 10♋ | 11♍ | 10♎ | 11♐ | 11♑ |
| 13♏ | 12♐ | 13♑ | 14♓ | 14♈ | 14♊ | 14♋ | 12♌ | 13♎ | 12♏ | 14♑ | 13♒ |
| 16♐ | 15♑ | 15♒ | 16♈ | 16♉ | 16♋ | 16♌ | 14♍ | 15♏ | 15♐ | 16♒ | 16♓ |
| 18♑ | 17♒ | 18♓ | 19♉ | 18♊ | 18♌ | 18♍ | 16♎ | 17♐ | 17♑ | 19♓ | 18♈ |
| 21♒ | 19♓ | 20♈ | 21♊ | 20♋ | 20♍ | 20♎ | 19♏ | 20♑ | 20♒ | 21♈ | 21♉ |
| 23♓ | 22♈ | 22♉ | 23♋ | 22♌ | 23♎ | 22♏ | 21♐ | 22♒ | 22♓ | 23♉ | 23♊ |
| 25♈ | 24♉ | 24♊ | 25♌ | 24♍ | 25♏ | 25♐ | 24♑ | 25♓ | 25♈ | 25♊ | 25♋ |
| 28♉ | 26♊ | 26♋ | 27♍ | 26♎ | 28♐ | 27♑ | 26♒ | 27♈ | 27♉ | 27♋ | 27♌ |
| 30♊ | 28♋ | 28♌ | 29♎ | 29♏ | 30♑ | 30♒ | 29♓ | 29♉ | 29♊ | 29♌ | 29♍ |
|  |  | 31♍ |  | 31♐ |  |  | 31♈ |  | 31♋ |  | 31♎ |

## 1921

| JAN. | FEB. | MAR. | APR. | MAY | JUNE | JULY | AUG. | SEPT. | OCT. | NOV. | DEC. |
|---|---|---|---|---|---|---|---|---|---|---|---|
| 2♏ | 1♐ | 3♑ | 2♒ | 1♓ | 3♉ | 2♊ | 1♋ | 1♍ | 3♏ | 1♐ | 1♑ |
| 5♐ | 3♑ | 5♒ | 4♓ | 4♈ | 5♊ | 4♋ | 3♌ | 3♎ | 5♐ | 3♑ | 3♒ |
| 7♑ | 6♒ | 8♓ | 6♈ | 6♉ | 7♋ | 6♌ | 5♍ | 5♏ | 7♑ | 6♒ | 6♓ |
| 10♒ | 8♓ | 10♈ | 9♉ | 8♊ | 9♌ | 8♍ | 7♎ | 7♐ | 10♒ | 8♓ | 8♈ |
| 12♓ | 11♈ | 13♉ | 11♊ | 10♋ | 11♍ | 10♎ | 9♏ | 10♑ | 12♓ | 11♈ | 11♉ |
| 15♈ | 13♉ | 15♊ | 13♋ | 13♌ | 13♎ | 12♏ | 11♐ | 12♒ | 15♈ | 13♉ | 13♊ |
| 17♉ | 16♊ | 17♋ | 15♌ | 15♍ | 15♏ | 15♐ | 14♑ | 15♓ | 17♉ | 16♊ | 15♋ |
| 19♊ | 18♋ | 19♌ | 17♍ | 17♎ | 18♐ | 17♑ | 16♒ | 17♈ | 19♊ | 18♋ | 17♌ |
| 21♋ | 20♌ | 21♍ | 20♎ | 19♏ | 20♑ | 20♒ | 19♓ | 20♉ | 22♋ | 20♌ | 19♍ |
| 23♌ | 22♍ | 23♎ | 22♏ | 21♐ | 23♒ | 22♓ | 21♈ | 22♊ | 24♌ | 22♍ | 21♎ |
| 25♍ | 24♎ | 25♏ | 24♐ | 24♑ | 25♓ | 25♈ | 24♉ | 24♋ | 26♍ | 24♎ | 24♏ |
| 27♎ | 26♏ | 28♐ | 26♑ | 26♒ | 28♈ | 27♉ | 26♊ | 26♌ | 28♎ | 26♏ | 26♐ |
| 30♏ | 28♐ | 30♑ | 29♒ | 29♓ | 30♉ | 30♊ | 28♋ | 28♍ | 30♏ | 29♐ | 28♑ |
|  |  |  |  | 31♈ |  |  | 30♌ | 30♎ |  |  | 31♒ |

| Libra | Scorpio | Sagittarius | Capricorn | Aquarius | Pisces |
|---|---|---|---|---|---|
| ♎ | ♏ | ♐ | ♑ | ♒ | ♓ |

## 1922

| JAN. | FEB. | MAR. | APR. | MAY | JUNE | JULY | AUG. | SEPT. | OCT. | NOV. | DEC. |
|---|---|---|---|---|---|---|---|---|---|---|---|
| 2♓ | 1♈ | 3♉ | 1♊ | 1♋ | 1♍ | 1♎ | 1♐ | 2♒ | 2♓ | 1♈ | 1♉ |
| 5♈ | 3♉ | 5♊ | 4♋ | 3♌ | 4♎ | 3♏ | 4♑ | 5♓ | 5♈ | 3♉ | 3♊ |
| 7♉ | 6♊ | 7♋ | 6♌ | 5♍ | 6♏ | 5♐ | 6♒ | 7♈ | 7♉ | 6♊ | 5♋ |
| 9♊ | 8♋ | 10♌ | 8♍ | 7♎ | 8♐ | 7♑ | 8♓ | 10♉ | 10♊ | 8♋ | 8♌ |
| 12♋ | 10♌ | 12♍ | 10♎ | 9♏ | 10♑ | 10♒ | 11♈ | 12♊ | 12♋ | 10♌ | 10♍ |
| 14♌ | 12♍ | 13♎ | 12♏ | 11♐ | 12♒ | 12♓ | 14♉ | 14♋ | 14♌ | 13♍ | 12♎ |
| 16♍ | 14♎ | 16♏ | 14♐ | 14♑ | 15♓ | 15♈ | 16♊ | 17♌ | 16♍ | 15♎ | 14♏ |
| 18♎ | 16♏ | 18♐ | 16♑ | 16♒ | 17♈ | 17♉ | 18♋ | 19♍ | 18♎ | 17♏ | 16♐ |
| 20♏ | 18♐ | 20♑ | 19♒ | 19♓ | 20♉ | 20♊ | 20♌ | 21♎ | 20♏ | 19♐ | 18♑ |
| 22♐ | 21♑ | 22♒ | 21♓ | 21♈ | 22♊ | 22♋ | 22♍ | 23♏ | 22♐ | 21♑ | 21♒ |
| 24♑ | 23♒ | 25♓ | 24♈ | 24♉ | 24♋ | 24♌ | 24♎ | 25♐ | 24♑ | 23♒ | 23♓ |
| 27♒ | 26♓ | 27♈ | 26♉ | 26♊ | 27♌ | 26♍ | 26♏ | 27♑ | 27♒ | 26♓ | 25♈ |
| 29♓ | 28♈ | 30♉ | 28♊ | 28♋ | 29♍ | 28♎ | 29♐ | 30♒ | 29♓ | 28♈ | 28♉ |
|  |  |  |  | 30♌ |  | 30♏ | 31♑ |  |  |  | 30♊ |

## 1923

| JAN. | FEB. | MAR. | APR. | MAY | JUNE | JULY | AUG. | SEPT. | OCT. | NOV. | DEC. |
|---|---|---|---|---|---|---|---|---|---|---|---|
| 2♋ | 2♍ | 2♍ | 2♏ | 2♐ | 2♒ | 2♓ | 1♈ | 2♊ | 2♋ | 1♌ | 3♎ |
| 4♌ | 4♎ | 4♎ | 4♐ | 4♑ | 5♓ | 4♈ | 3♉ | 5♋ | 4♌ | 3♍ | 5♏ |
| 6♍ | 7♏ | 6♏ | 6♑ | 6♒ | 7♈ | 7♉ | 6♊ | 7♌ | 7♍ | 5♎ | 7♐ |
| 8♎ | 9♐ | 8♐ | 9♒ | 8♓ | 10♉ | 10♊ | 8♋ | 9♍ | 9♎ | 7♏ | 9♑ |
| 10♏ | 11♑ | 10♑ | 11♓ | 11♈ | 12♊ | 12♋ | 11♌ | 11♎ | 11♏ | 9♐ | 11♒ |
| 12♐ | 13♒ | 12♒ | 14♈ | 13♉ | 15♋ | 14♌ | 13♍ | 13♏ | 13♐ | 11♑ | 13♓ |
| 15♑ | 16♓ | 15♓ | 16♉ | 16♊ | 17♌ | 16♍ | 15♎ | 15♐ | 15♑ | 13♒ | 15♈ |
| 17♒ | 18♈ | 17♈ | 19♊ | 18♋ | 19♍ | 19♎ | 17♏ | 17♑ | 17♒ | 16♓ | 18♉ |
| 19♓ | 21♉ | 20♉ | 21♋ | 21♌ | 21♎ | 21♏ | 19♐ | 20♒ | 19♓ | 18♈ | 20♊ |
| 22♈ | 23♊ | 22♊ | 23♌ | 23♍ | 24♏ | 23♐ | 21♑ | 22♓ | 22♈ | 20♉ | 23♋ |
| 24♉ | 26♋ | 25♋ | 26♍ | 25♎ | 26♐ | 25♑ | 23♒ | 24♈ | 24♉ | 23♊ | 25♌ |
| 27♊ | 28♌ | 27♌ | 28♎ | 27♏ | 28♑ | 27♒ | 26♓ | 27♉ | 27♊ | 26♋ | 28♍ |
| 29♋ |  | 29♍ | 30♏ | 29♐ | 30♒ | 29♓ | 28♈ | 29♊ | 29♋ | 28♌ | 30♎ |
| 31♌ |  | 31♎ |  | 31♑ |  | 31♈ | 31♉ |  |  | 30♍ |  |

| *Key:* | Aries | Taurus | Gemini | Cancer | Leo | Virgo |
|---|---|---|---|---|---|---|
| | ♈ | ♉ | ♊ | ♋ | ♌ | ♍ |

## 1924

| JAN. | FEB. | MAR. | APR. | MAY | JUNE | JULY | AUG. | SEPT. | OCT. | NOV. | DEC. |
|---|---|---|---|---|---|---|---|---|---|---|---|
| 1♏ | 1♑ | 2♒ | 3♈ | 2♉ | 1♊ | 1♋ | 2♍ | 1♎ | 2♐ | 1♑ | 2♓ |
| 3♐ | 3♒ | 4♓ | 5♉ | 5♊ | 4♋ | 3♌ | 4♎ | 3♏ | 4♑ | 3♒ | 4♈ |
| 5♑ | 6♓ | 6♈ | 8♊ | 7♋ | 6♌ | 6♍ | 7♏ | 5♐ | 6♒ | 5♓ | 7♉ |
| 7♒ | 8♈ | 9♉ | 10♋ | 10♌ | 9♍ | 8♎ | 9♐ | 7♑ | 9♓ | 7♈ | 9♊ |
| 9♓ | 10♉ | 11♊ | 13♌ | 12♍ | 11♎ | 10♏ | 11♑ | 9♒ | 11♈ | 9♉ | 12♋ |
| 12♈ | 13♊ | 14♋ | 15♍ | 15♎ | 13♏ | 12♐ | 13♒ | 11♓ | 13♉ | 12♊ | 14♌ |
| 14♉ | 15♋ | 16♌ | 17♎ | 17♏ | 15♐ | 14♑ | 15♓ | 14♈ | 16♊ | 14♋ | 17♍ |
| 17♊ | 18♌ | 19♍ | 19♏ | 19♐ | 17♑ | 16♒ | 17♈ | 16♉ | 18♋ | 17♌ | 19♎ |
| 19♋ | 20♍ | 21♎ | 21♐ | 21♑ | 19♒ | 19♓ | 19♉ | 18♊ | 21♌ | 19♍ | 21♏ |
| 21♌ | 22♎ | 23♏ | 23♑ | 23♒ | 21♓ | 21♈ | 22♊ | 21♋ | 23♍ | 22♎ | 23♐ |
| 24♍ | 24♏ | 25♐ | 25♒ | 25♓ | 23♈ | 23♉ | 24♋ | 23♌ | 25♎ | 24♏ | 25♑ |
| 26♎ | 27♐ | 27♑ | 28♓ | 27♈ | 26♉ | 26♊ | 27♌ | 25♍ | 27♏ | 26♐ | 27♒ |
| 28♏ | 29♑ | 29♒ | 30♈ | 30♉ | 28♊ | 28♋ | 29♍ | 28♎ | 30♐ | 28♑ | 29♓ |
| 30♐ |  | 31♓ |  |  |  | 31♌ |  | 30♏ |  | 30♒ |  |

## 1925

| JAN. | FEB. | MAR. | APR. | MAY | JUNE | JULY | AUG. | SEPT. | OCT. | NOV. | DEC. |
|---|---|---|---|---|---|---|---|---|---|---|---|
| 1♈ | 2♊ | 1♊ | 2♌ | 2♍ | 1♎ | 1♏ | 1♑ | 2♓ | 1♈ | 2♊ | 2♋ |
| 3♉ | 4♋ | 4♋ | 5♍ | 5♎ | 3♏ | 3♐ | 3♒ | 4♈ | 3♉ | 4♋ | 4♌ |
| 5♊ | 7♌ | 6♌ | 7♎ | 7♏ | 5♐ | 5♑ | 5♓ | 6♉ | 6♊ | 7♌ | 7♍ |
| 8♋ | 9♍ | 9♍ | 9♏ | 9♐ | 7♑ | 7♒ | 7♈ | 8♊ | 8♋ | 9♍ | 9♎ |
| 11♌ | 12♎ | 11♎ | 12♐ | 11♑ | 9♒ | 9♓ | 9♉ | 11♋ | 10♌ | 12♎ | 12♏ |
| 13♍ | 14♏ | 13♏ | 14♑ | 13♒ | 11♓ | 11♈ | 12♊ | 13♌ | 13♍ | 14♏ | 14♐ |
| 15♎ | 16♐ | 15♐ | 16♒ | 15♓ | 14♈ | 13♉ | 14♋ | 16♍ | 15♎ | 16♐ | 16♑ |
| 18♏ | 18♑ | 17♑ | 18♓ | 17♈ | 16♉ | 16♊ | 17♌ | 18♎ | 18♏ | 18♑ | 18♒ |
| 20♐ | 20♒ | 20♒ | 20♈ | 20♉ | 18♊ | 18♋ | 19♍ | 20♏ | 20♐ | 20♒ | 20♓ |
| 22♑ | 22♓ | 22♓ | 23♉ | 22♊ | 21♋ | 21♌ | 22♎ | 23♐ | 22♑ | 23♓ | 22♈ |
| 24♒ | 24♈ | 24♈ | 25♊ | 25♋ | 23♌ | 23♍ | 24♏ | 25♑ | 24♒ | 25♈ | 24♉ |
| 26♓ | 27♉ | 26♉ | 27♋ | 27♌ | 26♍ | 26♎ | 26♐ | 27♒ | 26♓ | 27♉ | 27♊ |
| 28♈ |  | 28♊ | 30♌ | 30♍ | 28♎ | 28♏ | 29♑ | 29♓ | 28♈ | 29♊ | 29♋ |
| 30♉ |  | 31♋ |  |  |  | 30♐ | 31♒ |  | 31♉ |  | 31♌ |

| Libra | Scorpio | Sagittarius | Capricorn | Aquarius | Pisces |
|---|---|---|---|---|---|
| ♎ | ♏ | ♐ | ♑ | ♒ | ♓ |

## 1926

| JAN. | FEB. | MAR. | APR. | MAY | JUNE | JULY | AUG. | SEPT. | OCT. | NOV. | DEC. |
|------|------|------|------|-----|------|------|------|-------|------|------|------|
| 3♍ | 2♎ | 1♎ | 2♐ | 1♑ | 2♓ | 1♈ | 2♊ | 1♋ | 3♍ | 2♎ | 1♍ |
| 5♎ | 4♏ | 3♏ | 4♑ | 4♒ | 4♈ | 3♉ | 4♋ | 3♌ | 5♎ | 4♏ | 4♐ |
| 8♏ | 7♐ | 6♐ | 6♒ | 6♓ | 6♉ | 6♊ | 7♌ | 6♍ | 8♏ | 6♐ | 6♑ |
| 10♐ | 9♑ | 8♑ | 9♓ | 8♈ | 8♊ | 8♋ | 9♍ | 8♎ | 10♐ | 9♑ | 8♒ |
| 12♑ | 11♒ | 10♒ | 11♈ | 10♉ | 11♋ | 11♌ | 12♎ | 11♏ | 13♑ | 11♒ | 10♓ |
| 14♒ | 13♓ | 12♓ | 13♉ | 12♊ | 13♌ | 13♍ | 14♏ | 13♐ | 15♒ | 13♓ | 13♈ |
| 16♓ | 15♈ | 14♈ | 15♊ | 14♋ | 16♍ | 16♎ | 17♐ | 15♑ | 17♓ | 15♈ | 15♉ |
| 18♈ | 17♉ | 16♉ | 17♋ | 17♌ | 18♎ | 18♏ | 19♑ | 17♒ | 19♈ | 17♉ | 17♊ |
| 20♉ | 19♊ | 18♊ | 20♌ | 19♍ | 21♏ | 20♐ | 21♒ | 20♓ | 21♉ | 19♊ | 19♋ |
| 23♊ | 21♋ | 21♋ | 22♍ | 22♎ | 23♐ | 23♑ | 23♓ | 21♈ | 23♊ | 22♋ | 21♌ |
| 25♋ | 24♌ | 23♌ | 25♎ | 24♏ | 25♑ | 25♒ | 25♈ | 23♉ | 25♋ | 24♌ | 24♍ |
| 28♌ | 26♍ | 26♍ | 27♏ | 27♐ | 27♒ | 27♓ | 27♉ | 26♊ | 28♌ | 26♍ | 26♎ |
| 30♍ | | 28♎ | 29♐ | 29♑ | 29♓ | 29♈ | 29♊ | 28♋ | 30♍ | 29♎ | 29♏ |
| | | 31♏ | | 31♒ | | 31♉ | | 30♌ | | | 31♐ |

## 1927

| JAN. | FEB. | MAR. | APR. | MAY | JUNE | JULY | AUG. | SEPT. | OCT. | NOV. | DEC. |
|------|------|------|------|-----|------|------|------|-------|------|------|------|
| 2♑ | 1♒ | 3♓ | 1♈ | 2♊ | 1♋ | 1♌ | 2♎ | 1♏ | 3♑ | 1♒ | 1♓ |
| 5♒ | 3♓ | 4♈ | 3♉ | 4♋ | 3♌ | 3♍ | 4♏ | 3♐ | 5♒ | 4♓ | 3♈ |
| 7♓ | 5♈ | 6♉ | 5♊ | 7♌ | 6♍ | 5♎ | 7♐ | 5♑ | 7♓ | 6♈ | 5♉ |
| 9♈ | 7♉ | 9♊ | 7♋ | 9♍ | 8♎ | 8♏ | 9♑ | 8♒ | 9♈ | 8♉ | 7♊ |
| 11♉ | 9♊ | 11♋ | 9♌ | 12♎ | 11♏ | 10♐ | 11♒ | 10♓ | 11♉ | 10♊ | 9♋ |
| 13♊ | 12♋ | 13♌ | 12♍ | 14♏ | 13♐ | 13♑ | 13♓ | 12♈ | 13♊ | 12♋ | 11♌ |
| 15♋ | 14♌ | 16♍ | 14♎ | 17♐ | 15♑ | 15♒ | 15♈ | 14♉ | 15♋ | 14♌ | 14♍ |
| 18♌ | 16♍ | 18♎ | 17♏ | 19♑ | 18♒ | 17♓ | 18♉ | 16♊ | 18♌ | 16♍ | 16♎ |
| 20♍ | 19♎ | 21♏ | 19♐ | 21♒ | 20♓ | 19♈ | 20♊ | 18♋ | 20♍ | 19♎ | 19♏ |
| 23♎ | 21♏ | 23♐ | 22♑ | 24♓ | 22♈ | 21♉ | 22♋ | 20♌ | 23♎ | 21♏ | 21♐ |
| 25♏ | 24♐ | 26♑ | 24♒ | 26♈ | 24♉ | 23♊ | 24♌ | 23♍ | 25♏ | 24♐ | 24♑ |
| 28♐ | 26♑ | 28♒ | 26♓ | 28♉ | 26♊ | 26♋ | 27♍ | 25♎ | 28♐ | 26♑ | 26♒ |
| 30♑ | 28♒ | 30♓ | 28♈ | 30♊ | 28♋ | 28♌ | 29♎ | 28♏ | 30♑ | 29♒ | 28♓ |
| | | | 30♉ | | | 30♍ | | 30♐ | | | 30♈ |

| Key: | Aries | Taurus | Gemini | Cancer | Leo | Virgo |
|------|-------|--------|--------|--------|-----|-------|
| | ♈ | ♉ | ♊ | ♋ | ♌ | ♍ |

## 1928

| JAN. | FEB. | MAR. | APR. | MAY | JUNE | JULY | AUG. | SEPT. | OCT. | NOV. | DEC. |
|---|---|---|---|---|---|---|---|---|---|---|---|
| 1♉ | 2♋ | 2♌ | 1♍ | 1♎ | 2♐ | 2♑ | 3♓ | 1♈ | 1♉ | 1♋ | 1♌ |
| 4♊ | 4♌ | 5♍ | 3♎ | 3♏ | 4♑ | 4♒ | 5♈ | 3♉ | 3♊ | 2♌ | 3♍ |
| 6♋ | 6♍ | 7♎ | 6♏ | 6♐ | 7♒ | 6♓ | 7♉ | 5♊ | 5♋ | 5♍ | 5♎ |
| 8♌ | 9♎ | 10♏ | 8♐ | 8♑ | 9♓ | 9♈ | 9♊ | 8♋ | 7♌ | 8♎ | 7♏ |
| 10♍ | 11♏ | 12♐ | 11♑ | 11♒ | 11♈ | 11♉ | 11♋ | 10♌ | 9♍ | 10♏ | 10♐ |
| 12♎ | 14♐ | 15♑ | 13♒ | 13♓ | 14♉ | 13♊ | 13♌ | 12♍ | 12♎ | 13♐ | 13♑ |
| 15♏ | 16♑ | 17♒ | 16♓ | 15♈ | 16♊ | 16♋ | 15♍ | 14♎ | 14♏ | 15♑ | 15♒ |
| 17♐ | 19♒ | 19♓ | 18♈ | 17♉ | 18♋ | 17♌ | 18♎ | 17♏ | 16♐ | 18♒ | 17♓ |
| 20♑ | 21♓ | 21♈ | 20♉ | 19♊ | 20♌ | 19♍ | 20♏ | 19♐ | 19♑ | 20♓ | 20♈ |
| 22♒ | 23♈ | 23♉ | 22♊ | 21♋ | 22♍ | 22♎ | 23♐ | 22♑ | 22♒ | 22♓ | 22♉ |
| 24♓ | 25♉ | 25♊ | 24♋ | 23♌ | 24♎ | 24♏ | 25♑ | 24♒ | 24♓ | 25♉ | 24♊ |
| 27♈ | 27♊ | 27♋ | 26♌ | 26♍ | 27♏ | 27♐ | 28♒ | 26♓ | 26♈ | 27♉ | 26♋ |
| 29♉ | 29♋ | 30♌ | 28♍ | 28♎ | 29♐ | 29♑ | 30♓ | 29♈ | 28♉ | 29♋ | 28♌ |
| 31♊ | | | | 30♏ | | 31♒ | | | 30♊ | | 30♍ |

## 1929

| JAN. | FEB. | MAR. | APR. | MAY | JUNE | JULY | AUG. | SEPT. | OCT. | NOV. | DEC. |
|---|---|---|---|---|---|---|---|---|---|---|---|
| 1♎ | 3♐ | 2♐ | 1♑ | 1♒ | 2♈ | 1♉ | 2♋ | 2♍ | 2♎ | 3♐ | 2♑ |
| 4♏ | 5♑ | 4♑ | 3♒ | 3♓ | 4♉ | 3♊ | 4♌ | 4♎ | 4♏ | 5♑ | 5♒ |
| 6♐ | 8♒ | 7♒ | 6♓ | 5♈ | 6♊ | 5♋ | 6♍ | 7♏ | 6♐ | 8♒ | 8♓ |
| 9♑ | 10♓ | 9♒ | 8♈ | 8♉ | 8♋ | 7♌ | 8♎ | 9♐ | 9♑ | 10♓ | 10♈ |
| 11♒ | 12♈ | 12♓ | 10♉ | 10♊ | 10♌ | 9♍ | 9♏ | 11♑ | 11♒ | 13♓ | 12♈ |
| 14♓ | 15♉ | 14♈ | 12♊ | 12♋ | 12♍ | 12♎ | 13♐ | 14♒ | 14♓ | 15♉ | 14♊ |
| 16♈ | 17♊ | 16♉ | 14♋ | 14♌ | 14♎ | 14♏ | 15♑ | 16♓ | 16♈ | 17♊ | 16♋ |
| 18♉ | 19♋ | 18♋ | 16♌ | 16♍ | 17♏ | 16♐ | 18♒ | 19♈ | 18♉ | 19♋ | 18♌ |
| 20♊ | 21♌ | 20♌ | 19♍ | 18♎ | 19♐ | 19♑ | 20♓ | 21♉ | 21♊ | 21♌ | 20♍ |
| 22♋ | 23♍ | 22♍ | 21♎ | 20♏ | 22♑ | 21♒ | 23♈ | 23♊ | 23♋ | 23♍ | 23♎ |
| 24♌ | 25♎ | 25♎ | 23♏ | 23♐ | 24♒ | 24♓ | 25♉ | 25♋ | 25♌ | 25♎ | 25♏ |
| 27♍ | 27♏ | 27♏ | 26♐ | 25♑ | 27♓ | 26♈ | 27♊ | 28♌ | 27♍ | 28♏ | 27♐ |
| 29♎ | | 29♐ | 28♑ | 28♒ | 29♈ | 29♉ | 29♋ | 30♍ | 29♎ | 30♐ | 30♑ |
| 31♏ | | | | 30♓ | | 31♊ | 31♌ | | 31♏ | | |

| Libra | Scorpio | Sagittarius | Capricorn | Aquarius | Pisces |
|---|---|---|---|---|---|
| ♎ | ♏ | ♐ | ♑ | ♒ | ♓ |

## 1930

| JAN. | FEB. | MAR. | APR. | MAY | JUNE | JULY | AUG. | SEPT. | OCT. | NOV. | DEC. |
|---|---|---|---|---|---|---|---|---|---|---|---|
| 1♒ | 3♈ | 2♈ | 3♊ | 2♋ | 3♍ | 2♎ | 3♐ | 1♑ | 1♒ | 2♈ | 2♉ |
| 4♓ | 5♉ | 4♉ | 5♋ | 4♌ | 5♎ | 4♏ | 5♑ | 4♒ | 4♓ | 5♉ | 5♊ |
| 6♈ | 7♊ | 6♓ | 7♌ | 6♍ | 7♏ | 6♐ | 8♒ | 6♓ | 6♈ | 7♊ | 7♋ |
| 9♉ | 9♋ | 9♈ | 9♍ | 8♎ | 9♐ | 9♑ | 10♓ | 9♈ | 9♉ | 9♋ | 9♌ |
| 11♊ | 11♌ | 11♉ | 11♎ | 11♏ | 12♑ | 11♒ | 13♈ | 11♉ | 11♊ | 12♌ | 11♍ |
| 13♋ | 13♍ | 13♊ | 13♏ | 13♐ | 14♒ | 14♓ | 15♉ | 14♊ | 13♋ | 14♍ | 13♎ |
| 15♌ | 15♎ | 15♋ | 16♐ | 15♑ | 17♓ | 16♈ | 17♊ | 16♋ | 15♌ | 16♎ | 15♏ |
| 17♍ | 17♏ | 17♌ | 18♑ | 18♒ | 19♈ | 19♉ | 20♋ | 18♌ | 17♍ | 18♏ | 17♐ |
| 19♎ | 20♐ | 19♍ | 20♒ | 20♓ | 21♉ | 21♊ | 22♌ | 20♍ | 19♎ | 20♐ | 20♑ |
| 21♏ | 22♑ | 22♎ | 23♓ | 23♈ | 24♊ | 23♋ | 24♍ | 22♎ | 22♏ | 22♑ | 22♒ |
| 23♐ | 25♒ | 24♏ | 25♈ | 25♉ | 26♋ | 25♌ | 26♎ | 24♐ | 24♑ | 25♒ | 25♓ |
| 26♑ | 27♓ | 27♐ | 28♉ | 27♊ | 28♌ | 27♍ | 28♏ | 26♑ | 26♒ | 27♓ | 27♈ |
| 29♒ |  | 29♑ | 30♊ | 29♋ | 30♍ | 29♎ | 30♐ | 29♑ | 28♒ | 30♈ | 30♉ |
| 31♓ |  | 31♒ |  | 31♌ |  | 31♏ |  |  | 31♓ |  |  |

## 1931

| JAN. | FEB. | MAR. | APR. | MAY | JUNE | JULY | AUG. | SEPT. | OCT. | NOV. | DEC. |
|---|---|---|---|---|---|---|---|---|---|---|---|
| 1♊ | 2♌ | 1♌ | 2♎ | 1♏ | 2♑ | 1♒ | 3♈ | 1♉ | 1♊ | 2♌ | 2♍ |
| 3♋ | 4♍ | 3♍ | 4♏ | 3♐ | 4♒ | 4♓ | 5♉ | 4♊ | 4♋ | 4♍ | 4♎ |
| 5♌ | 6♎ | 5♎ | 6♐ | 5♑ | 6♓ | 6♈ | 8♊ | 6♋ | 6♌ | 6♎ | 6♏ |
| 7♍ | 8♏ | 7♏ | 8♑ | 8♒ | 9♈ | 9♉ | 10♋ | 8♌ | 8♍ | 8♏ | 8♐ |
| 9♎ | 10♐ | 9♐ | 10♒ | 10♓ | 11♉ | 11♊ | 12♌ | 10♍ | 10♎ | 10♐ | 10♑ |
| 11♏ | 12♑ | 12♑ | 13♓ | 13♈ | 14♊ | 13♋ | 14♍ | 12♎ | 12♏ | 12♑ | 12♒ |
| 14♐ | 15♒ | 14♒ | 15♈ | 15♉ | 16♋ | 16♌ | 16♎ | 14♏ | 14♐ | 15♒ | 14♓ |
| 16♑ | 17♓ | 16♓ | 18♉ | 17♊ | 18♌ | 18♍ | 18♏ | 17♐ | 16♑ | 17♓ | 17♈ |
| 18♒ | 20♈ | 19♈ | 20♊ | 20♋ | 20♍ | 20♎ | 20♐ | 19♑ | 18♒ | 20♈ | 19♉ |
| 21♈ | 22♉ | 22♉ | 23♋ | 22♌ | 22♎ | 22♏ | 22♑ | 21♒ | 21♓ | 22♉ | 22♊ |
| 23♈ | 25♊ | 24♊ | 25♌ | 24♍ | 25♏ | 24♐ | 25♒ | 24♓ | 23♈ | 25♊ | 24♋ |
| 26♉ | 27♋ | 26♋ | 27♍ | 26♎ | 27♐ | 26♑ | 27♓ | 26♈ | 26♉ | 27♋ | 27♌ |
| 28♊ |  | 28♌ | 29♎ | 28♏ | 29♑ | 28♒ | 30♈ | 29♉ | 28♊ | 29♌ | 29♍ |
| 31♋ |  | 31♍ |  | 30♐ |  | 31♓ |  |  | 31♋ |  | 31♎ |

| Key: | Aries | Taurus | Gemini | Cancer | Leo | Virgo |
|---|---|---|---|---|---|---|
|  | ♈ | ♉ | ♊ | ♋ | ♌ | ♍ |

## 1932

| JAN. | FEB. | MAR. | APR. | MAY | JUNE | JULY | AUG. | SEPT. | OCT. | NOV. | DEC. |
|---|---|---|---|---|---|---|---|---|---|---|---|
| 2♏ | 3♑ | 1♑ | 2♓ | 1♈ | 3♊ | 3♋ | 1♌ | 2♎ | 1♏ | 2♑ | 1♒ |
| 4♐ | 5♒ | 3♒ | 4♈ | 4♉ | 5♋ | 5♌ | 3♍ | 4♏ | 3♐ | 4♒ | 3♓ |
| 6♑ | 7♓ | 5♓ | 7♉ | 7♊ | 8♌ | 7♍ | 6♎ | 6♐ | 5♑ | 6♓ | 6♈ |
| 8♒ | 10♈ | 8♈ | 9♊ | 9♋ | 10♍ | 9♎ | 8♏ | 8♑ | 8♒ | 9♈ | 8♉ |
| 11♓ | 12♉ | 10♉ | 12♋ | 11♌ | 12♎ | 11♏ | 10♐ | 10♒ | 10♓ | 11♉ | 11♊ |
| 13♈ | 15♊ | 13♊ | 14♌ | 14♍ | 14♏ | 14♐ | 12♑ | 13♓ | 12♈ | 14♊ | 13♋ |
| 16♉ | 17♋ | 15♋ | 16♍ | 16♎ | 16♐ | 16♑ | 14♒ | 15♈ | 15♉ | 16♋ | 16♌ |
| 18♊ | 19♌ | 18♌ | 18♎ | 18♏ | 18♑ | 18♒ | 16♓ | 18♉ | 17♊ | 19♌ | 18♍ |
| 21♋ | 21♍ | 20♍ | 20♏ | 20♐ | 20♒ | 20♓ | 19♈ | 20♊ | 20♋ | 21♍ | 20♎ |
| 23♌ | 23♎ | 22♎ | 22♐ | 22♑ | 23♓ | 22♈ | 21♉ | 23♋ | 22♌ | 23♎ | 23♏ |
| 25♍ | 26♏ | 24♏ | 24♑ | 24♒ | 25♈ | 25♉ | 24♊ | 25♌ | 25♍ | 25♏ | 25♐ |
| 27♎ | 28♐ | 26♐ | 27♒ | 26♓ | 28♉ | 27♊ | 26♋ | 27♍ | 27♎ | 27♐ | 27♑ |
| 29♏ |  | 28♑ | 29♓ | 29♈ | 30♊ | 30♋ | 29♌ | 29♎ | 29♏ | 29♑ | 29♒ |
| 31♐ |  | 30♒ |  | 31♉ |  | 31♍ |  |  | 31♐ |  | 31♓ |

## 1933

| JAN. | FEB. | MAR. | APR. | MAY | JUNE | JULY | AUG. | SEPT. | OCT. | NOV. | DEC. |
|---|---|---|---|---|---|---|---|---|---|---|---|
| 2♈ | 1♉ | 3♊ | 2♋ | 1♌ | 2♎ | 2♏ | 2♐ | 1♒ | 2♈ | 1♉ | 1♊ |
| 5♉ | 3♊ | 5♋ | 4♌ | 4♍ | 5♏ | 4♐ | 4♑ | 3♓ | 5♉ | 3♊ | 3♋ |
| 7♊ | 6♋ | 8♌ | 6♍ | 6♎ | 7♐ | 6♑ | 7♒ | 5♈ | 7♊ | 6♋ | 6♌ |
| 10♋ | 8♌ | 10♍ | 9♎ | 8♏ | 9♑ | 8♒ | 9♓ | 7♉ | 10♋ | 8♌ | 8♍ |
| 12♌ | 11♍ | 12♎ | 11♏ | 10♐ | 11♒ | 10♓ | 11♈ | 10♊ | 12♌ | 11♍ | 11♎ |
| 14♍ | 13♎ | 14♏ | 13♐ | 12♑ | 13♓ | 12♈ | 13♉ | 12♋ | 15♍ | 13♎ | 13♏ |
| 17♎ | 15♏ | 16♐ | 15♑ | 14♒ | 15♈ | 15♉ | 16♊ | 15♌ | 17♎ | 15♏ | 15♐ |
| 19♏ | 17♐ | 19♑ | 17♒ | 16♓ | 17♉ | 17♊ | 18♋ | 17♍ | 19♏ | 18♐ | 17♑ |
| 21♐ | 19♑ | 21♒ | 19♓ | 19♈ | 20♊ | 20♋ | 21♌ | 20♎ | 21♐ | 20♑ | 19♒ |
| 23♑ | 21♒ | 23♓ | 22♈ | 21♉ | 22♋ | 22♌ | 23♍ | 22♏ | 23♑ | 22♒ | 21♓ |
| 25♒ | 24♓ | 25♈ | 24♉ | 24♊ | 25♌ | 25♍ | 25♎ | 24♐ | 25♒ | 24♓ | 23♈ |
| 27♓ | 26♈ | 28♉ | 26♊ | 26♋ | 27♍ | 27♎ | 28♏ | 26♑ | 27♓ | 26♈ | 26♉ |
| 30♈ | 28♉ | 30♊ | 29♋ | 29♌ | 30♎ | 29♏ | 30♐ | 28♒ | 30♈ | 28♉ | 28♊ |
|  |  |  |  | 31♍ |  | 31♐ |  | 30♓ |  |  | 31♋ |

| Libra | Scorpio | Sagittarius | Capricorn | Aquarius | Pisces |
|---|---|---|---|---|---|
| ♎ | ♏ | ♐ | ♑ | ♒ | ♓ |

## 1934

| JAN. | FEB. | MAR. | APR. | MAY | JUNE | JULY | AUG. | SEPT. | OCT. | NOV. | DEC. |
|---|---|---|---|---|---|---|---|---|---|---|---|
| 2♌ | 1♍ | 3♎ | 1♏ | 1♐ | 1♒ | 3♈ | 1♉ | 2♋ | 2♌ | 1♍ | 1♎ |
| 5♍ | 3♎ | 5♏ | 3♐ | 3♑ | 3♓ | 5♉ | 3♊ | 5♌ | 5♍ | 3♎ | 3♏ |
| 7♎ | 6♏ | 7♐ | 5♑ | 5♒ | 5♈ | 7♊ | 6♋ | 7♍ | 7♎ | 6♏ | 5♐ |
| 9♏ | 8♐ | 9♑ | 7♒ | 7♓ | 8♉ | 10♋ | 8♌ | 10♎ | 9♏ | 8♐ | 7♑ |
| 11♐ | 10♑ | 11♒ | 10♓ | 9♈ | 10♊ | 12♌ | 11♍ | 12♏ | 12♐ | 10♑ | 9♒ |
| 13♑ | 12♒ | 13♓ | 12♈ | 11♉ | 12♋ | 15♍ | 13♎ | 14♐ | 14♑ | 12♒ | 11♓ |
| 15♒ | 14♓ | 15♈ | 14♉ | 14♊ | 15♌ | 17♎ | 16♏ | 17♑ | 16♒ | 14♓ | 14♈ |
| 17♓ | 16♈ | 18♉ | 16♊ | 16♋ | 17♍ | 20♏ | 18♐ | 19♒ | 18♓ | 16♈ | 16♉ |
| 20♈ | 18♉ | 20♊ | 19♋ | 19♌ | 20♎ | 22♐ | 20♑ | 21♓ | 20♈ | 19♉ | 18♊ |
| 22♉ | 21♊ | 22♋ | 21♌ | 21♍ | 22♏ | 24♑ | 22♒ | 23♈ | 22♉ | 21♊ | 21♋ |
| 24♊ | 23♋ | 25♌ | 24♍ | 24♎ | 24♐ | 26♒ | 24♓ | 25♉ | 24♊ | 23♋ | 23♌ |
| 27♋ | 26♌ | 27♍ | 26♎ | 26♏ | 26♑ | 28♓ | 26♈ | 27♊ | 27♋ | 26♌ | 26♍ |
| 29♌ | 28♍ | 30♎ | 28♏ | 28♐ | 28♒ | 30♈ | 28♉ | 29♋ | 29♌ | 28♍ | 28♎ |
|  |  |  |  | 30♑ | 30♓ |  | 31♊ |  |  |  | 30♏ |

## 1935

| JAN. | FEB. | MAR. | APR. | MAY | JUNE | JULY | AUG. | SEPT. | OCT. | NOV. | DEC. |
|---|---|---|---|---|---|---|---|---|---|---|---|
| 2♐ | 2♒ | 2♒ | 2♈ | 2♉ | 2♋ | 2♌ | 1♍ | 2♏ | 2♐ | 3♒ | 2♓ |
| 4♑ | 4♓ | 4♓ | 4♉ | 4♊ | 5♌ | 5♍ | 3♎ | 5♐ | 4♑ | 5♓ | 4♈ |
| 6♒ | 6♈ | 6♈ | 6♊ | 6♋ | 7♍ | 7♎ | 6♏ | 7♑ | 6♒ | 7♈ | 6♉ |
| 8♓ | 8♉ | 8♉ | 9♋ | 8♌ | 10♎ | 10♏ | 8♐ | 9♒ | 9♓ | 9♉ | 8♊ |
| 10♈ | 11♊ | 10♊ | 11♌ | 11♍ | 12♏ | 12♐ | 11♑ | 11♓ | 11♈ | 11♊ | 11♋ |
| 12♉ | 13♋ | 12♋ | 14♍ | 13♎ | 15♐ | 14♑ | 13♒ | 13♈ | 12♉ | 13♋ | 13♌ |
| 14♊ | 16♌ | 15♌ | 16♎ | 16♏ | 17♑ | 16♒ | 15♓ | 15♉ | 15♊ | 15♌ | 15♍ |
| 17♋ | 18♍ | 17♍ | 19♏ | 18♐ | 19♒ | 18♓ | 17♈ | 17♊ | 17♋ | 18♍ | 18♎ |
| 19♌ | 21♎ | 20♎ | 21♐ | 20♑ | 21♓ | 20♈ | 19♉ | 19♋ | 19♌ | 20♎ | 20♏ |
| 22♍ | 23♏ | 22♏ | 23♑ | 23♒ | 23♈ | 22♉ | 21♊ | 22♌ | 22♍ | 23♏ | 23♐ |
| 24♎ | 25♐ | 25♐ | 25♒ | 25♓ | 25♉ | 25♊ | 23♋ | 24♍ | 24♎ | 25♐ | 25♑ |
| 27♏ | 28♑ | 27♑ | 27♓ | 27♈ | 27♊ | 27♋ | 26♌ | 27♎ | 27♏ | 28♑ | 27♒ |
| 29♐ |  | 29♒ | 30♈ | 29♉ | 30♋ | 29♌ | 28♍ | 29♏ | 29♐ | 30♒ | 29♓ |
| 31♑ |  | 31♓ |  | 31♊ |  |  | 31♎ |  | 31♑ |  | 31♈ |

| | | | | | | |
|---|---|---|---|---|---|---|
| *Key:* | Aries | Taurus | Gemini | Cancer | Leo | Virgo |
| | ♈ | ♉ | ♊ | ♋ | ♌ | ♍ |

## 1936

| JAN. | FEB. | MAR. | APR. | MAY | JUNE | JULY | AUG. | SEPT. | OCT. | NOV. | DEC. |
|---|---|---|---|---|---|---|---|---|---|---|---|
| 3♉ | 1♊ | 1♋ | 3♍ | 2♎ | 1♏ | 1♐ | 2♒ | 2♈ | 2♉ | 2♋ | 2♌ |
| 5♊ | 3♋ | 4♌ | 5♎ | 5♏ | 4♐ | 3♑ | 4♓ | 4♉ | 4♊ | 5♌ | 4♍ |
| 7♋ | 6♌ | 6♍ | 8♏ | 7♐ | 6♑ | 6♒ | 6♈ | 7♊ | 6♋ | 7♍ | 7♎ |
| 9♌ | 8♍ | 9♎ | 10♐ | 10♑ | 8♒ | 8♓ | 8♉ | 9♋ | 8♌ | 9♎ | 9♏ |
| 12♍ | 10♎ | 11♏ | 12♑ | 12♒ | 10♓ | 10♈ | 10♊ | 11♌ | 11♍ | 12♏ | 12♐ |
| 14♎ | 13♏ | 14♐ | 15♒ | 14♓ | 13♈ | 12♉ | 12♋ | 13♍ | 13♎ | 14♐ | 14♑ |
| 17♏ | 15♐ | 16♑ | 17♓ | 16♈ | 15♉ | 14♊ | 15♌ | 16♎ | 16♏ | 17♑ | 17♒ |
| 19♐ | 18♑ | 18♒ | 19♈ | 18♉ | 17♊ | 16♋ | 17♍ | 18♏ | 18♐ | 19♒ | 19♓ |
| 21♑ | 20♒ | 21♓ | 21♉ | 20♊ | 19♋ | 18♌ | 20♎ | 21♐ | 21♑ | 22♓ | 21♈ |
| 24♒ | 22♓ | 23♈ | 23♊ | 22♋ | 21♌ | 21♍ | 22♏ | 23♑ | 23♒ | 24♈ | 23♐ |
| 26♓ | 24♈ | 24♉ | 25♋ | 25♌ | 23♍ | 23♎ | 25♐ | 26♒ | 25♓ | 26♉ | 25♑ |
| 28♈ | 26♉ | 27♊ | 27♌ | 27♍ | 26♎ | 26♏ | 27♑ | 28♓ | 27♈ | 28♊ | 27♒ |
| 30♉ | 28♊ | 29♋ | 30♍ | 30♎ | 28♏ | 28♐ | 29♒ | 30♈ | 29♉ | 30♋ | 29♌ |
|  |  | 31♌ |  |  |  | 31♑ | 31♓ |  | 31♊ |  |  |

## 1937

| JAN. | FEB. | MAR. | APR. | MAY | JUNE | JULY | AUG. | SEPT. | OCT. | NOV. | DEC. |
|---|---|---|---|---|---|---|---|---|---|---|---|
| 1♍ | 2♏ | 1♏ | 3♑ | 2♒ | 1♓ | 3♉ | 1♊ | 1♌ | 1♍ | 2♏ | 2♐ |
| 3♎ | 4♐ | 4♐ | 5♒ | 5♓ | 3♈ | 5♊ | 3♋ | 4♍ | 3♎ | 4♐ | 4♑ |
| 5♏ | 7♑ | 6♑ | 7♓ | 7♈ | 5♉ | 7♋ | 5♌ | 6♎ | 6♏ | 7♑ | 7♒ |
| 8♐ | 9♒ | 9♒ | 9♈ | 9♉ | 7♊ | 9♌ | 7♍ | 8♏ | 8♐ | 9♒ | 9♓ |
| 10♑ | 11♓ | 11♓ | 11♉ | 11♊ | 9♋ | 11♍ | 9♎ | 11♐ | 11♑ | 12♓ | 11♈ |
| 13♒ | 14♈ | 13♈ | 13♊ | 13♋ | 11♌ | 13♎ | 12♏ | 13♑ | 13♒ | 14♈ | 14♉ |
| 15♓ | 16♉ | 15♉ | 15♋ | 15♌ | 13♍ | 16♏ | 14♐ | 15♒ | 15♓ | 16♉ | 16♊ |
| 17♈ | 18♊ | 17♊ | 18♌ | 17♍ | 16♎ | 18♐ | 17♑ | 18♓ | 18♈ | 18♊ | 18♋ |
| 19♉ | 20♋ | 19♋ | 20♍ | 19♎ | 18♏ | 21♑ | 19♒ | 20♈ | 20♉ | 20♋ | 20♌ |
| 21♊ | 22♌ | 21♌ | 22♎ | 22♏ | 21♐ | 23♒ | 22♓ | 22♉ | 22♊ | 22♌ | 22♍ |
| 24♋ | 24♍ | 24♍ | 25♏ | 25♐ | 23♑ | 25♓ | 24♈ | 24♊ | 24♋ | 24♍ | 24♎ |
| 26♌ | 27♎ | 26♎ | 27♐ | 27♑ | 26♒ | 28♈ | 26♉ | 26♋ | 26♌ | 27♎ | 26♏ |
| 28♍ |  | 28♏ | 30♑ | 30♒ | 28♓ | 30♉ | 28♊ | 29♌ | 28♍ | 29♏ | 29♐ |
| 30♎ |  | 31♐ |  |  | 30♈ |  | 30♋ |  | 30♎ |  | 31♑ |

| Libra | Scorpio | Sagittarius | Capricorn | Aquarius | Pisces |
|---|---|---|---|---|---|
| ♎ | ♏ | ♐ | ♑ | ♒ | ♓ |

## 1938

| JAN. | FEB. | MAR. | APR. | MAY | JUNE | JULY | AUG. | SEPT. | OCT. | NOV. | DEC. |
|---|---|---|---|---|---|---|---|---|---|---|---|
| 3♒ | 2♓ | 1♓ | 2♉ | 1♊ | 2♌ | 1♍ | 2♏ | 1♐ | 3♒ | 2♓ | 1♈ |
| 5♓ | 4♈ | 3♈ | 4♊ | 3♋ | 4♍ | 3♎ | 4♐ | 3♑ | 5♓ | 4♈ | 4♉ |
| 8♈ | 6♉ | 5♉ | 6♋ | 5♌ | 6♎ | 5♏ | 7♑ | 6♒ | 8♈ | 6♉ | 6♊ |
| 10♉ | 8♊ | 8♊ | 8♌ | 7♍ | 8♏ | 8♐ | 9♒ | 8♓ | 10♉ | 9♊ | 8♋ |
| 12♊ | 10♋ | 10♋ | 10♍ | 10♎ | 11♐ | 10♑ | 12♓ | 10♈ | 12♊ | 11♋ | 10♌ |
| 14♋ | 12♌ | 12♌ | 12♎ | 12♏ | 13♑ | 13♒ | 14♈ | 13♉ | 14♋ | 13♌ | 12♍ |
| 16♌ | 15♍ | 14♍ | 15♏ | 14♐ | 16♒ | 15♓ | 16♉ | 15♊ | 16♌ | 15♍ | 14♎ |
| 18♍ | 17♎ | 16♎ | 17♐ | 17♑ | 18♓ | 18♈ | 19♊ | 17♋ | 19♍ | 17♎ | 16♏ |
| 20♎ | 19♏ | 18♏ | 20♑ | 19♒ | 21♈ | 20♉ | 21♋ | 19♌ | 21♎ | 19♏ | 19♐ |
| 23♏ | 21♐ | 21♐ | 22♒ | 22♓ | 23♉ | 22♊ | 23♌ | 21♍ | 23♏ | 22♐ | 21♑ |
| 25♐ | 24♑ | 23♑ | 25♓ | 24♈ | 25♊ | 24♋ | 25♍ | 23♎ | 25♐ | 24♑ | 24♒ |
| 28♑ | 26♒ | 26♒ | 27♈ | 27♉ | 27♋ | 26♌ | 27♎ | 26♏ | 28♑ | 27♒ | 26♓ |
| 30♒ | | 28♓ | 29♉ | 29♊ | 29♌ | 28♍ | 29♏ | 28♐ | 30♒ | 29♓ | 29♈ |
| | | 31♈ | | 31♋ | | 31♎ | | | | | 31♉ |

## 1939

| JAN. | FEB. | MAR. | APR. | MAY | JUNE | JULY | AUG. | SEPT. | OCT. | NOV. | DEC. |
|---|---|---|---|---|---|---|---|---|---|---|---|
| 2♊ | 1♋ | 2♌ | 1♍ | 2♏ | 1♐ | 3♒ | 2♓ | 3♉ | 3♊ | 1♋ | 3♍ |
| 4♋ | 3♌ | 4♍ | 3♎ | 4♐ | 3♑ | 5♓ | 4♈ | 5♊ | 5♋ | 3♌ | 5♎ |
| 6♌ | 5♍ | 6♎ | 5♏ | 7♑ | 6♒ | 8♈ | 7♉ | 8♋ | 7♌ | 5♍ | 7♏ |
| 8♍ | 7♎ | 8♏ | 7♐ | 9♒ | 8♓ | 10♉ | 9♊ | 10♌ | 9♍ | 7♎ | 9♐ |
| 10♎ | 9♏ | 11♐ | 9♑ | 12♓ | 11♈ | 13♊ | 11♋ | 12♍ | 11♎ | 10♏ | 11♑ |
| 13♏ | 11♐ | 13♑ | 12♒ | 14♈ | 13♉ | 15♋ | 13♌ | 14♎ | 13♏ | 12♐ | 14♒ |
| 15♐ | 14♑ | 16♒ | 14♓ | 17♉ | 17♊ | 17♌ | 15♍ | 16♏ | 15♐ | 14♑ | 16♓ |
| 18♑ | 16♒ | 18♓ | 17♈ | 19♊ | 17♋ | 19♍ | 17♎ | 18♐ | 18♑ | 16♒ | 19♈ |
| 20♒ | 19♓ | 21♈ | 19♉ | 21♋ | 19♌ | 21♎ | 19♏ | 20♑ | 20♒ | 19♓ | 21♉ |
| 23♓ | 21♈ | 23♉ | 22♊ | 23♌ | 21♍ | 23♏ | 22♐ | 23♒ | 23♓ | 21♈ | 24♊ |
| 25♈ | 24♉ | 25♊ | 24♋ | 25♍ | 24♎ | 25♐ | 24♑ | 25♓ | 25♈ | 24♉ | 26♋ |
| 28♉ | 26♊ | 28♋ | 26♌ | 27♎ | 26♏ | 28♑ | 26♒ | 28♈ | 27♉ | 26♊ | 28♌ |
| 30♊ | 28♋ | 30♌ | 28♍ | 30♏ | 28♐ | 30♒ | 29♓ | 30♉ | 30♊ | 28♋ | 30♍ |
| | | | 30♎ | | 30♑ | | 31♈ | | 30♌ | | |

| | *Key:* | Aries | Taurus | Gemini | Cancer | Leo | Virgo |
|---|---|---|---|---|---|---|---|
| | | ♈ | ♉ | ♊ | ♋ | ♌ | ♍ |

## 1940

| JAN. | FEB. | MAR. | APR. | MAY | JUNE | JULY | AUG. | SEPT. | OCT. | NOV. | DEC. |
|---|---|---|---|---|---|---|---|---|---|---|---|
| 1♎ | 2♐ | 2♑ | 1♒ | 1♓ | 2♉ | 2♊ | 3♌ | 1♍ | 2♏ | 1♐ | 3♒ |
| 3♏ | 4♑ | 5♒ | 3♓ | 3♈ | 4♊ | 4♋ | 5♍ | 3♎ | 4♐ | 3♑ | 5♓ |
| 5♐ | 6♒ | 7♓ | 6♈ | 6♉ | 7♋ | 6♌ | 7♎ | 5♏ | 7♑ | 5♒ | 7♈ |
| 8♑ | 9♓ | 10♈ | 8♉ | 8♊ | 9♌ | 8♍ | 9♏ | 7♐ | 9♒ | 8♓ | 10♉ |
| 10♒ | 11♈ | 12♉ | 11♊ | 10♋ | 11♍ | 10♎ | 11♐ | 9♑ | 11♓ | 10♈ | 13♊ |
| 13♓ | 14♉ | 15♊ | 13♋ | 13♌ | 13♎ | 13♏ | 13♑ | 12♒ | 14♈ | 13♉ | 15♋ |
| 15♈ | 16♊ | 17♋ | 15♌ | 15♍ | 15♏ | 15♐ | 15♒ | 14♓ | 16♉ | 15♊ | 17♌ |
| 18♉ | 19♋ | 19♌ | 18♍ | 17♎ | 17♐ | 17♑ | 18♓ | 17♈ | 19♊ | 18♋ | 19♍ |
| 20♊ | 21♌ | 21♍ | 20♎ | 19♏ | 20♑ | 19♒ | 20♈ | 19♉ | 21♋ | 20♌ | 22♎ |
| 22♋ | 23♍ | 23♎ | 22♏ | 21♐ | 22♒ | 22♓ | 23♉ | 22♊ | 24♌ | 22♍ | 24♏ |
| 24♌ | 25♎ | 25♏ | 24♐ | 23♑ | 24♓ | 24♈ | 25♊ | 24♋ | 26♍ | 24♎ | 26♐ |
| 26♍ | 27♏ | 27♐ | 26♑ | 25♒ | 27♈ | 27♉ | 28♋ | 26♌ | 28♎ | 26♏ | 28♑ |
| 28♎ | 29♐ | 29♑ | 28♒ | 28♓ | 29♉ | 29♊ | 30♌ | 28♍ | 30♏ | 28♐ | 30♒ |
| 30♏ |  |  |  | 30♈ |  | 31♋ |  | 30♎ |  | 30♑ |  |

## 1941

| JAN. | FEB. | MAR. | APR. | MAY | JUNE | JULY | AUG. | SEPT. | OCT. | NOV. | DEC. |
|---|---|---|---|---|---|---|---|---|---|---|---|
| 1♓ | 3♉ | 2♉ | 1♊ | 1♋ | 2♍ | 1♎ | 1♐ | 2♒ | 2♓ | 3♉ | 2♊ |
| 4♈ | 5♊ | 5♊ | 3♋ | 3♌ | 4♎ | 3♏ | 4♑ | 4♓ | 4♈ | 5♊ | 5♋ |
| 6♉ | 8♋ | 7♋ | 6♌ | 5♍ | 6♏ | 5♐ | 6♒ | 7♈ | 6♉ | 8♋ | 7♌ |
| 9♊ | 10♌ | 9♌ | 8♍ | 7♎ | 8♐ | 7♑ | 8♓ | 9♉ | 9♊ | 10♌ | 10♍ |
| 11♋ | 12♍ | 11♍ | 10♎ | 9♏ | 10♑ | 9♒ | 10♈ | 12♊ | 11♋ | 13♍ | 12♎ |
| 13♌ | 14♎ | 13♎ | 12♏ | 11♐ | 12♒ | 12♓ | 13♉ | 14♋ | 14♌ | 15♎ | 14♏ |
| 16♍ | 16♏ | 16♏ | 14♐ | 13♑ | 14♓ | 14♈ | 15♊ | 16♌ | 16♍ | 17♏ | 16♐ |
| 18♎ | 18♐ | 18♐ | 16♑ | 16♒ | 17♈ | 16♉ | 18♋ | 19♍ | 18♎ | 19♐ | 18♑ |
| 20♏ | 20♑ | 20♑ | 18♒ | 18♓ | 19♉ | 19♊ | 20♌ | 21♎ | 20♏ | 21♑ | 20♒ |
| 22♐ | 23♒ | 22♒ | 21♓ | 20♈ | 22♊ | 21♋ | 22♍ | 23♏ | 22♐ | 23♒ | 22♓ |
| 24♑ | 25♓ | 24♓ | 23♈ | 23♉ | 24♋ | 24♌ | 25♎ | 24♐ | 24♑ | 25♓ | 25♈ |
| 26♒ | 27♈ | 27♈ | 26♉ | 25♊ | 26♌ | 26♍ | 27♏ | 27♑ | 26♒ | 27♈ | 27♉ |
| 29♓ |  | 29♉ | 28♊ | 28♋ | 28♍ | 28♎ | 29♐ | 29♒ | 29♓ | 30♉ | 30♊ |
| 31♈ |  |  |  | 30♌ |  | 30♏ | 31♑ |  | 31♈ |  |  |

| Libra | Scorpio | Sagittarius | Capricorn | Aquarius | Pisces |
|---|---|---|---|---|---|
| ♎ | ♏ | ♐ | ♑ | ♒ | ♓ |

## 1942

| JAN. | FEB. | MAR. | APR. | MAY | JUNE | JULY | AUG. | SEPT. | OCT. | NOV. | DEC. |
|---|---|---|---|---|---|---|---|---|---|---|---|
| 1♋ | 2♍ | 2♍ | 2♏ | 2♐ | 2♒ | 2♓ | 3♉ | 1♊ | 1♋ | 3♍ | 2♎ |
| 4♌ | 5♎ | 4♎ | 4♐ | 4♑ | 4♓ | 4♈ | 5♋ | 4♋ | 4♌ | 5♎ | 4♏ |
| 6♍ | 7♏ | 6♏ | 6♑ | 6♒ | 7♈ | 6♉ | 8♋ | 6♌ | 6♍ | 7♏ | 7♐ |
| 8♎ | 9♐ | 8♐ | 9♒ | 8♓ | 9♉ | 9♊ | 10♌ | 9♍ | 8♎ | 9♐ | 9♑ |
| 11♏ | 11♑ | 10♑ | 11♓ | 10♈ | 12♊ | 11♋ | 13♍ | 11♎ | 11♏ | 11♑ | 11♒ |
| 13♐ | 13♒ | 12♒ | 13♈ | 13♉ | 14♋ | 14♌ | 15♎ | 13♏ | 13♐ | 13♒ | 13♓ |
| 15♑ | 15♓ | 15♓ | 16♉ | 15♊ | 17♌ | 16♍ | 17♏ | 15♐ | 15♑ | 15♓ | 15♈ |
| 17♒ | 17♈ | 17♈ | 18♊ | 18♋ | 19♍ | 19♎ | 19♐ | 18♑ | 17♒ | 18♈ | 17♉ |
| 19♓ | 20♉ | 19♉ | 21♋ | 20♌ | 21♎ | 21♏ | 21♑ | 20♒ | 19♓ | 20♉ | 20♊ |
| 21♈ | 22♊ | 22♊ | 23♌ | 23♍ | 24♏ | 23♐ | 23♒ | 22♓ | 21♈ | 22♊ | 22♋ |
| 23♉ | 25♋ | 24♋ | 25♍ | 25♎ | 26♐ | 25♑ | 25♓ | 24♈ | 24♉ | 25♋ | 25♌ |
| 26♊ | 27♌ | 27♌ | 28♎ | 27♏ | 28♑ | 27♒ | 28♈ | 26♉ | 26♊ | 27♌ | 27♍ |
| 29♋ |  | 29♍ | 30♏ | 29♐ | 30♒ | 29♓ | 30♉ | 29♊ | 29♋ | 30♍ | 30♎ |
| 31♌ |  | 31♎ |  | 31♑ |  | 31♈ |  |  | 31♌ |  |  |

## 1943

| JAN. | FEB. | MAR. | APR. | MAY | JUNE | JULY | AUG. | SEPT. | OCT. | NOV. | DEC. |
|---|---|---|---|---|---|---|---|---|---|---|---|
| 1♏ | 1♑ | 1♑ | 1♓ | 1♈ | 2♊ | 1♋ | 3♍ | 1♎ | 1♏ | 2♑ | 1♒ |
| 3♐ | 3♒ | 3♒ | 3♈ | 3♉ | 4♋ | 4♌ | 5♎ | 4♏ | 3♐ | 4♒ | 3♓ |
| 5♑ | 5♓ | 5♓ | 6♉ | 5♊ | 6♌ | 6♍ | 7♏ | 6♐ | 5♑ | 6♓ | 5♈ |
| 7♒ | 8♈ | 7♈ | 8♊ | 8♋ | 9♍ | 9♎ | 10♐ | 8♑ | 8♒ | 8♈ | 7♉ |
| 9♓ | 10♉ | 9♉ | 10♋ | 10♌ | 11♎ | 11♏ | 12♑ | 10♒ | 10♓ | 10♉ | 10♊ |
| 11♈ | 12♊ | 11♊ | 13♌ | 13♍ | 14♏ | 13♐ | 14♒ | 12♓ | 12♈ | 12♊ | 12♋ |
| 13♉ | 15♋ | 14♋ | 15♍ | 15♎ | 16♐ | 15♑ | 16♓ | 14♈ | 14♉ | 15♋ | 15♌ |
| 16♊ | 17♌ | 16♌ | 18♎ | 17♏ | 18♑ | 17♒ | 18♈ | 16♉ | 16♊ | 17♌ | 17♍ |
| 18♋ | 20♍ | 19♍ | 20♏ | 20♐ | 20♒ | 19♓ | 20♉ | 19♊ | 18♋ | 20♍ | 20♎ |
| 21♌ | 22♎ | 21♎ | 22♐ | 22♑ | 22♓ | 21♈ | 22♊ | 21♋ | 21♌ | 22♎ | 22♏ |
| 23♍ | 24♏ | 24♏ | 24♑ | 24♒ | 24♈ | 24♉ | 25♋ | 24♌ | 23♍ | 25♏ | 24♐ |
| 26♎ | 27♐ | 26♐ | 26♒ | 26♓ | 26♉ | 27♊ | 27♌ | 26♍ | 26♎ | 27♐ | 26♑ |
| 28♏ |  | 28♑ | 28♓ | 28♈ | 29♊ | 28♋ | 30♍ | 29♎ | 28♏ | 29♑ | 28♒ |
| 30♐ |  | 30♒ |  | 30♉ |  | 31♌ |  |  | 30♐ |  | 30♓ |

| Key: | Aries | Taurus | Gemini | Cancer | Leo | Virgo |
|---|---|---|---|---|---|---|
|  | ♈ | ♉ | ♊ | ♋ | ♌ | ♍ |

## 1944

| JAN. | FEB. | MAR. | APR. | MAY | JUNE | JULY | AUG. | SEPT. | OCT. | NOV. | DEC. |
|---|---|---|---|---|---|---|---|---|---|---|---|
| 2♈ | 2♊ | 1♊ | 2♌ | 1♍ | 3♏ | 2♐ | 1♑ | 2♓ | 1♈ | 2♊ | 1♋ |
| 4♉ | 5♋ | 3♋ | 4♍ | 4♎ | 5♐ | 5♑ | 3♒ | 4♈ | 3♉ | 4♋ | 3♌ |
| 6♊ | 7♌ | 5♌ | 7♎ | 6♏ | 7♑ | 7♒ | 5♓ | 6♉ | 5♊ | 6♌ | 6♍ |
| 8♋ | 10♍ | 8♍ | 9♏ | 9♐ | 9♒ | 9♓ | 7♈ | 8♊ | 7♋ | 9♍ | 8♎ |
| 11♌ | 12♎ | 10♎ | 11♐ | 11♑ | 12♓ | 11♈ | 9♉ | 10♋ | 10♌ | 11♎ | 11♏ |
| 13♍ | 15♏ | 13♏ | 14♑ | 13♒ | 14♈ | 13♉ | 11♊ | 12♌ | 12♍ | 14♏ | 13♐ |
| 16♎ | 17♐ | 15♐ | 16♒ | 15♓ | 16♉ | 15♊ | 14♋ | 15♍ | 15♎ | 16♐ | 16♑ |
| 18♏ | 19♑ | 18♑ | 18♓ | 17♈ | 18♊ | 18♋ | 16♌ | 17♎ | 17♏ | 18♑ | 18♒ |
| 21♐ | 21♒ | 20♒ | 20♈ | 20♉ | 20♋ | 20♌ | 19♍ | 20♏ | 20♐ | 21♒ | 20♓ |
| 23♑ | 23♓ | 22♓ | 22♉ | 22♊ | 23♌ | 22♍ | 21♎ | 22♐ | 22♑ | 23♓ | 22♈ |
| 25♒ | 25♈ | 24♈ | 24♊ | 24♋ | 25♍ | 25♎ | 24♏ | 25♑ | 24♒ | 25♈ | 24♉ |
| 27♓ | 27♉ | 26♉ | 27♋ | 26♌ | 28♎ | 27♏ | 26♐ | 27♒ | 26♓ | 27♉ | 26♊ |
| 29♈ | 28♊ | 28♊ | 29♌ | 29♍ | 30♏ | 30♐ | 29♑ | 29♓ | 29♈ | 29♊ | 29♋ |
| 31♉ |  | 30♋ |  | 31♎ |  |  | 31♒ |  | 31♉ |  | 31♌ |

## 1945

| JAN. | FEB. | MAR. | APR. | MAY | JUNE | JULY | AUG. | SEPT. | OCT. | NOV. | DEC. |
|---|---|---|---|---|---|---|---|---|---|---|---|
| 2♍ | 1♎ | 3♏ | 2♐ | 1♑ | 2♓ | 2♈ | 2♊ | 3♌ | 2♍ | 1♎ | 1♏ |
| 5♎ | 4♏ | 5♐ | 4♑ | 4♒ | 4♈ | 4♉ | 4♋ | 5♍ | 5♎ | 3♏ | 3♐ |
| 7♏ | 6♐ | 8♑ | 6♒ | 6♓ | 6♉ | 6♊ | 6♌ | 7♎ | 7♏ | 6♐ | 6♑ |
| 10♐ | 8♑ | 10♒ | 9♓ | 8♈ | 8♊ | 8♋ | 9♍ | 10♏ | 10♐ | 8♑ | 8♒ |
| 12♑ | 11♒ | 12♓ | 11♈ | 10♉ | 10♋ | 10♌ | 11♎ | 12♐ | 12♑ | 11♒ | 10♓ |
| 14♒ | 13♓ | 14♈ | 13♉ | 12♊ | 13♌ | 12♍ | 14♏ | 15♑ | 15♒ | 13♓ | 13♈ |
| 16♓ | 15♈ | 16♉ | 15♊ | 14♋ | 15♍ | 15♎ | 16♐ | 17♒ | 17♓ | 15♈ | 17♉ |
| 18♈ | 17♉ | 18♊ | 17♋ | 16♌ | 17♎ | 17♏ | 19♑ | 19♓ | 19♈ | 17♉ | 19♊ |
| 20♉ | 19♊ | 20♋ | 19♌ | 18♍ | 20♏ | 20♐ | 21♒ | 21♈ | 21♉ | 19♊ | 21♋ |
| 23♊ | 21♋ | 22♌ | 21♎ | 21♏ | 22♐ | 22♑ | 23♓ | 23♉ | 23♊ | 21♋ | 23♌ |
| 25♋ | 23♌ | 25♍ | 24♏ | 24♐ | 25♑ | 24♒ | 25♈ | 25♊ | 25♋ | 23♌ | 25♎ |
| 27♌ | 26♍ | 28♎ | 26♐ | 26♑ | 27♒ | 27♓ | 27♉ | 28♋ | 27♌ | 26♍ | 28♏ |
| 30♍ | 28♎ | 30♏ | 29♐ | 29♒ | 29♓ | 29♈ | 29♊ | 30♌ | 29♍ | 28♎ | 31♐ |
|  |  |  |  | 31♓ |  | 31♉ | 31♋ |  | 31♎ |  |  |

| Libra | Scorpio | Sagittarius | Capricorn | Aquarius | Pisces |
|---|---|---|---|---|---|
| ♎ | ♏ | ♐ | ♑ | ♒ | ♓ |

## 1946

| JAN. | FEB. | MAR. | APR. | MAY | JUNE | JULY | AUG. | SEPT. | OCT. | NOV. | DEC. |
|---|---|---|---|---|---|---|---|---|---|---|---|
| 2♑ | 1♒ | 2♓ | 1♈ | 2♊ | 1♋ | 2♍ | 1♎ | 2♐ | 2♑ | 1♒ | 1♓ |
| 4♒ | 3♓ | 4♈ | 3♉ | 4♋ | 3♌ | 5♎ | 3♏ | 5♑ | 5♒ | 3♓ | 3♈ |
| 7♓ | 5♈ | 7♉ | 5♊ | 6♌ | 5♍ | 7♏ | 6♐ | 7♒ | 7♓ | 6♈ | 5♉ |
| 9♈ | 7♉ | 9♊ | 7♋ | 9♍ | 7♎ | 10♐ | 8♑ | 10♓ | 9♈ | 8♉ | 7♊ |
| 11♉ | 9♊ | 11♋ | 9♌ | 11♎ | 10♏ | 12♑ | 11♒ | 12♈ | 11♉ | 10♊ | 9♋ |
| 13♊ | 12♋ | 13♌ | 11♍ | 14♏ | 12♐ | 15♒ | 13♓ | 14♉ | 13♊ | 12♋ | 11♌ |
| 15♋ | 14♌ | 15♍ | 14♎ | 16♐ | 15♑ | 17♓ | 15♈ | 16♊ | 15♋ | 14♌ | 13♍ |
| 17♌ | 16♍ | 18♎ | 16♏ | 19♑ | 17♒ | 19♈ | 18♉ | 18♋ | 18♌ | 16♍ | 16♎ |
| 20♍ | 18♎ | 20♏ | 19♐ | 21♒ | 20♓ | 21♉ | 20♊ | 20♌ | 20♍ | 18♎ | 18♏ |
| 22♎ | 21♏ | 23♐ | 21♑ | 23♓ | 22♈ | 24♊ | 22♋ | 23♍ | 22♎ | 21♏ | 20♐ |
| 24♏ | 23♐ | 25♑ | 24♒ | 26♈ | 24♉ | 26♋ | 24♌ | 25♎ | 24♏ | 23♐ | 23♑ |
| 27♐ | 26♑ | 27♒ | 26♓ | 28♉ | 26♊ | 28♌ | 26♍ | 27♏ | 27♐ | 26♑ | 25♒ |
| 29♑ | 28♒ | 30♓ | 28♈ | 30♊ | 28♋ | 30♍ | 28♎ | 30♐ | 29♑ | 28♒ | 28♓ |
|  |  |  | 30♉ |  | 30♌ |  | 31♏ |  |  |  | 30♈ |

## 1947

| JAN. | FEB. | MAR. | APR. | MAY | JUNE | JULY | AUG. | SEPT. | OCT. | NOV. | DEC. |
|---|---|---|---|---|---|---|---|---|---|---|---|
| 2♉ | 2♋ | 1♋ | 2♍ | 1♎ | 2♐ | 2♑ | 1♒ | 2♈ | 2♉ | 2♋ | 2♌ |
| 4♊ | 4♌ | 3♌ | 4♎ | 4♏ | 5♑ | 5♒ | 3♓ | 4♉ | 4♊ | 4♌ | 4♍ |
| 6♋ | 6♍ | 6♍ | 6♏ | 6♐ | 7♒ | 7♓ | 6♈ | 7♊ | 6♋ | 6♍ | 6♎ |
| 8♌ | 8♎ | 8♎ | 9♐ | 8♑ | 10♓ | 10♈ | 8♉ | 9♋ | 8♌ | 9♎ | 8♏ |
| 10♍ | 11♏ | 10♏ | 11♑ | 11♒ | 12♈ | 12♉ | 10♊ | 11♌ | 10♍ | 11♏ | 10♐ |
| 12♎ | 13♐ | 12♐ | 14♒ | 14♓ | 14♉ | 14♊ | 12♋ | 13♍ | 12♎ | 13♐ | 13♑ |
| 14♏ | 16♑ | 15♑ | 16♓ | 16♈ | 17♊ | 16♋ | 14♌ | 15♎ | 14♏ | 16♑ | 15♒ |
| 17♐ | 18♒ | 17♒ | 18♈ | 18♉ | 19♋ | 18♌ | 16♍ | 17♏ | 17♐ | 18♒ | 18♓ |
| 19♑ | 20♓ | 20♓ | 21♉ | 20♊ | 21♌ | 20♍ | 19♎ | 19♐ | 19♑ | 21♓ | 20♈ |
| 22♒ | 23♈ | 22♈ | 23♊ | 22♋ | 23♍ | 22♎ | 21♏ | 22♑ | 22♒ | 23♈ | 23♉ |
| 24♓ | 25♉ | 24♉ | 25♋ | 24♌ | 25♎ | 24♏ | 23♐ | 24♒ | 24♓ | 25♉ | 25♊ |
| 27♈ | 27♊ | 26♊ | 27♌ | 26♍ | 27♏ | 27♐ | 26♑ | 27♓ | 27♈ | 27♊ | 27♋ |
| 29♉ |  | 29♋ | 29♍ | 29♎ | 30♐ | 29♑ | 28♒ | 29♈ | 29♉ | 30♋ | 29♌ |
| 31♊ |  | 31♌ |  | 31♏ |  |  | 31♓ |  | 31♊ |  | 31♍ |

*Key:*   Aries   Taurus   Gemini   Cancer   Leo   Virgo

        ♈      ♉      ♊      ♋      ♌      ♍

## 1948

| JAN. | FEB. | MAR. | APR. | MAY | JUNE | JULY | AUG. | SEPT. | OCT. | NOV. | DEC. |
|---|---|---|---|---|---|---|---|---|---|---|---|
| 2♎ | 1♏ | 1♐ | 2♒ | 2♓ | 1♈ | 1♉ | 2♋ | 2♍ | 2♎ | 2♐ | 2♑ |
| 4♍ | 3♐ | 4♑ | 5♓ | 5♈ | 4♉ | 3♊ | 4♌ | 4♎ | 4♏ | 4♑ | 4♒ |
| 7♐ | 5♑ | 6♒ | 7♈ | 7♉ | 6♊ | 5♋ | 6♍ | 6♏ | 6♐ | 7♒ | 7♓ |
| 9♑ | 8♒ | 9♓ | 10♉ | 9♊ | 8♋ | 7♌ | 8♎ | 8♐ | 8♑ | 9♓ | 9♈ |
| 12♒ | 10♓ | 11♈ | 12♊ | 12♋ | 10♌ | 9♍ | 10♎ | 11♑ | 11♒ | 12♈ | 12♉ |
| 14♓ | 13♈ | 14♉ | 14♋ | 14♌ | 12♍ | 11♎ | 12♐ | 13♒ | 13♓ | 14♉ | 14♊ |
| 17♈ | 15♉ | 16♊ | 17♌ | 16♍ | 14♎ | 14♏ | 15♑ | 16♓ | 16♈ | 17♊ | 16♋ |
| 19♉ | 18♊ | 18♋ | 19♍ | 18♎ | 16♏ | 16♐ | 17♒ | 18♈ | 18♉ | 19♋ | 18♌ |
| 21♊ | 20♋ | 20♌ | 21♎ | 20♏ | 19♐ | 18♑ | 20♓ | 21♉ | 20♊ | 21♌ | 21♍ |
| 23♋ | 22♌ | 22♍ | 23♏ | 22♐ | 21♑ | 21♒ | 22♈ | 23♊ | 23♋ | 23♍ | 23♎ |
| 25♌ | 24♍ | 24♎ | 25♐ | 25♑ | 23♒ | 23♓ | 25♉ | 25♋ | 25♌ | 25♎ | 25♏ |
| 27♍ | 26♎ | 26♏ | 27♑ | 27♒ | 26♓ | 26♈ | 27♊ | 28♌ | 27♍ | 28♏ | 27♐ |
| 29♎ | 28♏ | 29♐ | 30♒ | 30♓ | 28♈ | 28♉ | 29♋ | 30♍ | 29♎ | 30♐ | 29♑ |
|  |  | 31♑ |  |  |  | 31♊ | 31♌ |  | 31♏ |  |  |

## 1949

| JAN. | FEB. | MAR. | APR. | MAY | JUNE | JULY | AUG. | SEPT. | OCT. | NOV. | DEC. |
|---|---|---|---|---|---|---|---|---|---|---|---|
| 1♒ | 2♈ | 1♈ | 2♊ | 2♋ | 1♌ | 2♎ | 3♐ | 1♑ | 1♒ | 2♈ | 2♉ |
| 3♓ | 4♉ | 4♉ | 5♋ | 4♌ | 3♍ | 4♏ | 5♑ | 3♒ | 3♓ | 4♉ | 4♊ |
| 6♈ | 7♊ | 6♊ | 7♌ | 6♍ | 5♎ | 6♐ | 7♒ | 6♓ | 5♈ | 7♊ | 6♋ |
| 8♉ | 9♋ | 9♋ | 9♍ | 9♎ | 7♏ | 9♑ | 9♓ | 8♈ | 8♉ | 9♋ | 9♌ |
| 10♊ | 11♌ | 11♌ | 11♎ | 11♏ | 9♐ | 11♒ | 12♈ | 11♉ | 11♊ | 12♌ | 11♍ |
| 13♋ | 13♍ | 13♍ | 13♏ | 13♐ | 11♑ | 13♓ | 14♉ | 13♊ | 13♋ | 14♍ | 13♎ |
| 15♌ | 15♎ | 15♎ | 15♐ | 15♑ | 13♒ | 16♈ | 17♊ | 16♋ | 15♌ | 16♎ | 15♏ |
| 17♍ | 17♏ | 17♏ | 17♑ | 17♒ | 16♓ | 18♉ | 19♋ | 18♌ | 17♍ | 18♏ | 17♐ |
| 19♎ | 19♐ | 19♐ | 20♒ | 19♓ | 18♈ | 21♊ | 22♌ | 20♍ | 20♎ | 20♐ | 19♑ |
| 21♏ | 22♑ | 21♑ | 22♓ | 22♈ | 21♉ | 23♋ | 24♍ | 22♎ | 22♏ | 22♑ | 22♒ |
| 23♐ | 24♒ | 23♒ | 25♈ | 24♉ | 23♊ | 25♌ | 26♎ | 24♏ | 24♐ | 24♒ | 24♓ |
| 26♑ | 27♓ | 26♓ | 27♉ | 27♊ | 26♋ | 27♍ | 28♏ | 26♐ | 26♑ | 27♓ | 26♈ |
| 28♒ |  | 28♈ | 30♊ | 29♋ | 28♌ | 29♎ | 30♐ | 28♑ | 28♒ | 29♈ | 29♉ |
| 30♓ |  | 31♉ |  | 30♍ |  | 31♏ |  |  | 30♓ |  | 31♊ |

| Libra | Scorpio | Sagittarius | Capricorn | Aquarius | Pisces |
|---|---|---|---|---|---|
| ♎ | ♏ | ♐ | ♑ | ♒ | ♓ |

## 1950

| JAN. | FEB. | MAR. | APR. | MAY | JUNE | JULY | AUG. | SEPT. | OCT. | NOV. | DEC. |
|---|---|---|---|---|---|---|---|---|---|---|---|
| 3♋ | 1♌ | 1♌ | 2♎ | 1♏ | 1♑ | 1♒ | 2♈ | 1♉ | 3♋ | 2♌ | 1♍ |
| 5♌ | 4♍ | 3♍ | 4♏ | 3♐ | 3♒ | 3♓ | 4♉ | 3♊ | 5♌ | 4♍ | 4♎ |
| 7♍ | 6♎ | 5♎ | 6♐ | 5♑ | 6♓ | 5♈ | 7♊ | 6♋ | 8♍ | 6♎ | 6♏ |
| 9♎ | 8♏ | 7♏ | 8♑ | 7♒ | 8♈ | 8♉ | 9♋ | 8♌ | 10♎ | 8♏ | 8♐ |
| 12♏ | 10♐ | 9♐ | 10♒ | 9♓ | 11♉ | 10♊ | 12♌ | 10♍ | 12♏ | 10♐ | 10♑ |
| 14♐ | 12♑ | 11♑ | 12♓ | 12♈ | 13♊ | 13♋ | 14♍ | 12♎ | 14♐ | 12♑ | 12♒ |
| 16♑ | 14♒ | 14♒ | 15♈ | 14♉ | 16♋ | 15♌ | 16♎ | 15♏ | 16♑ | 14♒ | 14♓ |
| 18♒ | 17♓ | 16♓ | 17♉ | 17♊ | 18♌ | 18♍ | 18♏ | 17♐ | 18♒ | 17♓ | 16♈ |
| 20♓ | 19♈ | 18♈ | 20♊ | 19♋ | 20♍ | 20♎ | 20♐ | 19♑ | 20♓ | 19♈ | 19♉ |
| 23♈ | 22♉ | 21♉ | 22♋ | 22♌ | 22♎ | 22♏ | 22♑ | 21♒ | 23♈ | 21♉ | 21♊ |
| 25♉ | 24♊ | 23♊ | 25♌ | 24♍ | 25♏ | 24♐ | 25♒ | 23♓ | 25♉ | 24♊ | 24♋ |
| 28♊ | 27♋ | 26♋ | 27♍ | 26♎ | 27♐ | 26♑ | 27♓ | 25♈ | 28♊ | 27♋ | 26♌ |
| 30♋ |  | 28♌ | 29♎ | 28♏ | 29♑ | 28♒ | 29♈ | 28♉ | 30♋ | 29♌ | 29♍ |
|  |  | 30♍ |  | 30♐ |  | 30♓ |  | 30♊ |  |  | 31♎ |

## 1951

| JAN. | FEB. | MAR. | APR. | MAY | JUNE | JULY | AUG. | SEPT. | OCT. | NOV. | DEC. |
|---|---|---|---|---|---|---|---|---|---|---|---|
| 2♏ | 1♐ | 2♑ | 2♓ | 2♈ | 1♉ | 3♋ | 2♌ | 3♎ | 2♏ | 1♐ | 2♒ |
| 4♐ | 3♑ | 4♒ | 5♈ | 4♉ | 3♊ | 5♌ | 4♍ | 5♏ | 4♐ | 3♑ | 4♓ |
| 6♑ | 5♒ | 6♓ | 7♉ | 7♊ | 6♋ | 8♍ | 6♎ | 7♐ | 7♑ | 5♒ | 6♈ |
| 8♒ | 7♓ | 8♈ | 10♊ | 9♋ | 8♌ | 10♎ | 9♏ | 9♑ | 9♒ | 7♓ | 9♉ |
| 10♓ | 9♈ | 11♉ | 12♋ | 12♌ | 11♍ | 13♏ | 11♐ | 11♒ | 11♓ | 9♈ | 11♊ |
| 13♈ | 11♉ | 13♊ | 15♌ | 14♍ | 13♎ | 15♐ | 13♑ | 13♓ | 13♈ | 12♉ | 14♋ |
| 15♉ | 14♊ | 16♋ | 17♍ | 17♎ | 15♏ | 17♑ | 15♒ | 16♈ | 15♉ | 14♊ | 16♌ |
| 18♊ | 16♋ | 18♌ | 19♎ | 19♏ | 17♐ | 19♒ | 17♓ | 18♉ | 18♊ | 16♋ | 19♍ |
| 20♋ | 19♌ | 21♍ | 21♏ | 21♐ | 19♑ | 21♓ | 19♈ | 20♊ | 20♋ | 19♌ | 21♎ |
| 23♌ | 21♍ | 23♎ | 23♐ | 23♑ | 21♒ | 23♈ | 21♉ | 23♋ | 23♌ | 21♍ | 23♏ |
| 25♍ | 23♎ | 25♏ | 25♑ | 25♒ | 23♓ | 25♉ | 24♊ | 25♌ | 25♍ | 24♎ | 26♐ |
| 27♎ | 26♏ | 27♐ | 27♒ | 27♓ | 25♈ | 28♊ | 26♋ | 28♍ | 27♎ | 26♏ | 28♑ |
| 29♏ | 28♐ | 29♑ | 30♓ | 29♈ | 28♉ | 30♋ | 29♌ | 30♎ | 30♏ | 28♐ | 30♒ |
|  |  | 31♒ |  |  | 30♊ |  | 31♍ |  |  | 30♑ |  |

| Key: | Aries | Taurus | Gemini | Cancer | Leo | Virgo |
|---|---|---|---|---|---|---|
|  | ♈ | ♉ | ♊ | ♋ | ♌ | ♍ |

## 1952

| JAN. | FEB. | MAR. | APR. | MAY | JUNE | JULY | AUG. | SEPT. | OCT. | NOV. | DEC. |
|---|---|---|---|---|---|---|---|---|---|---|---|
| 1♓ | 1♉ | 2♊ | 1♋ | 1♌ | 2♎ | 2♏ | 2♑ | 1♒ | 2♈ | 1♉ | 3♋ |
| 3♈ | 4♊ | 5♋ | 3♌ | 3♍ | 4♏ | 4♐ | 4♒ | 3♓ | 4♉ | 3♊ | 5♌ |
| 5♉ | 6♋ | 7♌ | 6♍ | 6♎ | 7♐ | 6♑ | 6♓ | 5♈ | 7♊ | 5♋ | 8♍ |
| 7♊ | 9♌ | 10♍ | 8♎ | 8♏ | 9♑ | 8♒ | 8♈ | 7♉ | 9♋ | 8♌ | 10♎ |
| 10♋ | 11♍ | 12♎ | 11♏ | 10♐ | 11♒ | 10♓ | 11♉ | 10♊ | 11♌ | 10♍ | 13♏ |
| 12♌ | 14♎ | 14♏ | 13♐ | 12♑ | 13♓ | 12♈ | 13♊ | 12♋ | 14♍ | 13♎ | 15♐ |
| 15♍ | 16♏ | 17♐ | 15♑ | 14♒ | 15♈ | 14♉ | 15♋ | 15♌ | 16♎ | 15♏ | 17♑ |
| 17♎ | 18♐ | 19♑ | 17♒ | 16♓ | 17♉ | 17♊ | 18♌ | 17♍ | 19♏ | 17♐ | 19♒ |
| 20♏ | 20♑ | 21♒ | 19♓ | 19♈ | 19♊ | 19♋ | 20♍ | 19♎ | 21♐ | 20♑ | 21♓ |
| 22♐ | 22♒ | 23♓ | 21♈ | 21♉ | 22♋ | 22♌ | 23♎ | 22♏ | 23♑ | 22♒ | 23♈ |
| 24♑ | 24♓ | 25♈ | 24♉ | 23♊ | 24♌ | 24♍ | 25♏ | 24♐ | 26♒ | 24♓ | 25♉ |
| 26♒ | 27♈ | 27♉ | 26♊ | 26♋ | 27♍ | 27♎ | 28♐ | 26♑ | 28♓ | 26♈ | 28♊ |
| 28♓ | 29♉ | 29♊ | 28♋ | 28♌ | 29♎ | 29♏ | 30♑ | 28♒ | 30♈ | 28♉ | 30♋ |
| 30♈ | | | | 31♍ | | 31♐ | | 30♓ | | 30♊ | |

## 1953

| JAN. | FEB. | MAR. | APR. | MAY | JUNE | JULY | AUG. | SEPT. | OCT. | NOV. | DEC. |
|---|---|---|---|---|---|---|---|---|---|---|---|
| 1♌ | 3♎ | 2♎ | 1♏ | 3♑ | 1♒ | 1♓ | 1♉ | 2♋ | 1♌ | 3♎ | 2♏ |
| 4♍ | 5♏ | 4♏ | 3♐ | 5♒ | 3♓ | 3♈ | 3♊ | 4♌ | 4♍ | 5♏ | 5♐ |
| 6♎ | 8♐ | 7♐ | 5♑ | 7♓ | 5♈ | 5♉ | 5♋ | 7♍ | 6♎ | 8♐ | 7♑ |
| 9♏ | 10♑ | 9♑ | 8♒ | 9♈ | 7♉ | 7♊ | 8♌ | 9♎ | 9♏ | 10♑ | 9♒ |
| 11♐ | 12♒ | 11♒ | 10♓ | 11♉ | 9♊ | 9♋ | 10♍ | 11♏ | 11♐ | 12♒ | 12♓ |
| 13♑ | 14♓ | 13♓ | 12♈ | 13♊ | 12♋ | 12♌ | 13♎ | 14♐ | 13♑ | 14♓ | 14♈ |
| 15♒ | 16♈ | 15♈ | 14♉ | 15♋ | 14♌ | 14♍ | 15♏ | 16♑ | 16♒ | 17♈ | 16♉ |
| 17♓ | 18♉ | 17♉ | 16♊ | 18♌ | 17♍ | 16♎ | 18♐ | 19♒ | 18♓ | 19♉ | 18♊ |
| 19♈ | 20♊ | 19♊ | 18♋ | 20♍ | 19♎ | 19♏ | 20♑ | 21♓ | 20♈ | 21♊ | 20♋ |
| 22♉ | 22♋ | 22♋ | 20♌ | 23♎ | 22♏ | 21♐ | 22♒ | 23♈ | 22♉ | 23♋ | 22♌ |
| 24♊ | 25♌ | 24♌ | 23♍ | 25♏ | 24♐ | 24♑ | 24♓ | 25♉ | 24♊ | 25♌ | 25♍ |
| 26♋ | 27♍ | 27♍ | 26♎ | 28♐ | 26♑ | 26♒ | 26♈ | 27♊ | 26♋ | 27♍ | 27♎ |
| 29♌ | | 29♎ | 28♏ | 30♑ | 28♒ | 28♓ | 28♉ | 29♋ | 29♌ | 30♎ | 30♏ |
| 31♍ | | | 30♐ | | | 30♈ | 30♊ | | 31♍ | | |

| Libra | Scorpio | Sagittarius | Capricorn | Aquarius | Pisces |
|---|---|---|---|---|---|
| ♎ | ♏ | ♐ | ♑ | ♒ | ♓ |

## 1954

| | JAN. | FEB. | MAR. | APR. | MAY | JUNE | JULY | AUG. | SEPT. | OCT. | NOV. | DEC. |
|---|---|---|---|---|---|---|---|---|---|---|---|---|
| | 1♐ | 2♒ | 2♒ | 2♈ | 2♉ | 2♋ | 2♌ | 3♎ | 1♏ | 1♐ | 2♒ | 2♓ |
| | 4♑ | 4♓ | 4♓ | 4♉ | 4♊ | 4♌ | 4♍ | 5♏ | 4♐ | 4♑ | 5♓ | 4♈ |
| | 6♒ | 6♈ | 6♈ | 6♊ | 6♋ | 6♍ | 6♎ | 8♐ | 6♑ | 6♒ | 7♈ | 6♉ |
| | 8♓ | 8♉ | 8♉ | 8♋ | 8♌ | 9♎ | 9♏ | 10♑ | 9♒ | 8♓ | 9♉ | 8♊ |
| | 10♈ | 11♊ | 10♊ | 11♌ | 10♍ | 12♏ | 11♐ | 12♒ | 11♓ | 11♈ | 11♊ | 10♋ |
| | 12♉ | 13♋ | 12♋ | 13♍ | 13♎ | 14♐ | 14♑ | 15♓ | 13♈ | 13♉ | 13♋ | 12♌ |
| | 14♊ | 15♌ | 14♌ | 15♎ | 15♏ | 16♑ | 16♒ | 17♈ | 15♉ | 14♊ | 15♌ | 15♍ |
| | 16♋ | 17♍ | 17♍ | 18♏ | 18♐ | 19♒ | 18♓ | 19♉ | 17♊ | 17♋ | 17♍ | 17♎ |
| | 19♌ | 20♎ | 19♎ | 20♐ | 20♑ | 21♓ | 21♈ | 21♊ | 19♋ | 19♌ | 20♎ | 20♏ |
| | 21♍ | 22♏ | 22♏ | 23♑ | 23♒ | 23♈ | 23♉ | 23♋ | 22♌ | 21♍ | 22♏ | 22♐ |
| | 24♎ | 25♐ | 24♐ | 25♒ | 25♓ | 25♉ | 25♊ | 25♌ | 24♍ | 24♎ | 25♐ | 25♑ |
| | 26♏ | 27♑ | 27♑ | 28♓ | 27♈ | 27♊ | 27♋ | 28♍ | 26♎ | 26♏ | 27♑ | 27♒ |
| | 29♐ | 29♒ | 29♒ | 30♈ | 29♉ | 29♋ | 29♌ | 30♎ | 29♏ | 29♐ | 30♓ | 29♓ |
| | 31♑ | | 31♓ | | 31♊ | | 31♍ | | | 31♒ | | |

## 1955

| | JAN. | FEB. | MAR. | APR. | MAY | JUNE | JULY | AUG. | SEPT. | OCT. | NOV. | DEC. |
|---|---|---|---|---|---|---|---|---|---|---|---|---|
| | 1♈ | 1♊ | 2♋ | 1♌ | 3♎ | 1♏ | 1♐ | 2♒ | 1♓ | 1♈ | 1♊ | 1♋ |
| | 3♉ | 3♋ | 5♌ | 3♍ | 5♏ | 4♐ | 4♑ | 5♓ | 2♈ | 3♉ | 3♋ | 3♌ |
| | 5♊ | 5♌ | 7♍ | 5♎ | 8♐ | 6♑ | 6♒ | 8♈ | 6♉ | 5♊ | 5♌ | 5♍ |
| | 7♋ | 7♍ | 9♎ | 8♏ | 10♑ | 9♒ | 9♓ | 9♉ | 8♊ | 7♋ | 8♍ | 7♎ |
| | 9♌ | 10♎ | 12♏ | 10♐ | 13♒ | 11♓ | 11♈ | 11♊ | 10♋ | 9♌ | 10♎ | 10♏ |
| | 11♍ | 12♏ | 14♐ | 13♑ | 15♓ | 14♈ | 13♉ | 14♋ | 12♌ | 11♍ | 12♏ | 12♐ |
| | 13♎ | 15♐ | 17♑ | 15♒ | 17♈ | 16♉ | 15♊ | 16♌ | 14♍ | 14♎ | 15♐ | 15♑ |
| | 16♏ | 17♑ | 19♒ | 18♓ | 19♉ | 18♊ | 17♋ | 18♍ | 16♎ | 16♏ | 17♑ | 17♒ |
| | 18♐ | 20♒ | 21♓ | 20♈ | 21♊ | 20♋ | 19♌ | 19♎ | 18♐ | 18♐ | 20♒ | 20♓ |
| | 21♑ | 22♓ | 23♈ | 22♉ | 23♋ | 22♌ | 21♍ | 22♏ | 21♑ | 21♑ | 22♓ | 22♈ |
| | 23♒ | 24♈ | 26♉ | 24♊ | 25♌ | 24♍ | 24♎ | 25♐ | 23♒ | 23♒ | 25♈ | 24♉ |
| | 26♓ | 26♉ | 28♊ | 26♋ | 28♍ | 26♎ | 26♏ | 27♑ | 26♓ | 26♓ | 27♉ | 26♊ |
| | 28♈ | 28♊ | 30♋ | 28♌ | 30♎ | 29♏ | 28♐ | 30♒ | 28♈ | 28♈ | 29♊ | 28♋ |
| | 30♉ | | | 30♍ | | | 31♑ | | | 30♉ | | 30♌ |

| *Key:* | Aries | Taurus | Gemini | Cancer | Leo | Virgo |
|---|---|---|---|---|---|---|
| | ♈ | ♉ | ♊ | ♋ | ♌ | ♍ |

## 1956

| JAN. | FEB. | MAR. | APR. | MAY | JUNE | JULY | AUG. | SEPT. | OCT. | NOV. | DEC. |
|---|---|---|---|---|---|---|---|---|---|---|---|
| 1♍ | 2♏ | 3♐ | 2♑ | 2♒ | 3♈ | 2♉ | 1♊ | 1♌ | 1♍ | 1♏ | 1♐ |
| 3♎ | 5♐ | 5♑ | 4♒ | 4♓ | 5♉ | 5♊ | 3♋ | 3♍ | 3♎ | 4♐ | 3♑ |
| 6♏ | 7♑ | 8♒ | 7♓ | 6♈ | 7♊ | 7♋ | 5♌ | 6♎ | 5♏ | 6♑ | 6♒ |
| 8♐ | 10♒ | 10♓ | 9♈ | 9♉ | 9♋ | 9♌ | 7♍ | 8♏ | 7♐ | 9♒ | 8♓ |
| 11♑ | 12♓ | 13♈ | 11♉ | 11♊ | 11♌ | 11♍ | 9♎ | 10♐ | 10♑ | 11♓ | 11♈ |
| 13♒ | 14♈ | 15♉ | 13♊ | 13♋ | 13♍ | 13♎ | 11♏ | 12♑ | 12♒ | 14♈ | 13♉ |
| 16♓ | 17♉ | 17♊ | 16♋ | 15♌ | 15♎ | 15♏ | 14♐ | 15♒ | 15♓ | 16♉ | 16♊ |
| 18♈ | 19♊ | 19♋ | 18♌ | 17♍ | 18♏ | 18♐ | 16♑ | 17♓ | 17♈ | 18♊ | 18♋ |
| 20♉ | 21♋ | 21♌ | 20♍ | 19♎ | 20♐ | 20♑ | 19♒ | 20♈ | 20♉ | 20♋ | 20♌ |
| 23♊ | 23♌ | 23♍ | 22♎ | 21♏ | 23♑ | 22♒ | 21♓ | 22♉ | 22♊ | 22♌ | 22♍ |
| 25♋ | 25♍ | 26♎ | 24♏ | 24♐ | 25♒ | 25♓ | 24♈ | 24♊ | 24♋ | 24♍ | 24♎ |
| 27♌ | 27♎ | 28♏ | 27♐ | 26♑ | 28♓ | 27♈ | 26♉ | 27♋ | 26♌ | 27♎ | 26♏ |
| 29♍ | 29♏ | 30♐ | 29♑ | 29♒ | 30♈ | 30♉ | 28♊ | 29♌ | 28♍ | 29♏ | 28♐ |
| 31♎ | | | | 31♓ | | | 30♋ | | 30♎ | | 31♑ |

## 1957

| JAN. | FEB. | MAR. | APR. | MAY | JUNE | JULY | AUG. | SEPT. | OCT. | NOV. | DEC. |
|---|---|---|---|---|---|---|---|---|---|---|---|
| 2♒ | 1♓ | 3♈ | 1♉ | 1♊ | 2♌ | 1♍ | 2♏ | 2♑ | 2♒ | 1♓ | 1♈ |
| 5♓ | 4♈ | 5♉ | 4♊ | 3♋ | 4♍ | 3♎ | 4♐ | 5♒ | 5♓ | 3♈ | 3♉ |
| 7♈ | 6♉ | 8♊ | 6♋ | 5♌ | 6♎ | 5♏ | 6♑ | 7♓ | 7♈ | 6♉ | 6♊ |
| 10♉ | 8♊ | 10♋ | 8♌ | 8♍ | 8♏ | 8♐ | 9♒ | 10♈ | 10♉ | 8♊ | 8♋ |
| 12♊ | 10♋ | 12♌ | 10♍ | 10♎ | 10♐ | 10♑ | 11♓ | 12♉ | 12♊ | 11♋ | 10♌ |
| 14♋ | 12♌ | 14♍ | 12♎ | 12♏ | 13♑ | 12♒ | 14♈ | 15♊ | 14♋ | 13♌ | 12♍ |
| 16♌ | 14♍ | 16♎ | 14♏ | 14♐ | 15♒ | 15♓ | 16♉ | 17♋ | 15♌ | 15♍ | 14♎ |
| 18♍ | 16♎ | 18♏ | 17♐ | 16♑ | 18♓ | 17♈ | 19♊ | 19♌ | 19♍ | 17♎ | 16♏ |
| 20♎ | 19♏ | 20♐ | 19♑ | 19♒ | 20♈ | 20♉ | 21♋ | 21♍ | 21♎ | 19♏ | 19♐ |
| 22♏ | 21♐ | 23♑ | 21♒ | 21♓ | 22♉ | 22♊ | 23♌ | 23♎ | 23♏ | 21♐ | 21♑ |
| 25♐ | 23♑ | 25♒ | 24♓ | 24♈ | 25♊ | 24♋ | 25♍ | 25♏ | 25♐ | 23♑ | 23♒ |
| 27♑ | 26♒ | 28♓ | 26♈ | 26♉ | 27♋ | 26♌ | 27♎ | 27♐ | 27♑ | 26♒ | 26♓ |
| 29♒ | 28♓ | 30♈ | 29♉ | 28♊ | 29♌ | 28♍ | 29♏ | 30♑ | 29♒ | 28♓ | 28♈ |
| | | | | 31♋ | | 30♎ | 31♐ | | | | 31♉ |

| Libra | Scorpio | Sagittarius | Capricorn | Aquarius | Pisces |
|---|---|---|---|---|---|
| ♎ | ♏ | ♐ | ♑ | ♒ | ♓ |

## 1958

| JAN. | FEB. | MAR. | APR. | MAY | JUNE | JULY | AUG. | SEPT. | OCT. | NOV. | DEC. |
|---|---|---|---|---|---|---|---|---|---|---|---|
| 2♊ | 1♋ | 2♌ | 1♍ | 2♏ | 1♐ | 2♒ | 1♓ | 2♉ | 2♊ | 1♋ | 3♍ |
| 4♋ | 3♌ | 4♍ | 3♎ | 4♐ | 3♑ | 5♓ | 3♈ | 5♊ | 5♋ | 3♌ | 5♎ |
| 6♌ | 5♍ | 6♎ | 5♏ | 6♑ | 5♒ | 7♈ | 6♉ | 7♋ | 7♌ | 5♍ | 7♏ |
| 8♍ | 7♎ | 8♏ | 7♐ | 9♒ | 7♓ | 10♉ | 9♊ | 10♌ | 9♍ | 8♎ | 9♐ |
| 11♎ | 9♏ | 10♐ | 9♑ | 11♓ | 10♈ | 12♊ | 11♋ | 12♍ | 11♎ | 10♏ | 11♑ |
| 13♏ | 11♐ | 13♑ | 11♒ | 14♈ | 12♉ | 15♋ | 13♌ | 14♎ | 13♏ | 12♐ | 13♒ |
| 15♐ | 13♑ | 15♒ | 14♓ | 16♉ | 15♊ | 17♌ | 15♍ | 16♏ | 15♐ | 14♑ | 15♓ |
| 17♑ | 16♒ | 17♓ | 16♈ | 18♊ | 17♋ | 19♍ | 17♎ | 18♐ | 17♑ | 16♒ | 18♈ |
| 19♒ | 18♓ | 20♈ | 19♉ | 21♋ | 19♌ | 21♎ | 19♏ | 20♑ | 19♒ | 18♓ | 20♉ |
| 22♓ | 21♈ | 23♉ | 21♊ | 23♌ | 21♍ | 24♏ | 21♐ | 22♒ | 22♓ | 21♈ | 23♊ |
| 24♈ | 23♉ | 25♊ | 24♋ | 25♍ | 24♎ | 26♐ | 24♑ | 25♓ | 24♈ | 23♉ | 25♋ |
| 27♉ | 26♊ | 27♋ | 26♌ | 28♎ | 26♏ | 28♑ | 26♒ | 27♈ | 27♉ | 26♊ | 28♌ |
| 29♊ | 28♋ | 30♌ | 28♍ | 30♏ | 28♐ | 30♒ | 28♓ | 30♉ | 29♊ | 28♋ | 30♍ |
|  |  |  | 30♎ |  | 30♑ | 31♓ | 31♈ |  |  | 30♌ |  |

## 1959

| JAN. | FEB. | MAR. | APR. | MAY | JUNE | JULY | AUG. | SEPT. | OCT. | NOV. | DEC. |
|---|---|---|---|---|---|---|---|---|---|---|---|
| 1♎ | 2♐ | 1♐ | 1♒ | 1♓ | 2♉ | 2♊ | 1♋ | 2♍ | 1♎ | 2♐ | 1♑ |
| 3♏ | 4♑ | 3♑ | 4♓ | 3♈ | 5♊ | 5♋ | 3♌ | 4♎ | 3♏ | 4♑ | 3♒ |
| 5♐ | 6♒ | 5♒ | 6♈ | 6♉ | 7♋ | 7♌ | 6♍ | 6♏ | 6♐ | 6♒ | 6♓ |
| 7♑ | 8♓ | 7♓ | 9♉ | 8♊ | 10♌ | 9♍ | 8♎ | 8♐ | 8♑ | 8♓ | 8♈ |
| 10♒ | 11♈ | 10♈ | 11♊ | 11♋ | 12♍ | 12♎ | 10♏ | 10♑ | 10♒ | 11♈ | 11♉ |
| 12♓ | 13♉ | 12♉ | 14♋ | 13♌ | 14♎ | 14♏ | 12♐ | 13♒ | 12♓ | 13♉ | 13♊ |
| 14♈ | 16♊ | 15♊ | 16♌ | 16♍ | 16♏ | 16♐ | 14♑ | 15♓ | 14♈ | 16♊ | 15♋ |
| 17♉ | 18♋ | 17♋ | 18♍ | 18♎ | 19♐ | 18♑ | 16♒ | 17♈ | 17♉ | 18♋ | 18♌ |
| 19♊ | 20♌ | 20♌ | 21♎ | 20♏ | 21♑ | 20♒ | 18♓ | 19♉ | 19♊ | 21♌ | 20♍ |
| 22♋ | 23♍ | 22♍ | 23♏ | 22♐ | 23♒ | 22♓ | 21♈ | 22♊ | 22♋ | 23♍ | 23♎ |
| 24♌ | 25♎ | 24♎ | 25♐ | 24♑ | 25♓ | 24♈ | 23♉ | 24♋ | 25♌ | 25♎ | 25♏ |
| 26♍ | 27♏ | 26♏ | 27♑ | 26♒ | 27♈ | 26♉ | 26♊ | 27♌ | 27♍ | 27♏ | 27♐ |
| 28♎ | 28♐ | 28♐ | 29♒ | 28♓ | 29♉ | 29♊ | 28♋ | 29♍ | 29♎ | 29♐ | 29♑ |
| 31♏ |  | 30♑ |  | 31♈ |  | 31♋ | 31♌ |  | 31♏ |  | 31♒ |

Key:  Aries  Taurus  Gemini  Cancer  Leo  Virgo
♈  ♉  ♊  ♋  ♌  ♍

## 1960

| JAN. | FEB. | MAR. | APR. | MAY | JUNE | JULY | AUG. | SEPT. | OCT. | NOV. | DEC. |
|---|---|---|---|---|---|---|---|---|---|---|---|
| 2♓ | 1♈ | 1♉ | 3♋ | 2♌ | 1♍ | 1♎ | 2♐ | 2♒ | 1♓ | 2♉ | 2♊ |
| 4♈ | 3♉ | 4♊ | 5♌ | 5♍ | 4♎ | 3♏ | 4♑ | 4♓ | 4♈ | 4♊ | 4♋ |
| 7♉ | 5♊ | 6♋ | 8♍ | 7♎ | 6♏ | 5♐ | 6♒ | 6♈ | 6♉ | 7♋ | 7♌ |
| 9♊ | 8♋ | 9♌ | 10♎ | 9♏ | 8♐ | 7♑ | 8♓ | 8♉ | 8♊ | 9♌ | 9♍ |
| 12♋ | 10♌ | 11♍ | 12♏ | 11♐ | 10♑ | 9♒ | 10♈ | 11♊ | 11♋ | 12♍ | 12♎ |
| 14♌ | 13♍ | 13♎ | 14♐ | 13♑ | 12♒ | 11♓ | 12♉ | 13♋ | 13♌ | 14♎ | 14♏ |
| 17♍ | 15♎ | 16♏ | 16♑ | 15♒ | 14♓ | 13♈ | 14♊ | 16♌ | 16♍ | 17♏ | 16♐ |
| 19♎ | 17♏ | 18♐ | 18♒ | 18♓ | 16♈ | 15♉ | 17♋ | 18♍ | 18♎ | 19♐ | 18♑ |
| 21♏ | 19♐ | 20♑ | 20♓ | 20♈ | 18♉ | 18♊ | 19♌ | 21♎ | 20♏ | 21♑ | 20♒ |
| 23♐ | 22♑ | 22♒ | 23♈ | 22♉ | 21♊ | 21♋ | 22♍ | 23♏ | 22♐ | 23♒ | 22♓ |
| 25♑ | 24♒ | 24♓ | 25♉ | 25♊ | 23♋ | 23♌ | 24♎ | 25♐ | 24♑ | 25♓ | 24♈ |
| 27♒ | 26♓ | 26♈ | 27♊ | 27♋ | 26♌ | 26♍ | 27♏ | 27♑ | 27♒ | 27♈ | 27♉ |
| 29♓ | 28♈ | 29♉ | 30♋ | 30♌ | 28♍ | 28♎ | 29♐ | 29♒ | 29♓ | 29♉ | 29♊ |
|  |  | 31♊ |  |  |  | 30♏ | 31♑ |  | 31♈ |  |  |

## 1961

| JAN. | FEB. | MAR. | APR. | MAY | JUNE | JULY | AUG. | SEPT. | OCT. | NOV. | DEC. |
|---|---|---|---|---|---|---|---|---|---|---|---|
| 1♋ | 2♍ | 1♍ | 2♏ | 2♐ | 2♒ | 2♓ | 2♉ | 1♊ | 3♌ | 2♍ | 2♎ |
| 3♌ | 4♎ | 4♎ | 3♐ | 4♑ | 4♓ | 4♈ | 4♊ | 3♋ | 5♍ | 4♎ | 4♏ |
| 6♍ | 7♏ | 6♏ | 7♑ | 6♒ | 6♈ | 6♉ | 6♋ | 6♌ | 7♎ | 6♏ | 6♐ |
| 8♎ | 9♐ | 8♐ | 9♒ | 8♓ | 9♉ | 8♊ | 9♌ | 8♍ | 10♏ | 9♐ | 9♑ |
| 10♏ | 11♑ | 10♑ | 11♓ | 10♈ | 11♊ | 11♋ | 12♍ | 11♎ | 13♐ | 11♑ | 11♒ |
| 13♐ | 13♒ | 12♒ | 13♈ | 12♉ | 13♋ | 13♌ | 14♎ | 13♏ | 15♑ | 13♒ | 13♓ |
| 15♑ | 15♓ | 15♓ | 15♉ | 15♊ | 16♌ | 16♍ | 17♏ | 15♐ | 17♒ | 16♓ | 15♈ |
| 17♒ | 17♈ | 17♈ | 17♊ | 17♋ | 18♍ | 18♎ | 19♐ | 18♑ | 19♓ | 18♈ | 17♉ |
| 19♓ | 19♉ | 19♉ | 20♋ | 20♌ | 21♎ | 21♏ | 21♑ | 20♒ | 21♈ | 20♉ | 19♊ |
| 21♈ | 22♊ | 21♊ | 22♌ | 22♍ | 23♏ | 23♐ | 23♒ | 22♓ | 23♉ | 22♊ | 22♋ |
| 23♉ | 24♋ | 23♋ | 25♍ | 25♎ | 26♐ | 25♑ | 25♓ | 24♈ | 26♊ | 24♋ | 24♌ |
| 25♊ | 27♌ | 26♌ | 27♎ | 27♏ | 28♑ | 27♒ | 27♈ | 26♉ | 28♋ | 27♌ | 26♍ |
| 28♋ |  | 28♍ | 30♏ | 29♐ | 30♒ | 29♓ | 30♉ | 28♊ | 30♌ | 29♍ | 29♎ |
| 30♌ |  | 31♎ |  | 31♑ |  | 31♈ |  | 30♋ |  |  | 31♏ |

| Libra | Scorpio | Sagittarius | Capricorn | Aquarius | Pisces |
|---|---|---|---|---|---|
| ♎ | ♏ | ♐ | ♑ | ♒ | ♓ |

## 1962

| JAN. | FEB. | MAR. | APR. | MAY | JUNE | JULY | AUG. | SEPT. | OCT. | NOV. | DEC. |
|---|---|---|---|---|---|---|---|---|---|---|---|
| 3♐ | 1♑ | 1♑ | 1♓ | 1♈ | 1♊ | 1♋ | 2♍ | 1♎ | 3♐ | 2♑ | 1♒ |
| 5♑ | 3♒ | 3♒ | 3♈ | 3♉ | 3♋ | 3♌ | 4♎ | 3♏ | 5♑ | 4♒ | 3♓ |
| 7♒ | 5♓ | 5♓ | 5♉ | 5♊ | 6♌ | 6♍ | 7♏ | 6♐ | 8♒ | 6♓ | 5♈ |
| 9♓ | 7♈ | 7♈ | 7♊ | 7♋ | 8♍ | 8♎ | 9♐ | 8♑ | 10♓ | 8♈ | 8♉ |
| 11♈ | 10♉ | 9♉ | 10♋ | 9♌ | 11♎ | 11♏ | 12♑ | 10♒ | 12♈ | 10♉ | 10♊ |
| 13♉ | 12♊ | 11♊ | 12♌ | 12♍ | 13♏ | 13♐ | 14♒ | 12♓ | 14♉ | 12♊ | 12♋ |
| 16♊ | 14♋ | 13♋ | 15♍ | 14♎ | 16♐ | 16♑ | 16♓ | 14♈ | 16♊ | 14♋ | 14♌ |
| 18♋ | 17♌ | 16♌ | 17♎ | 16♏ | 18♐ | 17♒ | 18♈ | 16♉ | 18♋ | 17♌ | 16♍ |
| 20♌ | 19♍ | 18♍ | 20♏ | 18♐ | 20♑ | 19♓ | 20♉ | 18♊ | 20♌ | 19♍ | 19♎ |
| 23♍ | 22♎ | 21♎ | 22♐ | 20♑ | 22♒ | 22♈ | 22♊ | 20♋ | 23♍ | 21♎ | 21♏ |
| 25♎ | 24♏ | 23♏ | 24♑ | 22♒ | 24♓ | 24♉ | 23♋ | 21♌ | 25♎ | 24♏ | 24♐ |
| 28♏ | 26♐ | 26♐ | 27♒ | 24♓ | 26♈ | 26♊ | 25♌ | 23♍ | 28♏ | 26♐ | 26♑ |
| 30♐ |  | 28♑ | 29♓ | 26♈ | 28♉ | 27♋ | 28♍ | 25♎ | 30♐ | 29♑ | 28♒ |
|  |  | 30♒ |  | 28♉ | 30♋ | 29♌ | 30♎ | 28♏ |  |  | 31♓ |
|  |  |  |  | 30♊ |  | 30♍ |  | 30♐ |  |  |  |

## 1963

| JAN. | FEB. | MAR. | APR. | MAY | JUNE | JULY | AUG. | SEPT. | OCT. | NOV. | DEC. |
|---|---|---|---|---|---|---|---|---|---|---|---|
| 2♈ | 2♊ | 1♊ | 2♌ | 2♍ | 1♎ | 3♐ | 2♑ | 3♓ | 2♈ | 1♉ | 2♋ |
| 4♉ | 4♋ | 4♋ | 5♍ | 4♎ | 3♏ | 5♑ | 4♒ | 5♈ | 4♉ | 3♊ | 4♌ |
| 6♊ | 7♌ | 6♌ | 7♎ | 7♏ | 6♐ | 8♒ | 7♓ | 7♉ | 6♊ | 5♋ | 6♍ |
| 8♋ | 9♍ | 8♍ | 10♏ | 9♐ | 8♑ | 10♓ | 9♈ | 9♊ | 8♋ | 7♌ | 9♎ |
| 10♌ | 11♎ | 11♎ | 12♐ | 12♑ | 10♒ | 12♈ | 10♉ | 11♋ | 10♌ | 9♍ | 11♏ |
| 13♍ | 14♏ | 13♏ | 15♑ | 14♒ | 13♓ | 14♉ | 13♊ | 13♌ | 13♍ | 11♎ | 14♐ |
| 15♎ | 16♐ | 16♐ | 17♒ | 16♓ | 15♈ | 16♊ | 15♋ | 15♍ | 15♎ | 14♏ | 16♑ |
| 18♏ | 19♑ | 18♑ | 19♓ | 19♈ | 17♉ | 18♋ | 17♌ | 18♎ | 18♏ | 16♐ | 19♒ |
| 20♐ | 21♒ | 21♒ | 21♈ | 21♉ | 19♊ | 21♌ | 19♍ | 20♏ | 20♐ | 19♑ | 21♓ |
| 22♑ | 23♓ | 23♓ | 23♉ | 23♊ | 21♋ | 23♍ | 22♎ | 23♐ | 22♑ | 21♒ | 23♈ |
| 25♒ | 25♈ | 25♈ | 25♊ | 25♋ | 23♌ | 25♎ | 24♏ | 25♑ | 24♒ | 24♓ | 25♉ |
| 27♓ | 27♉ | 27♉ | 27♋ | 27♌ | 25♍ | 28♏ | 27♐ | 27♒ | 26♓ | 26♈ | 27♊ |
| 29♈ |  | 29♊ | 29♌ | 30♍ | 28♎ | 30♐ | 29♑ | 30♓ | 28♈ | 28♉ | 29♋ |
| 31♉ |  | 31♋ |  |  | 30♏ |  | 31♒ |  | 30♉ | 30♊ | 31♌ |

| *Key:* | Aries | Taurus | Gemini | Cancer | Leo | Virgo |
|---|---|---|---|---|---|---|
|  | ♈ | ♉ | ♊ | ♋ | ♌ | ♍ |

## 1964

| JAN. | FEB. | MAR. | APR. | MAY | JUNE | JULY | AUG. | SEPT. | OCT. | NOV. | DEC. |
|---|---|---|---|---|---|---|---|---|---|---|---|
| 3♍ | 1♎ | 2♏ | 1♐ | 1♑ | 2♓ | 2♈ | 2♊ | 1♋ | 2♍ | 1♎ | 3♐ |
| 5♎ | 4♏ | 5♐ | 3♑ | 3♒ | 4♈ | 4♉ | 4♋ | 3♌ | 4♎ | 3♏ | 5♑ |
| 7♏ | 6♐ | 7♑ | 6♒ | 6♓ | 6♉ | 6♊ | 6♌ | 5♍ | 7♏ | 5♐ | 8♒ |
| 10♐ | 9♑ | 10♒ | 8♓ | 8♈ | 8♊ | 8♋ | 8♍ | 7♎ | 9♐ | 8♑ | 10♓ |
| 12♑ | 11♒ | 12♓ | 10♈ | 10♉ | 10♋ | 10♌ | 10♎ | 9♏ | 11♑ | 10♒ | 13♈ |
| 15♒ | 13♓ | 14♈ | 13♉ | 12♊ | 12♌ | 12♍ | 13♏ | 12♐ | 14♒ | 13♓ | 15♉ |
| 17♓ | 16♈ | 16♉ | 15♊ | 14♋ | 15♍ | 14♎ | 15♐ | 14♑ | 16♓ | 15♈ | 17♊ |
| 19♈ | 18♉ | 18♊ | 17♋ | 16♌ | 17♎ | 16♏ | 18♑ | 17♒ | 19♈ | 17♉ | 19♋ |
| 22♉ | 20♊ | 20♋ | 19♌ | 18♍ | 19♏ | 19♐ | 20♒ | 19♓ | 21♉ | 19♊ | 21♌ |
| 24♊ | 22♋ | 23♌ | 21♍ | 21♎ | 22♐ | 22♑ | 23♓ | 21♈ | 23♊ | 21♋ | 23♍ |
| 26♋ | 24♌ | 25♍ | 23♎ | 23♏ | 24♑ | 24♒ | 25♈ | 23♉ | 25♋ | 23♌ | 25♎ |
| 28♌ | 26♍ | 27♎ | 26♏ | 25♐ | 27♒ | 26♓ | 27♉ | 26♊ | 27♌ | 26♍ | 27♏ |
| 30♍ | 29♎ | 29♏ | 28♐ | 28♑ | 29♓ | 29♈ | 29♊ | 28♋ | 29♍ | 28♎ | 30♐ |
|  |  |  |  | 30♒ |  | 31♉ |  | 30♌ |  | 30♏ |  |

## 1965

| JAN. | FEB. | MAR. | APR. | MAY | JUNE | JULY | AUG. | SEPT. | OCT. | NOV. | DEC. |
|---|---|---|---|---|---|---|---|---|---|---|---|
| 1♑ | 3♓ | 2♓ | 1♈ | 2♊ | 1♋ | 2♍ | 1♎ | 2♐ | 1♑ | 3♓ | 2♈ |
| 4♒ | 5♈ | 4♈ | 3♉ | 4♋ | 3♌ | 4♎ | 3♏ | 4♑ | 4♒ | 5♈ | 5♉ |
| 6♓ | 7♉ | 7♉ | 5♊ | 7♌ | 5♍ | 7♏ | 5♐ | 6♒ | 6♓ | 7♉ | 7♊ |
| 9♈ | 10♊ | 9♊ | 7♋ | 9♍ | 7♎ | 9♐ | 8♑ | 9♓ | 9♈ | 9♊ | 9♋ |
| 11♉ | 12♋ | 11♋ | 9♌ | 11♎ | 9♏ | 11♑ | 10♒ | 11♈ | 11♉ | 12♋ | 11♌ |
| 13♊ | 14♌ | 13♌ | 11♍ | 13♏ | 12♐ | 14♒ | 13♓ | 14♉ | 13♊ | 14♌ | 13♍ |
| 15♋ | 16♍ | 15♍ | 14♎ | 15♐ | 14♑ | 16♓ | 15♈ | 16♊ | 16♋ | 16♍ | 15♎ |
| 17♌ | 18♎ | 17♎ | 16♏ | 18♑ | 17♒ | 19♈ | 18♉ | 18♋ | 18♌ | 18♎ | 18♏ |
| 19♍ | 20♏ | 19♏ | 18♐ | 20♒ | 19♓ | 21♉ | 20♊ | 20♌ | 20♍ | 20♏ | 20♐ |
| 21♎ | 22♐ | 22♐ | 21♑ | 23♓ | 22♈ | 24♊ | 22♋ | 22♍ | 22♎ | 23♐ | 22♑ |
| 24♏ | 25♑ | 24♑ | 23♒ | 25♈ | 24♉ | 26♋ | 24♌ | 25♎ | 24♏ | 25♑ | 25♒ |
| 26♐ | 27♒ | 27♒ | 26♓ | 28♉ | 26♊ | 28♌ | 26♍ | 27♏ | 26♐ | 27♒ | 27♓ |
| 29♑ |  | 29♓ | 28♈ | 30♊ | 28♋ | 30♍ | 28♎ | 29♐ | 29♑ | 30♓ | 30♈ |
| 31♒ |  |  | 30♉ |  | 30♌ |  | 30♏ |  | 31♒ |  |  |

| Libra | Scorpio | Sagittarius | Capricorn | Aquarius | Pisces |
|---|---|---|---|---|---|
| ♎ | ♏ | ♐ | ♑ | ♒ | ♓ |

## 1966

| JAN. | FEB. | MAR. | APR. | MAY | JUNE | JULY | AUG. | SEPT. | OCT. | NOV. | DEC. |
|---|---|---|---|---|---|---|---|---|---|---|---|
| 1♉ | 2♋ | 1♋ | 2♍ | 1♎ | 2♐ | 1♑ | 3♓ | 1♈ | 1♉ | 2♋ | 2♌ |
| 4♊ | 4♌ | 4♌ | 4♎ | 3♏ | 4♑ | 4♒ | 5♈ | 4♉ | 4♊ | 4♌ | 4♍ |
| 6♋ | 6♍ | 6♍ | 6♏ | 6♐ | 7♒ | 6♓ | 8♉ | 6♊ | 6♋ | 7♍ | 6♎ |
| 8♌ | 8♎ | 7♎ | 8♐ | 8♑ | 9♓ | 9♈ | 10♊ | 9♋ | 8♌ | 9♎ | 8♏ |
| 10♍ | 10♏ | 10♏ | 10♑ | 10♒ | 12♈ | 11♉ | 12♋ | 11♌ | 10♍ | 11♏ | 10♐ |
| 12♎ | 12♐ | 12♐ | 13♒ | 13♓ | 14♉ | 14♊ | 14♌ | 13♍ | 12♎ | 13♐ | 12♑ |
| 14♏ | 15♑ | 14♑ | 15♓ | 15♈ | 16♊ | 16♋ | 16♍ | 15♎ | 14♏ | 15♑ | 15♒ |
| 16♐ | 17♒ | 17♒ | 18♈ | 18♉ | 19♋ | 18♌ | 18♎ | 17♏ | 16♐ | 17♒ | 17♓ |
| 19♑ | 20♓ | 19♓ | 20♉ | 20♊ | 21♌ | 20♍ | 20♏ | 19♐ | 19♑ | 20♓ | 20♈ |
| 21♒ | 22♈ | 22♈ | 23♊ | 22♋ | 23♍ | 22♎ | 23♐ | 21♑ | 21♒ | 22♈ | 22♉ |
| 24♓ | 25♉ | 24♉ | 25♋ | 24♌ | 25♎ | 24♏ | 25♑ | 24♒ | 23♓ | 25♉ | 25♊ |
| 26♈ | 27♊ | 26♊ | 27♌ | 26♍ | 27♏ | 26♐ | 27♒ | 26♓ | 26♈ | 27♊ | 27♋ |
| 29♉ |  | 29♋ | 29♍ | 29♎ | 29♐ | 29♑ | 30♓ | 29♈ | 28♉ | 29♋ | 29♌ |
| 31♊ |  | 31♌ |  | 31♏ |  | 31♒ |  |  | 31♊ |  | 31♍ |

## 1967

| JAN. | FEB. | MAR. | APR. | MAY | JUNE | JULY | AUG. | SEPT. | OCT. | NOV. | DEC. |
|---|---|---|---|---|---|---|---|---|---|---|---|
| 2♎ | 1♏ | 2♐ | 1♑ | 3♓ | 1♈ | 1♉ | 2♋ | 1♌ | 1♍ | 1♏ | 1♐ |
| 4♏ | 3♐ | 4♑ | 3♒ | 5♈ | 4♉ | 4♊ | 5♌ | 3♍ | 3♎ | 3♐ | 3♑ |
| 7♐ | 5♑ | 7♒ | 5♓ | 8♉ | 6♊ | 6♋ | 7♍ | 5♎ | 5♏ | 5♑ | 5♒ |
| 9♑ | 7♒ | 9♓ | 8♈ | 10♊ | 9♋ | 8♌ | 9♎ | 7♏ | 7♐ | 7♒ | 7♓ |
| 11♒ | 10♓ | 12♈ | 10♉ | 12♋ | 11♌ | 11♍ | 11♏ | 9♐ | 9♑ | 10♓ | 9♈ |
| 13♓ | 12♈ | 14♉ | 13♊ | 15♌ | 13♍ | 13♎ | 13♐ | 12♑ | 11♒ | 12♈ | 12♉ |
| 16♈ | 15♉ | 17♊ | 15♋ | 17♍ | 15♎ | 15♏ | 15♑ | 14♒ | 13♓ | 14♉ | 14♊ |
| 18♉ | 17♊ | 19♋ | 17♌ | 19♎ | 17♏ | 18♐ | 18♒ | 16♓ | 16♈ | 17♊ | 17♋ |
| 21♊ | 20♋ | 21♌ | 20♍ | 21♏ | 20♐ | 20♑ | 20♓ | 18♈ | 18♉ | 19♋ | 19♌ |
| 23♋ | 22♌ | 23♍ | 22♎ | 23♐ | 22♑ | 22♒ | 22♈ | 21♉ | 20♊ | 22♌ | 22♍ |
| 25♌ | 24♍ | 25♎ | 24♏ | 25♑ | 24♒ | 24♓ | 25♉ | 23♊ | 22♋ | 24♍ | 24♎ |
| 27♍ | 26♎ | 27♏ | 26♐ | 27♒ | 26♓ | 27♈ | 27♊ | 26♋ | 24♌ | 27♎ | 26♏ |
| 30♎ | 28♏ | 29♐ | 28♑ | 30♓ | 29♈ | 29♉ | 30♋ | 28♌ | 26♍ | 29♏ | 28♐ |
|  |  |  | 30♒ |  |  | 31♊ |  |  | 28♎ |  | 30♑ |

| *Key:* | Aries | Taurus | Gemini | Cancer | Leo | Virgo |
|---|---|---|---|---|---|---|
|  | ♈ | ♉ | ♊ | ♋ | ♌ | ♍ |

## 1968

| JAN. | FEB. | MAR. | APR. | MAY | JUNE | JULY | AUG. | SEPT. | OCT. | NOV. | DEC. |
|---|---|---|---|---|---|---|---|---|---|---|---|
| 1♒ | 2♈ | 3♉ | 2♊ | 2♋ | 3♍ | 2♎ | 1♏ | 1♑ | 3♓ | 1♈ | 1♉ |
| 3♓ | 5♉ | 5♊ | 4♋ | 4♋ | 5♎ | 4♏ | 3♐ | 3♒ | 5♈ | 4♉ | 3♊ |
| 6♈ | 7♊ | 8♋ | 7♌ | 6♍ | 7♏ | 6♐ | 5♑ | 5♓ | 7♉ | 6♊ | 6♋ |
| 8♉ | 10♋ | 10♌ | 9♍ | 9♎ | 9♐ | 8♑ | 7♒ | 8♈ | 10♊ | 9♋ | 8♌ |
| 11♊ | 12♌ | 13♍ | 11♎ | 11♏ | 11♐ | 10♒ | 9♓ | 10♉ | 12♋ | 11♌ | 11♍ |
| 13♋ | 14♍ | 15♎ | 13♏ | 13♐ | 13♑ | 13♓ | 11♈ | 12♊ | 15♌ | 14♍ | 13♎ |
| 16♌ | 16♎ | 17♏ | 15♐ | 15♑ | 15♓ | 15♈ | 14♉ | 15♋ | 17♍ | 16♎ | 15♏ |
| 18♍ | 18♏ | 19♐ | 17♑ | 17♒ | 18♈ | 17♉ | 16♊ | 17♌ | 19♎ | 18♏ | 17♐ |
| 20♎ | 21♐ | 21♑ | 19♒ | 19♓ | 20♉ | 20♊ | 19♋ | 20♍ | 22♎ | 20♐ | 19♑ |
| 22♏ | 23♑ | 23♒ | 22♓ | 21♈ | 23♊ | 22♋ | 21♌ | 22♎ | 24♐ | 22♑ | 21♒ |
| 24♐ | 25♒ | 25♓ | 24♈ | 24♉ | 25♋ | 25♌ | 24♍ | 24♏ | 26♑ | 24♒ | 23♓ |
| 26♑ | 27♓ | 28♈ | 27♉ | 26♊ | 28♌ | 27♍ | 26♎ | 26♐ | 28♒ | 26♓ | 26♈ |
| 29♒ | 29♈ | 30♉ | 29♊ | 29♋ | 30♍ | 29♎ | 28♏ | 28♑ | 30♓ | 28♈ | 28♉ |
| 31♓ |  |  |  | 31♌ |  |  | 30♐ | 30♒ |  |  | 31♊ |

## 1969

| JAN. | FEB. | MAR. | APR. | MAY | JUNE | JULY | AUG. | SEPT. | OCT. | NOV. | DEC. |
|---|---|---|---|---|---|---|---|---|---|---|---|
| 2♋ | 1♌ | 3♍ | 1♎ | 1♏ | 1♑ | 1♒ | 1♈ | 2♊ | 2♋ | 1♌ | 1♍ |
| 5♌ | 3♍ | 5♎ | 4♏ | 3♐ | 3♒ | 3♓ | 4♉ | 5♋ | 5♌ | 4♍ | 3♎ |
| 7♍ | 6♎ | 7♏ | 6♐ | 5♑ | 5♓ | 5♈ | 6♊ | 7♌ | 7♍ | 6♎ | 6♏ |
| 9♎ | 8♏ | 9♐ | 8♑ | 7♒ | 8♈ | 7♉ | 9♋ | 10♍ | 10♎ | 8♏ | 8♐ |
| 12♏ | 10♐ | 11♑ | 10♒ | 9♓ | 10♉ | 10♊ | 11♌ | 12♎ | 12♏ | 10♐ | 10♑ |
| 14♐ | 12♑ | 14♒ | 12♓ | 11♈ | 13♊ | 12♋ | 14♍ | 15♏ | 14♐ | 12♑ | 12♒ |
| 16♑ | 14♒ | 16♓ | 14♈ | 14♉ | 15♋ | 15♌ | 16♎ | 17♏ | 16♑ | 14♒ | 14♓ |
| 18♒ | 16♓ | 18♈ | 17♉ | 16♊ | 18♌ | 17♍ | 18♏ | 19♑ | 18♒ | 17♓ | 16♈ |
| 20♓ | 18♈ | 20♉ | 19♊ | 19♋ | 20♍ | 20♎ | 20♐ | 21♒ | 20♓ | 19♈ | 18♉ |
| 22♈ | 21♉ | 23♊ | 21♋ | 21♌ | 22♎ | 22♏ | 23♑ | 23♓ | 22♈ | 21♉ | 20♊ |
| 24♉ | 23♊ | 25♋ | 24♌ | 24♍ | 25♏ | 24♐ | 25♒ | 25♈ | 25♉ | 23♊ | 23♋ |
| 27♊ | 26♋ | 28♌ | 26♍ | 26♎ | 27♐ | 26♑ | 27♓ | 27♉ | 27♊ | 26♋ | 26♌ |
| 29♋ | 28♌ | 30♍ | 29♎ | 28♏ | 29♑ | 28♒ | 29♈ | 30♊ | 30♋ | 28♌ | 28♍ |
|  |  |  |  | 30♐ |  | 30♓ | 31♉ |  |  |  | 31♎ |

| Libra | Scorpio | Sagittarius | Capricorn | Aquarius | Pisces |
|---|---|---|---|---|---|
| ♎ | ♏ | ♐ | ♑ | ♒ | ♓ |

## 1970

| JAN. | FEB. | MAR. | APR. | MAY | JUNE | JULY | AUG. | SEPT. | OCT. | NOV. | DEC. |
|---|---|---|---|---|---|---|---|---|---|---|---|
| 2♏ | 1♐ | 2♑ | 3♓ | 2♈ | 3♊ | 2♋ | 1♌ | 2♎ | 2♏ | 1♐ | 2♒ |
| 4♐ | 3♑ | 4♒ | 5♈ | 4♉ | 5♋ | 5♌ | 3♍ | 5♏ | 4♐ | 3♑ | 4♓ |
| 6♑ | 5♒ | 6♓ | 7♉ | 6♊ | 7♌ | 7♍ | 6♎ | 7♐ | 7♑ | 5♒ | 7♈ |
| 8♒ | 7♓ | 8♈ | 9♊ | 9♋ | 10♍ | 10♎ | 8♏ | 9♑ | 9♒ | 7♓ | 9♉ |
| 10♓ | 9♈ | 10♉ | 11♋ | 11♌ | 12♎ | 12♏ | 11♐ | 12♒ | 11♓ | 9♈ | 11♊ |
| 12♈ | 11♉ | 12♊ | 14♌ | 14♍ | 15♏ | 14♐ | 13♑ | 14♓ | 13♈ | 11♉ | 13♋ |
| 15♉ | 13♊ | 15♋ | 16♍ | 16♎ | 17♐ | 17♑ | 15♒ | 15♈ | 15♉ | 14♊ | 15♌ |
| 17♊ | 16♋ | 17♌ | 19♎ | 18♏ | 19♑ | 19♒ | 17♓ | 18♉ | 17♊ | 16♋ | 18♍ |
| 19♋ | 18♌ | 20♍ | 21♏ | 21♐ | 21♒ | 21♓ | 19♈ | 20♊ | 19♋ | 18♌ | 20♎ |
| 22♌ | 21♍ | 22♎ | 23♐ | 23♑ | 23♓ | 23♈ | 21♉ | 22♋ | 22♌ | 21♍ | 23♏ |
| 24♍ | 23♎ | 25♏ | 26♑ | 25♒ | 25♈ | 25♉ | 23♊ | 24♌ | 24♍ | 23♎ | 25♐ |
| 27♎ | 26♏ | 27♐ | 28♒ | 27♓ | 28♉ | 27♊ | 26♋ | 27♍ | 27♎ | 26♏ | 28♑ |
| 29♏ | 28♐ | 29♑ | 30♓ | 29♈ | 30♊ | 29♋ | 28♌ | 30♎ | 29♏ | 28♐ | 30♒ |
|  |  | 31♒ |  | 31♉ |  |  | 31♍ |  |  | 30♑ |  |

*Key:*

| Aries | Taurus | Gemini | Cancer | Leo | Virgo |
|---|---|---|---|---|---|
| ♈ | ♉ | ♊ | ♋ | ♌ | ♍ |

| Libra | Scorpio | Sagittarius | Capricorn | Aquarius | Pisces |
|---|---|---|---|---|---|
| ♎ | ♏ | ♐ | ♑ | ♒ | ♓ |

*Mirror, mirror, tell me,*
*Am I pretty or plain?*
*Or am I downright ugly*
*And ugly to remain?*

*Shall I marry a gentleman?*
*Shall I marry a clown?*
*Or shall I marry old Knives-and-Scissors*
*Shouting through the town?*

Your ascendant—the sign that was rising on the Eastern horizon at the time of your birth—is the next important factor in your chart after your sun and moon. If the description of your Sun Sign doesn't seem to fit you, it may be that you've an ascendant that overpowers it. For instance, a Leo ascendant may tend to dominate the weaker characteristics of an Aquarius or a Pisces. (There we go again, picking on those poor Pisces!) The sun represents the basic, main expression of the self and the ascendant determines how it manifests itself to the world—your way of walking, your actions, your physical body, the way you talk, and so forth. So if you're vain about physical appearances, check out his or her ascendant and you'll find out why he or she is so beautiful. (Or ugly.)

ARIES RISING: You're enthusiastic, ardent, energetic, forceful, aggressive, impulsive, impatient. Usually tall and wiry with bright, lively eyes.

TAURUS RISING: You could be on the husky or stocky side, but have a pleasant, melodious voice to make up for it.

Aesthetic, you appreciate the arts, especially music. But you have that propensity to weight problems, because you love rich foods, too.

**GEMINI RISING:** Airy, quick, easily distracted, you can adjust to almost any situation. (Just start throwing the keys into the middle of the room when you're around.) Tendency to overcome is the one where you put off till tomorrow what you could do today. You also scatter and waste a lot of energy. But you're tall, slender, and so people like you anyway.

**CANCER RISING:** You're maternal, home-loving, affectionate, emotional, sensitive and intuitive. People find you easy to confide in. You're apt to be full-bosomed with tendencies toward gaining weight in the midsection.

**LEO RISING:** You're queenly (or kingly), regal, magnetic, dramatic, colorful, energetic, enthusiastic, have a sunny disposition, narrow hips and broad shoulders. (The girls have narrow shoulders with wider hips.) You're beautiful, Leo!

**VIRGO RISING:** Slender, with a well-distributed figure (discreetly proportioned, shall we say), you're fair with thin lips, but you manage to be talkative on any and all subjects. Very critical!

**LIBRA RISING:** All-round, well-balanced, tasteful, you have great propriety, hate vulgarity and always employ excellent taste. You've a well-proportioned body and you're a joy to be with.

**SCORPIO RISING:** Demanding, domineering, temperamental, intense, sensuous, resourceful, passionate, mysterious, with a propensity to overindulge in food and drink—wow! How can you be so many things? Also have high cheekbones, good structure and keen, penetrating eyes.

**SAGITTARIUS RISING:** You're extroverted, loquacious, eager, active, and apt to exaggerate. To tell whoppers, if you want to know the truth! You have lovely legs.

**CAPRICORN RISING:** You're angular-looking, have thin, good bones, high cheekbones and a triangular face. Your skin can turn sallow from worry and poor eating and you wouldn't want that to happen, so you'd better take care of yourself. You often show one side of yourself to the public, but keep another one inaccessibly private.

**AQUARIUS RISING:** This makes you unconventional, vital and interested in people and life around you. You're a "doer." You have lovely but slightly irregular features. You are apt to be temperamental and careless about taking offense at others' remarks. Who cares what *they* say? You do, and it's time you stopped!

**PISCES RISING:** You are dual-natured (two fishes swimming in opposite directions), romantic, emotional, a dreamer, have a tendency to bloat and are prone to acquire a double chin. But you're such a great lover, nobody ever notices it.

# HOW TO FIND THE PLACEMENT OF ASCENDANT AT THE TIME OF YOUR BIRTH

### January 1
#### Approximate Time of Birth

| A.M. | | P.M. | |
|---|---|---|---|
| 12:30 | Libra | 1:10 | Taurus |
| 3:05 | Scorpio | 2:50 | Gemini |
| 5:35 | Sagittarius | 5:05 | Cancer |
| 7:50 | Capricorn | 7:30 | Leo |
| 9:25 | Aquarius | 10:05 | Virgo |
| 10:45 | Pisces | | |
| 11:55 | Aries | | |

### January 15
#### Approximate Time of Birth

| A.M. | | P.M. | |
|---|---|---|---|
| 2:05 | Scorpio | 12:10 | Taurus |
| 4:35 | Sagittarius | 1:50 | Gemini |
| 6:50 | Capricorn | 4:05 | Cancer |
| 8:25 | Aquarius | 6:30 | Leo |
| 9:45 | Pisces | 9:05 | Virgo |
| 10:55 | Aries | 11:30 | Libra |

### February 1
#### Approximate Time of Birth

| A.M. | | P.M. | |
|---|---|---|---|
| 1:05 | Scorpio | 12:50 | Gemini |
| 3:35 | Sagittarius | 3:05 | Cancer |
| 5:50 | Capricorn | 5:30 | Leo |
| 7:25 | Aquarius | 8:05 | Virgo |
| 8:45 | Pisces | 10:30 | Libra |
| 9:55 | Aries | | |
| 11:10 | Taurus | | |

### February 15
#### Approximate Time of Birth

| A.M. | | P.M. | |
|---|---|---|---|
| 12:05 | Scorpio | 2:05 | Cancer |
| 2:35 | Sagittarius | 4:30 | Leo |
| 4:50 | Capricorn | 7:05 | Virgo |
| 6:25 | Aquarius | 9:30 | Libra |
| 7:45 | Pisces | | |
| 8:55 | Aries | | |
| 10:10 | Taurus | | |
| 11:50 | Gemini | | |

### March 1
#### Approximate Time of Birth

| A.M. | | P.M. | |
|---|---|---|---|
| 1:35 | Sagittarius | 1:05 | Cancer |
| 3:50 | Capricorn | 3:30 | Leo |
| 5:25 | Aquarius | 6:05 | Virgo |
| 6:45 | Pisces | 8:30 | Libra |
| 7:55 | Aries | 11:05 | Scorpio |
| 9:10 | Taurus | | |
| 10:50 | Gemini | | |

### March 15
#### Approximate Time of Birth

| A.M. | | P.M. | |
|---|---|---|---|
| 12:35 | Sagittarius | 12:05 | Cancer |
| 2:50 | Capricorn | 2:30 | Leo |
| 4:25 | Aquarius | 5:05 | Virgo |
| 5:45 | Pisces | 7:30 | Libra |
| 6:55 | Aries | 10:05 | Scorpio |
| 8:10 | Taurus | | |
| 9:50 | Gemini | | |

### April 1
#### Approximate Time of Birth

| A.M. | | P.M. | |
|---|---|---|---|
| 1:50 | Capricorn | 1:30 | Leo |
| 3:25 | Aquarius | 4:05 | Virgo |
| 4:45 | Pisces | 6:30 | Libra |
| 5:55 | Aries | 9:05 | Scorpio |
| 7:10 | Taurus | 11:35 | Sagittarius |
| 8:50 | Gemini | | |
| 11:05 | Cancer | | |

### April 15
#### Approximate Time of Birth

| A.M. | | P.M. | |
|---|---|---|---|
| 12:30 | Capricorn | 12:30 | Leo |
| 2:55 | Aquarius | 3:05 | Virgo |
| 3:45 | Pisces | 5:30 | Libra |
| 4:55 | Aries | 8:05 | Scorpio |
| 6:10 | Taurus | 10:35 | Sagittarius |
| 7:50 | Gemini | | |
| 10:05 | Cancer | | |

## May 1
### Approximate Time of Birth

| A.M. | | P.M. | |
|------|------|------|------|
| 1:25 | Aquarius | 2:05 | Virgo |
| 2:45 | Pisces | 4:30 | Libra |
| 3:55 | Aries | 7:05 | Scorpio |
| 5:10 | Taurus | 9:35 | Sagittarius |
| 6:50 | Gemini | 11:50 | Capricorn |
| 9:05 | Cancer | | |
| 11:30 | Leo | | |

## July 1
### Approximate Time of Birth

| A.M. | | P.M. | |
|------|------|------|------|
| 1:10 | Taurus | 12:30 | Libra |
| 2:50 | Gemini | 3:05 | Scorpio |
| 5:05 | Cancer | 5:35 | Sagittarius |
| 7:30 | Leo | 7:50 | Capricorn |
| 10:05 | Virgo | 9:25 | Aquarius |
| | | 10:45 | Pisces |
| | | 11:55 | Aries |

## May 15
### Approximate Time of Birth

| A.M. | | P.M. | |
|------|------|------|------|
| 12:25 | Aquarius | 1:05 | Virgo |
| 1:45 | Pisces | 3:30 | Libra |
| 2:55 | Aries | 6:05 | Scorpio |
| 4:10 | Taurus | 8:35 | Sagittarius |
| 5:50 | Gemini | 10:50 | Capricorn |
| 8:05 | Cancer | | |
| 10:30 | Leo | | |

## July 15
### Approximate Time of Birth

| A.M. | | P.M. | |
|------|------|------|------|
| 12:10 | Taurus | 2:05 | Scorpio |
| 1:50 | Gemini | 4:35 | Sagittarius |
| 4:05 | Cancer | 6:50 | Capricorn |
| 6:30 | Leo | 8:25 | Aquarius |
| 9:05 | Virgo | 9:45 | Pisces |
| 11:30 | Libra | 10:55 | Aries |

## June 1
### Approximate Time of Birth

| A.M. | | P.M. | |
|------|------|------|------|
| 12:45 | Pisces | 12:05 | Virgo |
| 1:55 | Aries | 2:30 | Libra |
| 3:10 | Taurus | 5:05 | Scorpio |
| 4:50 | Gemini | 7:35 | Sagittarius |
| 7:05 | Cancer | 9:50 | Capricorn |
| 9:30 | Leo | 11:25 | Aquarius |

## August 1
### Approximate Time of Birth

| A.M. | | P.M. | |
|------|------|------|------|
| 12:50 | Gemini | 1:05 | Scorpio |
| 3:05 | Cancer | 3:35 | Sagittarius |
| 5:30 | Leo | 5:50 | Capricorn |
| 8:05 | Virgo | 7:25 | Aquarius |
| 10:30 | Libra | 8:45 | Pisces |
| | | 9:55 | Aries |
| | | 11:10 | Taurus |

## June 15
### Approximate Time of Birth

| A.M. | | P.M. | |
|------|------|------|------|
| 12:55 | Aries | 1:30 | Libra |
| 2:10 | Taurus | 4:05 | Scorpio |
| 3:50 | Gemini | 6:35 | Sagittarius |
| 6:05 | Cancer | 8:50 | Capricorn |
| 8:30 | Leo | 10:25 | Aquarius |
| 11:05 | Virgo | 11:45 | Pisces |

## August 15
### Approximate Time of Birth

| A.M. | | P.M. | |
|------|------|------|------|
| 2:05 | Cancer | 12:05 | Scorpio |
| 4:30 | Leo | 2:35 | Sagittarius |
| 7:05 | Virgo | 4:50 | Capricorn |
| 9:30 | Libra | 6:25 | Aquarius |
| | | 7:45 | Pisces |
| | | 8:55 | Aries |
| | | 10:10 | Taurus |
| | | 11:50 | Gemini |

### September 1
#### Approximate Time of Birth

| A.M. | | P.M. | |
|---|---|---|---|
| 1:05 | Cancer | 1:35 | Sagittarius |
| 3:30 | Leo | 3:50 | Capricorn |
| 6:06 | Virgo | 5:25 | Aquarius |
| 8:30 | Libra | 6:45 | Pisces |
| 11:05 | Scorpio | 7:55 | Aries |
| | | 9:10 | Taurus |
| | | 10:50 | Gemini |

### November 1
#### Approximate Time of Birth

| A.M. | | P.M. | |
|---|---|---|---|
| 2:05 | Virgo | 1:25 | Aquarius |
| 4:30 | Libra | 2:45 | Pisces |
| 7:05 | Scorpio | 3:55 | Aries |
| 9:35 | Sagittarius | 5:10 | Taurus |
| 11:50 | Capricorn | 6:50 | Gemini |
| | | 9:05 | Cancer |
| | | 11:30 | Leo |

### September 15
#### Approximate Time of Birth

| A.M. | | P.M. | |
|---|---|---|---|
| 12:05 | Cancer | 12:35 | Sagittarius |
| 2:30 | Leo | 2:50 | Capricorn |
| 5:05 | Virgo | 4:25 | Aquarius |
| 7:30 | Libra | 5:45 | Pisces |
| 10:05 | Scorpio | 6:55 | Aries |
| | | 8:10 | Taurus |
| | | 9:50 | Gemini |

### November 15
#### Approximate Time of Birth

| A.M. | | P.M. | |
|---|---|---|---|
| 1:05 | Virgo | 12:25 | Aquarius |
| 3:30 | Libra | 1:45 | Pisces |
| 6:06 | Scorpio | 2:55 | Aries |
| 8:35 | Sagittarius | 4:10 | Taurus |
| 10:50 | Capricorn | 5:50 | Gemini |
| | | 8:05 | Cancer |
| | | 10:30 | Leo |

### October 1
#### Approximate Time of Birth

| A.M. | | P.M. | |
|---|---|---|---|
| 1:30 | Leo | 1:50 | Capricorn |
| 4:05 | Virgo | 3:25 | Aquarius |
| 6:30 | Libra | 4:45 | Pisces |
| 9:05 | Scorpio | 5:55 | Aries |
| 11:35 | Sagittarius | 7:10 | Taurus |
| | | 8:50 | Gemini |
| | | 11:05 | Cancer |

### December 1
#### Approximate Time of Birth

| A.M. | | P.M. | |
|---|---|---|---|
| 12:05 | Virgo | 12:45 | Pisces |
| 2:30 | Libra | 1:55 | Aries |
| 5:05 | Scorpio | 3:10 | Taurus |
| 7:35 | Sagittarius | 4:50 | Gemini |
| 9:50 | Capricorn | 7:05 | Cancer |
| 11:25 | Aquarius | 9:30 | Leo |

### October 15
#### Approximate Time of Birth

| A.M. | | P.M. | |
|---|---|---|---|
| 12:30 | Leo | 12:50 | Capricorn |
| 3:05 | Virgo | 2:25 | Aquarius |
| 5:30 | Libra | 3:45 | Pisces |
| 8:05 | Scorpio | 4:55 | Aries |
| 10:35 | Sagittarius | 6:10 | Taurus |
| | | 7:50 | Gemini |
| | | 10:05 | Cancer |

### December 15
#### Approximate Time of Birth

| A.M. | | P.M. | |
|---|---|---|---|
| 1:30 | Libra | 12:55 | Aries |
| 4:05 | Scorpio | 2:10 | Taurus |
| 6:35 | Sagittarius | 3:50 | Gemini |
| 8:50 | Capricorn | 6:06 | Cancer |
| 10:25 | Aquarius | 8:30 | Leo |
| 11:45 | Pisces | 11:05 | Virgo |

*I sent a letter to my love*
*And on the way I dropped it;*
*A little puppy picked it up*
*And put it in his pocket.*
*It isn't you, it isn't you,*
*But it is you.*

Speech, writing, reading, the mind, gesticulation—all forms of communication—as well as the nervous system are ruled by Mercury. It is the medium through which we have contact with that world which lies outside ourselves, the bridge over which we transport our thoughts to others and receive theirs in return. Were there no Mercury there would be no communication with anyone, we would all walk around as strangers, alienated from each other, unable to ever understand or make ourselves understood. You can see, we're sure, how important this planet is to one's love life.

MERCURY IN ARIES: Well, your mind leaves nothing to be desired. It's a keen one, and just loaded with all sorts of creative new ideas. Very inventive in the romantic area, you have the knack of being a good writer of love-letters, and in your sex life you are among the most spontaneous and least inhibited in the Zodiac.

MERCURY IN TAURUS: You have very set ideas, which is a trait that also carries over into your sex life. You are overly stubborn and have quite shrewd values in life, especially in monetary matters. You like your sex linked up with money. Need we say more?

117

**MERCURY IN GEMINI:** You love to be on the move, and have much to offer on the superficial level to a sex partner. If you're going to offer more, you'd better have some good planetary placements to compensate for the roving eye this configuration gives you.

**MERCURY IN CANCER:** You will always be an attractive sex partner, so thank your stars that this placement keeps you looking young well on in life. You may, however, suffer from emotional conflicts love and sex bring you and you are apt to be changeable in *affaires de coeur.*

**MERCURY IN LEO:** You are big-hearted and open, easy to get along with and able to offer yourself generously with no holds barred. Uninhibited sexually, you really know how to respond and can be an expert initiator as well. These factors make you a desirable sex partner.

**MERCURY IN VIRGO:** You may have health problems or at least be inclined to worry about your health to the extent that it can interfere with your sex life. Guard against being overly nervous and shy of the opposite sex.

**MERCURY IN LIBRA:** You are at ease with the opposite sex and like to cooperate with romantic and sexual encounters, though you prefer being the pursued one rather than the pursuer. You are desirable and a warm sex partner.

**MERCURY IN SCORPIO:** You are secretive about your affairs and do not confide the truth to people easily. You penetrate to the core of a person in sexual liaisons, and are able to extract a vital essence from them no one else seems able to even comprehend.

**MERCURY IN SAGITTARIUS:** Impulsive and free-wheeling, you are apt to be caught in all sorts of romantic escapades, and your life is full of adventure in sex and love. You like to be on the move and your many travels bring you an abundance of opportunity for sexual experimentation.

**MERCURY IN CAPRICORN:** You are ambitious and very practical. You have the ability to draw the right person or persons to you and will always gain in the material sense from your sex encounters. You are thorough and systematic about your life and leave no stones unturned; therefore you will always have a provision for the sex side of your nature's expression.

MERCURY IN AQUARIUS: From your large circle of friends in social gatherings, political and welfare work, you will always have the faculty of drawing appropriate partners to you and you will never be a wallflower. You are balanced and know that sex has its proper place in your life. You do not have a tendency to go overboard but are moderate and well-ordered in your sex life.

MERCURY IN PISCES: You must guard against taking on other people's problems and woes—you have enough of your own. You have an innate understanding of others, and are empathetic and sympathetic, intuitive and psychic. These are traits which serve you well in your love life, and can be used to great advantage with the opposite sex.

## HOW TO FIND THE PLACEMENT OF MERCURY AT THE TIME OF YOUR BIRTH

Mercury changes signs so often it would take a whole separate book for its tables, but this tiny planet is situated so closely to the sun, there is a way you can get a general idea of where it was at the time of your birth. Because it never is more than 28° from the sun and there are only 30° in each sign, it can never be more than one sign away from your Sun Sign if not occupying that same position. So check all three signs, the one before, the one after and your Sun Sign itself and through your own "rectification" decide which one fits you best.

*Whistle, daughter, whistle,*
  *And you shall have a sheep.*
*Mother, I cannot whistle,*
  *Neither can I sleep.*

*Whistle, daughter, whistle,*
  *And you shall have a cow.*
*Mother, I cannot whistle,*
  *Neither know I how.*

*Whistle, daughter, whistle,*
  *And you shall have a man.*
*Mother, I cannot whistle,*
  *But I'll do the best I can.*

Venus is, of course, the planet that exerts the greatest direct influence over your sex life. Finding out where Venus was at the date of your birth will give you a good yardstick regarding your sex nature since Venus traditionally rules love and beauty, and plays a great influence in things erotic. Venus represents feelings of affection, influences attractions and the desire and capacity for love. It brings about the aspects which affect romance, marriage, divorce, intimacy, friendships, sense stimulants and a host of others all related to that great mystery that remains uppermost in most of our minds.

VENUS IN ARIES: Watch out, heedless one, this placement can make you fickle and ever in search of new and exciting conquests. Idealistic to a fault, your enthusiasm is as great at its height as your dampened spirits are when the affair has cooled. You'd better be wary of hasty marriage; you're just the fool who'll rush in where angels fear to tread. You always think you know best, but most often your judgment is decidedly *not* the best. However, on the positive side, you have an enormous capacity to become completely involved in the life of another; you are wonderful as a lover, intense, passionate, giving, selfless, romantic. One of your main assets is also one of your main faults; you take people too much on faith. Thus, while you are open, honest and guileless, you tend to go too heavily on appearances, and to jump to conclusions. For you your lover must be the be all and end all of your existence; you demand and need to receive absolute devotion in return or you will be sorely disappointed in love and ever on the lookout for something better to fire your interests.

VENUS IN TAURUS: This person, while slow to give his affections, is nevertheless demonstrative and quite earthy and voluptuous in his responses and inclinations once he has given his heart and committed himself. A more steadfast partner would be hard to find—the loved one should feel great security emanating from the Venus in Taurus native's capacity to give of his charm, steadfastness and strong Venusian emotions. For Venus is in domicile in Taurus; that is, it is one of the two strongest placements of the planet in the whole Zodiac. Thus here we see an ideal—a balance and a harmony. Badly aspected (that is, making adverse angles to other planets in a chart) the Venus in Taurus native could very easily become jealous, possessive and clinging. Infidelity is hard to tolerate for these people. They expect the same devotion from the partner that they themselves are capable of giving. Venus is in such fortunate a placement in Taurus that in addition to love it usually also brings a marriage for money—an added boon. Oftentimes it is not easy to get something going with a Venus in Taurus native—they are, as we have said, slow to give of their affections. It is therefore wise to take it slow, and to try to become a habit with them first. Gradually you will have endeared yourself to them, as they grow fond of that which is a part of their environment. Lucky indeed is the Venus in Taurus native, luckier still the one who is fortunate enough to tie up with him.

VENUS IN GEMINI: This is one of the most complex placements of Venus. You are very changeable and fickle, you love to experiment, you can never really be sure where you in actuality stand. You love to play games, both with others and with yourself. The intellectual predominates in you, you are ruled by your mind rather than by your groin, which is not to say that you are incapable of feeling, either. However, love, sex and everything romantic come to you first as purely mental things, a kick if you will. You like to play a thing around in your mind, and create fantasies, seeing yourself in varied amatory poses and performing assorted erotic techniques with the partner of the opposite sex long before contact has actually been made. You have the decided feeling that you can be all things to all people. In short, you would like to seduce the whole world. There's no end to your unpredictability and changeability—one day you will groove with somebody and the next day you won't, it's as simple as that. A dress, a pair of glasses, a funky suit worn by the member of the opposite sex will turn you on one day and turn you off the next. You have no explanations for it, it just happens that way. Added to all this, you can be in love with several people at once—two would be your usual minimum quota. Whoever heard of being in love with less than two people at once? Never a Venus in Gemini native. He's the one with a girl in every port, or she is the charmer driving six guys up the wall, each one sure he is the one and only. An example: a Venus in Gemini acquaintance of ours recently decided to become an unwed mother. She had all of her devoted lovers begging to take the responsibility for the baby's paternity. Last we heard of her she was in an unwed mothers' home. She never did make up her mind, she was so busy being in love with love and going through her daily changeabouts. One thing to always bear in mind with a Venus in Gemini native is that he will never lose his desire to experiment. He may lose his desire for you, though. But it's a great quality while it's still you he experiments with.

VENUS IN CANCER: The home and family mean everything to you, and you seek the perfect mate. You are so idealistic that you are frequently one of the most unfaithful, and sometimes even promiscuous among your friends, which is actually opposed to your nature and principles. For your peccadilloes you pay a great price, that of extreme guilt and remorse, since you so long for the complete love, the one final consummate love that will lift you above the commonplace and give stature and meaning to your life. If fortunate to a degree, you are at least relatively secure, but your restless moody nature will never really feel at peace, until you have found the love that is the beginning and end of your existence. One thing about you is that you will never desert the home front except in cases of dire emergency, where circumstances have become completely intolerable. But watch out that your guilts do not put your partner wise to you—in more than one case we have seen homes break up because the spouse of the Venus in Cancer native "got wise" and didn't care to put up with the untenable situation any longer. You Venus in Cancer natives too often wear your hearts on your sleeves and should be more discreet about your behavior and feelings. Overly sensitive, you can become a *kvetch* and a disappointment to your partner. On the positive side, your capacity to love is enormous. Should you be fortunate enough to make the right choices in your love partner, you will be an ideal mate—sensitive, emotional, romantic, affectionate, loving, tender, in complete harmony and fusion, in oneness sexually with your mate.

VENUS IN LEO: You are a born showman, in the boudoir, across a dinner table, at a party, a discotheque, anywhere you appear in romantic situations. Furthermore, you have a way of turning everything into an advantage: where a situation would not be especially fortuitous or profitable romantically for someone else, you know how to fix it so everything works for you. Lavish, open, good-hearted, you love to bestow expensive gifts, buy flowers, diamonds, furs, cars—nothing is too good for you to lavish on your loved one. This is equally true of Venus in Leo women as it is of the men. The women with this aspect will go overboard buying outlandish items for their boyfriends. The native with this aspect is passionate, undaunted, loyal, idealistic, conscious of his desirability and magnetism for the opposite sex.

VENUS IN VIRGO: Well, here we go again, Virgo the Virgin, chaste, pristine, refined, neat, orderly, concise, terse, laconic, discriminatory, clean, sincere, dutiful, tasteful, pure of mind . . . don't you often get tired of hearing how dull you are sexually? Lucky for you there are few genuine All-Virgo types, and that other aspects can jazz you up to some extent, because you'd be an awful bore otherwise. Still, a touch of Virgo often gives the balance some natures need. For instance, suppose your sun in Scorpio was too strong; well, in that case, Venus in Virgo would be the perfect agent to modify it. It would soften you and add a prudence to your nature, a clear-thinkingness. It would retard some of those strong emotions, for Venus in Virgo tends to be restrained emotionally. This native is cautious and will usually postpone marriage till late in life, if choosing to undertake the venture at all. Venus in Virgo can be dangerous when the intellect gets out of hand, convincing the native he is missing out on something—then he will push himself into many promiscuous affairs, unfelt and uninvolved, in order to try to feel something which he is sure he has missed. This can be a sad and frustrating placement unless modified by other more favorable aspects in the chart. But once the Venus in Virgo native has been able to find and feel love, he will never give up and will be one of the strongest and most eloquent spokesmen the lover has ever found.

VENUS IN LIBRA: Here again we have an ideal placement for Venus, it being in domicile once again, as it is in Taurus. Venus in Libra natives are ideal lovers and mates, they are among the most charming members of the Zodiac, and are avid for love and romance. Love is an art to them, and they thrive on the many varied applications of the art of seduction. It would be unwise in any way to emphasize the vulgar or appetitive aspects of sex with a native having this aspect —save that approach for someone with Venus in Capricorn, who will respond to the lusty, earthy and even scatological aspects of sex. For your Venus in Libra native—exuding good taste and refinement, together with a voluptuous approach in lovemaking—likes to make sure that even the surroundings are charming and lovely where their affairs take place. Be sure you vary your amatory techniques with them; be subtle and soigné. Make love a continual feast, with all the accouterments of beauty and charm. Avoid the humdrum, show little courtesies and you will be generously rewarded with this native's appreciation.

VENUS IN SCORPIO: A Venus in Scorpio is restless to a fault, particularly when the sexual stone has been left unturned; that is to say, he has an enormous need to prove his physical desirability and cannot rest until he has done so. This requires him always to make a speedy and highly charged physical conquest, in which he can show himself to be aggressive, intense, romantic and passionate. It is often difficult for others to understand why this person has such a great need to prove himself, for he is usually highly endowed with both charm and allure, and from all appearances lacks nothing in the way of self-esteem. But such is not the case; this native is often one of the most insecure people, sexually speaking, you are likely to find anywhere. And so throughout his life he will have this pressing and urgent need, which is not only sexual but also pathological. Possessive to a fault, the Venus in Scorpio is heedless of others' opinions, and should learn caution and prudence or he will continue to go through life being hurt and unfulfilled. In a native negatively aspected, there is the tendency to become involved with someone much the lower in either rank, class or intellect, someone who will make the Venus in Scorpio feel degraded and guilt-ridden. This native often fluctuates between feelings of exaltation and remorse regarding sex, and has difficulty reconciling his enormous sexual appetites. He will likely profit financially from marriage, but will probably not be satisfied with one partner for any great length of time.

VENUS IN SAGITTARIUS: Honesty is the keynote of these people. Unafraid of any consequences, fearless, determined, these people will risk all when they feel they are right—which is most of the time. Very strong in their convictions, they are not known for tact but rather for complete bluntness. This quality can either endear them or have a drastic effect upon the partner or love object. But for the most part, Venus in Sagittarius is a perspicacious placement, causing the natives to have humor, charm, appeal, magnetism, sociability, generosity and straightforwardness. They are idealistic regarding love and sex, and need spiritual fulfillment in love as well as companionship to feel truly happy. They make great "pals" and often function in this role better than any other Venus placement. He is devoted in love, and once he falls (it may take him a considerable time to do so, however) he is a devoted lover. However, he desires freedom and the person he chooses to ally himself with will have to understand his need for individuality and a life of his own.

VENUS IN CAPRICORN: This is apt to be a confusing placement for Venus—the native is never quite sure of where he stands, and is torn and in conflict most of the time. Highly ambitious, snobbish even, the native will desire an alliance from which he can benefit socially and materially. Failing to find this, he will flirt with other areas of the romantic, in a way that could be lustful and robust, alternating with taunting and teasing, a routine in which he delights. Afraid of real commitment, this person will instead cater to his own ego, standing back and admiring his own flirtatiousness and sexiness. He shies away from marriage until the right chance for advancement comes his way. He is most discerning and discriminating of what is right for him, and able to juggle his life so his sexual appetites will be satisfied perfectly while he is busy manipulating circumstances to suit his other ends. Aware, shrewd, flirtatious, difficult to know, he is not one to plunge headlong into anything romantic; he knows exactly where he is going and how he is doing every minute. Calculating, spoiled, he seldom gives himself away. It takes one to know one, and this is about the only time this native will have to cop out, when he's busted by one like himself.

VENUS IN AQUARIUS: A person having Venus in Aquarius is honest and good-natured, direct, straightforward and dependable. If he commits himself, he means it, no tricks, lies, deceits here; you can count on a truthful and sincere relationship. The person will be giving and kindly, often self-sacrificing. Should a suitable love object fail to come his way, his outlet will be other sexual affairs in which his chief attraction will be that of beauty and physical attractiveness. Physical appearance is most important to this person, and is the chief thing that first impresses him in his sexual exploits. After the initial impression (strong shoulders, silky smooth skin, a firm bustline, for instance) has arrested his attention, he will then turn to qualities of character and see if those measure up to his standards. If they do, he will pursue his honest, sincere and straightforward relationship—

if not, he will go on to (a) satisfying his physical desire minimally, (b) continuing with his search for a better ideal. Men having this placement are irresistible little boys that women always want to mother; women are flirtatious and magnetic to the opposite sex.

VENUS IN PISCES: This person desires complete fusion in the love object, so much so that he is continually disappointed in love, since rarely does he find anyone who can live up to his high ideals. Sensitive, he is often hurt in love, feeling he is giving more than he is receiving, which is usually the case, but it is always his own fault not to have exercised the proper judgment, to have made poor choices from the start. He is so ardent and seeks love to such an extent, that he fails to read danger signals, and is thus constantly disappointed and left crying in his beer. When this person is fortunate enough to find the love he craves, he completely immerses himself in the other and is devoted and fulfilled; sexually he craves spirituality, a merging of body, mind and soul, where he blends and becomes one with his partner. Sensual and passionate, he usually finds rare moments of the fusion he seeks, and will have to endure many clandestine and illegal unions while seeking his ideal.

# HOW TO FIND THE PLACEMENT OF VENUS
## AT THE TIME OF YOUR BIRTH

## VENUS IN ARIES

| YEAR | FROM — TO | YEAR | FROM — TO | YEAR | FROM — TO |
|---|---|---|---|---|---|
| 1900 | Feb. 11 — Mar. 10 | 1923 | Apr. 27 — May 21 | 1946 | Mar. 12 — Apr. 3 |
| 1901 | Mar. 30 — Apr. 22 | 1924 | Feb. 13 — Mar. 8 | 1947 | Apr. 24 — May 19 |
| 1902 | May 7 — May 31 | 1925 | Mar. 28 — Apr. 20 | 1948 | Feb. 11 — Mar. 6 |
| 1903 | Mar. 1 — Mar. 23 | 1926 | May 7 — June 2 | 1949 | Mar. 26 — Apr. 19 |
| 1904 | Apr. 13 — May 11 | 1927 | Feb. 27 — Mar. 22 | 1950 | May 3 — May 30 |
| 1905 | Feb. 1 — Mar. 5 | 1928 | Apr. 12 — May 5 | 1951 | Feb. 25 — Mar. 20 |
| | May 9 — May 27 | 1929 | Feb. 3 — Mar. 27 | 1952 | Apr. 10 — May 3 |
| 1906 | Mar. 11 — Apr. 7 | | Apr. 20 — June 2 | 1953 | Feb. 2 — Mar. 14 |
| 1907 | Apr. 28 — May 22 | 1930 | Mar. 13 — Apr. 5 | | May 31 — June 4 |
| 1908 | Feb. 14 — Mar. 9 | 1931 | Apr. 27 — May 21 | 1954 | Mar. 11 — Apr. 3 |
| 1909 | Mar. 29 — Apr. 20 | 1932 | Feb. 13 — Mar. 9 | 1955 | Apr. 25 — May 19 |
| 1910 | May 2 — May 31 | 1933 | Mar. 28 — Apr. 20 | 1956 | Feb. 11 — Mar. 7 |
| 1911 | Feb. 28 — Mar. 23 | 1934 | May 6 — June 2 | 1957 | M; Apr. 18 |
| 1912 | Apr. 3 — May 6 | 1935 | Feb. 28 — Mar. 22 | 1958 | May 5 — May 31 |
| 1913 | Feb. 3 — Mar. 5 | 1936 | Apr. 12 — May 5 | 1959 | Feb. 24 — Mar. 20 |
| | May 2 — May 30 | 1937 | Feb. 3 — Mar. 9 | 1960 | Apr. 9 — May 3 |
| 1914 | Mar. 14 — Apr. 5 | | Apr. 15 — June 4 | 1961 | Feb. 2 — June 5 |
| 1915 | May 1 — May 25 | 1938 | Mar. 13 — Apr. 5 | 1962 | Mar. 11 — Apr. 3 |
| 1916 | Feb. 12 — Mar. 9 | 1939 | Apr. 26 — May 20 | 1963 | Mar. 24 — May 18 |
| 1917 | Mar. 1 — Apr. 20 | 1940 | Feb. 13 — Mar. 8 | 1964 | Feb. 11 — Mar. 7 |
| 1918 | May 7 — June 2 | 1941 | Mar. 27 — Apr. 19 | 1965 | Mar. 25 — Apr. 18 |
| 1919 | Feb. 27 — Mar. 22 | 1942 | May 6 — June 1 | 1966 | May 5 — May 31 |
| 1920 | Apr. 12 — May 6 | 1943 | Feb. 26 — Mar. 21 | 1967 | Feb. 24 — Mar. 19 |
| 1921 | Feb. 3 — Mar. 6 | 1944 | Apr. 11 — May 4 | 1968 | Apr. 9 — May 2 |
| | Apr. 25 — June 1 | 1945 | Feb. 2 — Mar. 10 | 1969 | Feb. 2 — June 5 |
| 1922 | Mar. 13 — Apr. 6 | | Apr. 8 — June 4 | 1970 | Mar. 10 — Apr. 2 |

# VENUS IN TAURUS

| YEAR | FROM | TO | YEAR | FROM | TO | YEAR | FROM | TO |
|------|------|-----|------|------|-----|------|------|-----|
| 1900 | Mar. 11 — | Apr. 5 | 1923 | May 22 — | June 14 | 1946 | Apr. 5 — | Apr. 29 |
| 1901 | Apr. 23 — | May 15 | 1924 | Mar. 9 — | Apr. 4 | 1947 | May 20 — | June 13 |
| 1902 | June 1 — | June 30 | 1925 | Apr. 21 — | May 15 | 1948 | Mar. 7 — | Apr. 1 |
| 1903 | Mar. 24 — | Apr. 17 | 1926 | June 3 — | June 28 | 1949 | Apr. 20 — | May 13 |
| 1904 | May 12 — | May 31 | 1927 | Mar. 23 — | Apr. 16 | 1950 | May 31 — | June 26 |
| 1905 | Mar. 6 — | May 8 | 1928 | May 6 — | May 29 | 1951 | Mar. 21 — | Apr. 14 |
|      | May 28 — | July 7 | 1929 | Mar. 8 — | Apr. 19 | 1952 | May 4 — | May 28 |
| 1906 | Apr. 8 — | Apr. 28 |      | June 3 — | July 7 | 1953 | Mar. 15 — | Mar. 30 |
| 1907 | May 23 — | June 16 | 1930 | Apr. 6 — | Apr. 30 |      | June 5 — | July 6 |
| 1908 | Mar. 10 — | Apr. 6 | 1931 | May 22 — | June 14 | 1954 | Apr. 4 — | Apr. 28 |
| 1909 | Apr. 21 — | May 16 | 1932 | Mar. 10 — | Apr. 4 | 1955 | May 20 — | June 12 |
| 1910 | June 1 — | June 29 | 1933 | Apr. 21 — | May 15 | 1956 | Mar. 8 — | Apr. 3 |
| 1911 | Mar. 24 — | Apr. 20 | 1934 | June 3 — | June 28 | 1957 | Apr. 19 — | Mar. 12 |
| 1912 | May 7 — | May 31 | 1935 | Mar. 23 — | Apr. 16 | 1958 | June 1 — | June 26 |
| 1913 | Mar. 6 — | May 1 | 1936 | May 6 — | May 29 | 1959 | Mar. 21 — | Apr. 14 |
|      | May 31 — | July 7 | 1937 | Mar. 10 — | Mar. 28 | 1960 | May 4 — | May 27 |
| 1914 | Apr. 6 — | May 1 |      | June 6 — | July 7 | 1961 | June 6 — | July 6 |
| 1915 | May 26 — | June 15 | 1938 | Apr. 6 — | Apr. 29 | 1962 | Apr. 4 — | Apr. 27 |
| 1916 | Mar. 10 — | Apr. 5 | 1939 | May 21 — | June 14 | 1963 | May 19 — | June 12 |
| 1917 | Apr. 21 — | May 15 | 1940 | Mar. 9 — | Apr. 4 | 1964 | Mar. 8 — | Apr. 3 |
| 1918 | June 3 — | June 28 | 1941 | Apr. 20 — | May 14 | 1965 | Apr. 19 — | May 12 |
| 1919 | Mar. 23 — | Apr. 16 | 1942 | June 2 — | June 27 | 1966 | June 1 — | June 25 |
| 1920 | May 7 — | May 31 | 1943 | Mar. 22 — | Apr. 15 | 1967 | Mar. 20 — | Apr. 13 |
| 1921 | Mar. 7 — | Apr. 24 | 1944 | May 5 — | May 28 | 1968 | May 3 — | May 27 |
|      | June 2 — | July 7 | 1945 | Mar. 11 — | Apr. 7 | 1969 | June 6 — | July 6 |
| 1922 | Apr. 7 — | Apr. 30 |      | June 5 — | July 7 | 1970 | Apr. 3 — | Apr. 26 |

## VENUS IN GEMINI

| YEAR | FROM | TO | YEAR | FROM | TO | YEAR | FROM | TO |
|------|------|-----|------|------|-----|------|------|-----|
| 1900 | Apr. 6 — May 5 | | 1925 | May 16 — June 8 | | 1948 | Apr. 2 — May 1 | |
| 1901 | May 16 — June 10 | | 1926 | June 29 — July 23 | | 1949 | May 14 — June 6 | |
| 1902 | July 1 — July 19 | | 1927 | Apr. 17 — May 11 | | 1950 | June 27 — July 21 | |
| 1903 | Apr. 18 — May 18 | | 1928 | May 30 — June 23 | | 1951 | Apr. 15 — May 10 | |
| 1904 | June 1 — June 24 | | 1929 | July 8 — Aug. 4 | | 1952 | May 29 — June 21 | |
| 1905 | July 8 — Aug. 5 | | 1930 | May 1 — May 24 | | 1953 | July 7 — Aug. 3 | |
| 1906 | Apr. 29 — May 26 | | 1931 | June 15 — July 19 | | 1954 | Apr. 29 — May 23 | |
| 1907 | June 17 — July 14 | | 1932 | Apr. 5 — May 6 | | 1955 | June 13 — July 7 | |
| 1908 | Apr. 7 — May 3 | | | July 14 — July 28 | | 1956 | Apr. 4 — May 7 | |
| 1909 | May 17 — June 9 | | 1933 | May 16 — June 8 | | | June 23 — Aug. 3 | |
| 1910 | June 30 — July 24 | | 1934 | June 29 — July 23 | | 1957 | May 13 — June 6 | |
| 1911 | Apr. 21 — May 12 | | 1935 | Apr. 17 — May 11 | | 1958 | June 27 — July 21 | |
| 1912 | June 7 — June 21 | | 1936 | May 30 — June 23 | | 1959 | Apr. 15 — May 10 | |
| 1913 | July 8 — Aug. 5 | | 1937 | July 8 — Aug. 4 | | 1960 | June 22 — July 15 | |
| 1914 | May 2 — May 25 | | 1938 | Apr. 30 — May 24 | | 1961 | July 7 — Aug. 3 | |
| 1915 | June 16 — July 10 | | 1939 | June 15 — July 9 | | 1962 | Apr. 28 — May 22 | |
| 1916 | Apr. 6 — May 5 | | 1940 | Apr. 3 — May 6 | | 1963 | June 13 — July 6 | |
| 1917 | May 16 — June 9 | | | July 6 — Aug. 1 | | 1964 | Apr. 4 — May 8 | |
| 1918 | June 29 — July 24 | | 1941 | May 15 — June 7 | | | June 18 — Aug. 4 | |
| 1919 | Apr. 17 — May 12 | | 1942 | June 28 — July 22 | | 1965 | May 13 — June 5 | |
| 1920 | June 1 — June 21 | | 1943 | Apr 16 — May 10 | | 1966 | June 26 — July 21 | |
| 1921 | July 8 — Aug. 5 | | 1944 | May 29 — June 22 | | 1967 | Apr. 14 — May 9 | |
| 1922 | May 1 — May 25 | | 1945 | July 8 — Aug. 3 | | 1968 | May 28 — June 20 | |
| 1923 | June 15 — July 9 | | 1946 | Apr. 30 — May 23 | | 1969 | July 7 — Aug. 2 | |
| 1924 | Apr. 5 — May 5 | | 1947 | June 14 — July 7 | | 1970 | Apr. 27 — May 21 | |

## VENUS IN CANCER

| YEAR | FROM | TO | YEAR | FROM | TO | YEAR | FROM | TO |
|------|------|-----|------|------|-----|------|------|-----|
| 1900 | May 6 — Sept. 8 | | 1925 | June 9 — July 3 | | 1948 | May 2 — Sept. 4 | |
| 1901 | June 11 — July 4 | | 1926 | July 24 — Aug. 17 | | 1949 | June 7 — July 1 | |
| 1902 | July 20 — Aug. 19 | | 1927 | May 12 — June 7 | | 1950 | July 22 — Aug. 15 | |
| 1903 | May 19 — June 5 | | 1928 | June 24 — July 17 | | 1951 | May 11 — June 6 | |
| 1904 | June 26 — July 22 | | 1929 | Aug. 5 — Aug. 30 | | 1952 | June 22 — July 16 | |
| 1905 | Aug. 6 — Aug. 31 | | 1930 | May 25 — June 18 | | 1953 | Aug. 4 — Aug. 29 | |
| 1906 | May 27 — June 19 | | 1931 | July 10 — Aug. 3 | | 1954 | May 24 — June 17 | |
| 1907 | July 14 — Aug. 8 | | 1932 | May 7 — July 13 | | 1955 | July 8 — July 31 | |
| 1908 | May 4 — Sept. 8 | | | July 29 — Sept. 8 | | 1956 | May 8 — June 22 | |
| 1909 | June 10 — July 3 | | 1933 | June 9 — July 3 | | | Aug. 4 — Sept. 7 | |
| 1910 | July 25 — Aug. 18 | | 1934 | July 24 — Aug. 30 | | 1957 | June 7 — June 30 | |
| 1911 | May 13 — June 8 | | 1935 | May 12 — June 7 | | 1958 | July 22 — Aug. 15 | |
| 1912 | June 22 — July 22 | | 1936 | June 24 — July 17 | | 1959 | May 11 — June 6 | |
| 1913 | Aug. 6 — Aug. 31 | | 1937 | Aug. 5 — Aug. 30 | | 1960 | June 22 — July 15 | |
| 1914 | May 26 — July 19 | | 1938 | May 25 — June 18 | | 1961 | Aug. 4 — Aug. 29 | |
| 1915 | July 11 — Aug. 3 | | 1939 | July 10 — Aug. 2 | | 1962 | May 23 — June 16 | |
| 1916 | May 6 — Sept. 9 | | 1940 | May 7 — July 5 | | 1963 | July 7 — July 31 | |
| 1917 | June 10 — July 1 | | | Aug. 2 — Sept. 8 | | 1964 | May 9 — June 17 | |
| 1918 | July 25 — Aug. 16 | | 1941 | June 8 — July 7 | | | Aug. 5 — Sept. 7 | |
| 1919 | May 13 — June 7 | | 1942 | July 23 — Aug. 16 | | 1965 | June 6 — June 30 | |
| 1920 | June 22 — July 18 | | 1943 | May 11 — June 6 | | 1966 | July 22 — Aug. 15 | |
| 1921 | Aug. 6 — Aug. 31 | | 1944 | June 23 — July 16 | | 1967 | May 10 — June 6 | |
| 1922 | May 26 — June 19 | | 1945 | Aug. 4 — Aug. 30 | | 1968 | June 21 — July 15 | |
| 1923 | July 10 — Aug. 3 | | 1946 | Mar. 24 — June 17 | | 1969 | Aug. 3 — Aug. 28 | |
| 1924 | May 6 — Sept. 8 | | 1947 | July 8 — Aug. 1 | | 1970 | May 22 — June 15 | |

## VENUS IN LEO

| YEAR | FROM | TO | YEAR | FROM | TO | YEAR | FROM | TO |
|------|------|-----|------|------|-----|------|------|-----|
| 1900 | Sept. 9 — | Oct. 8 | 1925 | July 4 — | July 27 | 1949 | July 2 — | July 25 |
| 1901 | July 13 — | July 26 | 1926 | Aug. 18 — | Sept. 11 | 1950 | Aug. 16 — | Sept. 9 |
| 1902 | Aug. 20 — | Sept. 10 | 1927 | June 8 — | July 7 | 1951 | June 7 — | July 7 |
| 1903 | June 6 — | July 7 | 1928 | July 18 — | Aug. 11 | 1952 | July 11 — | Aug. 9 |
| 1904 | July 23 — | Aug. 14 | 1929 | Aug. 31 — | Sept. 25 | 1953 | Aug. 30 — | Sept. 23 |
| 1905 | Sept. 1 — | Sept. 30 | 1930 | June 19 — | July 14 | 1954 | June 18 — | July 12 |
| 1906 | June 21 — | July 15 | 1931 | Aug. 4 — | Aug. 27 | 1955 | Aug. 1 — | Aug. 25 |
| 1907 | Aug. 9 — | Aug. 23 | 1932 | Sept. 9 — | Oct. 7 | 1956 | Sept. 8 — | Oct. 5 |
| 1908 | Sept. 9 — | Oct. 7 | 1933 | July 4 — | July 27 | 1957 | July 1 — | July 25 |
| 1909 | July 4 — | July 26 | 1934 | Aug. 31 — | Sept. 11 | 1958 | Aug. 16 — | Sept. 9 |
| 1910 | Aug. 19 — | Sept. 12 | 1935 | June 8 — | July 7 | 1959 | June 7 — | July 8 |
| 1911 | June 9 — | July 7 | 1936 | July 18 — | Aug. 11 | | Sept. 20 — | Sept. 24 |
| 1912 | July 23 — | Aug. 7 | 1937 | Aug. 31 — | Sept. 25 | 1960 | July 16 — | Aug. 8 |
| 1913 | Sept. 1 — | Sept. 26 | 1938 | June 19 — | July 14 | 1961 | Aug. 30 — | Sept. 23 |
| 1914 | June 20 — | July 15 | 1939 | Aug. 3 — | Aug. 26 | 1962 | June 17 — | July 12 |
| 1915 | Aug. 4 — | Aug. 28 | 1940 | Sept. 9 — | Oct. 6 | 1963 | Aug. 1 — | Aug. 24 |
| 1916 | Sept. 9 — | Oct. 3 | 1941 | July 3 — | July 26 | 1964 | Sept. 8 — | Oct. 5 |
| 1917 | July 2 — | July 28 | 1942 | Aug. 17 — | Sept. 10 | 1965 | July 1 — | July 25 |
| 1918 | Aug. 17 — | Sept. 11 | 1943 | June 8 — | July 7 | 1966 | Aug. 16 — | Sept. 8 |
| 1919 | June 8 — | July 8 | 1944 | July 17 — | Aug. 20 | 1967 | June 7 — | July 8 |
| 1920 | July 19 — | Aug. 11 | 1945 | Aug. 31 — | Sept. 24 | | Sept. 9 — | Oct. 1 |
| 1921 | Sept. 1 — | Sept. 22 | 1946 | June 18 — | July 12 | 1968 | July 16 — | Aug. 8 |
| 1922 | June 20 — | July 14 | 1947 | Aug. 2 — | Aug. 25 | 1969 | Aug. 29 — | Sept. 22 |
| 1923 | Aug.4 — | Aug. 27 | 1948 | Sept. 5 — | Oct. 4 | 1970 | June 16 — | July 10 |
| 1924 | Sept. 9 — | Oct. 7 | | | | | | |

## VENUS IN VIRGO

| YEAR | FROM | TO | YEAR | FROM | TO | YEAR | FROM | TO |
|------|------|-----|------|------|-----|------|------|-----|
| 1900 | Oct. 9 — Oct. 31 | | 1923 | Aug. 28 — Sept. 20 | | 1948 | Oct. 5 — Oct. 30 | |
| 1901 | July 27 — Aug. 23 | | 1924 | Oct. 8 — Nov. 2 | | 1949 | July 26 — Aug.19 | |
| 1902 | Sept. 11 — Oct. 6 | | 1925 | July 28 — Aug. 21 | | 1950 | Sept. 10 — Oct. 3 | |
| 1903 | July 8 — Aug. 17 | | 1926 | Sept. 12 — Oct. 5 | | 1951 | July 8 — Nov. 9 | |
| | Sept. 7 — Nov. 8 | | 1927 | July 8 — Nov. 9 | | 1952 | Aug. 10 — Sept. 2 | |
| 1904 | Aug. 15 — Sept. 18 | | 1928 | Aug. 12 — Sept. 4 | | 1953 | Sept. 24 — Oct. 18 | |
| 1905 | Oct. 1 — Oct. 14 | | 1929 | Sept. 26 — Oct. 19 | | 1954 | July 13 — Aug. 8 | |
| 1906 | July 16 — Aug. 10 | | 1930 | July 15 — Aug. 9 | | 1955 | Aug. 26 — Sept. 18 | |
| 1907 | Aug. 24 — Sept. 23 | | 1931 | Aug. 28 — Sept. 20 | | 1956 | Oct. 6 — Oct. 31 | |
| 1908 | Oct. 6 — Oct. 31 | | 1932 | Oct. 8 — Nov. 2 | | 1957 | July 26 — Aug. 19 | |
| 1909 | July 29 — Aug. 20 | | 1933 | July 28 — Aug. 21 | | 1958 | Sept. 10 — Oct. 3 | |
| 1910 | Sept. 13 — Oct. 6 | | 1934 | Sept. 12 — Oct. 5 | | 1959 | July 9 — Sept. 19 | |
| 1911 | July 8 — Nov. 8 | | 1935 | July 8 — Nov. 9 | | | Sept. 25 — Nov. 9 | |
| 1912 | Aug. 8 — Aug. 31 | | 1936 | Aug. 12 — Sept. 4 | | 1960 | Aug. 9 — Sept. 2 | |
| 1913 | Sept. 27 — Oct. 19 | | 1937 | Sept. 26 — Oct. 19 | | 1961 | Sept. 24 — Oct. 17 | |
| 1914 | July 16 — Aug. 18 | | 1938 | July 15 — Aug. 9 | | 1962 | July 13 — Aug. 8 | |
| 1915 | Aug. 29 — Sept. 21 | | 1939 | Aug. 27 — Sept. 20 | | 1963 | Aug. 25 — Sept. 17 | |
| 1916 | Oct. 4 — Nov. 2 | | 1940 | Oct. 7 — Nov. 1 | | 1964 | Oct. 6 — Oct. 30 | |
| 1917 | July 29 — Aug. 21 | | 1941 | July 27 — Aug. 20 | | 1965 | July 26 — Aug. 19 | |
| 1918 | Sept. 12 — Sept. 30 | | 1942 | Sept. 11 — Oct. 4 | | 1966 | Sept. 9 — Oct. 2 | |
| 1919 | July 9 — Aug. 22 | | 1943 | July 8 — Nov. 9 | | 1967 | July 9 — Sept. 8 | |
| | Aug. 28 — Nov. 8 | | 1944 | Aug. 11 — Sept. 3 | | | Oct. 2 — Nov. 9 | |
| 1920 | Aug. 12 — Aug. 31 | | 1945 | Sept. 25 — Oct. 18 | | 1968 | Aug. 9 — Sept. 1 | |
| 1921 | Sept. 23 — Oct. 20 | | 1946 | July 13 — Aug. 7 | | 1969 | Sept. 23 — Oct. 17 | |
| 1922 | July 15 — Aug. 9 | | 1947 | Aug. 26 — Sept. 18 | | 1970 | July 11 — Aug. 5 | |

## VENUS IN LIBRA

| YEAR | FROM | TO | YEAR | FROM | TO | YEAR | FROM | TO |
|---|---|---|---|---|---|---|---|---|
| 1900 | Nov. 1 — Nov. 26 | | 1923 | Sept. 21 — Oct. 14 | | 1947 | Sept. 19 — Oct. 12 | |
| 1901 | Aug. 24 — Sept. 15 | | 1924 | Nov. 3 — Nov. 26 | | 1948 | Oct. 31 — Nov. 24 | |
| 1902 | Oct. 6 — Oct. 29 | | 1925 | Aug. 22 — Sept. 15 | | 1949 | Aug. 20 — Sept. 13 | |
| 1903 | Aug. 18 — Sept. 6 Nov. 9 — Dec. 9 | | 1926 | Oct. 6 — Oct. 29 | | 1950 | Oct. 4 — Oct. 27 | |
| 1904 | Sept. 10 — Sept. 30 | | 1927 | Nov. 10 — Dec. 9 | | 1951 | Nov. 10 — Dec. 7 | |
| 1905 | Oct. 15 — Nov. 22 | | 1928 | Sept. 5 — Sept. 28 | | 1952 | Sept. 3 — Sept. 27 | |
| 1906 | Aug. 11 — Sept. 7 | | 1929 | Oct. 20 — Nov. 12 | | 1953 | Oct. 19 — Nov. 11 | |
| 1907 | Sept. 24 — Oct. 13 | | 1930 | Aug. 10 — Sept. 6 | | 1954 | Aug. 9 — Sept. 6 | |
| 1908 | Nov. 1 — Nov. 25 | | 1931 | Sept. 21 — Oct. 14 | | 1955 | Sept. 19 — Nov. 12 | |
| 1909 | Aug. 21 — Sept. 16 | | 1932 | Nov. 3 — Nov. 26 | | 1956 | Nov. 1 — Nov. 25 | |
| 1910 | Oct. 6 — Oct. 30 | | 1933 | Aug. 22 — Sept. 15 | | 1957 | Aug. 20 — Sept. 13 | |
| 1911 | Nov. 9 — Dec. 7 | | 1934 | Oct. 6 — Oct. 29 | | 1958 | Oct. 4 — Oct. 27 | |
| 1912 | Sept. 1 — Sept. 29 | | 1935 | Nov. 10 — Dec. 8 | | 1959 | Nov. 10 — Dec. 7 | |
| 1913 | Oct. 20 — Nov. 13 | | 1936 | Sept. 5 — Sept. 28 | | 1960 | Sept. 3 — Sept. 26 | |
| 1914 | Aug. 19 — Sept. 6 | | 1937 | Oct. 20 — Nov. 12 | | 1961 | Oct. 18 — Nov. 10 | |
| 1915 | Sept. 22 — Oct. 12 | | 1938 | Aug. 10 — Sept. 7 | | 1962 | Aug. 9 — Sept. 16 | |
| 1916 | Nov. 3 — Nov. 22 | | 1939 | Sept. 21 — Oct. 14 | | 1963 | Sept. 18 — Oct. 11 | |
| 1917 | Aug. 22 — Sept. 11 | | 1940 | Nov. 2 — Nov. 26 | | 1964 | Oct. 31 — Nov. 24 | |
| 1918 | Oct. 1 — Oct. 29 | | 1941 | Aug. 21 — Sept. 14 | | 1965 | Aug. 20 — Sept. 13 | |
| 1919 | Aug. 23 — Aug. 27 Nov. 9 — Dec. 8 | | 1942 | Oct. 5 — Oct. 28 | | 1966 | Oct. 3 — Oct. 26 | |
| 1920 | Sept. 1 — Sept. 29 | | 1943 | Nov. 10 — Dec. 7 | | 1967 | Nov. 10 — Dec. 6 | |
| 1921 | Oct. 21 — Nov. 13 | | 1944 | Sept. 4 — Sept. 27 | | 1968 | Sept. 2 — Sept. 26 | |
| 1922 | Aug. 10 — Sept. 6 | | 1945 | Oct. 19 — Nov. 11 | | 1969 | Oct. 18 — Nov. 10 | |
| | | | 1946 | Aug. 8 — Sept. 3 | | 1970 | Aug. 6 — Sept. 1 | |

## VENUS IN SCORPIO

| YEAR | FROM | TO | YEAR | FROM | TO | YEAR | FROM | TO |
|------|------|-----|------|------|-----|------|------|-----|
| 1900 | Nov. 27 — Dec. 22 | | 1924 | Nov. 27 — Dec. 21 | | 1947 | Oct. 13 — Nov. 5 | |
| 1901 | Sept. 16 — Oct. 14 | | 1925 | Sept. 16 — Oct. 11 | | 1948 | Nov. 25 — Dec. 19 | |
| 1902 | Oct. 30 — Nov. 22 | | 1926 | Oct. 30 — Nov. 22 | | 1949 | Sept. 14 — Oct. 8 | |
| 1903 | Dec. 10 — Dec. 31 | | 1927 | Dec. 10 — Dec. 31 | | 1950 | Oct. 28 — Nov. 20 | |
| 1904 | Jan. 1 — Jan. 4 | | 1928 | Jan. 1 — Jan. 3 | | 1951 | Dec. 8 — Dec. 31 | |
| | Oct. 1 — Oct. 24 | | | Sept. 29 — Oct. 23 | | 1952 | Jan. 1 — Jan. 2 | |
| 1905 | Nov. 23 — Dec. 11 | | 1929 | Nov. 13 — Dec. 6 | | | Sept. 28 — Oct. 21 | |
| 1906 | Sept. 8 — Oct. 8 | | 1930 | Sept. 7 — Oct. 11 | | 1953 | Nov. 12 — Dec. 5 | |
| | Dec. 18 — Dec. 24 | | | Nov. 22 — Dec. 31 | | 1954 | Sept. 7 — Oct. 22 | |
| 1907 | Oct. 14 — Nov. 8 | | 1931 | Jan. 1 — Jan. 3 | | | Oct. 27 — Dec. 31 | |
| 1908 | Nov. 26 — Dec. 21 | | | Oct. 15 — Nov. 7 | | 1955 | Jan. 1 — Jan. 5 | |
| 1909 | Sept. 17 — Oct. 19 | | 1932 | Nov. 27 — Dec. 21 | | | Oct. 13 — Nov. 5 | |
| 1910 | Oct. 31 — Nov. 22 | | 1933 | Sept. 16 — Oct. 11 | | 1956 | Dec. 26 — Dec. 31 | |
| 1911 | Dec. 8 — Dec. 31 | | 1934 | Oct. 30 — Nov. 22 | | 1957 | Sept. 14 — Oct. 9 | |
| 1912 | Jan. 1 — Jan. 4 | | 1935 | Dec. 9 — Dec. 31 | | 1958 | Oct. 28 — Nov. 20 | |
| | Sept. 20 — Oct. 22 | | 1936 | Jan. 1 — Jan. 3 | | 1959 | Dec. 8 — Dec. 31 | |
| 1913 | Nov. 14 — Dec. 7 | | | Sept. 29 — Oct. 23 | | 1960 | Jan. 1 Only | |
| 1914 | Sept. 7 — Oct. 6 | | 1937 | Nov. 13 — Dec. 6 | | | Sept. 27 — Oct. 21 | |
| | Dec. 5 — Dec. 31 | | 1938 | Sept. 8 — Oct. 13 | | 1961 | Nov. 11 — Dec. 4 | |
| 1915 | Oct. 13 — Nov. 8 | | | Nov. 16 — Dec. 31 | | 1962 | Sept. 7 — Dec. 31 | |
| 1916 | Nov. 23 — Dec. 21 | | 1939 | Jan. 1 — Jan. 4 | | 1963 | Jan. 1 — Jan. 6 | |
| 1917 | Sept. 12 — Oct. 11 | | | Oct. 15 — Nov. 7 | | | Oct. 12 — Nov. 5 | |
| 1918 | Oct. 30 — Nov. 22 | | 1940 | Nov. 27 — Dec. 20 | | 1964 | Nov. 25 — Dec. 18 | |
| 1919 | Dec. 9 — Dec. 31 | | 1941 | Sept. 15 — Oct. 10 | | 1965 | Sept. 14 — Oct. 9 | |
| 1920 | Jan. 1 — Jan. 3 | | 1942 | Oct. 29 — Nov. 21 | | 1966 | Oct. 27 — Nov. 19 | |
| | Sept. 30 — Oct. 20 | | 1943 | Dec. 8 — Dec. 31 | | 1967 | Dec. 7 — Dec. 31 | |
| 1921 | Nov. 14 — Dec. 7 | | 1944 | Jan. 1 — Jan. 2 | | 1968 | Jan. 1 Only | |
| 1922 | Sept. 7 — Oct. 10 | | | Sept. 28 — Oct. 22 | | | Sept. 27 — Oct. 20 | |
| | Nov. 29 — Dec. 31 | | 1945 | Nov. 12 — Dec. 5 | | 1969 | Nov. 11 — Dec. 4 | |
| 1923 | Jan. 1 Only | | 1946 | Sept. 4 — Oct. 4 | | 1970 | Sept. 2 — Oct. 2 | |
| | Oct. 15 — Nov. 7 | | | | | | | |

## VENUS IN SAGITTARIUS

| YEAR | FROM — TO | YEAR | FROM — TO | YEAR | FROM — TO |
|------|-----------|------|-----------|------|-----------|
| 1900 | Dec. 23 — Dec. 31 | 1924 | Dec. 22 — Dec. 31 | 1949 | Jan. 1 — Jan. 12 |
| 1901 | Jan. 1 — Jan. 17 | 1925 | Jan. 1 — Jan. 14 | | Oct. 9 — Nov. 3 |
| | Oct. 15 — Nov. 7 | | Oct. 12 — Nov. 6 | 1950 | Nov. 21 — Dec. 14 |
| 1902 | Nov. 23 — Dec. 22 | 1926 | Nov. 23 — Dec. 16 | 1951 | No Transit of Sign |
| 1903 | No Transit of Sign | 1927 | No Transit of Sign | | During 1951 |
| | During 1903 | | During 1927 | 1952 | Jan. 3 — Jan. 27 |
| 1904 | Jan. 4 — Jan. 29 | 1928 | Jan. 4 — Jan. 28 | | Oct. 22 — Nov. 15 |
| | Oct. 26 — Nov. 22 | | Oct. 24 — Nov. 16 | 1953 | Dec. 6 — Dec. 29 |
| 1905 | Dec. 11 — Dec. 25 | 1929 | Dec. 7 — Dec. 30 | 1954 | Oct. 23 — Oct. 26 |
| 1906 | Oct. 9 — Dec. 17 | 1930 | Oct. 12 — Nov. 21 | 1955 | Jan. 6 — Feb. 5 |
| | Dec. 25 — Dec. 30 | 1931 | Jan. 4 — Feb. 6 | | Nov. 6 — Nov. 29 |
| 1907 | Jan. 1 — Feb. 6 | | Nov. 8 — Dec. 1 | 1956 | No Transit of Sign |
| | Nov. 9 — Dec. 2 | 1932 | Dec. 22 — Dec. 31 | | During 1956 |
| 1908 | Dec. 22 — Dec. 31 | 1933 | Jan. 1 — Jan. 14 | 1957 | Jan. 1 — Jan. 12 |
| 1909 | Jan. 1 — Jan. 12 | | Oct. 12 — Nov. 6 | | Oct. 10 — Nov. 5 |
| | Oct. 20 — Nov. 7 | 1934 | Nov. 23 — Dec. 16 | 1958 | Nov. 21 — Dec. 13 |
| 1910 | Nov. 23 — Dec. 18 | 1935 | No Transit of Sign | 1959 | No Transit of Sign |
| 1911 | No Transit of Sign | | During 1935 | | During 1959 |
| | During 1911 | 1936 | Jan. 4 — Jan. 28 | 1960 | Jan. 2 — Jan. 26 |
| 1912 | Jan. 5 — Jan. 29 | | Oct. 24 — Nov. 16 | | Oct. 22 — Nov. 14 |
| | Oct. 23 — Nov. 17 | 1937 | Dec. 7 — Dec. 30 | 1961 | Dec. 5 — Dec. 28 |
| 1913 | Dec. 8 — Dec. 31 | 1938 | Oct. 14 — Nov. 15 | 1962 | No Transit of Sign |
| 1914 | Oct. 7 — Dec. 31 | 1939 | Jan. 4 — Feb. 6 | | During 1962 |
| 1915 | Jan. 1 — Feb. 6 | | Nov. 8 — Dec. 1 | 1963 | Jan. 2 — Feb. 5 |
| | Nov. 9 — Dec. 2 | 1940 | Dec. 21 — Dec. 31 | | Nov. 6 — Nov. 29 |
| 1916 | Dec. 22 — Dec. 31 | 1941 | Oct. 11 — Nov. 5 | 1964 | Dec. 19 — Dec. 31 |
| 1917 | Jan. 1 — Jan. 17 | 1942 | Nov. 22 — Dec. 15 | 1965 | Jan. 1 — Jan. 11 |
| | Oct. 12 — Nov. 1 | 1943 | No Transit of Sign | | Oct. 10 — Nov. 5 |
| 1918 | Nov. 23 — Dec. 19 | | During 1943 | 1966 | Nov. 20 — Dec. 13 |
| 1919 | No Transit of Sign | 1944 | Jan. 3 — Jan. 27 | 1967 | No Transit of Sign |
| | During 1919 | | Oct. 23 — Nov. 15 | | During 1967 |
| 1920 | Jan. 4 — Jan. 31 | 1945 | Dec. 6 — Dec. 29 | 1968 | Jan. 2 — Jan. 26 |
| | Oct. 21 — Nov. 17 | 1946 | Oct. 5 — Dec. 31 | | Oct. 21 — Nov. 14 |
| 1921 | Dec. 8 — Dec. 21 | 1947 | Jan. 1 — Feb. 2 | 1969 | Dec. 5 — Dec. 27 |
| 192? | ?ct. 11 — Nov. 28 | | Nov. 6 — Nov. 29 | 1970 | Oct. 3 — Dec. 31 |
| 1923 | Jan. 2 — Feb. 6 | 1948 | Dec. 20 — Dec. 31 | | |
| | Nov. 8 — Dec.1 | | | | |

## VENUS IN CAPRICORN

| YEAR | FROM | TO |
|------|------|-----|
| 1900 | No Transit of Sign During 1900 | |
| 1901 | Jan. 18 — Feb. 8 | |
| | Nov. 8 — Dec. 5 | |
| 1902 | Dec. 23 — Dec. 31 | |
| 1903 | Jan. 1 — Jan. 10 | |
| 1904 | Jan. 30 — Feb. 29 | |
| | Nov. 23 — Dec. 12 | |
| 1905 | No Transit of Sign During 1905 | |
| 1906 | Jan. 2 — Jan. 25 | |
| 1907 | Feb. 7 — Mar. 6 | |
| | Dec. 3 — Dec. 26 | |
| 1908 | No Transit of Sign During 1908 | |
| 1909 | Jan. 13 — Feb. 8 | |
| | Nov. 8 — Dec. 5 | |
| 1910 | Dec. 17 — Dec. 31 | |
| 1911 | Jan. 1 — Jan. 15 | |
| 1912 | Jan. 30 — Feb. 23 | |
| | Nov. 18 — Dec. 12 | |
| 1913 | No Transit of Sign During 1913 | |
| 1914 | Jan. 1 — Jan. 20 | |
| 1915 | Feb. 7 — Mar. 6 | |
| | Dec. 3 — Dec. 26 | |
| 1916 | No Transit of Sign During 1916 | |
| 1917 | Jan. 18 — Feb. 7 | |
| | Nov. 2 — Dec. 5 | |
| 1918 | Dec. 20 — Dec. 31 | |
| 1919 | Jan. 1 — Jan. 9 | |
| 1920 | Feb. 1 — Feb. 22 | |
| | Nov. 18 — Dec. 11 | |
| 1921 | No Transit of Sign During 1921 | |
| 1922 | Jan. 1 — Jan. 24 | |
| 1923 | Feb. 7 — Mar. 5 | |
| | Dec. 2 — Dec. 25 | |
| 1924 | No Transit of Sign During 1924 | |
| 1925 | Jan. 15 — Feb. 7 | |
| | Nov. 7 — Dec. 5 | |
| 1926 | Dec. 17 — Dec. 31 | |
| 1927 | Jan. 1 — Jan. 8 | |
| 1928 | Jan. 29 — Feb. 22 | |
| | Nov. 17 — Dec. 11 | |
| 1929 | Dec. 31 Only | |
| 1930 | Jan. 1 — Jan. 23 | |
| 1931 | Feb. 7 — Mar. 5 | |
| | Dec. 2 — Dec. 25 | |
| 1932 | Jan. 1 — Jan. 18 | |
| 1933 | Jan. 15 — Feb. 7 | |
| | Nov. 7 — Dec. 5 | |
| 1934 | Dec. 18 — Dec. 31 | |
| 1935 | Jan. 1 — Jan. 8 | |
| 1936 | Jan. 26 — Feb. 22 | |
| | Nov. 17 — Dec. 11 | |
| 1937 | Dec. 31 Only | |
| 1938 | Jan. 1 — Jan. 23 | |
| 1939 | Feb. 7 — Mar. 5 | |
| | Dec. 2 — Dec. 25 | |
| 1940 | No Transit of Sign During 1940 | |
| 1941 | Jan. 14 — Feb. 6 | |
| | Nov. 6 — Dec. 5 | |
| 1942 | Dec. 16 — Dec. 31 | |
| 1943 | Jan. 1 — Jan. 7 | |
| 1944 | Jan. 1 — Feb. 22 | |
| | Nov. 16 — Dec. 9 | |
| 1945 | Dec. 30 — Dec. 31 | |
| 1946 | Jan. 1 — Jan. 22 | |
| 1947 | Feb. 3 — Mar. 2 | |
| | Nov. 30 — Dec. 23 | |
| 1948 | No Transit of Sign During 1948 | |
| 1949 | Jan. 13 — Feb. 5 | |
| | Nov. 4 — Dec. 1 | |
| 1950 | Dec. 15 — Dec. 31 | |
| 1951 | Jan. 1 — Jan. 7 | |
| 1952 | Jan. 28 — Feb. 20 | |
| | Nov. 16 — Dec. 10 | |
| 1953 | Dec. 30 — Dec. 31 | |
| 1954 | Jan. 1 — Jan. 21 | |
| 1955 | Feb. 6 — Mar. 4 | |
| | Nov. 30 — Dec. 23 | |
| 1956 | No Transit of Sign During 1956 | |
| 1957 | Jan. 13 — Feb. 5 | |
| | Nov. 6 — Dec. 6 | |
| 1958 | Dec. 14 — Dec. 31 | |
| 1959 | Jan. 1 — Jan. 6 | |
| 1960 | Jan. 27 — Feb. 20 | |
| | Nov. 15 — Dec. 9 | |
| 1961 | Dec. 29 — Dec. 31 | |
| 1962 | Jan. 1 — Jan. 21 | |
| 1963 | Feb. 6 — Mar. 3 | |
| | Nov. 30 — Dec. 23 | |
| 1964 | No Transit of Sign During 1964 | |
| 1965 | Jan. 12 — Feb. 3 | |
| | Nov. 6 — Dec. 7 | |
| 1966 | Feb. 6 — Feb. 25 | |
| | Dec. 14 — Dec. 31 | |
| 1967 | Jan. 1 — Jan. 6 | |
| 1968 | Jan. 27 — Feb. 19 | |
| | Nov. 15 — Dec. 9 | |
| 1969 | Dec. 28 — Dec. 31 | |
| 1970 | Jan. 1 — Jan. 20 | |

## VENUS IN AQUARIUS

| YEAR | FROM — TO | YEAR | FROM — TO | YEAR | FROM — TO |
|------|-----------|------|-----------|------|-----------|
| 1900 | Jan. 1 — Jan. 19 | 1923 | Mar. 6 — Mar. 31 | 1947 | Mar. 3 — Mar. 29 |
| 1901 | Feb. 10 — Mar. 5 | | Dec. 26 — Dec. 31 | | Dec. 24 — Dec. 31 |
| | Dec. 6 — Dec. 31 | 1924 | Jan. 1 — Jan. 19 | 1948 | Jan. 1 — Jan. 17 |
| 1902 | Jan. 1 — Jan. 11 | 1925 | Feb. 8 — Mar. 3 | 1949 | Feb. 6 — Mar. 1 |
| | Feb. 7 — Apr. 4 | | Dec. 6 — Dec. 13 | | Dec. 2 — Dec. 31 |
| 1903 | Jan. 11 — Feb. 4 | 1926 | Jan. 1 — Apr. 5 | 1950 | Jan. 1 — Jan. 5 |
| 1904 | Feb. 24 — Mar. 19 | 1927 | Jan. 9 — Feb. 1 | 1951 | Jan. 8 — Jan. 31 |
| | Dec. 13 — Dec. 31 | 1928 | Feb. 23 — Mar. 17 | 1952 | Feb. 21 — Mar. 16 |
| 1905 | Jan. 1 — Jan. 7 | | Dec. 12 — Dec. 31 | | Dec. 11 — Dec. 31 |
| 1906 | Jan. 26 — Feb. 18 | 1929 | Jan. 1 — Jan. 5 | 1953 | Jan. 1 — Jan. 4 |
| 1907 | Mar. 7 — Apr. 1 | 1930 | Jan. 24 — Feb. 16 | 1954 | Jan. 22 — Feb. 14 |
| | Dec. 27 — Dec. 31 | 1931 | Mar. 6 — Mar. 31 | 1955 | Mar. 5 — Mar. 29 |
| 1908 | Jan. 1 — Jan. 20 | | Dec. 26 — Dec. 31 | 1956 | Jan. 1 — Jan. 17 |
| 1909 | Feb. 9 — Mar. 4 | 1932 | Jan. 1 — Jan. 19 | 1957 | Feb. 6 — Mar. 1 |
| | Dec. 6 — Dec. 31 | 1933 | Feb. 8 — Mar. 3 | | Dec. 7 — Dec. 31 |
| 1910 | Jan. 1 — Jan. 20 | | Dec. 6 — Dec. 25 | 1958 | Jan. 1 — Apr. 6 |
| | Jan. 29 — Apr. 4 | 1934 | Jan. 1 — Apr. 6 | 1959 | Jan. 7 — Jan. 30 |
| 1911 | Jan. 16 — Jan. 27 | 1935 | Jan. 9 — Feb. 1 | 1960 | Dec. 10 — Dec. 31 |
| 1912 | Feb. 24 — Mar. 18 | 1936 | Feb. 23 — Mar. 17 | 1961 | Jan. 1 — Jan. 4 |
| | Dec. 13 — Dec. 31 | | Dec. 12 — Dec. 31 | 1962 | Jan. 22 — Feb. 14 |
| 1913 | Jan. 1 — Jan. 6 | 1937 | Jan. 1 — Jan. 6 | 1963 | Mar. 4 — Mar. 29 |
| 1914 | Jan. 25 — Feb. 17 | 1938 | Jan. 24 — Feb. 16 | | Dec. 24 — Dec. 31 |
| 1915 | Mar. 7 — Apr. 1 | 1939 | Mar. 6 — Mar. 31 | 1964 | Jan. 1 — Jan. 16 |
| | Dec. 27 — Dec. 31 | | Dec. 26 — Dec. 31 | 1965 | Feb. 4 — Feb. 28 |
| 1916 | Jan. 1 — Jan. 19 | 1940 | Jan. 1 — Jan. 18 | | Dec. 8 — Dec. 31 |
| 1917 | Feb. 8 — Mar. 4 | 1941 | Feb. 7 — Mar. 2 | 1966 | Jan. 1 — Feb. 5 |
| | Dec. 6 — Dec. 31 | | Dec. 6 — Dec. 31 | | Feb. 26 — Apr. 6 |
| 1918 | Jan. 1 — Apr. 5 | 1942 | Jan. 1 — Apr. 6 | 1967 | Jan. 7 — Jan. 30 |
| 1919 | Jan. 10 — Feb. 2 | 1943 | Jan. 1 — Jan. 31 | 1968 | Feb. 20 — Mar. 15 |
| 1920 | Feb. 23 — Mar. 18 | 1944 | Feb. 22 — Mar. 16 | | Dec. 10 — Dec. 31 |
| | Dec. 12 — Dec. 31 | | Dec. 10 — Dec. 31 | 1969 | Jan. 1 — Jan. 4 |
| 1921 | Jan. 1 — Jan. 3 | 1945 | Jan. 1 — Jan. 5 | 1970 | Jan. 21 — Feb. 13 |
| 1922 | Jan. 25 — Feb. 16 | 1946 | Jan. 23 — Feb. 15 | | |

## VENUS IN PISCES

| YEAR | FROM | TO | YEAR | FROM | TO | YEAR | FROM | TO |
|---|---|---|---|---|---|---|---|---|
| 1900 | Jan. 20 — Feb. 13 | | 1923 | Apr. 1 — Apr. 26 | | 1947 | Mar. 30 — Apr. 23 | |
| 1901 | Mar. 6 — Mar. 29 | | 1924 | Jan. 20 — Feb. 12 | | 1948 | Jan. 18 — Feb. 10 | |
| 1902 | Jan. 12 — Feb. 6 | | 1925 | Mar. 4 — Mar. 27 | | 1949 | Mar. 2 — Mar. 25 | |
| | Apr. 5 — May 6 | | 1926 | Apr. 6 — May 6 | | 1950 | Jan. 6 — Feb. 9 | |
| 1903 | Feb. 4 — Feb. 27 | | 1927 | Feb. 2 — Feb. 26 | | 1951 | Feb. 1 — Feb. 24 | |
| 1904 | Mar. 20 — Apr. 12 | | 1928 | Mar. 18 — Apr. 11 | | 1952 | Mar. 7 — Apr. 9 | |
| 1905 | Jan. 8 — Feb. 2 | | 1929 | Jan. 6 — Feb. 2 | | 1953 | Jan. 5 — Feb. 1 | |
| 1906 | Feb. 19 — Mar. 14 | | 1930 | Feb. 17 — Mar. 12 | | 1954 | Feb. 15 — Mar. 10 | |
| 1907 | Apr. 2 — Apr. 27 | | 1931 | Apr. 1 — Apr. 26 | | 1955 | Mar. 30 — Apr. 24 | |
| 1908 | Jan. 21 — Feb. 13 | | 1932 | Jan. 20 — Feb. 12 | | 1956 | Jan. 18 — Feb. 10 | |
| 1909 | Mar. 5 — Mar. 28 | | 1933 | Mar. 4 — Mar. 27 | | 1957 | Mar. 2 — Mar. 25 | |
| 1910 | Jan. 16 — Jan. 28 | | 1934 | Apr. 7 — May 6 | | 1958 | Apr. 7 — May 4 | |
| | Apr. 5 — May 6 | | 1935 | Feb. 2 — Feb. 27 | | 1959 | Jan. 31 — Feb. 23 | |
| 1911 | Feb. 3 — Feb. 27 | | 1936 | Mar. 18 — Apr. 11 | | 1960 | Mar. 16 — Apr. 8 | |
| 1912 | Mar. 19 — Apr. 12 | | 1937 | Jan. 7 — Feb. 2 | | 1961 | Jan. 5 — Feb. 1 | |
| 1913 | Jan. 7 — Feb. 2 | | 1938 | Feb. 17 — Mar. 12 | | 1962 | Feb. 15 — Mar. 10 | |
| 1914 | Feb. 18 — Mar. 13 | | 1939 | Apr. 1 — Apr. 25 | | 1963 | Mar. 30 — Apr. 23 | |
| 1915 | Apr. 2 — Apr. 26 | | 1940 | Jan. 19 — Feb. 12 | | 1964 | Jan. 17 — Feb. 10 | |
| 1916 | Jan. 20 — Feb. 13 | | 1941 | Mar. 3 — Mar. 26 | | 1965 | Mar. 1 — Mar. 24 | |
| 1917 | Mar. 5 — Mar. 28 | | 1942 | Apr. 7 — May 5 | | 1966 | Apr. 7 — May 4 | |
| 1918 | Apr. 6 — May 6 | | 1943 | Feb. 1 — Feb. 25 | | 1967 | Jan. 31 — Feb. 23 | |
| 1919 | Feb. 3 — Feb. 26 | | 1944 | Mar. 17 — Apr. 10 | | 1968 | Mar. 16 — Apr. 8 | |
| 1920 | Mar. 19 — Apr. 11 | | 1945 | Jan. 6 — Feb. 1 | | 1969 | Jan. 5 — Feb. 1 | |
| 1921 | Jan. 7 — Feb. 2 | | 1946 | Feb. 16 — Mar. 11 | | 1970 | Feb. 14 — Mar. 9 | |
| 1922 | Feb. 17 — Mar. 12 | | | | | | | |

*A woman, a spaniel, and a walnut tree,*
*The more you beat them the better they be.*

The position of Mars in your chart indicates the velocity of your sex drive as this planet signifies matter emerging through solar activity, and rules creativity, new energy, and new forms. Well-positioned, it can be a great creative force in one's life; ill-positioned, since it is "the warrior," it can cause you to provoke fights, act boisterous, unpleasant, cruel and sometimes in a bullying manner. Mars badly aspected can be one of the most detrimental factors for your sex drive; for instance, a Mars which makes bad aspects to the moon in a chart can cause destruction and evil, anger and ill will. Well-placed, it is a courageous and powerful help to the native and can endow him with great confidence and power.

MARS IN ARIES: This can give you rashness, enthusiasm, impulsiveness, and a taste for adventure. You will be prone to sudden and violent love affairs; you will have a taste for the thrilling and even the outrageous. You are passionate and heedless of consequences.

MARS IN TAURUS: You will have a persistence and constancy in your sex drive and in your sex energies. Often sex is connected with money for you, or financial gain. You will either marry for money or gain from your sexual alliances. You would make a good hooker or gigolo.

MARS IN GEMINI: Energetic and athletic, you are a bedroom athlete par excellence. You'll often tend to be sarcastic with your mate and tire easily of alliances and liaisons. You're easily bored in sex and prefer the new and inventive.

MARS IN CANCER: You are prone to emotional panegyrics and go in for exhibitions of emotions as well as frequent misunderstandings with your partner. Although you have a strong sex drive it is often thwarted and unfulfilled. You are a difficult person to reach. You like to use your imagination in sex and often fantasize another sexual situation altogether from the one in which you are engaged, since you are so frequently dissatisfied with your present sexual circumstances.

MARS IN LEO: You are dynamic and energetic, quick in your sexual responses, uncomplicated in enjoying healthy relations. Beware of your temper and fiery nature.

MARS IN VIRGO: You are apt to have a taste for the bizzare and unusual. You could be a good sex pervert. Hopefully you will have other aspects favorably placed which will balance out your sex nature. When you engage in sex with those beneath you, you must beware your self-image doesn't get out of hand.

MARS IN LIBRA: You are very enthusiastic and cooperative in bed, and you enjoy every area of good sex relations. You must beware, though, of a bad temper that could alienate you from your sex partner. Your marriage could be frequently jeopardized, but then you do have the bedroom in which you can mend old grudges.

MARS IN SCORPIO: You know what you want and where you are going and will always get your way in sex. You are a good manipulator and can always come up with an interesting idea of how to satisfy your appetites when there seems no solution in sight. Really an inventive little creature. You will never pine away for long, for sex will always come your way.

MARS IN SAGITTARIUS: You are impulsive and have a fondness for movement and travel. You will encounter frequent sexual escapades on your many trips through the world. Never idle for long, you attract the opposite sex easily.

MARS IN CAPRICORN: You will desire to elevate yourself through your sex conquests and adventures. You seek self-aggrandizement or self-improvement. This is sometimes an advantage, sometimes a disadvantage, depending on your other aspects.

MARS IN AQUARIUS: You are an hospitable person who finds many opportunities for sex, but you are discriminating and do not indulge as often as others might. Your sex appetite is generally conservative.

MARS IN PISCES: Your sex life will be a source of trouble to you, and will often make you unhappy and melancholy. You somehow do not know how to integrate sex properly into the rest of your life and balance it. Often it will be of too great a mental importance to you, and you will feel frustrated.

# HOW TO FIND THE PLACEMENT OF MARS
## AT THE TIME OF YOUR BIRTH

| 1890 Date | Zodiacal Sign |
|---|---|
| Jan. 1 — Feb. 28 | Scorpio |
| Feb. 29 — June 16 | Sagittarius |
| June 17 — July 21 | Scorpio |
| July 22 — Sept. 23 | Sagittarius |
| Sept. 24 — Nov. 4 | Capricorn |
| Nov. 5 — Dec. 16 | Aquarius |
| Dec. 17 — Dec. 31 | Pisces |

### 1891

| Date | Zodiacal Sign |
|---|---|
| Jan. 1 — Jan. 25 | Pisces |
| Jan. 26 — Mar. 7 | Aries |
| Mar. 8 — Apr. 19 | Taurus |
| Apr. 20 — June 3 | Gemini |
| June 4 — July 19 | Cancer |
| July 20 — Sept. 4 | Leo |
| Sept. 5 — Oct. 21 | Virgo |
| Oct. 22 — Dec. 7 | Libra |
| Dec. 8 — Dec. 31 | Scorpio |

### 1892

| Date | Zodiacal Sign |
|---|---|
| Jan. 1 — Feb. 24 | Scorpio |
| Feb. 25 — Mar. 13 | Sagittarius |
| Mar. 14 — May 6 | Capricorn |
| May 7 — Nov. 8 | Aquarius |
| Nov. 9 — Dec. 27 | Pisces |
| Dec. 28 — Dec. 31 | Aries |

### 1893

| Date | Zodiacal Sign |
|---|---|
| Jan. 1 — Feb. 10 | Aries |
| Feb. 11 — Mar. 28 | Taurus |
| Mar. 29 — May 13 | Gemini |
| May 14 — June 29 | Cancer |
| June 30 — Aug. 15 | Leo |
| Aug. 16 — Oct. 1 | Virgo |
| Oct. 2 — Nov. 16 | Libra |
| Nov. 17 — Dec. 31 | Scorpio |

### 1894

| Date | Zodiacal Sign |
|---|---|
| Jan. 1 — Feb. 13 | Sagittarius |
| Feb. 14 — Mar. 27 | Capricorn |
| Mar. 28 — May 9 | Aquarius |
| May 10 — June 22 | Pisces |

| 1894 Date | Zodiacal Sign |
|---|---|
| June 23 — Aug. 18 | Aries |
| Aug. 19 — Oct. 12 | Taurus |
| Oct. 13 — Dec. 30 | Aries |
| Dec. 31 | Taurus |

### 1895

| Date | Zodiacal Sign |
|---|---|
| Jan. 1 — Mar. 1 | Taurus |
| Mar. 2 — Apr. 21 | Gemini |
| Apr. 22 — June 10 | Cancer |
| June 11 — July 28 | Leo |
| July 29 — Sept. 13 | Virgo |
| Sept. 14 — Oct. 30 | Libra |
| Oct. 31 — Dec. 11 | Scorpio |
| Dec. 12 — Dec. 31 | Sagittarius |

### 1896

| Date | Zodiacal Sign |
|---|---|
| Jan. 1 — Jan. 22 | Sagittarius |
| Jan. 23 — Mar. 2 | Capricorn |
| Mar. 3 — Apr. 11 | Aquarius |
| Apr. 12 — May 21 | Pisces |
| May 22 — July 1 | Aries |
| July 2 — Aug. 15 | Taurus |
| Aug. 16 — Dec. 31 | Gemini |

### 1897

| Date | Zodiacal Sign |
|---|---|
| Jan. 1 — Mar. 21 | Gemini |
| Mar. 22 — May 17 | Cancer |
| May 18 — July 8 | Leo |
| July 9 — Aug. 25 | Virgo |
| Aug. 26 — Oct. 9 | Libra |
| Oct. 10 — Nov. 21 | Scorpio |
| Nov. 22 — Dec. 31 | Sagittarius |

### 1898

| Date | Zodiacal Sign |
|---|---|
| Jan. 1 | Sagittarius |
| Jan. 2 — Feb. 10 | Capricorn |
| Feb. 11 — Mar. 20 | Aquarius |
| Mar. 21 — Apr. 28 | Pisces |
| Apr. 29 — June 6 | Aries |
| June 7 — July 18 | Taurus |
| July 19 — Sept. 2 | Gemini |
| Sept. 3 — Oct. 30 | Cancer |
| Oct. 31 — Dec. 31 | Leo |

| 1899 | Date | Zodiacal Sign |
|---|---|---|
| | Jan. 1 — Jan. 15 | Leo |
| | Jan. 16 — Apr. 14 | Cancer |
| | Apr. 15 — June 15 | Leo |
| | June 16 — Aug. 5 | Virgo |
| | Aug. 6 — Sept. 20 | Libra |
| | Sept. 21 — Nov. 2 | Scorpio |
| | Nov. 3 — Dec. 13 | Sagittarius |
| | Dec. 14 — Dec. 31 | Capricorn |

| 1900 | | |
|---|---|---|
| | Jan. 1 — Feb. 28 | Aquarius |
| | Mar. 1 — Apr. 7 | Pisces |
| | Apr. 8 — May 16 | Aries |
| | May 17 — June 26 | Taurus |
| | June 27 — Aug. 9 | Gemini |
| | Aug. 10 — Sept. 26 | Cancer |
| | Sept. 27 — Nov. 22 | Leo |
| | Nov. 23 — Dec. 31 | Virgo |

| 1901 | | |
|---|---|---|
| | Jan. 1 — Mar. 1 | Virgo |
| | Mar. 2 — May 10 | Leo |
| | May 11 — July 13 | Virgo |
| | July 14 — Aug. 31 | Libra |
| | Sept. 1 — Oct. 14 | Scorpio |
| | Oct. 15 — Nov. 23 | Sagittarius |
| | Nov. 24 — Dec. 31 | Capricorn |

| 1902 | | |
|---|---|---|
| | Jan. 1 | Capricorn |
| | Jan. 2 — Feb. 8 | Aquarius |
| | Feb. 9 — Mar. 17 | Pisces |
| | Mar. 18 — Apr. 26 | Aries |
| | Apr. 27 — June 6 | Taurus |
| | June 7 — July 20 | Gemini |
| | July 21 — Sept. 4 | Cancer |
| | Sept. 5 — Oct. 23 | Leo |
| | Oct. 24 — Dec. 19 | Virgo |
| | Dec. 20 — Dec. 31 | Libra |

| 1903 | | |
|---|---|---|
| | Jan. 1 — Apr. 19 | Libra |
| | Apr. 20 — May 30 | Virgo |
| | May 31 — Aug. 6 | Libra |
| | Aug. 7 — Sept. 22 | Scorpio |
| | Sept. 23 — Nov. 2 | Sagittarius |
| | Nov. 3 — Dec. 11 | Capricorn |
| | Dec. 12 — Dec. 31 | Aquarius |

| 1904 | Date | Zodiacal Sign |
|---|---|---|
| | Jan. 1 — Jan. 19 | Aquarius |
| | Jan. 20 — Feb. 26 | Pisces |
| | Feb. 27 — Apr. 6 | Aries |
| | Apr. 7 — May 17 | Taurus |
| | May 18 — June 30 | Gemini |
| | July 1 — Aug. 14 | Cancer |
| | Aug. 15 — Oct. 1 | Leo |
| | Oct. 2 — Nov. 19 | Virgo |
| | Nov. 20 — Dec. 31 | Libra |

| 1905 | | |
|---|---|---|
| | Jan. 1 — Jan. 13 | Libra |
| | Jan. 14 — Aug. 21 | Scorpio |
| | Aug. 22 — Oct. 7 | Sagittarius |
| | Oct. 8 — Nov. 17 | Capricorn |
| | Nov. 18 — Dec. 27 | Aquarius |
| | Dec. 28 — Dec. 31 | Pisces |

| 1906 | | |
|---|---|---|
| | Jan. 1 — Feb. 4 | Pisces |
| | Feb. 5 — Mar. 16 | Aries |
| | Mar. 17 — Apr. 28 | Taurus |
| | Apr. 29 — June 11 | Gemini |
| | June 12 — July 27 | Cancer |
| | July 28 — Sept. 12 | Leo |
| | Sept. 13 — Oct. 29 | Virgo |
| | Oct. 30 — Dec. 16 | Libra |
| | Dec. 17 — Dec. 31 | Scorpio |

| 1907 | | |
|---|---|---|
| | Jan. 1 — Feb. 4 | Scorpio |
| | Feb. 5 — Apr. 1 | Sagittarius |
| | Apr. 2 — Oct. 13 | Capricorn |
| | Oct. 14 — Nov. 28 | Aquarius |
| | Nov. 29 — Dec. 31 | Pisces |

| 1908 | | |
|---|---|---|
| | Jan. 1 — Jan. 10 | Pisces |
| | Jan. 11 — Feb. 22 | Aries |
| | Feb. 23 — Apr. 6 | Taurus |
| | Apr. 7 — May 22 | Gemini |
| | May 23 — July 7 | Cancer |
| | July 8 — Aug. 23 | Leo |
| | Aug. 24 — Oct. 9 | Virgo |
| | Oct. 10 — Nov. 25 | Libra |
| | Nov. 26 — Dec. 31 | Scorpio |

| 1909 Date | Zodiacal Sign |
|---|---|
| Jan. 1 — Jan. 9 | Scorpio |
| Jan. 10 — Feb. 23 | Sagittarius |
| Feb. 24 — Apr. 9 | Capricorn |
| Apr. 10 — May 25 | Aquarius |
| May 26 — July 20 | Pisces |
| July 21 — Sept. 26 | Aries |
| Sept. 27 — Nov. 20 | Pisces |
| Nov. 21 — Dec. 31 | Aries |

**1910**

| Date | Zodiacal Sign |
|---|---|
| Jan. 1 — Feb. 22 | Aries |
| Feb. 23 — Mar. 13 | Taurus |
| Mar. 14 — May 1 | Gemini |
| May 2 — June 18 | Cancer |
| June 19 — Aug. 5 | Leo |
| Aug. 6 — Sept. 21 | Virgo |
| Sept. 22 — Nov. 6 | Libra |
| Nov. 7 — Dec. 19 | Scorpio |
| Dec. 20 — Dec. 31 | Sagittarius |

**1911**

| Date | Zodiacal Sign |
|---|---|
| Jan. 1 — Jan. 31 | Sagittarius |
| Feb. 1 — Mar. 13 | Capricorn |
| Mar. 14 — Apr. 22 | Aquarius |
| Apr. 23 — June 2 | Pisces |
| June 3 — July 15 | Aries |
| July 16 — Sept. 5 | Taurus |
| Sept. 6 — Nov. 29 | Gemini |
| Nov. 30 — Dec. 31 | Taurus |

**1912**

| Date | Zodiacal Sign |
|---|---|
| Jan. 1 — Jan. 30 | Taurus |
| Jan. 31 — Apr. 4 | Gemini |
| Apr. 5 — May 27 | Cancer |
| May 28 — July 16 | Leo |
| July 17 — Sept. 2 | Virgo |
| Sept. 3 — Oct. 17 | Libra |
| Oct. 18 — Nov. 29 | Scorpio |
| Nov. 30 — Dec. 31 | Sagittarius |

**1913**

| Date | Zodiacal Sign |
|---|---|
| Jan. 1 — Jan. 10 | Sagittarius |
| Jan. 11 — Feb. 18 | Capricorn |
| Feb. 19 — Mar. 29 | Aquarius |
| Mar. 30 — May 7 | Pisces |
| May 8 — June 16 | Aries |
| June 17 — July 28 | Taurus |
| July 29 — Sept. 15 | Gemini |
| Sept. 16 — Dec. 31 | Cancer |

| 1914 Date | Zodiacal Sign |
|---|---|
| Jan. 1 — May 1 | Cancer |
| May 2 — June 25 | Leo |
| June 26 — Aug. 14 | Virgo |
| Aug. 15 — Sept. 28 | Libra |
| Sept. 29 — Nov. 10 | Scorpio |
| Nov. 11 — Dec. 21 | Sagittarius |
| Dec. 22 — Dec. 31 | Capricorn |

**1915**

| Date | Zodiacal Sign |
|---|---|
| Jan. 1 — Jan. 29 | Capricorn |
| Jan. 30 — Mar. 9 | Aquarius |
| Mar. 10 — Apr. 16 | Pisces |
| Apr. 17 — May 25 | Aries |
| May 26 — July 5 | Taurus |
| July 6 — Aug. 18 | Gemini |
| Aug. 19 — Oct. 7 | Cancer |
| Oct. 8 — Dec. 31 | Leo |

**1916**

| Date | Zodiacal Sign |
|---|---|
| Jan. 1 — May 28 | Leo |
| May 29 — July 22 | Virgo |
| July 23 — Sept. 8 | Libra |
| Sept. 9 — Oct. 21 | Scorpio |
| Oct. 22 — Dec. 1 | Sagittarius |
| Dec. 2 — Dec. 31 | Capricorn |

**1917**

| Date | Zodiacal Sign |
|---|---|
| Jan. 1 — Jan. 9 | Capricorn |
| Jan. 10 — Feb. 16 | Aquarius |
| Feb. 17 — Mar. 26 | Pisces |
| Mar. 27 — May 4 | Aries |
| May 5 — June 14 | Taurus |
| June 15 — July 27 | Gemini |
| July 28 — Sept. 11 | Cancer |
| Sept. 12 — Nov. 1 | Leo |
| Nov. 2 — Dec. 31 | Virgo |

**1918**

| Date | Zodiacal Sign |
|---|---|
| Jan. 1 — Jan. 10 | Virgo |
| Jan. 11 — Feb. 25 | Libra |
| Feb. 26 — June 23 | Virgo |
| June 24 — Aug. 16 | Libra |
| Aug. 17 — Sept. 30 | Scorpio |
| Oct. 1 — Nov. 10 | Sagittarius |
| Nov. 11 — Dec. 19 | Capricorn |
| Dec. 20 — Dec. 31 | Aquarius |

**1919**

| Date | Zodiacal Sign |
|---|---|
| Jan. 1 — Jan. 26 | Aquarius |
| Jan. 27 — Mar. 6 | Pisces |
| Mar. 7 — Apr. 14 | Aries |

| 1919 | Date | Zodiacal Sign |
|---|---|---|
| | Apr. 15 — May 25 | Taurus |
| | May 26 — July 8 | Gemini |
| | July 9 — Aug. 22 | Cancer |
| | Aug. 23 — Oct. 9 | Leo |
| | Oct. 10 — Nov. 29 | Virgo |
| | Nov. 30 — Dec. 31 | Libra |

**1920**

| | | |
|---|---|---|
| | Jan. 1 — Jan. 31 | Libra |
| | Feb. 1 — Apr. 23 | Scorpio |
| | Apr. 24 — July 10 | Libra |
| | July 11 — Sept. 4 | Scorpio |
| | Sept. 5 — Oct. 18 | Sagittarius |
| | Oct. 19 — Nov. 27 | Capricorn |
| | Nov. 28 — Dec. 31 | Aquarius |

**1921**

| | | |
|---|---|---|
| | Jan. 1 — Jan. 4 | Aquarius |
| | Jan. 5 — Feb. 12 | Pisces |
| | Feb. 13 — Mar. 24 | Aries |
| | Mar. 25 — May 5 | Taurus |
| | May 6 — June 9 | Gemini |
| | June 20 — Aug. 2 | Cancer |
| | Aug. 3 — Sept. 18 | Leo |
| | Sept. 19 — Nov. 6 | Virgo |
| | Nov. 7 — Dec. 25 | Libra |
| | Dec. 26 — Dec. 31 | Scorpio |

**1922**

| | | |
|---|---|---|
| | Jan. 1 — Feb. 18 | Scorpio |
| | Feb. 19 — Sept. 13 | Sagittarius |
| | Sept. 14 — Oct. 30 | Capricorn |
| | Oct. 31 — Dec. 11 | Aquarius |
| | Dec. 12 — Dec. 31 | Pisces |

**1923**

| | | |
|---|---|---|
| | Jan. 1 — Jan. 20 | Pisces |
| | Jan. 21 — Mar. 3 | Aries |
| | Mar. 4 — Apr. 15 | Taurus |
| | Apr. 16 — May 30 | Gemini |
| | May 31 — July 15 | Cancer |
| | July 16 — Aug. 31 | Leo |
| | Sept. 1 — Oct. 17 | Virgo |
| | Oct. 18 — Dec. 3 | Libra |
| | Dec. 4 — Dec. 31 | Scorpio |

| 1924 | Date | Zodiacal Sign |
|---|---|---|
| | Jan. 1 — Feb. 19 | Scorpio |
| | Feb. 20 — Mar. 6 | Sagittarius |
| | Mar. 7 — Apr. 24 | Capricorn |
| | Apr. 25 — June 24 | Aquarius |
| | June 25 — Aug. 24 | Pisces |
| | Aug. 25 — Oct. 19 | Aquarius |
| | Oct. 20 — Dec. 18 | Pisces |
| | Dec. 19 — Dec. 31 | Aries |

**1925**

| | | |
|---|---|---|
| | Jan. 1 — Feb. 4 | Aries |
| | Feb. 5 — Mar. 23 | Taurus |
| | Mar. 24 — May 9 | Gemini |
| | May 10 — June 25 | Cancer |
| | June 26 — Aug. 12 | Leo |
| | Aug. 13 — Sept. 28 | Virgo |
| | Sept. 29 — Nov. 13 | Libra |
| | Nov. 14 — Dec. 27 | Scorpio |
| | Dec. 28 — Dec. 31 | Sagittarius |

**1926**

| | | |
|---|---|---|
| | Jan. 1 — Feb. 8 | Sagittarius |
| | Feb. 9 — Mar. 22 | Capricorn |
| | Mar. 23 — May 3 | Aquarius |
| | May 4 — June 14 | Pisces |
| | June 15 — July 31 | Aries |
| | Aug. 1 — Dec. 31 | Taurus |

**1927**

| | | |
|---|---|---|
| | Jan. 1 — Feb. 21 | Taurus |
| | Feb. 22 — Apr. 16 | Gemini |
| | Apr. 17 — June 5 | Cancer |
| | June 6 — July 24 | Leo |
| | July 25 — Sept. 10 | Virgo |
| | Sept. 11 — Oct. 25 | Libra |
| | Oct. 26 — Dec. 7 | Scorpio |
| | Dec. 8 — Dec. 31 | Sagittarius |

**1928**

| | | |
|---|---|---|
| | Jan. 1 — Jan. 18 | Sagittarius |
| | Jan. 19 — Feb. 27 | Capricorn |
| | Feb. 28 — Apr. 7 | Aquarius |
| | Apr. 8 — May 16 | Pisces |
| | May 17 — June 25 | Aries |
| | June 26 — Aug. 8 | Taurus |
| | Aug. 9 — Oct. 2 | Gemini |
| | Oct. 3 — Dec. 19 | Cancer |
| | Dec. 20 — Dec. 31 | Gemini |

| 1929 Date | Zodiacal Sign |
|---|---|
| Jan. 1 — Mar. 10 | Gemini |
| Mar. 11 — May 12 | Cancer |
| May 13 — July 3 | Leo |
| July 4 — Aug. 21 | Virgo |
| Aug. 22 — Oct. 5 | Libra |
| Oct. 6 — Nov. 18 | Scorpio |
| Nov. 19 — Dec. 28 | Sagittarius |
| Dec. 29 — Dec. 31 | Capricorn |

### 1930

| | |
|---|---|
| Jan. 1 — Feb. 6 | Capricorn |
| Feb. 7 — Mar. 16 | Aquarius |
| Mar. 17 — Apr. 24 | Pisces |
| Apr. 25 — June 2 | Aries |
| June 3 — July 14 | Taurus |
| July 15 — Aug. 27 | Gemini |
| Aug. 28 — Oct. 20 | Cancer |
| Oct. 21 — Dec. 31 | Leo |

### 1931

| | |
|---|---|
| Jan. 1 — Feb. 15 | Leo |
| Feb. 16 — Mar. 29 | Cancer |
| Mar. 30 — June 9 | Leo |
| June 10 — July 31 | Virgo |
| Aug. 1 — Sept. 16 | Libra |
| Sept. 17 — Oct. 29 | Scorpio |
| Oct. 30 — Dec. 9 | Sagittarius |
| Dec. 10 — Dec. 31 | Capricorn |

### 1932

| | |
|---|---|
| Jan. 1 — Jan. 17 | Capricorn |
| Jan. 18 — Feb. 24 | Aquarius |
| Feb. 25 — Apr. 2 | Pisces |
| Apr. 3 — May 11 | Aries |
| May 12 — June 21 | Taurus |
| June 22 — Aug. 3 | Gemini |
| Aug. 4 — Sept. 19 | Cancer |
| Sept. 20 — Nov. 12 | Leo |
| Nov. 13 — Dec. 31 | Virgo |

### 1933

| | |
|---|---|
| Jan. 1 — July 5 | Virgo |
| July 6 — Aug. 25 | Libra |
| Aug. 26 — Oct. 8 | Scorpio |
| Oct. 9 — Nov. 18 | Sagittarius |
| Nov. 19 — Dec. 27 | Capricorn |
| Dec. 28 — Dec. 31 | Aquarius |

| 1934 Date | Zodiacal Sign |
|---|---|
| Jan. 1 — Feb. 3 | Aquarius |
| Feb. 4 — Mar. 13 | Pisces |
| Mar. 14 — Apr. 21 | Aries |
| Apr. 22 — June 1 | Taurus |
| June 2 — July 14 | Gemini |
| July 15 — Aug. 29 | Cancer |
| Aug. 30 — Oct. 17 | Leo |
| Oct. 18 — Dec. 10 | Virgo |
| Dec. 11 — Dec. 31 | Libra |

### 1935

| | |
|---|---|
| Jan. 1 — July 28 | Libra |
| July 29 — Sept. 15 | Scorpio |
| Sept. 16 — Oct. 27 | Sagittarius |
| Oct. 28 — Dec. 6 | Capricorn |
| Dec. 7 — Dec. 31 | Aquarius |

### 1936

| | |
|---|---|
| Jan. 1 — Jan. 13 | Aquarius |
| Jan. 14 — Feb. 21 | Pisces |
| Feb. 22 — Mar. 31 | Aries |
| Apr. 1 — May 12 | Taurus |
| May 13 — June 24 | Gemini |
| June 25 — Aug. 9 | Cancer |
| Aug. 10 — Sept. 25 | Leo |
| Sept. 26 — Nov. 13 | Virgo |
| Nov. 14 — Dec. 31 | Libra |

### 1937

| | |
|---|---|
| Jan. 1 — Mar. 12 | Scorpio |
| Mar. 13 — May 13 | Sagittarius |
| May 14 — Aug. 7 | Scorpio |
| Aug. 8 — Sept. 29 | Sagittarius |
| Sept. 30 — Nov. 10 | Capricorn |
| Nov. 11 — Dec. 20 | Aquarius |
| Dec. 21 — Dec. 31 | Pisces |

### 1938

| | |
|---|---|
| Jan. 1 — Jan. 29 | Pisces |
| Jan. 30 — Mar. 11 | Aries |
| Mar. 12 — Apr. 22 | Taurus |
| Apr. 23 — June 6 | Gemini |
| June 7 — July 21 | Cancer |
| July 22 — Sept. 6 | Leo |
| Sept. 7 — Oct. 24 | Virgo |
| Oct. 25 — Dec. 10 | Libra |
| Dec. 11 — Dec. 31 | Scorpio |

| 1939 Date | Zodiacal Sign |
|---|---|
| Jan. 1 — Jan. 28 | Scorpio |
| Jan. 29 — Mar. 20 | Sagittarius |
| Mar. 21 — May 23 | Capricorn |
| May 24 — July 20 | Aquarius |
| July 21 — Sept. 23 | Capricorn |
| Sept. 24 — Nov. 18 | Aquarius |
| Nov. 19 — Dec. 31 | Pisces |

**1940**

| Jan. 1 — Jan. 2 | Pisces |
|---|---|
| Jan. 3 — Feb. 16 | Aries |
| Feb. 17 — Mar. 31 | Taurus |
| Apr. 1 — May 16 | Gemini |
| May 17 — July 2 | Cancer |
| July 3 — Aug. 18 | Leo |
| Aug. 19 — Oct. 4 | Virgo |
| Oct. 5 — Nov. 19 | Libra |
| Nov. 20 — Dec. 31 | Scorpio |

**1941**

| Jan. 1 — Jan. 3 | Scorpio |
|---|---|
| Jan. 4 — Feb. 16 | Sagittarius |
| Feb. 17 — Apr. 1 | Capricorn |
| Apr. 2 — May 15 | Aquarius |
| May 16 — July 1 | Pisces |
| July 2 — Dec. 31 | Aries |

**1942**

| Jan. 1 — Jan. 10 | Aries |
|---|---|
| Jan. 11 — Mar. 6 | Taurus |
| Mar. 7 — Apr. 25 | Gemini |
| Apr. 26 — June 13 | Cancer |
| June 14 — July 31 | Leo |
| Aug. 1 — Sept. 16 | Virgo |
| Sept. 17 — Oct. 31 | Libra |
| Nov. 1 — Dec. 14 | Scorpio |
| Dec. 14 — Dec. 31 | Sagittarius |

**1943**

| Jan. 1 — Jan. 25 | Sagittarius |
|---|---|
| Jan. 26 — Mar. 7 | Capricorn |
| Mar. 8 — Apr. 16 | Aquarius |
| Apr. 17 — May 26 | Pisces |
| May 27 — June 6 | Aries |
| June 7 — Aug. 22 | Taurus |
| Aug. 23 — Dec. 31 | Gemini |

| 1944 Date | Zodiacal Sign |
|---|---|
| Jan. 1 — Mar. 27 | Gemini |
| Mar. 28 — May 21 | Cancer |
| May 22 — July 11 | Leo |
| July 12 — Aug. 28 | Virgo |
| Aug. 29 — Oct. 12 | Libra |
| Oct. 13 — Nov. 24 | Scorpio |
| Nov. 25 — Dec. 31 | Sagittarius |

**1945**

| Jan. 1 — Jan. 4 | Sagittarius |
|---|---|
| Jan. 5 — Feb. 13 | Capricorn |
| Feb. 14 — Mar. 24 | Aquarius |
| Mar. 25 — May 1 | Pisces |
| May 2 — June 10 | Aries |
| June 11 — July 22 | Taurus |
| July 23 — Sept. 6 | Gemini |
| Sept. 7 — Nov. 10 | Cancer |
| Nov. 11 — Dec. 25 | Leo |
| Dec. 26 — Dec. 31 | Cancer |

**1946**

| Jan. 1 — Apr. 21 | Cancer |
|---|---|
| Apr. 22 — June 19 | Leo |
| June 20 — Aug. 8 | Virgo |
| Aug. 9 — Sept. 23 | Libra |
| Sept. 24 — Nov. 5 | Scorpio |
| Nov. 6 — Dec. 16 | Sagittarius |
| Dec. 17 — Dec. 31 | Capricorn |

**1947**

| Jan. 1 — Jan. 24 | Capricorn |
|---|---|
| Jan. 25 — Mar. 3 | Aquarius |
| Mar. 4 — Apr. 10 | Pisces |
| Apr. 11 — May 20 | Aries |
| May 21 — June 30 | Taurus |
| July 1 — Aug. 12 | Gemini |
| Aug. 13 — Sept. 30 | Cancer |
| Oct. 1 — Nov. 30 | Leo |
| Dec. 1 — Dec. 31 | Virgo |

**1948**

| Jan. 1 — Feb. 11 | Virgo |
|---|---|
| Feb. 12 — May 17 | Leo |
| May 18 — July 16 | Virgo |
| July 17 — Sept. 2 | Libra |
| Sept. 3 — Oct. 16 | Scorpio |
| Oct. 17 — Nov. 25 | Sagittarius |
| Nov. 26 — Dec. 31 | Capricorn |

| 1949 Date | Zodiacal Sign |
|---|---|
| Jan. 1 — Jan. 3 | Capricorn |
| Jan. 4 — Feb. 10 | Aquarius |
| Feb. 11 — Mar. 20 | Pisces |
| Mar. 21 — Apr. 29 | Aries |
| Apr. 30 — June 9 | Taurus |
| June 10 — July 22 | Gemini |
| July 23 — Sept. 6 | Cancer |
| Sept. 7 — Oct. 26 | Leo |
| Oct. 27 — Dec. 25 | Virgo |
| Dec. 26 — Dec. 31 | Libra |

### 1950

| | |
|---|---|
| Jan. 1 — Mar. 27 | Libra |
| Mar. 28 — June 10 | Virgo |
| June 11 — Aug. 9 | Libra |
| Aug. 10 — Sept. 24 | Scorpio |
| Sept. 25 — Nov. 5 | Sagittarius |
| Nov. 6 — Dec. 14 | Capricorn |
| Dec. 15 — Dec. 31 | Aquarius |

### 1951

| | |
|---|---|
| Jan. 1 — Jan. 21 | Aquarius |
| Jan. 22 — Feb. 28 | Pisces |
| Mar. 1 — Apr. 9 | Aries |
| Apr. 10 — May 20 | Taurus |
| May 21 — July 2 | Gemini |
| July 3 — Aug. 17 | Cancer |
| Aug. 18 — Oct. 3 | Leo |
| Oct. 4 — Nov. 23 | Virgo |
| Nov. 24 — Dec. 31 | Libra |

### 1952

| | |
|---|---|
| Jan. 1 — Jan. 19 | Libra |
| Jan. 20 — Aug. 26 | Scorpio |
| Aug. 27 — Oct. 11 | Sagittarius |
| Oct. 12 — Nov. 20 | Capricorn |
| Nov. 21 — Dec. 29 | Aquarius |
| Dec. 30 — Dec. 31 | Pisces |

### 1953

| | |
|---|---|
| Jan. 1 — Feb. 7 | Pisces |
| Feb. 8 — Mar. 19 | Aries |
| Mar. 20 — Apr. 30 | Taurus |
| May 1 — June 13 | Gemini |
| June 14 — July 28 | Cancer |
| July 29 — Sept. 13 | Leo |
| Sept. 14 — Oct. 31 | Virgo |
| Nov. 1 — Dec. 19 | Libra |
| Dec. 20 — Dec. 31 | Scorpio |

| 1954 Date | Zodiacal Sign |
|---|---|
| Jan. 1 — Feb. 8 | Scorpio |
| Feb. 9 — Apr. 11 | Sagittarius |
| Apr. 12 — July 2 | Capricorn |
| July 3 — Aug. 23 | Sagittarius |
| Aug. 24 — Oct. 20 | Capricorn |
| Oct. 21 — Dec. 3 | Aquarius |
| Dec. 4 — Dec. 31 | Pisces |

### 1955

| | |
|---|---|
| Jan. 1 — Jan. 14 | Pisces |
| Jan. 15 — Feb. 25 | Aries |
| Feb. 26 — Apr. 9 | Taurus |
| Apr. 10 — May 25 | Gemini |
| May 26 — July 10 | Cancer |
| July 11 — Aug. 26 | Leo |
| Aug. 27 — Oct. 12 | Virgo |
| Oct. 13 — Nov. 28 | Libra |
| Nov. 29 — Dec. 31 | Scorpio |

### 1956

| | |
|---|---|
| Jan. 1 — Jan. 13 | Scorpio |
| Jan. 14 — Feb. 27 | Sagittarius |
| Feb. 28 — Apr. 13 | Capricorn |
| Apr. 14 — June 2 | Aquarius |
| June 3 — Dec. 5 | Pisces |
| Dec. 6 — Dec. 31 | Aries |

### 1957

| | |
|---|---|
| Jan. 1 — Feb. 27 | Aries |
| Feb. 28 — Mar. 16 | Taurus |
| Mar. 17 — May 3 | Gemini |
| May 4 — June 20 | Cancer |
| June 21 — Aug. 7 | Leo |
| Aug. 8 — Sept. 23 | Virgo |
| Sept. 24 — Nov. 7 | Libra |
| Nov. 8 — Dec. 22 | Scorpio |
| Dec. 23 — Dec. 31 | Sagittarius |

### 1958

| | |
|---|---|
| Jan. 1 — Feb. 2 | Sagittarius |
| Feb. 3 — Mar. 16 | Capricorn |
| Mar. 17 — Apr. 26 | Aquarius |
| Apr. 27 — June 6 | Pisces |
| June 7 — July 20 | Aries |
| July 21 — Sept. 20 | Taurus |
| Sept. 21 — Oct. 28 | Gemini |
| Oct. 29 — Dec. 31 | Taurus |

| 1959 Date | Zodiacal Sign |
|---|---|
| Jan. 1 — Feb. 9 | Taurus |
| Feb. 10 — Apr. 9 | Gemini |
| Apr. 10 — May 31 | Cancer |
| June 1 — July 19 | Leo |
| July 20 — Sept. 4 | Virgo |
| Sept. 5 — Oct. 20 | Libra |
| Oct. 21 — Dec. 2 | Scorpio |
| Dec. 3 — Dec. 31 | Sagittarius |

**1960**

| | |
|---|---|
| Jan. 1 — Jan. 13 | Sagittarius |
| Jan. 14 — Feb. 22 | Capricorn |
| Feb. 23 — Apr. 1 | Aquarius |
| Apr. 2 — May 10 | Pisces |
| May 11 — June 19 | Aries |
| June 20 — Aug. 1 | Taurus |
| Aug. 2 — Sept. 20 | Gemini |
| Sept. 21 — Dec. 31 | Cancer |

**1961**

| | |
|---|---|
| Jan. 1 — May 5 | Cancer |
| May 6 — June 27 | Leo |
| June 28 — Aug. 16 | Virgo |
| Aug. 17 — Sept. 30 | Libra |
| Oct. 1 — Nov. 12 | Scorpio |
| Nov. 13 — Dec. 23 | Sagittarius |
| Dec. 24 — Dec. 31 | Capricorn |

**1962**

| | |
|---|---|
| Jan. 1 — Jan. 31 | Capricorn |
| Feb. 1 — Mar. 11 | Aquarius |
| Mar. 12 — Apr. 18 | Pisces |
| Apr. 19 — May 27 | Aries |
| May 28 — July 8 | Taurus |
| July 9 — Aug. 21 | Gemini |
| Aug. 22 — Oct. 10 | Cancer |
| Oct. 11 — Dec. 31 | Leo |

**1963**

| | |
|---|---|
| Jan. 1 — June 2 | Leo |
| June 3 — July 26 | Virgo |
| July 27 — Sept. 11 | Libra |
| Sept. 12 — Oct. 24 | Scorpio |
| Oct. 25 — Dec. 4 | Sagittarius |
| Dec. 5 — Dec. 31 | Capricorn |

| 1964 Date | Zodiacal Sign |
|---|---|
| Jan. 1 — Jan. 12 | Capricorn |
| Jan. 13 — Feb. 19 | Aquarius |
| Feb. 20 — Mar. 28 | Pisces |
| Mar. 29 — May 6 | Aries |
| May 7 — June 16 | Taurus |
| June 17 — July 29 | Gemini |
| July 30 — Sept. 14 | Cancer |
| Sept. 15 — Nov. 5 | Leo |
| Nov. 6 — Dec. 31 | Virgo |

**1965**

| | |
|---|---|
| Jan. 1 — June 28 | Virgo |
| June 29 — Aug. 19 | Libra |
| Aug. 20 — Oct. 3 | Scorpio |
| Oct. 4 — Nov. 13 | Sagittarius |
| Nov. 14 — Dec. 22 | Capricorn |
| Dec. 23 — Dec. 31 | Aquarius |

**1966**

| | |
|---|---|
| Jan. 1 — Jan. 29 | Aquarius |
| Jan. 30 — Mar. 8 | Pisces |
| Mar. 9 — Apr. 16 | Aries |
| Apr. 17 — May 27 | Taurus |
| May 28 — July 10 | Gemini |
| July 11 — Aug. 24 | Cancer |
| Aug. 25 — Oct. 11 | Leo |
| Oct. 12 — Dec. 3 | Virgo |
| Dec. 4 — Dec. 31 | Libra |

**1967**

| | |
|---|---|
| Jan. 1 — Feb. 11 | Libra |
| Feb. 12 — Mar. 31 | Scorpio |
| Apr. 1 — July 18 | Libra |
| July 19 — Sept. 9 | Scorpio |
| Sept. 10 — Oct. 22 | Sagittarius |
| Oct. 23 — Nov. 30 | Capricorn |
| Dec. 1 — Dec. 31 | Aquarius |

**1968**

| | |
|---|---|
| Jan. 1 — Jan. 8 | Aquarius |
| Jan. 9 — Feb. 16 | Pisces |
| Feb. 17 — Mar. 26 | Aries |
| Mar. 27 — May 7 | Taurus |
| May 8 — June 20 | Gemini |
| June 21 — Aug. 4 | Cancer |
| Aug. 5 — Sept. 20 | Leo |
| Sept. 21 — Oct. 8 | Virgo |
| Oct. 9 — Dec. 28 | Libra |
| Dec. 29 — Dec. 31 | Scorpio |

| 1969 Date | Zodiacal Sign | 1970 Date | Zodiacal Sign |
|-----------|---------------|-----------|---------------|
| Jan. 1 — Feb. 24 | Scorpio | Jan. 1 — Jan. 23 | Pisces |
| Feb. 25 — Sept. 20 | Sagittarius | Jan. 24 — Mar. 6 | Aries |
| Sept. 21 — Nov. 3 | Capricorn | Mar. 7 — Apr. 17 | Taurus |
| Nov. 4 — Dec. 13 | Aquarius | Apr. 18 — June 1 | Gemini |
| Dec. 14 — Dec. 31 | Pisces | June 2 — July 17 | Cancer |
| | | July 18 — Sept. 2 | Leo |
| | | Sept. 3 — Oct. 19 | Virgo |
| | | Oct. 20 — Dec. 5 | Libra |
| | | Dec. 6 — Dec. 31 | Scorpio |

*If I am to marry rich,*
*Let me hear a cock crow.*
*If I am to marry poor,*
*Let me hear a hammer blow.*

Fame and fortune, generosity, honors, fulfillment of ambitions, good luck—all of these are bestowed by the beneficent planet Jupiter when it is well aspected—even the happy endings to love affairs. Whereas the moon is involved with the subconscious, Jupiter signifies the superconsciousness. Emotions are expanded in scope, we are enabled understanding of the causes underlying things and man is greater able to develop his fineness of character through Jupiter's beneficial rays.

JUPITER IN ARIES: You're full of big ideas and, what's more, they work out. You travel a lot and know how to implement your dynamic plans in a subdued way that is never unpleasant to those around you, including your loved one.

JUPITER IN TAURUS: You're impressed with exteriors and always put a lot into yours because you're endowed with the ability to make lots of money. You're generous and share the bounty with your partner.

JUPITER IN GEMINI: You're blessed with a keen intellect, would make a good writer, love change and moving about, and are quite a pleasant person to be around. Your happy love life bears witness to this.

JUPITER IN CANCER: You love the home and family and that is where your greatest expression of love takes place. You're deeply romantic and emotional, a good combination for a good lover.

JUPITER IN LEO: You take a lot of pride in yourself and in your lover and/or wife and family. You love to go out and be seen with that special person and you make a good business leader, too.

JUPITER IN VIRGO: You're a tedious worker and make an excellent provider to your loved ones. You do well, like nice things and are very particular, especially in the romance area.

JUPITER IN LIBRA: You have great taste, are artistic, and a popular person with a good disposition. You're loyal in matters of marriage, generous and make a great asset as a partner in anything, especially the sack.

JUPITER IN SCORPIO: You're intuitive and philosophic and you know how to share your ideas in such a way that others can benefit by them, too. You're a clever person, perceptive and could have exceptional judicial capabilities. You're also a sexy, amorous lover.

JUPITER IN SAGITTARIUS: You're concerned with the good of others, like to know that everyone is happy, are fun to be around with your jovial, gregarious personality, love to travel and are often intuitive and successful in way-out business ventures. Can be an exciting love partner, too.

JUPITER IN CAPRICORN: You're very big with the "establishment" because you know how to make it in society, say the right things, dress right, and travel in the right circles. You're more likely a proponent of the "popular" view, nothing that's too freaky, but that will get you a lot of votes if you happen to be a politician—which you could be successfully. You're the ideal mate for someone who's looking to get loved and to get ahead, too.

JUPITER IN AQUARIUS: You're interested in social reform for the good of all mankind and will probably get actively involved in government or anything you can to instrument these changes. You know how to make friends in the right places to help make it possible. For anyone interested in a "humane" lover, you're it.

JUPITER IN PISCES: You really care about people and what's going on in the world but there may be an uptightness in you that makes you withdraw when it comes to really being effectual. You're good for anyone who's looking for sympathy, understanding and great love in their romantic partnership.

## HOW TO FIND THE PLACEMENT OF JUPITER AT THE TIME OF YOUR BIRTH

| Date | Zodiacal Sign |
|------|---------------|
| Jan. 1, 1890 to Feb. 24, 1890 | Capricorn |
| Feb. 25, 1890 to Mar. 7, 1891 | Aquarius |
| Mar. 8, 1891 to Mar. 16, 1892 | Pisces |
| Mar. 17, 1892 to Mar. 24, 1893 | Aries |
| Mar. 25, 1893 to Aug. 20, 1893 | Taurus |
| Aug. 21, 1893 to Oct. 19, 1893 | Gemini |
| Oct. 20, 1893 to Apr. 1, 1894 | Taurus |
| Apr. 2, 1894 to Aug. 18, 1894 | Gemini |
| Aug. 19, 1894 to Jan. 1, 1895 | Cancer |
| Jan. 2, 1895 to Apr. 10, 1895 | Gemini |
| Apr. 11, 1895 to Sept. 4, 1895 | Cancer |
| Sept. 5, 1895 to Feb. 29, 1896 | Leo |
| Mar. 1, 1896 to Apr. 17, 1896 | Cancer |
| Apr. 18, 1896 to Sept. 27, 1896 | Leo |
| Sept. 28, 1896 to Oct. 27, 1897 | Virgo |
| Oct. 28, 1897 to Nov. 26, 1898 | Libra |
| Nov. 27, 1898 to Dec. 25, 1899 | Scorpio |
| Dec. 26, 1899 to Jan. 18, 1901 | Sagittarius |
| Jan. 19, 1901 to Feb. 6, 1902 | Capricorn |
| Feb. 7, 1902 to Feb. 19, 1903 | Aquarius |
| Feb. 20, 1903 to Feb. 29, 1904 | Pisces |

| Date | Zodiacal Sign |
|---|---|
| Mar. 1, 1904 to Aug. 8, 1904 | Aries |
| Aug. 9, 1904 to Aug. 31, 1904 | Taurus |
| Sept. 1, 1904 to Mar. 7, 1905 | Aries |
| Mar. 8, 1905 to July 20, 1905 | Taurus |
| July 21, 1905 to Dec. 4, 1905 | Gemini |
| Dec. 5, 1905 to Mar. 9, 1906 | Taurus |
| Mar. 10, 1906 to July 30, 1906 | Gemini |
| July 31, 1906 to Aug. 18, 1907 | Cancer |
| Aug. 19, 1907 to Sept. 11, 1908 | Leo |
| Sept. 12, 1908 to Oct. 11, 1909 | Virgo |
| Oct. 12, 1909 to Nov. 11, 1910 | Libra |
| Nov. 12, 1910 to Dec. 9, 1911 | Scorpio |
| Dec. 10, 1911 to Jan. 2, 1913 | Sagittarius |
| Jan. 3, 1913 to Jan. 21, 1914 | Capricorn |
| Jan. 22, 1914 to Feb. 3, 1915 | Aquarius |
| Feb. 4, 1915 to Feb. 11, 1916 | Pisces |
| Feb. 12, 1916 to June 25, 1916 | Aries |
| June 26, 1916 to Oct. 26, 1916 | Taurus |
| Oct. 27, 1916 to Feb. 12, 1917 | Aries |
| Feb. 13, 1917 to June 29, 1917 | Taurus |
| June 30, 1917 to July 12, 1918 | Gemini |
| July 13, 1918 to Aug. 1, 1919 | Cancer |
| Aug. 2, 1919 to Aug. 26, 1920 | Leo |
| Aug. 27, 1920 to Sept. 25, 1921 | Virgo |
| Sept. 26, 1921 to Oct. 26, 1922 | Libra |
| Oct. 27, 1922 to Nov. 24, 1923 | Scorpio |
| Nov. 25, 1923 to Dec. 17, 1924 | Sagittarius |
| Dec. 18, 1924 to Jan. 5, 1926 | Capricorn |
| Jan. 6, 1926 to Jan. 17, 1927 | Aquarius |
| Jan. 18, 1927 to June 5, 1927 | Pisces |
| June 6, 1927 to Sept. 10, 1927 | Aries |
| Sept. 11, 1927 to Jan. 22, 1928 | Pisces |
| Jan. 23, 1928 to June 3, 1928 | Aries |
| June 4, 1928 to June 11, 1929 | Taurus |
| June 12, 1929 to June 26, 1930 | Gemini |
| June 27, 1930 to July 16, 1931 | Cancer |
| July 17, 1931 to Aug. 10, 1932 | Leo |
| Aug. 11, 1932 to Sept. 9, 1933 | Virgo |
| Sept. 10, 1933 to Oct. 10, 1934 | Libra |
| Oct. 11, 1934 to Nov. 8, 1935 | Scorpio |
| Nov. 9, 1935 to Dec. 1, 1936 | Sagittarius |
| Dec. 2, 1936 to Dec. 19, 1937 | Capricorn |

| Date | Zodiacal Sign |
|------|---------------|
| Dec. 20, 1937 to May 13, 1938 | Aquarius |
| May 14, 1938 to July 29, 1938 | Pisces |
| July 30, 1938 to Dec. 28, 1938 | Aquarius |
| Dec. 29, 1938 to May 10, 1939 | Pisces |
| May 11, 1939 to Oct. 29, 1939 | Aries |
| Oct. 30, 1939 to Dec. 19, 1939 | Pisces |
| Dec. 20, 1939 to May 15, 1940 | Aries |
| May 16, 1940 to May 25, 1941 | Taurus |
| May 26, 1941 to June 9, 1942 | Gemini |
| June 10, 1942 to June 29, 1943 | Cancer |
| June 30, 1943 to July 25, 1944 | Leo |
| July 26, 1944 to Aug. 24, 1945 | Virgo |
| Aug. 25, 1945 to Sept. 24, 1946 | Libra |
| Sept. 25, 1946 to Oct. 23, 1947 | Scorpio |
| Oct. 24, 1947 to Nov. 14, 1948 | Sagittarius |
| Nov. 15, 1948 to Apr. 11, 1949 | Capricorn |
| Apr. 12, 1949 to June 26, 1949 | Aquarius |
| June 27, 1949 to Nov. 29, 1949 | Capricorn |
| Nov. 30, 1949 to Apr. 14, 1950 | Aquarius |
| Apr. 15, 1950 to Sept. 14, 1950 | Pisces |
| Sept. 15, 1950 to Dec. 1, 1950 | Aquarius |
| Dec. 2, 1950 to Apr. 20, 1951 | Pisces |
| Apr. 21, 1951 to Apr. 27, 1952 | Aries |
| Apr. 28, 1952 to May 8, 1953 | Taurus |
| May 9, 1953 to May 23, 1954 | Gemini |
| May 24, 1954 to June 11, 1955 | Cancer |
| June 12, 1955 to Nov. 16, 1955 | Leo |
| Nov. 17, 1955 to Jan. 17, 1956 | Virgo |
| Jan. 18, 1956 to July 6, 1956 | Leo |
| July 7, 1956 to Dec. 11, 1956 | Virgo |
| Dec. 12, 1956 to Feb. 18, 1957 | Libra |
| Feb. 19, 1957 to Aug. 5, 1957 | Virgo |
| Aug. 6, 1957 to Jan. 12, 1958 | Libra |
| Jan. 13, 1958 to Mar. 19, 1958 | Scorpio |
| Mar. 20, 1958 to Sept. 6, 1958 | Libra |
| Sept. 7, 1958 to Feb. 9, 1959 | Scorpio |
| Feb. 10, 1959 to Apr. 23, 1959 | Sagittarius |
| Apr. 24, 1959 to Oct. 4, 1959 | Scorpio |
| Oct. 5, 1959 to Feb. 29, 1960 | Sagittarius |
| Mar. 1, 1960 to June 9, 1960 | Capricorn |
| June 10, 1960 to Oct. 24, 1960 | Sagittarius |
| Oct. 25, 1960 to Mar. 14, 1961 | Capricorn |

| Date | Zodiacal Sign |
| --- | --- |
| Mar. 15, 1961 to Aug. 11, 1961 | Aquarius |
| Aug. 12, 1961 to Nov. 3, 1961 | Capricorn |
| Nov. 4, 1961 to Mar. 24, 1962 | Aquarius |
| Mar. 25, 1962 to Apr. 3, 1963 | Pisces |
| Apr. 4, 1963 to Apr. 11, 1964 | Aries |
| Apr. 12, 1964 to Apr. 21, 1965 | Taurus |
| Apr. 22, 1965 to Sept. 20, 1965 | Gemini |
| Sept. 21, 1965 to Nov. 16, 1965 | Cancer |
| Nov. 17, 1965 to May 4, 1966 | Gemini |
| May 5, 1966 to Sept. 26, 1966 | Cancer |
| Sept. 27, 1966 to Jan. 15, 1967 | Leo |
| Jan. 16, 1967 to May 22, 1967 | Cancer |
| May 23, 1967 to Oct. 18, 1967 | Leo |
| Oct. 19, 1967 to Feb. 26, 1968 | Virgo |
| Feb. 27, 1968 to June 14, 1968 | Leo |
| June 15, 1968 to Nov. 14, 1968 | Virgo |
| Nov. 15, 1968 to Mar. 29, 1969 | Libra |
| Mar. 30, 1969 to July 14, 1969 | Virgo |
| July 15, 1969 to Dec. 15, 1969 | Libra |
| Dec. 16, 1969 to Apr. 29, 1970 | Scorpio |
| Apr. 30, 1970 to Aug. 14, 1970 | Libra |
| Aug. 15, 1970 to Dec. 31, 1970 | Scorpio |

*The rats and the mice,*
*They made such a strife,*
*I was forc'd to go to*
*London, to buy me a wife.*

Saturn governs form and organization, in a paternal and often stern way, and represents the main factor of destiny in our lives. It is the great reaper, the lord of time, trying us often seemingly beyond our endurance. Tough a taskmaster as it is, one who has built his foundation solidly will be little shaken by Saturn, and one whose foundations are weak can profit from the hard lessons Saturn gives. Saturn is the great builder, the least understood planet in astrology. People often lose their patience regarding Saturn and tend to blame all adverse circumstances on its "negative influence." This is a misnomer, as Saturn should actually be looked upon as a blessing, for it is like a loving but stern father looking out for his child, wanting the child to profit from his own mistakes. In the love and romance area, it is Venus that will see to it that we attract a mate, but it is the character-building influence of Saturn that will help us to keep him or her.

SATURN IN ARIES: This tempers some of your innate irrationality and erratic qualities, helping you to apply all your genius and inventiveness to practical ventures. Brings your lovemaking habits more down-to-earth, too.

SATURN IN TAURUS: You can be stubborn but you're a tenacious sort of a beast. You're thrifty and not the wildest of lovers unless all is up with you and you're doing well financially.

**SATURN IN GEMINI:** Saturn's restrictions do not set well in Gemini. You can be a difficult, brooding person to be around. You probably look to your lover to pick you up.

**SATURN IN CANCER:** Here again, the home is affected, where you may find yourself limited in many ways; it can be financially or in your ability to relate to others emotionally. Makes it difficult for your partner.

**SATURN IN LEO:** You have great pride, sometimes too great, and because of it may be misunderstood in the romance department. Could make you miss out altogether. Limitations also are expressed here through family and children.

**SATURN IN VIRGO:** Because you're so intolerant of others, you're penalized often by other people's intolerance, especially your love partner's. Your accomplishments often go unrecognized and your greatest restriction occurs in the way you're underrated and underestimated in your profession.

**SATURN IN LIBRA:** Your greatest unhappiness takes place during your marriage or within any other partnership. You may find yourself with a mate who deprives you of your most basic pleasure—love. He or she could also be jealous or tyrannical.

**SATURN IN SCORPIO:** You're psychic, and have a great understanding of life and the afterlife. Unfortunately you often have to go through great suffering, such as a loss of your family, friends or loved one, perhaps even through death, in order to accomplish this. Your wisdom is tempered by your heartbreaking experiences but it leaves you a bit shopworn toward the end. Hope it's not too late by then.

**SATURN IN SAGITTARIUS:** Saturn gives a feeling of dependability and responsibility to all those wild, adventurous thoughts for which you're famous, and your philosophical bent may reap tangible fruits such as a book or two on your new school of religious thought. Can be a good mate for someone equally intellectual and far out.

SATURN IN CAPRICORN: You always achieve your goal, but it reaps you unpopularity and it's doubtful sometimes whether it's all worth it. Find a partner as seething with ambition as yourself to understand where you're at. No one else ever will.

SATURN IN AQUARIUS: Your dreams of revolutionizing the political scene to bring peace, goodwill and prosperity to all peoples have been thought of before and your ambition may be thwarted as others' have been. However, don't be disappointed or frustrated for your lover will lick your wounds as soon as you get home from the "march."

SATURN IN PISCES: This can be grim, full of melancholy and withdrawal. You think people are out to get you, and often they really are; you suffer early loss of family and loved ones and although you're psychic a lot of the time, you aren't even interested in knowing about your own prophecies about the future, it's all so dreary. Sure can be a drag for a love partner who's less than supersympathetic.

## HOW TO FIND THE PLACEMENT OF SATURN AT THE TIME OF YOUR BIRTH

| Date | Zodiacal Sign |
|------|---------------|
| Jan. 1, 1890 to Jan. 23, 1890 | Virgo |
| Jan. 24, 1890 to June 27, 1890 | Leo |
| June 28, 1890 to Dec. 26, 1891 | Virgo |
| Dec. 27, 1891 to Jan. 22, 1892 | Libra |
| Jan. 23, 1892 to Aug. 28, 1892 | Virgo |
| Aug. 29, 1892 to Nov. 6, 1894 | Libra |
| Nov. 7, 1894 to Feb. 6, 1897 | Scorpio |
| Feb. 7, 1897 to Apr. 9, 1897 | Sagittarius |
| Apr. 10, 1897 to Oct. 26, 1897 | Scorpio |
| Oct. 27, 1897 to Jan. 20, 1900 | Sagittarius |

| Date | Zodiacal Sign |
|------|---------------|
| Jan. 21, 1900 to July 18, 1900 | Capricorn |
| July 19, 1900 to Oct. 16, 1900 | Sagittarius |
| Oct. 17, 1900 to Jan. 19, 1903 | Capricorn |
| Jan. 20, 1903 to Apr. 12, 1905 | Aquarius |
| Apr. 13, 1905 to Aug. 16, 1905 | Pisces |
| Aug. 17, 1905 to Jan. 7, 1906 | Aquarius |
| Jan. 8, 1906 to Mar. 18, 1908 | Pisces |
| Mar. 19, 1908 to May 16, 1910 | Aries |
| May 17, 1910 to Dec. 14, 1910 | Taurus |
| Dec. 15, 1910 to Jan. 19, 1911 | Aries |
| Jan. 20, 1911 to July 6, 1912 | Taurus |
| July 7, 1912 to Nov. 30, 1912 | Gemini |
| Dec. 1, 1912 to Mar. 25, 1913 | Taurus |
| Mar. 26, 1913 to Aug. 24, 1914 | Gemini |
| Aug. 25, 1914 to Dec. 6, 1914 | Cancer |
| Dec. 7, 1914 to May 11, 1915 | Gemini |
| May 12, 1915 to Oct. 16, 1916 | Cancer |
| Oct. 17, 1916 to Dec. 7, 1916 | Leo |
| Dec. 8, 1916 to June 23, 1917 | Cancer |
| June 24, 1917 to Aug. 11, 1919 | Leo |
| Aug. 12, 1919 to Oct. 7, 1921 | Virgo |
| Oct. 8, 1921 to Dec. 19, 1923 | Libra |
| Dec. 20, 1923 to Apr. 5, 1924 | Scorpio |
| Apr. 6, 1924 to Sept. 13, 1924 | Libra |
| Sept. 14, 1924 to Dec. 2, 1926 | Scorpio |
| Dec. 3, 1926 to Mar. 29, 1929 | Sagittarius |
| Mar. 30, 1929 to May 4, 1929 | Capricorn |
| May 5, 1929 to Nov. 29, 1929 | Sagittarius |
| Nov. 30, 1929 to Feb. 22, 1932 | Capricorn |
| Feb. 23, 1932 to Aug. 12, 1932 | Aquarius |
| Aug. 13, 1932 to Nov. 18, 1932 | Capricorn |
| Nov. 19, 1932 to Feb. 13, 1935 | Aquarius |
| Feb. 14, 1935 to Apr. 24, 1937 | Pisces |
| Apr. 25, 1937 to Oct. 17, 1937 | Aries |
| Oct. 18, 1937 to Jan. 13, 1938 | Pisces |
| Jan. 14, 1938 to July 5, 1939 | Aries |
| July 6, 1939 to Sept. 21, 1939 | Taurus |
| Sept. 22, 1939 to Mar. 19, 1940 | Aries |
| Mar. 20, 1940 to May 7, 1942 | Taurus |
| May 8, 1942 to June 19, 1944 | Gemini |
| June 20, 1944 to Aug. 1, 1946 | Cancer |
| Aug. 2, 1946 to Sept. 18, 1948 | Leo |

| Date | Zodiacal Sign |
|------|---------------|
| Sept. 19, 1948 to Apr. 2, 1949 | Virgo |
| Apr. 3, 1949 to May 28, 1949 | Leo |
| May 29, 1949 to Nov. 19, 1950 | Virgo |
| Nov. 20, 1950 to Mar. 6, 1951 | Libra |
| Mar. 7, 1951 to Aug. 12, 1951 | Virgo |
| Aug. 13, 1951 to Oct. 21, 1953 | Libra |
| Oct. 22, 1953 to Jan. 11, 1956 | Scorpio |
| Jan. 12, 1956 to May 13, 1956 | Sagittarius |
| May 14, 1956 to Oct. 9, 1956 | Scorpio |
| Oct. 10, 1956 to Jan. 4, 1959 | Sagittarius |
| Jan. 5, 1959 to Jan. 9, 1962 | Capricorn |
| Jan. 10, 1962 to Dec. 16, 1964 | Aquarius |
| Dec. 17, 1964 to Mar. 2, 1967 | Pisces |
| Mar. 3, 1967 to Apr. 28, 1969 | Aries |
| Apr. 29, 1969 thru 1970 | Taurus |

*Jack and Jill*
*Went up the Hill,*
  *To fetch a Pail of Water;*
*Jack fell down*
*And broke his Crown,*
  *And Jill came tumbling after.*

Uranus, the revolutionary planet, is often known as the great upsetter, so determined is it to never let one condition endure for too long. It believes the old must give way to the new, that outworn values must be changed and replaced with those more timely. Under Uranus' influence great upheavals can occur overnight. It gives us insight into the laws of nature, often spreading its understanding in flashes, sometimes drastic and even disastrous. Resplendent with new and fascinating experiences which may lead to expansion of outlook, full of sudden changes in environment, Uranus is the innovator, the planet of electricity, and no wrong can ever stay hidden too long; when necessary Uranus will cause whole lifetime fabrics to collapse. When this happens it is usually because that fabric was essentially wrongly woven to begin with. Remember this when considering all the changes going on in our society today, and also that as far as the sexual and political revolution is concerned, the masses always resist change. Such Uranian inspired innovations as electricity and the horseless carriage which are commonplace today were catastrophic a few years ago. So rest assured that what's blowing people's minds today will be taken for granted as "establishment" values tomorrow.

URANUS IN ARIES: You are often difficult for your loved one to understand, as you're spontaneous in your actions,

163

quick, inventive in your thinking. You're adventuresome and like the unexpected. Careful that you don't get too far ahead of things. You may find it lonesome out there.

URANUS IN TAURUS: You're a restless lover, and apt to change careers often, too. You're temperamental, which accounts for these upsets and erratic changes. Watch unexpected financial upheavals.

URANUS IN GEMINI: You're on the move a lot, in your romances, too. You're difficult to understand, maybe because you're intellectually so far ahead of everybody else. Could prove very lonely for you, though.

URANUS IN CANCER: The unpredictable events of this aspect occur in the home, where you may have an eccentric living with you. Your mate, perhaps? Well, you're patient and imaginative so you should be able to deal with it.

URANUS IN LEO: You're impulsive, original, and like spur-of-the-moment affairs. The unpredictable in your life is often yourself. You're inventive and get good business hunches. Follow them through.

URANUS IN VIRGO: Here the unexpected occurs in your line of business. Love at the office, anyone? Let's hope it's something pleasant like that. It won't hinder your astuteness and dependability as an employee.

URANUS IN LIBRA: You get it in marriage or a partnership—the unexpected, that is. Watch out for things going haywire, though. You may spend some time in court but with your mental dexterity you'll give them a run for their money.

URANUS IN SCORPIO: You're secretive, intuitive and might even go so far as being psychic. You get a lot of the unexpected throughout your life, and so does your mate. Maybe he or she turns out to be a surprise. Or could it be you?

URANUS IN SAGITTARIUS: You travel a lot, are outdoorsy, inventive, creative and have advanced theories and philosophies on a lot of things, yet you're exceptionally traditional in the romance area.

URANUS IN CAPRICORN: Something unexpected may happen to you in your work, too. And depending on your profession, it may have a resounding effect on the rest of the world. Your ideas may be offbeat; however, your lover is not.

URANUS IN AQUARIUS: You'll apply your unexpected ideas to the betterment of society or in business. You have interesting—although a bit strange—friends. And out of this weird assortment, one is your partner. Sounds like it could be more a shock than a surprise, doesn't it? Expect a lot of unusual experiences in view of all this.

URANUS IN PISCES: You're extremely psychic, and about your love affairs, too. You'll spot him or her right off the bat. You get premonitions about him or her and about the world around you, too, and they're usually correct.

### HOW TO FIND THE PLACEMENT OF URANUS AT THE TIME OF YOUR BIRTH

| Date | Zodiacal Sign |
|------|---------------|
| Jan. 1, 1890 to Dec. 9, 1890 | Libra |
| Dec. 10, 1890 to Apr. 4, 1891 | Scorpio |
| Apr. 5, 1891 to Sept. 25, 1891 | Libra |
| Sept. 26, 1891 to Dec. 1, 1897 | Scorpio |
| Dec. 2, 1897 to July 3, 1898 | Sagittarius |
| July 4, 1898 to Sept. 10, 1898 | Scorpio |
| Sept. 11, 1898 to Dec. 19, 1904 | Sagittarius |
| Dec. 20, 1904 to Jan. 30, 1912 | Capricorn |
| Jan. 31, 1912 to Sept. 4, 1912 | Aquarius |
| Sept. 5, 1912 to Nov. 11, 1912 | Capricorn |
| Nov. 12, 1912 to Mar. 31, 1919 | Aquarius |
| Apr. 1, 1919 to Aug. 16, 1919 | Pisces |
| Aug. 17, 1919 to Jan. 21, 1920 | Aquarius |

| Date | Zodiacal Sign |
|------|---------------|
| Jan. 22, 1920 to Mar. 30, 1927 | Pisces |
| Mar. 31, 1927 to Nov. 4, 1927 | Aries |
| Nov. 5, 1927 to Jan. 12, 1928 | Pisces |
| Jan. 13, 1928 to June 6, 1934 | Aries |
| June 7, 1934 to Oct. 9, 1934 | Taurus |
| Oct. 10, 1934 to Mar. 28, 1935 | Aries |
| Mar. 29, 1935 to Aug. 6, 1941 | Taurus |
| Aug. 7, 1941 to Oct. 4, 1941 | Gemini |
| Oct. 5, 1941 to May 13, 1942 | Taurus |
| May 14, 1942 to Aug. 29, 1948 | Gemini |
| Aug. 30, 1948 to Nov. 11, 1948 | Cancer |
| Nov. 12, 1948 to June 9, 1949 | Gemini |
| June 10, 1949 to Aug. 23, 1955 | Cancer |
| Aug. 24, 1955 to Jan. 27, 1956 | Leo |
| Jan. 28, 1956 to June 8, 1956 | Cancer |
| June 9, 1956 to Oct. 31, 1961 | Leo |
| Nov. 1, 1961 to Jan. 11, 1962 | Virgo |
| Jan. 12, 1962 to Aug. 8, 1962 | Leo |
| Aug. 9, 1962 to Sept. 27, 1968 | Virgo |
| Sept. 28, 1968 to May 20, 1969 | Libra |
| May 21, 1969 to June 23, 1969 | Virgo |
| June 24, 1969 to Dec. 15, 1974 | Libra |

*Of all the sayings in the world*
*The one to see you through*
*Is, Never trouble trouble*
*Till trouble troubles you.*

Intuitive, sensitive, imaginative, those favorably aspected with Neptune's rays are mystics, dreamers, lovers of beauty and art, who are often involved in occupations that are ethereal and creative with an element of unreality such as painting, acting, space exploration, research or photography. Whereas Uranus inspires us with flashes of insight, it is Neptune that gives us the completed vision, and enables us to bring it into concrete reality. All great poets are Neptunian people as it is this planet that bestows one with the whole vast concept of a novel, a work of music or a poem. Neptune is known for the dissolving of boundaries and enormous expansion; successful businessmen have strong Neptunian aspects, for its favorable rays often endow them with the ability of knowing when to buy and sell at the right moment and great intuition in making instantaneous judgments. Neptune can be very helpful when it comes to picking out a love that will last a lifetime.

NEPTUNE IN TAURUS, 1874–1887: Sometimes oversensitive in your love life, you have good instincts for making money in business. You're into new concepts in both the material and art worlds and into advancements in the occult before anyone else is.

NEPTUNE IN GEMINI, 1887–1901: During this period of restlessness there was increased intellectual activity and the occult became more aptly expressed in books. You, too, probably feel an urge for changes as well as a desire for new ideals in commerce, communications and trade.

NEPTUNE IN CANCER, 1901–1915: This was a period of further nurturing of mysticism and the occult. You're probably sensitive, emotional and prone to be interested in the arts and the psychic sciences.

NEPTUNE IN LEO, 1915–1929: This period brought about new conditions in government. For the native, it tends to give you a restlessness, a lack of stability in love and a distaste for authority. You're eager for change but try to take your loved one into consideration when you go about drastically upsetting and redoing old conditions.

NEPTUNE IN VIRGO, 1929–1943: You're probably the metaphysical type as this was a period of great growth in the New Thought movements such as Science of Mind. There was also an increase in new concepts in health, diet, art and public service. Kind of like now.

NEPTUNE IN LIBRA, 1943–1956: This aspect is responsible for new ideas regarding marriage, which the hippies, a lot of whom were born during this period, seem to be bearing out. These strange alliances carry over onto a national level, too.

NEPTUNE IN SCORPIO, 1956–1970: A highly interesting time, when great technological progress is made, man reaches out to the planets and arrives on the moon, a time of great consciousness-expansion, progress in chemistry and science, but without much foresight into pollution, depletion of natural resources and other havoc being played with the environment that the coming generations will inevitably have to deal with.

Of course we can attribute a lot of the sex revolution going on right now to this Scorpian aspect, too, as it rules the genitalia. If we think the generation that came in during the '43 to '56 period is far out, wait until this one really gets its thing together.

NEPTUNE IN SAGITTARIUS, 1970–1984: Well, the pendulum swings both ways and this period will bring us new types of religion, added religious zeal, a further expansion of consciousness, desires for all kinds of exploration, revolutionary ideas of government and philosophy—just about everything that Orwell predicted.

NEPTUNE IN CAPRICORN, 1984–1996: Lots of the great concepts everyone's been coming up with will be implemented in politics and international affairs. There'll generally be a fuller amount of actualizing and realizing of goals and ambitions plus great revolutionary changes throughout the world. Throughout the ages, nothing seems as constant as change. What would we do without it?

## HOW TO FIND THE PLACEMENT OF NEPTUNE AT THE TIME OF YOUR BIRTH

| Date | Zodiacal Sign |
| --- | --- |
| Jan. 1, 1890 to July 19, 1901 | Gemini |
| July 20, 1901 to Dec. 25, 1901 | Cancer |
| Dec. 26, 1901 to May 19, 1902 | Gemini |
| May 20, 1902 to Sept. 22, 1914 | Cancer |
| Sept. 23, 1914 to Dec. 14, 1914 | Leo |
| Dec. 15, 1914 to July 18, 1915 | Cancer |
| July 19, 1915 to Mar. 19, 1916 | Leo |
| Mar. 20, 1916 to May 1, 1916 | Cancer |
| May 2, 1916 to Sept. 20, 1928 | Leo |
| Sept. 21, 1928 to Feb. 19, 1929 | Virgo |
| Feb. 20, 1929 to July 23, 1929 | Leo |
| July 24, 1929 to Oct. 3, 1942 | Virgo |
| Oct. 4, 1942 to Apr. 18, 1943 | Libra |
| Apr. 19, 1943 to Aug. 2, 1943 | Virgo |
| Aug. 3, 1943 to Dec. 22, 1955 | Libra |
| Dec. 23, 1955 to Mar. 10, 1956 | Scorpio |
| Mar. 11, 1956 to Oct. 18, 1956 | Libra |
| Oct. 19, 1956 to June 15, 1957 | Scorpio |
| June 16, 1957 to Aug. 4, 1957 | Libra |
| Aug. 5, 1957 to Mar. 4, 1970 | Scorpio |
| Mar. 5, 1970 to Aug. 10, 1970 | Sagittarius |
| Aug. 11, 1970 to Nov. 6, 1970 | Scorpio |

*There was a little girl,*
    *and she had a little curl*
*Right in the middle of her forehead;*

*When she was good,*
    *she was very, very good,*
*But when she was bad she was horrid.*

The mysterious and subterranean influence of the planet Pluto—though discovered as recently as March 13, 1930—has been felt in the world over the centuries. However, during the past few decades astrologers have been able to study the planet's forces to a greater extent and have come to see it as a major influence causing dramatic world changes.

Known as the "higher octave of Mars," Pluto is Latin for "the rich one." It traditionally rules the lower regions of the earth, the unknown, the dark forces breaking out into the light. It deals its bounties and blows in great measure and especially over the past and coming decades, its influence has and will continue to include areas of scientific discovery, atom smashing, excavation of the sea, cures from disease, and breakthroughs in the field of space exploration yet incomprehensible. Pluto symbolically means double-headed, exuding both life-giving and death-giving rays, and humanity in its evolution must experience both the negative and the positive vibrations of this planet—and all of them, for that matter.

Because this planet was so recently discovered its full impact will not be known to astrologers till perhaps the end of the century, so it would be presumptuous to try to summarize its effects upon the twelve signs yet. However, we do know several interesting facts about this fascinating planet and can generalize to a certain extent: It rules countries and

cities where ancient civilizations lie buried and where there
is volcanic or earthquake activity, such as Japan, Mexico,
Rome, Pompeii and San Francisco. We know that when Pluto
was in Gemini (from the years 1883 to 1914) it brought
about a cultivation of the intellect, a searching and inventiveness, good judgment, but also a feeling of unrest and of being
dual-natured and separated from the self. Pluto in Cancer
(1914–1938) gave conservatism to people and politics, a
perseverance, tenacity; it brought introspection, added intuition and a building upon old values, adapting them to new
times, coupled with a devotion to new causes, and a new
kind of subconscious awareness. When Pluto went into the
sign Leo around 1939 it brought dramatic world changes—
war, unrest and strife, heroism and bloodshed together with
increased scientific uncoverings. With Pluto now in the sign
of Virgo we can expect further mental changes and a gradual
cooling down. A greater balance and sense of world justice
will be achieved when Pluto enters the sign of Libra around
1972.

Some further investigations as to the nature of Pluto
reveal the following: its influence in a chart is greatest when
found in angular houses, which as you will remember, are
houses numbers one, four, seven and eleven. When Pluto and
Mars are aspected adversely to each other, extreme violence
can be the outcome, depending on the house and sign. In
spite of the revolutionary, often drastic nature of Pluto's
negative influence, if one looks prudently forward and stays
ahead of the game, one can avoid disaster and pursue a better
way of life.

If we're not aware, Pluto's influence often sneaks up on
us, until all of a sudden we perceive that changes have taken
place without our having been aware of them and we are
catapulted into reality. It's as if the changes that take place
under Pluto manifest themselves subconsciously and then
suddenly we consciously recognize them. When we look back
at crossroads in our lives, unrecognized at the time as such,
and see that a change of course of action could have altered
our whole life, a check of our progressions will probably
indicate that Pluto was transiting in a key position causing
this to happen.

Since Pluto is the planet of extremes, it can take us to the
heights of success and bliss or the depths of failure and ulti-

mate despair. As we said before, for the aware person, Pluto can be a constructive force of recognition. For others, less conscious, it can incite laziness and lethargy.

We have seen, and will continue to see, Pluto bringing us great revolutionary changes, unrest and strife. We can look upon this present age as a preparatory period in which upheavals, eruptions, fanaticism and revolutions will ultimately lead us to adopt new and more constructive modes of living. For instance, today the world has become increasingly aware of a sexual revolution which, while at first encompassing only small dimensions, soon burst forth to the worldwide proportions seen by the end of the sixties. So widespread has this revolution been that scarcely anyone has escaped its influence. Those with an upbringing tainted with Victorianism were shocked by the bold views the young flaunted; but by and large most people, aware that things are indeed "different" today than in the "olden days" have come around and are more tolerant and open about sexual matters than they had been previously.

Some planets have long-range effects on whole groups of people or nations, during a certain time. Uranus, for instance, stays in a sign seven years, Neptune fourteen years. Therefore a whole group of people will sometimes inherit a certain tendency. Those born with Pluto in Leo (1939–1957) comprise a lot of the young people who today are largely responsible for pioneering this new frankness and progressive attitude toward sex. They were the children of a group of hard-working, home-loving, conservative, short-haired people who were born with their Pluto in Cancer (1914–1938). More and more they are rejecting traditionally held values and creating new ones. That they sleep together and live together without benefit of clergy or state law sanction has become the rule rather than the exception. While premarital sex has always been in existence, never has it been dealt with as honestly as today. Young lovers make no bones about it, they live and love openly, with none of the old hypocrisy which once caused scandal, outrage, ostracism from society and a multitude of psychological problems with which to be dealt.

Time-honored views on marriage are being revamped and more and more the emphasis is being placed on the pursuit and achievement of meaningful relationships. The married as well as the unmarried are part of the new morality, being ever and increasingly more experimental about their relationships. And of course the popular market has been flooded with literature, plays and films celebrating our newfound freedom.

All of this has been refreshing as we came out of an age that was steeped in a combination of pristine Victorian standards packaged in a sterile Madison Avenue plastic. However, the pendulum swings both ways, and with all the far out things this generation brought us we'll bet a lot of people were beginning to think it had been broken. But in 1957 Pluto went into the sign Virgo. You know how uptight and puritanical that sign can be—we might just find ourselves in a few years at the extreme opposite end of the pendulum again. Virgo's rays also inspire intellectuality, mental superiority and good common sense. It brings the ability to logically vocalize one's views and is hard to beat in a debate. And so this new generation will not only have the innate courage of its convictions, but will demand proof of validity and truth.

Pluto also rules universal welfare urges, hence the preoccupation of the present generation with politics, protests, social conditions, efforts to end the war and oppression generally. Yet, adverse aspects of Pluto can mean disobedience and the breaking of laws through violence, and thus we have seen the kids sometimes get carried away in their means toward such a noble end.

The planet Pluto, astrologers have discovered, is an ever-increasing force with which to deal, for it causes changes in whatever sign it is in, and we will have to constantly stay on our toes if we are to meet its increasingly modern demands.

Pluto in Capricorn—1762–1777
Pluto in Aquarius—1777–1799
Pluto in Pisces—1799–1823
Pluto in Aries—1823–1852
Pluto in Taurus—1852–1884
Pluto in Gemini—1884–1914
Pluto in Cancer—1914–1939
Pluto in Leo—1939–1957
Pluto in Virgo—1957–1972
Pluto in Libra—1972–1984

# YOUR HOUSES

*One leaf for fame, one leaf for wealth,*
*One for a faithful lover,*
*And one leaf to bring glorious health,*
*And all in a four-leaf clover.*

From the tables in this book, locate your probable ascendant. As the time of year can vary things slightly, it's best to verify with a professional astrologer. But for approximation's sake, let's start thus: infallibly, your ascendant will always be placed in the first house. Let's assume you have Virgo rising. All right, it's in the first house. And let's say you have Sun in Leo, one sign back, which most likely places your Sun in Leo in the twelfth house.

Now you can go through all the tables, locating your various planets. Knowing that the signs proceed in orderly fashion beginning with Aries, ending with Pisces, each one occupying the succeeding house, you are now able to place your various planets on the wheel, where they will fall in the twelve houses.

Note: These house positions can vary slightly, one house lower or higher, due to degree and other factors, so we recommend that you either check with a professional astrologer or buy at a nominal price from your local bookstore a table of houses, in order to be able to rectify them.

The following information should serve as a guideline to you, pointing out the influences of the planets in the various houses, providing food for thought as to how well you know yourself.

## Sun in the Houses

SUN IN FIRST HOUSE: This aspect gives you radiant and joyful relationships, excellent health, strength and endurance, all of which aid you in achieving the maximum from your love and sex liaisons.

SUN IN SECOND HOUSE: Your generosity will help to make you a loving partner and you should bring much in the way of financial success to your mate.

SUN IN THIRD HOUSE: You'll have a penchant for making good contacts which may prove of strong sexual magnetism in your many travels. Your love life should sparkle plenty.

SUN IN FOURTH HOUSE: A favorable placement for love, which should endure well into advanced years. Yours is a fireside love nature.

SUN IN FIFTH HOUSE: You're happy at diversions and should meet your mate at a social gathering. You abound in good luck and will be blessed with especially lovely children.

SUN IN SIXTH HOUSE: Yours is not the strongest constitution, but if you take adequate care of your health and get enough rest, you should weather all storms, marital and otherwise.

SUN IN SEVENTH HOUSE: Yours will be a fortuitous marriage, the kind people envy and point to as ideal. You are one of the few in life to achieve this.

SUN IN EIGHTH HOUSE: You'll undoubtedly make good financial gain through your marriage. Marriage will increase your bank account a thousand-fold and it's likely you'll be in for other gratuities as well.

SUN IN NINTH HOUSE: You have high ambitions and should find the fulfillment of a conventional marriage somewhat less than your expectations.

SUN IN TENTH HOUSE: You will find yourself basking in public attention and your career will probably be more important than your marriage.

SUN IN ELEVENTH HOUSE: You'll have great happiness from friendships, which will prove more enduring than your love relationships, but eventually (later on in life), you'll find the realization of your dreams.

SUN IN TWELFTH HOUSE: You're afflicted with shyness and often steer clear of people because of a basic lack of confidence, which should cause some inhibitions in your love life as well.

## Moon in the Houses

MOON IN FIRST HOUSE: You bring a sensitivity and an emotional quality to your partner. However, you must guard against moodiness and changeability, and consider the effect this has on others.

MOON IN SECOND HOUSE: You should gain financially through your marriage partner or your mother. Money is of great importance to you and will be of primary consideration in your choice of partner.

MOON IN THIRD HOUSE: You're at your best when allowed full expression of your own line of thought instead of having to play to somebody else's. Don't take a back seat, but get out in the world, travel and mix, assert yourself.

MOON IN FOURTH HOUSE: You have a great love of home and family and are traditional in your views and ideals. Your old age should be especially happy.

MOON IN FIFTH HOUSE: You desire children above all else and you bring strong emotions to the love relationship; however, you must guard against unsteadiness and indecision.

MOON IN SIXTH HOUSE: Keep your head in a steady place or you'll be inclined to self-pity and psychosomatic ills.

You'd be happiest choosing a partner where you'll wield the controlling rein.

MOON IN SEVENTH HOUSE: You are unfortunately not the most decisive person in the world, thus you'll no doubt find yourself having many second, third and fourth thoughts, and will be wishing to get out of love entanglements almost as soon as you've gotten into them.

MOON IN EIGHTH HOUSE: You'll profit to financial advantage from your partner and will bring strong psychic ability to the relationship, enabling you to cope with many problems effectively.

MOON IN NINTH HOUSE: Your imagination can serve you well, but don't let it trip you up in marriage. Apply some common sense to your choice.

MOON IN TENTH HOUSE: You'll be hopping from job to job and won't want for opportunity to meet the opposite sex.

MOON IN ELEVENTH HOUSE: Friendships will be solid and enduring. You'd be best off choosing a marriage partner from among your friends rather than being carried away by the false glow of romance.

MOON IN TWELFTH HOUSE: You must overcome your sensitivity and learn to express your true inner thoughts and feelings if you're to score a success with the opposite sex.

### Mercury in the Houses

MERCURY IN FIRST HOUSE: Your restlessness and nervousness should be brought under control if you aim to achieve a good love relationship.

MERCURY IN SECOND HOUSE: Finances could be a problem with your mate and you must curb your impatience in this area to make things work between the two of you.

MERCURY IN THIRD HOUSE: If aspects to this house

are favorable, your reason will always guide your heart. If afflicted, you incline toward deceit and are apt to walk a fine line between fact and fantasy.

MERCURY IN FOURTH HOUSE: You are ever restlessly in search of the new and different in exciting emotions and love thrills, and may expect many changes in your relations with the opposite sex.

MERCURY IN FIFTH HOUSE: You're a pioneer and can stun the world (as well as your beloved) with your rhetoric. Love will develop your nature and give you just the right amount of rounding out you need.

MERCURY IN SIXTH HOUSE: You are inclined to be irritable and irascible and must often hold your temper in check if you want to maintain a solid love relationship. You have a tendency to spread yourself thin.

MERCURY IN SEVENTH HOUSE: Most likely you can look forward to an early marriage and a gifted mate who'll treat you well. There's the chance you may not respond in kind, however.

MERCURY IN EIGHTH HOUSE: Your penetrating intellect leaves no areas uncovered and you're particularly interested in sex in all its many aspects and will be an early experimenter who continues late into life.

MERCURY IN NINTH HOUSE: You have excellent qualities—sincerity, earnestness, forthrightness—all of which could make you a good partner, but if afflicted you will have to guard against profligacy.

MERCURY IN TENTH HOUSE: Your success in all your undertakings attracts many to you who'll be interested in you for a permanent partner. You'll undoubtedly experiment a good deal before you finally settle down—if you ever do.

MERCURY IN ELEVENTH HOUSE: You circulate in top company and are ambitious in your social life. Your mate should come from a cultured background.

MERCURY IN TWELFTH HOUSE: You keep your own counsel and few people know what goes on behind that mysterious facade. Your keen insight into others' problems makes you a sought-after companion.

## Venus in the Houses

VENUS IN FIRST HOUSE: You have a serene, lovely disposition and bring kindness, gentility and refinement to the love match.

VENUS IN SECOND HOUSE: You'll be lucky with money and all your alliances in the romantic vein will net you financial profit as well. You're at your best as gigolo or kept woman.

VENUS IN THIRD HOUSE: You're capable of seeing the other person's point of view and are ready and willing to compromise at all times. This makes you a very easy lover with whom to be.

VENUS IN FOURTH HOUSE: A happy home life in childhood will cause you to be complacent and you won't start looking for marriage till late in life.

VENUS IN FIFTH HOUSE: Your love affairs will be good matches and bring you happiness. Likewise, your children and your business deals will be equally successful.

VENUS IN SIXTH HOUSE: You are fond of art and a lovely home will be of prime importance to you. You will happily wait on your partner hand and foot.

VENUS IN SEVENTH HOUSE: Your marriage will be smooth and you will be able to more or less sit back and let your partner take over. Little seems required of you in return.

VENUS IN EIGHTH HOUSE: Financial gain through romantic alliance will no doubt happen in your case. Or you could win a legacy from a loved one's death.

VENUS IN NINTH HOUSE: Your keen intuition will lead you into many interesting adventures and into foreign lands, although you basically are a homebody and would prefer a more settled life than fate seems to decree you.

VENUS IN TENTH HOUSE: You're lucky and popular and will attain great success socially. The opposite sex enhances you at gatherings and will bring you gain in marriage as well.

VENUS IN ELEVENTH HOUSE: Some people might think of your circle of friends as freaky or far out but you wouldn't have it any other way, and among your iconoclast companions you'll never want for attention and romance.

VENUS IN TWELFTH HOUSE: Most of your love alliances are clandestine and often result in scandal and trouble. The mystical and occult hold great fascination for you and you are fond of consulting soothsayers to determine the romantic maneuvers of your life.

### Mars in the Houses

MARS IN FIRST HOUSE: Courage, pride and a strong will propel you into a positive attitude toward love, sex, and all things romantic. Your curious and outgoing nature will cause you to experiment a good deal sexually before you finally settle down to devoted domesticity.

MARS IN SECOND HOUSE: You'll always have to work extra hard for money and may have trouble holding onto it, but don't let that destroy your confidence in yourself and your desirability.

MARS IN THIRD HOUSE: Your impulsiveness and short temper often get you into trouble with your close associates. Lucky for you, you can usually breeze off on a long trip to permit cooling off.

MARS IN FOURTH HOUSE: Much strife follows you, and your domestic life is far from peaceful. You probably should never have let yourself in for marriage.

MARS IN FIFTH HOUSE: Your recklessness and moody restlessness, your desire for gambling and excitement can lead you into quarrels in the home. It's unlikely you'll have harmony in family relations.

MARS IN SIXTH HOUSE: You're accident-prone, which could work both for and against you in matters of love, so you'll just have to hold your breath and hope for the best.

MARS IN SEVENTH HOUSE: A rash early marriage will prove disastrous and result in much discord and legal entanglements. Once you are out of this phase you'll have interesting affairs. You'd be wise to live with someone and avoid the red tape, which to you could be a large headache.

MARS IN EIGHTH HOUSE: You must be careful to guard your health and finances, both of which will be troublesome in your family life. Strong possibility of legal difficulties and lawsuits, so watch your step.

MARS IN NINTH HOUSE: Travel will result in problems abroad. You will no doubt find your emotions strained with in-laws. Steer clear of them as much as possible.

MARS IN TENTH HOUSE: You're prone toward scandal and public scorn. The risks you are only too eager to take usually prove disastrous. Caution is advised.

MARS IN ELEVENTH HOUSE: Discord with friends and loved ones, many partners, restlessness and seeking in sex and romance.

MARS IN TWELFTH HOUSE: You align yourself with causes which can compensate for the lack of emotional satisfaction which afflicts you with the opposite sex.

### Jupiter in the Houses

JUPITER IN FIRST HOUSE: If well-aspected this brings great opportunity for advancement in life through influential people, and it's likely you'll marry well, too. If poorly aspected you must learn to control your impatience if you're to achieve a good relationship with your partner.

JUPITER IN SECOND HOUSE: You bring excellent qualities to a love relationship: kindness, sympathy, and a desire to be helpful. Probably you are not as appreciated as you should be.

JUPITER IN THIRD HOUSE: You're an asset to any family and are always ready to pitch in and do your share, however you do like change and will probably have a few extramarital affairs largely out of boredom.

JUPITER IN FOURTH HOUSE: You're devoted to the family and are a homebody. Good luck in real estate investments should be yours.

JUPITER IN FIFTH HOUSE: Sensuous and lustful, you desire acquisition and seek to profit in your love relationships as well.

JUPITER IN SIXTH HOUSE: Success in business, since you're a good organizer, is a foregone conclusion. However, things don't look as keen for you in the love area.

JUPITER IN SEVENTH HOUSE: You're traditional in your marriage outlook and will be a dutiful partner. Money should be plentiful in your union.

JUPITER IN EIGHTH HOUSE: Good for money. You can be an asset to your partner, for your intuition regarding speculation is accurate.

JUPITER IN NINTH HOUSE: Travel is one of the highlights of your life and you'll cover the globe many times over. You're best off with a partner who shares your passion for this as well as your love of the out-of-doors and sports.

JUPITER IN TENTH HOUSE: Your partner will find a trustworthy mate in you and one who'll be certain to carve a niche for himself in life.

JUPITER IN ELEVENTH HOUSE: If well-aspected you'll be lucky to find kindly-disposed lovers but if poorly aspected, your laziness will repel the opposite sex.

JUPITER IN TWELFTH HOUSE: Qualities of helpfulness, kindness and selflessness are assets you bring to your partner. You have a knack for extricating yourself from troubles.

### Saturn in the Houses

SATURN IN FIRST HOUSE: You should strive to overcome your timidity and to come out of yourself more; your serious nature can sometimes cause misunderstandings with those with whom you'd like to have a love relationship.

SATURN IN SECOND HOUSE: Don't let your apprehension and fears over money jeopardize your chances for successful relations with the opposite sex.

SATURN IN THIRD HOUSE: You may have obstacles impeding your education and upbringing, but have the strength to weather the storm and find yourself in a good position later in life. However, your domestic life will be troubled by in-laws and relatives.

SATURN IN FOURTH HOUSE: A sense of impending doom seems always to lie at the back of your mind and causes you much unhappiness which you can't seem to keep out of your dealings with the opposite sex.

SATURN IN FIFTH HOUSE: You have a tendency to deliberate, procrastinate and delay. You will never make a snap judgment regarding marriage, in fact you'll probably have to be dragged to the altar.

SATURN IN SIXTH HOUSE: Your critical and exacting nature makes you a difficult partner to live with. Perhaps you'd best forget it. You're one of the "unmarriageables," anyway.

SATURN IN SEVENTH HOUSE: You may tend to marry

someone a good deal older or younger than yourself, and you will experience many marital difficulties after the May-December charm has worn thin.

SATURN IN EIGHTH HOUSE: You aspire to acquire financial betterment through marriage, but you will find your hopes dashed.

SATURN IN NINTH HOUSE: You maintain a traditional view of marriage despite the fact that you may have delays in obtaining your ideal. You will probably be misunderstood by most people. It's not easy to know you.

SATURN IN TENTH HOUSE: You do not tolerate being put down and will easily become incensed if you feel you're not getting the respect you deserve. Why do you so often waste your time with unworthy people?

SATURN IN ELEVENTH HOUSE: The reserve in your nature is only a front. Inside you earnestly desire love and affection but constantly feel thwarted.

SATURN IN TWELFTH HOUSE: You have a tendency to isolate yourself from the rest of the world and to cut yourself off from people. You have many inward fears and feelings of emptiness and hopelessness.

### Uranus in the Houses

URANUS IN FIRST HOUSE: You're not easy to know or understand and are apt to be tactless and rude. You'll have to curb your desire to rule others if you're to have a solid relationship with another.

URANUS IN SECOND HOUSE: The two assets you'll bring to a marriage are financial solvency and an original mind in speculative ventures.

URANUS IN THIRD HOUSE: You are a wild iconoclast— unconventional, crazy, far out, apt to be a genius, brilliant and erratic. It would be near to impossible for a member of

the opposite sex to begin to penetrate you, and you'll make
a lot of lovers unhappy.

URANUS IN FOURTH HOUSE: Your home life will be
marked by numerous upsets and changes. No, you'll never
have that peaceful and ideal ménage of which you've dreamed.

URANUS IN FIFTH HOUSE: Your love affairs should be
interesting and off-beat. You're prone to head-over-heels love
at first sight and can tire of someone just as easily as you
initially accept him.

URANUS IN SIXTH HOUSE: You want things your way
and are often unable to compromise, making difficulties in
your home life.

URANUS IN SEVENTH HOUSE: Marry in haste, repent
not at leisure but also in haste is your pattern of behavior.
Although you might hit it lucky and see one of your snap
judgments materialize into a lasting marriage, it's unlikely.

URANUS IN EIGHTH HOUSE: Financial worries and
difficulties will plague you throughout your marriage, but
your own particular brand of faith will help you along.

URANUS IN NINTH HOUSE: The unexpected always happens in your life, so be prepared for anything in your relations with the opposite sex. You attract danger, adventure
and trouble, but you always have a ball doing it.

URANUS IN TENTH HOUSE: Probably you'll achieve
recognition and will be propelled before the public, which
could cause jealousy on the part of your mate.

URANUS IN ELEVENTH HOUSE: Be sure your partner
approves of your far out friends or it will make you unhappy,
since traveling in straight company is not your bag.

URANUS IN TWELFTH HOUSE: You have a great desire
to be unconventional and to break all restricting bonds, consequently you'll probably have many stimulating extramarital
affairs.

## *Neptune in the Houses*

NEPTUNE IN FIRST HOUSE: You are terribly vague and don't think things through well. Although you don't lack for imagination you nevertheless are changeable, moody and unreliable, weakening your potential as a love partner.

NEPTUNE IN SECOND HOUSE: Your carelessness and extremes regarding money can threaten you in a love relationship and cause anything with potential to suffer.

NEPTUNE IN THIRD HOUSE: You may be too wise for those around you; your psychic powers enable you to understand much others have no inkling of. This could cause you loneliness.

NEPTUNE IN FOURTH HOUSE: Your dreams are idealistic and often implausible and the home you dream of will be hard to come by.

NEPTUNE IN FIFTH HOUSE: Your idealism would never lead you to expect the kind of deception you will experience in love.

NEPTUNE IN SIXTH HOUSE: You tend toward psychosomatic illness and it would be wise to get to the root of your troubles before you go looking for marriage to compound your problems.

NEPTUNE IN SEVENTH HOUSE: You'll have to come down considerably in your ideals and learn to be content with a good deal less than you expected in marriage, particularly from the standpoint of finances.

NEPTUNE IN EIGHTH HOUSE: Many afflictions regarding money can cause you unhappiness and you'll hanker after better things than life seems to deal you.

NEPTUNE IN NINTH HOUSE: You may meet your mate on a trip. It would be best if you chose someone who shared your interest in the occult and mystical side of life.

NEPTUNE IN TENTH HOUSE: People think you're an oddball, which you are, but you've got a lot to offer life and a lot to give to another, so don't let them sell you short.

NEPTUNE IN ELEVENTH HOUSE: You lead an interesting off-beat life and always manage to meet your lovers in original circumstances.

NEPTUNE IN TWELFTH HOUSE: Don't idle away your time in useless fancies and self-indulgent daydreams. You're a mental and emotional masturbator and need to learn to give to others if you're to have a decent relationship along the line.

## Pluto in the Houses

PLUTO IN FIRST HOUSE: Enormous power to force yourself through life. Many important turning points producing marked effects on your character. Deep-cutting events. This is not a good placement for marriage, as the tendency is for the person to have a dual nature and to cause him to be full of contradictions. He has a great desire for experience, is inclined to be a reckless daredevil.

PLUTO IN SECOND HOUSE: This is a good aspect for finances and often stockbrokers and bankers have their Pluto placed here. It brings wealth in a sensational manner. The native is often a loner, secretive, and inaccessible.

PLUTO IN THIRD HOUSE: This aspect endows the native with a quick wit and speedy reflexes, a great need for self-expression, and inexhaustible energy for his highly original projects. A good placement for family life. A life-time student.

PLUTO IN FOURTH HOUSE: This aspect brings an inquiring mind and desire for adventure and freedom. Frequent changes will occur in life. The native would be suited for careers in physics, archaeology, and real estate. Wealth comes late in life. Probable misunderstanding with parents and frequent changes of residence.

PLUTO IN FIFTH HOUSE: There is a great sex force inherent here which may often be mischanneled into depravity, perversion or celibacy. It denotes virility, can also indicate several children, and the native here is usually impetuous, ardent, zealous, and often endowed with a talent for acting.

PLUTO IN SIXTH HOUSE: This is a good position for doctors, surgeons and healers who have a mission in life to care for the sick and needy, whose devotion is toward an ideal of duty toward mankind.

PLUTO IN SEVENTH HOUSE: This aspect will bring jealousy and unfaithfulness, struggles and separations in married life, many crises. It is a placement giving the forceful personality of many politicians. The native here seeks out many acquaintances but these seldom lead to the desired goal. Often separations that result lead to immediate alliances following, but usually these are ill-fated. Overturns, adventures and crises are tantamount throughout married life. Enemies are made through marriage. This placement is often associated with accidents and a disgraceful death.

PLUTO IN EIGHTH HOUSE: This aspect is held by numerous people who disappear strangely, whose often tragic or sudden death is under unusual circumstances such as in mine slides or through black magic. It is a placement which brings great danger to life and its natives are often self-destructive. It also influences medium-ship and ESP experiences and is the aspect of many occultists.

PLUTO IN NINTH HOUSE: This is a highly favorable position leading to growth and evolution, a desire to gain knowledge and self-improvement. Its natives are independent thinkers, often geniuses, who exude religious ardor and more often are founders of new religions. An undeveloped type having this aspect might be a shallow-thinking globe-trotter, while the highly developed native would be a pioneer and idealist.

PLUTO IN TENTH HOUSE: These people can often be rulers and dictators, as they are self-assertive and often domineering and dictatorial. They are difficult to know and more difficult to have a true friendship with. They are aggressive and immune to intended barbs. If well-aspected with Venus, this leads to an artistic bent. Often position, power and prestige are lost overnight. They are most often found in ruling positions.

PLUTO IN ELEVENTH HOUSE: This placement is good for doctors and priests. It denotes humanitarianism and love for fellow men. These people are idealists and reformers who give much to others.

PLUTO IN TWELFTH HOUSE: This is the poorest house in which Pluto can be posited. It is an evil influence fraught with many temptations. Most criminals have this unfortunately adverse aspect, which is also the position assigned to traitors, swindlers, sex deviates and black magicians. It brings inherited diseases, accidents, imprisonments, treachery and depravity. Coupled with some favorable aspects in a chart to counterbalance the negativity, these people might achieve success as jurors or detectives.

# And Even Heavier Yet . . .

*There was a man, he went mad,*
*He jumped into a paper bag;*
*The paper bag was too narrow,*
*He jumped into a wheelbarrow;*
*The wheelbarrow took on fire,*
*He jumped into a cow byre;*
*The cow byre was too nasty,*
*He jumped into an apple pasty;*
*The apple pasty was too sweet,*
*He jumped into Chester-le-Street;*
*Chester-le-Street was full of stones,*
*He fell down and broke his bones.*

Have you ever wondered why freaky and frustrating things always happen to you? Why your heart's desire is beyond your reach? Why you can't earn more money, find romance and happiness, gain good health?

*Lilith may be what is fouling up your life.*

Who is Lilith?

In the Talmud, she was known as "the mother of demons" and the "Queen of Evil." She is also called Lilah and Delilah, a destructive force in Adam's life, man's betrayer due to his own weakness.

The old Hebrew prophets were astrologers and much of the Hebraic and Judaeo-Christian lore can only rightfully be interpreted with a knowledge of astrology.

It is reported in the Talmud that Lilith and Adam fought; then she left and was overtaken by three angels. Jealousy over Adam's new partner, Eve, caused Lilith to swear revenge on their children.

Lilith, a mysterious and obscure element in astrology, is

called the "dark moon of the earth." She is seen only at intervals every six months—and then only her shadow is visible on the face of the sun.

Her name means "night"; she is also called the "night hag." She is given special power over childbirth. For instance, a tenth house afflicted by Lilith in one's native chart means death in childbirth.

It is especially bad if Lilith affects the rising sign of the chart, though all matters and people coming under the influence of Lilith's place in the chart will be affected negatively, so that the full measure of one's heart's desire will not be attained in that area. Lilith is the element which lures the vulnerable man to his doom.

She is particularly strong if residing in the native's twelfth house. Here one's self-undoing is through seemingly deliberate mistakes.

It is Lilith who is responsible for compulsiveness, fatal fascinations and attractions, unexpected financial losses, birth defects. She is associated with denial involving the house in which she appears, an influence which can be activated at intervals, for instance when a planetary conjunction or eclipse occurs.

Studying your natal chart and finding your Lilith can make you aware and cause you to better understand yourself. (For the means of finding your Lilith may we recommend *The Dark Moon Lilith* by Ivy Goldstein-Jacobsen.)

If Lilith is in an angular house, this can make the native charming to the opposite sex but cause trouble in marriage. Lilith in an angular house denies the greatest good. In the first house it brings physical defects to the native; in the fourth, family problems; in the seventh, trouble with one's partner or enemies; and the tenth, trouble with one's profession or with childbirth.

The next strongest (and consequently most negative) positions in which Lilith appears are the succedent houses (2, 5, 8, 11) affecting finances and possessions.

In cadent houses, Lilith functions weakest. For instance, in the sixth house, she will affect one's functioning to the degree that his own personal desires and will are always subordinate, and one is never free to do as he likes but will always be subject to another's wishes first. In the other cadent houses she also affects one's functioning in one way or another.

Loss of national resources and lives of members of the armed forces can be shown by Lilith. Other adverse trends can be demonstrated by Lilith in the stock market, the death rate, mining and real estate, wars. Congenital birth defects can be traced to Lilith by making a horoscope for the time of conception (your ascendant at birth is the position of your moon at conception, by the way).

The unfortunate thing about Lilith is that there isn't anyone who can escape her. While she can be intercepted and her influence at that particular time held back temporarily, sooner or later her negative power will be felt once again. Thus there is no getting away from her, but an awareness of her presence and waxing and waning influence can help one to be more understanding of the whys and wherefores of their lacks and failures.

Even today not that much is known about Lilith, yet it's something worth taking note of because it does have such an effect on our lives. It is certainly not well-known enough yet to be shown on the computer, but perhaps someday it will be. Remember, just a few years ago *astrology* wasn't on the computer. And don't feel overwhelmed if some of the more esoteric aspects of astrology are too far above your head. To someone, even if it's a being from another dimension, each and every one of us is just a novice.

*Star light, star bright*
*First star I see tonight*
*I wish I may, I wish I might*
*Have the wish I wish tonight.*

Simple zodiacal astrology alone, while both an art and a science, as well as a lifetime study, is only scratching the surface of the study of astrology.

There are other systems of astrology which have come down to us through the ages, notably through the Hindus, Chinese and Arabians. The ancients had what they called "fixed stars" as well as the "wandering" ones (which we know as our planets).

National and international events are difficult to foresee, using simple zodiacal astrology alone, as the influence of the planets is slow and often indecisive. Therefore, it is necessary to have access to the knowledge of fixed stars in order to foresee the trends, the radical and abrupt changes, the un-expected upheavals of the globe.

The fixed stars provide us with knowledge of an influence strong enough for events of large magnitude. The influence of the fixed stars is very sudden and dramatic, in contrast to the planets, whose influence is slow and progressive.

Actually, each of the fixed stars of the ancients is a sun in itself. One of the farthest of these fixed stars is Polaris, the North Star, forty-four light-years away from the earth.

In many ways the figures represented by the various con-stellations and fixed stars quite closely resemble the influence that star or constellation exerts. For instance, another fixed star, Canus Major, exerts strong influence on dogs, believe it or not. (The ancient Arabs, Chinese and Hindus were quite well-versed, psychic, aware people.)

The most powerful effect of a fixed star is when it falls either in conjunction or parallel to a planet in the chart of the native. Oppositions and squares are also to be reckoned with.

It is interesting to find the fixed stars which appear in the angular houses of a chart (first house: the self; fourth house: the home; seventh house: the partner; tenth house: the profession). Fixed stars falling in angular houses will bring the strongest influences to life. When planets and stars operate together in the same position of chart, the effect is magnified. Usually, the positing of the fixed stars in a chart is ignored by all but the most esoteric astrologers, but it is the fixed stars which exert the most drastic effect upon life, thus a study of the fixed stars is worth pursuing by those who wish to go deeper into astrology.

Stars are of varying "magnitudes" from first magnitude (the brightest) down to fifteenth (stars after the sixth magnitude are invisible to the naked eye). Some stars change their magnitudes within set periods. Collisions, for one thing, cause the extra brilliance of stars from time to time, and the strength of their influence correspondingly waxes and wanes. First magnitude stars confer honors. The fixed stars' influence, as with planets, are strongest when in angular houses and on cusps, weakest in cadent houses, strong when rising and setting.

Growth of religions is affected by the passage of the vernal equinox through our zodiacal constellations. Its entry into Taurus was associated with the golden calf and worship of Baal; its passage into Aries brought worship of the ram. Christianity began when the vernal equinox came close to Pisces and the followers of Jesus adopted the symbol of fish for its emblem.

Two thousand one hundred and sixty years is about the time the vernal equinox takes to pass through one sign— the influence is felt in periods of approximately seven hundred and twenty years each. Some say the much heralded Aquarian Age began after World War I, others are announcing it at present, and still others predict it for the year 2660. It is a difficult thing to correctly ascertain, but we may, through evidence and empirical data, gather that the latter date is liable to be more accurate.

It is also known that comets can herald war, pestilence, famine, earthquakes and other disasters, and that they are closely linked with other celestial phenomena which can be studied at close range by the esotericist. Yet another open field of study involves the lunar mansions, also an ancient system, older than either the "fixed star" system or our present "Sun Sign and planet" system, of which we have variants from Arabia, India and China. It is the Arab system which is most closely connected with the Ptolemic system. One interesting factor of the "lunar mansion" system is that by using it, the ancients could correctly predict a baby's sex before birth.

From the preceding material you can get an idea of what a varied and deep study astrology can be.

*There was an old woman*
*Who lived in a shoe,*
*She had so many children*
*She didn't know what to do.*

Are you single and hoping for marriage? Interested in knowing what your chances might be in the future? Look in your chart to see where your Mars and your Venus are placed, whether they are in fruitful signs. Here is a chart to guide you:

| *Barren Signs* | *Semi-Barren Signs* |
|---|---|
| Gemini | Aries |
| Leo | Sagittarius |
| Virgo | Capricorn |

| *Semi-Fruitful* | *Fruitful* |
|---|---|
| Taurus | Cancer |
| Libra | Scorpio |
| Aquarius | Pisces |

This is not to say that because your sun is in Virgo, for instance, that you are "barren." It is just a term astrologers use relating to the degree of fertility of each sign, and it's the sum total of all your planets again that determines exactly where you're at. If you come out on the plus side, the picture looks hopeful for you, and you'll probably end up with a mate and a houseful of kids.

Another guideline is to check the house in which your

Mars and Venus fall. (If you are not adept enough at astrology you may require a professional astrologer for this.) The best houses here would be the first, tenth and eleventh, making it most fortuitous for marriage, though the fourth, fifth and seventh are good also. Unfavorable houses for Mars and Venus, marriage-wise, would be the sixth, eighth and twelfth.

Finally, add up all the other planets in your chart, all the houses, everything, and see how many occur in fruitful signs, to get a general picture of just how hopeful your situation might be. Of course, there are still other aspects involved—many a time, such a seemingly slight asset as a semi-sextile can be a determining factor, so don't despair if things don't look that promising. Maybe the additional counseling of a good professional astrologer will help to point out to you that your number is yet to come up.

# TANTRA YOGA

*There was an old woman of Surrey,*
*Who was morn, noon, and night in a hurry;*
*    Called her husband a fool,*
*    Drove her children to school,*
*The worrying old woman of Surrey.*

Sex has often been referred to as one of America's greatest pastimes, second only to baseball, yet were the stipulations for being a lover nearly as rigid as those on the baseball diamond, there would not be many to qualify for the big league. Athletes and artists alike recognize the need for practice of a technique in order to develop their skills. It is hardly a rookie who walks up to the mound and pitches a deciding game in the World Series, but someone who has spent endless hours coordinating his body and practicing motor skills to ensure his preparedness.

Despite natural aptitude, an apprenticeship is required in every field of endeavor where the results desired are of a high level of achievement. Sex, however, one of the most important areas of existence, is a field which most people plunge into blind and hope for the best. Like the paramecium, their procedure of movement is hit or miss. Surprisingly, a lot of people do not even realize they can be better sex partners. The unlimited possibilities for development in this area have been little explored. Modern man, ignorant of the vast untapped potential of his sexuality, enjoying only partial fulfillment, has robbed himself of the full character and benefits of sex. Furthermore, when the organism does not function to its fullest capacity, hormonal balance as well as nerve and muscle tone suffer, and power and strength are lost. Many psychosomatic illnesses are the resulting side effects of the failure of sex to find its proper place in life.

We of the West have much to learn from the ancient wise men of the East, for they understand what most Westerners do not, that it is not a divided world we live in, but an interdependent, interpenetrating one. In their system of Yoga exercises they teach us a method whereby we can achieve a state that transcends duality, where there is no separation of subject and object, but where the knower, knowledge and the known are one. As the great mystic poet Ni'mat-Allah wrote:

> We are of the sea, and the sea is our essence;
> why then is there this duality between us?
> The world is an imaginary line before the sight;
> read well that line, for it was inscribed by us.

When man is divided from his experience, it is no wonder his pleasure is only partial and thus frustrating. Sex loses its intensity and power with the failure to attune oneself to this law. A reintegration is imperative if sex is to achieve the expression of which it is capable, with the union of the body, mind and spirit.

In India and Tibet for centuries masters have passed on to their pupils a sacred teaching called Tantra Yoga, which teaches that sex is the highest force in life, and that sexual intercourse, when correctly practiced, can endow man with the ultimate in ever-expanding powers and benefits. The Tantra system endows lovers with dynamism, spontaneity and vigor, leaving them refreshed, revitalized, rejuvenated and reintegrated, providing them with the means of unlimited heightening of energy.

Tantra, as adapted for Western use, can provide the practitioner with the power to elevate sex by making it the liberating force it was meant to be. In the Tantrik way sex becomes a revelation in depth, where the interpenetration of the sex centers at their highest affords the opportunity for transcendent physical, psychic and spiritual interchange, lifting the partners into a flowing stream of cosmic vitality and ecstasy. The Yogic system of development provides a series of exercises through which the body, mind and spirit may be developed into an effective instrument capable of executing the sexual performance at its peak. Most of the Yogic orders, however, demand vows of celibacy, with the exception of the Tantriks, who believe sex is one of the highest experiences in a man's life, an opportunity to transcend the mundane.

Instructions and procedures are given to the initiate in Tantra Yoga by the master according to the stage of development the pupil has reached in order that the dormant Kundalini or "serpent power" that lies coiled up at the base of the spine may be developed to its fullest. The Yogis have divided the spine into seven chakras or centers which start at the base of the spine and go to the top of the head and through which the Kundalini, during progressive meditation, is carried. It reaches the deity in the upper part of the head, where it stays for a while and then returns through the chakras, bringing an impowering and spiritualizing effect to each of them. Most Yogic orders, considering that the processes in the spine automatically take care of themselves in response to their asanas, pranayama and meditation, do not meditate directly on the serpent power; the Tantriks, however, do, causing the energies to flow to the fingertips, toes, throughout the entire body, stirring, energizing, and giving renewed current and life to the body and spirit. Through applying these same principles to his sex life, man can achieve potency enabling him to extend the ecstasy of the orgasm for an hour or more if he wishes.

Yoga is misinterpreted by some as a religion; nor is it a creed; rather it is a method through which man can realize himself and his union with the Universal Spirit, and acquaint himself with the basic Hindu attitude that everything contained in the universe—the air, water, earth and fire, all of the elements, the plants, the species, even the rocks and minerals—is composed of this same Divine Substance. The concept of this spirit, essence, life, call it whatever you will, is part of an ancient theory to which modern science with the discovery of the atom is starting to adhere and more.

Yoga can be practiced as either a religious or nonreligious experience, but none of its teachings will ever run counter to any other religious teachings so a person of any religious denomination can practice it with a clear conscience. Yoga is the study of you, your real self, who you really are.

All of the forces within that make you function both on a voluntary and involuntary level, your organs, muscles, bones, your conscious and subconscious minds, your soul or spirit, all that you are is encompassed in its study. And it also concerns itself with the forces outside and around you that act upon you and cause you to react. The chief aim of Yoga is to develop you to your highest peak of perfection, a place where you can maintain the lasting and rewarding relationship you desire with a person of the opposite sex.

Earlier we cited some alarming divorce statistics indicating that it is becoming increasingly difficult for love to endure the fast-paced, rapidly changing world we live in. Most of us have become so conditioned to a cutthroat society where we have to fight for everything we get that we not only view the world around us as competitive from a business standpoint, but have come to look upon all other men and/or women as menacing rivals to our love lives. Indeed, how many people do you know who live in a perpetual state of anxiety? If the elements don't get them and they aren't struck down by an automobile or a rabid Doberman pinscher, they're plagued with slow trading of the industrials or finding out their kids, barely off the pot, are on it again.

Through even a slight comprehension of Yoga, you will come to view the natural forces as well as society in general as friendly, and will also look upon members of your own sex as allies with whom you can take and receive, learn and teach. If this ancient science enables Yogis to walk in the jungles unharmed, perhaps it can do the same thing for you at carnivorous sales meetings, and help tame the savages one encounters at cocktail parties. (Perhaps you're familiar with a contemporary painting by Philip Kirkland entitled "Cocktail Party"; it shows a group of sociables partying it up, looking rather conventional in their suits and cocktail clothes, except that their heads have been replaced by pistols and revolvers.)

While only part of our society is armed today, the rest is certainly well-armored, to borrow a term Reich coined. But how many of us have an orgone box into which we can crawl for release? That's another nice thing about Yoga, you don't need any gadgets, gimmicks or fancy, expensive apparatus to perform the asanas. Just your own body, and you're free to do them anywhere and in just a limited amount of space.

Meditation, concentration and control of the thought processes are as important for everyday living—"as a man thinketh in his heart, so is he . . ."—as they are for your love life—". . . what a man takes in through contemplation, that he must pour out in love." The study of Yoga can aid in the building of a lasting relationship through helping you to develop the poise and confidence you need in your loved one both during times of togetherness and separation. Fear begets the thing feared and even causes people to react in the way your fear dictates. Remember what Job said? "The thing I feared has come upon me . . ." and it undoubtedly does. The resulting strength of will and self-reliance you will gain from your exercises will also help any tendencies you might have toward possessiveness, jealousy or any other unpleasant emotions that tend to drive lovers either berserk or, if they're not equally self-destructive, just away. Only that which we are willing to release can we truly hold; nor is there any way we can hang onto something that does not rightfully belong to us; nor any way anyone can take something away from us that is rightfully ours ("right?" meaning in accord with divine spiritual law).

In their unending pursuit to solve the great riddle of which came first, the chicken or the egg, many psychologists say that all-round marital harmony is founded upon a good sex life; yet there is always the other school that counters with the theory that a good sex life is based on all-round marital harmony. Whether a marriage finds its growth or deterioration in the kitchen, living room, bedroom or basement, suffice it to say that in any of the realms of domestic living represented in each of these areas a good sense of humor and a good-natured flexibility certainly contribute to compatibility and harmony. But how many people are capable of true, complete relaxation? It is certainly the first prerequisite of reason and clear thinking, for it is only in a relaxed state that the mind truly functions at peak level. And how many people do you know who can lie down and relax their limbs but cannot relax their minds? Complete relaxation can only be induced by a state where the mind as well as the body is loose and free from any destructive or negative thoughts such as prejudice, hatred, selfishness, greed, etc. Through the mental control gained in the practice of the postures, you will be able to rest from a job, transferring your energy from one department of your being to another, thus doubling your efficiency. This control of the prana or life force is also the basis of healing, when one is able to channel it to any organ or area of the body that may be malfunctioning.

Although a lot of people, including the late President John F. Kennedy, have talked about a national physical fitness program and millions of Americans already practice Yoga, we do not feel it has ever really received the recognition and acclaim in the West that it deserves. Yogic benefits that warrant the system far superior to any other method of self-improvement of which we are aware can be expounded upon for pages but we are restricted to having to just hit upon a few of the high points.

It can be said that you receive more for your money with Yoga, because certainly in our hustling, bustling society, time is money; Yoga saves you time because with the stretching and pulling technique involved in the postures you receive twice the benefit you would get from other exercises in the same amount of time. Most forms of calisthenics in which you repeat exercises rapidly and many times increase the heartbeat and cause unnecessary exertion and tiredness. The taut, hard muscles that result from these exercises make blood circulation difficult later in life, often leaving the practitioner stiff and rheumatic. Physical Yoga instead rejuvenates through a scientifically balanced system of stimulating and relaxing exercises, tones the muscles without making them hard and overdeveloped, while it massages, exercises and develops the internal organs and gives healthgiving treatments to the glands. To sum it up, Yoga can keep your body supple and agile while giving you added physical and mental control, increase your stamina and ability to endure extremes of temperatures, make you more resistant to disease, prolong youthfulness, delay the aging process while it develops you spiritually, making you equally beautiful on the inside as well as outside.

Certain precaution should be taken if you are overweight, elderly or not in shipshape condition physically. If you have high blood pressure, be particularly careful with the inverted positions such as the shoulder stand and headstand in which the blood rushes to the head. You may in this case want to refrain from such postures altogether. If you have any osteopathic problems, a slipped disc or some other pathological disablement, consult your doctor to determine which positions will not be detrimental, or if you are under the guidance of a reputable master, he may be able to help you to utilize the positions to cure certain of these ailments. If you're a geriatric, use discretion in the amount of exercises you do and the exertion you bring upon your system. If you're extremely fat, you may find it desirable to lose weight before you can really get into some of the more complicated positions. Don't try to master the more difficult postures right away. Remember, the Yogis have spent years acquiring the agility they now so readily demonstrate.

There are numerous divisions of Yoga, but we are going to concern ourselves here with Hatha or physical yoga; of necessity we will have to omit a lot of detail in the minimum amount of space we are able to devote to its practice in this book. However, the reader should bear in mind these two things: if the exercises shown herein are practiced properly and regularly, they are enough to provide a devotee with a lifetime of practice and no matter how small the effort you put into your Yoga, you will be well compensated in the richer and fuller way of life that results. If we only serve in this volume to introduce you to the pursuit of a study on which numerous books are available in bookstores and libraries, we will have done you an invaluable service. While Yoga is ultimately an individual study, we recommend that for the beginner it can be advantageous to study either privately or in a group under the guidance of a competent teacher or master until you have a firm grasp on the philosophy and a proficiency in the various techniques involved in the asanas. In many cities there are television programs where the postures are demonstrated which can be of great benefit to hasten your progress.

Begin your exercises by choosing a place to perform them that will be available on a regular basis, if this is at all possible. This area will then adopt a serenity which you will come to immediately associate with your Yoga practice, and the calm vibration there will help to put you in a receptive mood much more quickly as you begin your meditation practice each day. It is, of course, ideal to perform the asanas outdoors but in the beginning, unless you have a very isolated place and the climate is temperate, it could be distracting. After you become adept, you will be able to practice anywhere. Choose a quiet part of your home; if your quarters are large enough you might want to convert one room into a special meditation retreat. Otherwise a corner of the bedroom will probably offer the least distraction and the greatest calmness available.

As we said before, Yoga can be either religious or non-religious, so you can practice your exercises with as much or as little ritual as you desire. You may wish to create for your meditation an altar with a picture of any master or masters you might be following and place fresh flowers or incense around these for added inspiration. If you find the outdoors more inspiring, you may practice in front of a window overlooking a pleasant view; nature itself can become your shrine. Or if you find either of these distracting, you may prefer a starker surrounding and the handiwork of your own imagination. In any case, your meditation should be directed either eastward or northward.

Once you have established a proper place, fold a blanket or piece of material and cover it with either fur or silk, or if you prefer to be even more orthodox, you may use a wooden meditation platform an inch off the ground as the Yogis do. The reason for any of these is to insulate yourself from the earth currents. Make sure you are dressed in comfortable clothing that is loose and easy in which to move around. Dance leotards and tights work nicely, too.

Now you are ready to begin your exercises. The various schools of Hatha Yoga have innumerable ways of teaching the system which for the sake of simplification we have divided into the following three sections:

1) Asanas or postures.
2) Pranayama or breathing exercises.
3) Mantras or affirmations.

The entire system is a balanced one and in order to receive its threefold benefits to the body, mind and spirit every part of it must be practiced. It is the integration of all three of these activities which makes the system effective, for were the postures performed by themselves they would be merely physical and breathing exercises, the affirmations a series of rhetorical statements.

We suggest as a beginning asana the Sunworshipers exercise—also known as Salutation to the Sun or Soorya Namaskar, its Sanskrit name—which is made up of a series of twelve positions. After performing this asana it is easier to do the others but some people find it sufficient by itself, and receive great benefits doing no other than this exercise. The Yogis perform the Sunworshipers exercise facing the early morning sun; this is not advisable later in the day, however, as the rays could be harmful to the eyes. This asana is a combination of physical and breathing exercises. When you are adept at it, it is practiced in rounds, usually twelve during a session, while reciting the twelve names of the Lord Sun whom the Yogis regard as the Deity and sustainer of health, youth and longevity.

## POSITION No. 1

Face your shrine, window, or if it is possible, the sun which will also be eastward if you are practicing this in the morning. Stand erect with legs together, the body neither too stiff nor too relaxed, and fold the hands together in front of you with the tips of the fingers just below the lips. Now, if you want to set the tone for your asanas, you might want to recite some sort of mantra or affirmation. Here is a verse from the Sanskrit, "Salutation of the Dawn":

> Listen to the exhortation of the dawn
> Look to this day for it is life
> The very life of life!
> Within its brief course
>     lie all of the verities
>     and all of the realities
> Of your existence.
> The bliss of growth
> The glory of action
> The splendor of beauty;
> For yesterday is but a dream
> And tomorrow is only a vision;
> But today, well lived
> Makes every yesterday a dream of happiness
> And every tomorrow a vision of hope.
> Look well, therefore, to this day!
> Such is the Salutation of the dawn.

## POSITION No. 2

Inhale deeply and raise your arms above your head, bend-

ing back as far as possible without overbalancing. This keeps
the rib cage flexible and strengthens the spine.

## POSITION No. 3

Exhale completely and while doing so bend forward until the
hands are on the floor and in line with the feet or as near that as
possible. In the beginning you may bend your knees slightly
in order that you may touch your head against them. Later on,
though, the legs should be rigid. Keep the chin locked tightly
against the chest while in this position giving the thyroid a
treatment. The position also relieves pelvic congestion and
constipation.

## POSITION No. 4

Inhale and step as far backward as you can with the right
foot. Keep the hands and left foot planted firmly on the
ground while bending the head backward in an effort to look
up and back as far as possible. The left knee should be between the hands.

## POSITION No. 5

Inhale and hold the breath while moving the left leg back
with the right. Keep feet and legs together, toes bent, with
the knees and body off the floor and in a straight line, and
rest the hands on the floor with the arms straight.

## POSITION No. 6

Exhale and lower the body to the floor, allowing only the
feet, knees, hands, chest and forehead to touch the floor.

## POSITION No. 7

Inhale and arch backward as much as possible, bending the
spine to the maximum. This position is also known as the
Cobra pose or Bhujangasana and is particularly good for
women who might have any uterine-ovarian problems. It
also tones the ovaries and gives a beneficial treatment to the
uterus as well as a stretch to the spine and abdominal area.

## POSITION No. 8

Exhale and raise the body to a high arch while the feet
and hands remain on the floor.

POSITION No. 9

Inhale and place your right foot between your hands, the same as you did in Position No. 4. Left foot and knee remain on the floor, and don't forget to look up and back as far as you can.

POSITION No. 10

Exhale and bring the left leg up with the right one. Bring the head to the knees and place the hands beside the feet, the same as in Position No. 3.

POSITION No. 11

Repeating Position No. 2, raise the arms overhead and inhale while bending backward.

POSITION No. 12

Exhale, drop the hands; or if you wish you may clasp them for a momentary meditation as in Position No. 1; then relax.

Some of the postures you will encounter appear to be simple and easy, but when done correctly they are often much more difficult than they look. Remember that it is not just the posture alone from which the benefit is derived, not merely the going through of the motions, but from the concentration and attention you give to that particular part of the body that is being worked and treated. Any postures that you find difficult will become much easier through practice and soon you will be able to maintain all of them without discomfort. It is also important that you never continue an exercise so long that there is a strain on the body, and that you never exert yourself beyond your particular restrictions at that moment.

Whenever you feel the slightest bit tired, stop performing your asanas and assume the Corpse pose, also known as Savasana. Lie flat on your back, legs a foot or so apart, arms away from the body with the palms up. Close your eyes, let yourself go completely, jaws sagging, sighing, yawning, feeling delicious relaxation seep throughout your being while you surrender your body to gravity and your mind to peace. This is the time of the recharging of your batteries, the restoration of your energy.

Let your mind first examine your body to make sure every part of it is relaxed, fingers, toes, knees, thighs, pelvic area, chest, arms and head, going over it thoroughly to see that not one muscle is tense. Then make sure the mind does not reside on anything unpleasant, but rather seduce it into thinking of the most peaceful scene you can imagine, if you are compelled to think at all. Better you should let all thoughts roll by, ignoring them completely while the mind is occupied with nothing; even the most persistent ones will disappear on their own for want of attention. This relaxation in between asanas is as important as the asanas themselves, and is much of what makes the system so effective.

The following exercises can be divided into two categories. The first in which the body is bent forward are stimulating to the heart and nervous system and should not be done just before retiring, unless buffed out with some of the postures in Section Two. These are not accelerating but rather calming to the system and therefore desirable before going to sleep, as well as any other time of the day.

## Section One

COBRA POSE: (Bhujangasana)

This is described in Position No. 7 of Soorya Namaskar. It is beneficial to the suprarenal glands, massages the kidneys and flexes the spine while restoring vitality.

FISH POSE: (Matsyasana)

Lie on your back and, if you are able to, cross your legs into full lotus. Otherwise let them remain straight. Place the palms under the thighs and with the help of the elbows raise the chest, bending the neck backward as much as possible and rest on the top of the head. This is good for firming up the skin around the neck and the chin and also for limbering up the cervical and lumbar regions and releasing any tension in the shoulder muscles, thus increasing the circulation in all those parts. This exercise is especially good to do after the shoulder stand as it releases any cramps that might have come about.

LOCUST POSE: (Salabhasana)

Lie face-down with the palms upward and next to the body.

The chin should rest on the floor causing the head to be raised slightly. Slowly inhale and stiffen the body. Raise one leg, keeping the knee straight, and then rest and raise the other. This is half locust and when your back is strong enough, raise both legs for full locust.

## Bow Pose: (Dhanurasana)

Lying face-down, bend the legs over the thighs; reach back and catch each ankle with each hand and pull until the head, body and knees have risen off the floor causing the back to arch and the full weight of the body to rest on the abdomen. The breath should be held during this position. You may only be able to maintain it for a short while until the body is conditioned. This pose aids the digestion, appetite, circulation and can also help reduce excess weight. It is great for massaging the back muscles and when you are adept you will be able to rock in this position bringing an added benefit.

## Wheel Pose: (Chakrasana)

Lie down on the back, bend the arms and legs backward and walk the hands and feet inward until the body is arched and raised as high as it will go. Remain here until the legs, shoulders, arms, hips and spine are well stretched.

## Spinal Twist: (Ardha Matsendrasana)

The preparatory position for this posture is with the legs folded inward while in a sitting position, with the knees pulled tightly against the chest. The weight of the body should rest on the feet. Bend the right leg at the knee, placing the heel as firmly as you can against the perineum, that small area at the lowest part of the trunk between the genitals and the rectum, and bend the left leg at the knee and place the foot across the right leg, on the floor just next to the outside of the right thigh. Reach the right arm across the left knee and take hold of the left foot with the right hand. If you are able to, stretch the right arm back until you can catch onto the right thigh or else let it rest wherever it is comfortable until you have attained the desired flexibility. Then reverse the position. This pose brings an excellent stretch to the spine and abdominal region.

*Section Two*

PLOW POSE: (Halasana)

Lie flat on the back with the hands and palms pressed downward and close to the thighs. Without bending the legs and with great control raise the lower part of the body and back up and over until the toes touch the ground. Maintain this position as long as it is comfortable, making sure the legs remain in a straight line. This position gives a treatment to the neck and thyroid region and increases the circulation in the head and neck area, thereby rejuvenating tired, worn faces.

SHOULDER STAND: (Sarvangasana)

Once again lie flat on the back and gradually raise the legs, straight and close together, until the trunk, hips and legs are perpendicular to the floor. With the elbows placed firmly on the floor, support the back with both hands. The chin should be tightly locked against the chest. This also brings a benefit to the shoulder and neck area.

HEAD-KNEE POSE: (Janu Sirasana)

Sit on the floor and stretch the legs out in front of you, keeping them as straight as possible. Raise the arms and slowly bend forward until you are able to touch your toes or whatever other part of the leg is comfortable and not beyond your restrictions. Pull your body forward until your head touches your knees or comes as close as possible. Then slowly rise, keeping the arms above the head, and with great control lower the body back until you are lying in Savasana. For variation you can perform the exercise by bending the right leg and placing the heel against the perineum. Then reverse the position and have the left leg bent.

YOGA MUDRA:

Sit in lotus if you are able to with the arms folded in back of your body and bend forward as far as you can, resting the forehead on the floor. This gives a treatment to the internal organs and is very pleasant and relaxing as well.

HEADSTAND:  (Sirshasana)

We are going to describe two variations of this posture; the first one gives more benefits but it is also more difficult to master. Kneel down and bend forward and place the arms on the floor, folded across each other with the hands clasped over the opposite elbows, directly in front of you. Then open the hands and measure an exact triangle from the hands to the elbows. Interlace the fingers, forming a cup against which the head may secure itself while the elbows serve as a base enabling the forearms to balance the body. The frontal part of the head should be placed on the floor and against the hands with the body arched up in the beginning and only the feet touching the floor, similar to Position No. 8 in Soorya Namaskar. When you are secure enough, fold the knees into the body and slowly rise, balancing with the toes anytime you need to, until you are secure enough to rise. You should never have to kick yourself up, but should practice until you have the control to gracefully lift the legs and the whole body erect.

The second and easier variation begins with the body in a kneeling position. Bend forward, keeping the hands separated, and create a tripod by placing the head and hands at equal distance from each other on the floor. To rise you may climb the knees up on the elbows, if necessary, and rise into the headstand this way. This version may give you the strength you will need in the shoulders and back to accomplish the first headstand. This asana is excellent for the circulation, allowing a reversal of the blood mass which tends to accumulate in certain regions when we are in an upright position due to the pull of gravity. The brain is also nourished in this posture, and the shoulder, neck and back muscles are stretched and strengthened. It is an excellent treatment for the glands and internal organs and helps maintain youth and vitality as well as enhancing one's physical beauty.

Now that your body is limber and relaxed, we will begin work on the clearing of the mind, the brightening of the eyes and the expanded span of concentration and control over the nervous system that results from Pranayama. Start by sitting in a comfortable position and taking several deep, slow breaths, inhaling as long as you can without strain. Be careful that you do not make yourself dizzy. Concentrate on the beat of your heart and your breath itself. You will begin to feel in tune with yourself and aware of the strength and rhythm of your body.

Yogic breathing emphasizes an exhalation that is longer than the inhalation. In this retention exercise raise your right hand to your nose with the thumb blocking the right nostril. Do not press against the nostril but simply block it from underneath. The forefinger and second finger should be folded under and rest on the bridge of the nose while the third finger is used to block the left nostril and the little finger remains idle. You can start your inhalation/exhalation with a ratio of 1:2; that is, if you inhale for five seconds exhale for ten. Increase as you become more adept.

The next step is retention or a holding of the breath between the inhalation and exhalation. The retention should be double that of the exhalation so you might start with 1:4:2, two seconds inhalation, eight seconds retention and four seconds expiration. When you feel you can do more, increase your rhythm to perhaps 5:20:10 or 8:32:16.

There are other kinds of breathing exercises such as Bhramari or "beetle-droning breath," in which you exhale the air slowly making the buzzing sound of an insect. By making this droning sound you will cause a vibration to go through the head and mouth and eventually it will reverberate through the bones and the whole body. This exercise is good for the voice, increasing its resonance and making it more melodious, and is also beneficial to the circulation.

Another Pranayama is Sitkari. Fold the tongue so that the tip of it touches the upper palate. Then draw air through the mouth with a hissing sound, "si-si-si." Retain this breath as long as you can and slowly let it out through both nostrils.

Several postures are used for meditation, one of the oldest and most popular being the Padmasana or Lotus Seat. In order to assume this position bend the legs and place the right foot on the left thigh and the left foot on the right thigh, with the soles of the feet facing upward. The hands can be either in the lap, sitting on each knee with the palms upward or with the fingertips pointing to the earth. Some people also like the thumb and forefinger tips touching. The position itself has a calming effect on the mind and is also beneficial to meditation in that it brings all of the various members and currents of the body together in a more consolidated area.

If you are not yet up to the demands of the Lotus position you can probably manage Siddhasana, the pose of the spiritually enlightened; sit cross-legged, placing the left heel under the perineum and the right one above the left leg with the heel near the genitals with the foot turned upward. There is also Sukhasana or easy pose. All you do is sit on the floor in the ordinary cross-legged position, with your head, neck and trunk in a straight line.

Once you have found a comfortable seat you should begin by facing eastward or northward (hopefully you were able to place your shrine or happen to have your window in that direction). Your body should be relatively relaxed from the asanas you've just finished; and the Pranayama should have helped to still the mind. If you find you are still caught up in the mundane trivia of life, just let those thoughts flow on. Try to be detached from them, as if they were passing by on a stream and you are secure and calm on the bank nearby, watching.

This thought control, however, is one of the most difficult tasks in Yoga, and Easterners have likened the mind to a jumping monkey. But that is not all. The monkey is also intoxicated, making it all the more difficult to discipline. And then, as if that weren't enough, the monkey is bitten by a scorpion. And invaded by a demon. All this, the Easterners say, is what we have to cope with when we seek to discipline the mind. How, then, do we subdue it and bring this jumping, intoxicated, poisoned, possessed monkey under our control? You let him jump until he tires out; in time the alcohol wears off; the scorpion sting will fade; and the demon will be drowned in the spirit of your faith and peace. Finally the monkey ceases his jumping, and it is during our meditation that all this comes about, as he becomes interested in other things: mantras, affirmations, or perhaps you would like to enumerate your blessings in praise and thanks to the Divine Universal Provider in your own language. There are many things that can happen in meditation. You can talk to God or, perhaps better yet, you may want to listen. Many books have been written with prayers in English, Sanskrit and every language imaginable. Or you can just repeat the sound of the Universal Cosmic Consciousness, "Om," pronounced "A-U-M."

This book is geared toward astrology and lovers, and finding the perfect mate for you. So far you may feel we've dealt more with you than we have with love, lovers or lovemaking. However, this is where your love affair will begin. With you. Your first love affair must be with yourself, for if you don't think you're appealing and desirable nobody else ever will. If you have practiced all the exercises we've given you to bring yourself into a state of peace and love, you're sure to attract someone with like mind. Make sure you don't let anyone disturb this inner calm once you've found it and don't you disturb it yourself. The Yogis say that unpleasant, contemptuous words produce discord and bad vibrations while words uttered in peace and love create just the opposite.

The ancient Chinese *Book of Changes*, known as the *I Ching*, discourses on this subject in Hexagram No. 53, Chien/ Development (Gradual Progress):

"The development of events that lead to a girl's following a man to his home proceeds slowly. The various formalities must be disposed of before the marriage takes place. This principle of gradual development can be applied to other situations as well; it is always applicable where it is a matter of correct relationships of cooperation, as for instance in the appointment of an official. The development must be allowed to take its proper course. Hasty action would not be wise. This is also true, finally, of any effort to exert influence on others, for here too the essential factor is a correct way of development through cultivation of one's own personality. No influence such as that exerted by agitators has a lasting effect.

"Within the personality, too, development must follow the same course if lasting results are to be achieved. Gentleness that is adaptable, but at the same time penetrating, is the outer form that should proceed from inner calm.

"The very gradualness of the development makes it necessary to have perseverance, for perseverance alone prevents slow progress from dwindling to nothing."

It goes on in the section called "The Image" to conclude

that: "Thus the superior man abides in dignity and virtue, in order to improve the mores.

"No sudden influence or awakening is of lasting effect."

We mentioned earlier that we would go into Yoga and especially Tantra Yoga, the sexual aspect of the system. But obviously if, as we also said earlier, Tantrik doctrine is so esoteric that it is basically passed down from master to student, we can't expound much on that either. Then, you're probably asking, as did a popular rock and roll song a few years back, "Who, who, who, who . . . who wrote the book of love?" No one ever answered the group's question, probably because they didn't want to have to inform them that it was undoubtedly banned before it ever got to press, if anyone ever dared to attempt it in the repressed fifties. People like Reich, Freud, Jung, some of the greatest minds of the twentieth century, far from being preoccupied with the writing of the book of love, spent their time writing on why twentieth-century man was too repressed to even undertake and furthermore to master the act.

"Who, who, who, who . . . who wrote the book of love?" the group continued to ask repetitiously, as rock groups often do, apparently not aware of history, and the East; for in that ancient, sacred land it had been written thousands of years ago by Kalyana Malla, and was called the *Ananga Ranga* or *The Hindu Art of Love*. This book had been banned in the West, then treated with undue sensationalism when finally introduced. Both attitudes showed a deep misunderstanding of the work. It is basically a love manual to teach the readers how to be psychically pure and physically pleasant to each other; it was intended, when written, as a simple sincere effort to encourage monogamy and save people the monotony and satiety which so many people suffer.

On the following pages we have quoted from this book. You will notice that many of the Sanskrit names of the positions of intercourse are the same or similar to those of the Hatha postures. You will also better understand why we put so much emphasis on the agility and limberness the previous asanas provide. The Hindus maintain such pliability that they are able to assume the following positions while talking, caressing the partner, eating, drinking or even smoking a water pipe.

"There are five main Bandha or Asana—forms or postures

of congress—which appear in the following shape and each of these will require its own description successively and in due order.

"(A) Uttana-bandha (i.e., supine posture) is the great division so-called by men well-versed in the art of love, when a woman lies upon her back, and her husband sits close to her upon his hams. But is this all that can be said of it? No! no! there are eleven subdivisions:

"1. Samapada-uttana-bandha, is when the husband places his wife upon her back, raises both her legs, and placing them upon his shoulders, sits close to her and enjoys her.

"2. Nagara-uttana-bandha, is when the husband places his wife upon her back, sits between her legs, raises them both, keeping them on the other side of his waist, and thus enjoys her.

"3. Traivikrama-uttana-bandha, is when one of the wife's legs is left lying upon the bed or carpet, the other being placed upon the head of the husband, who supports himself upon both hands. This position is very admirable.

"4. Vyomapada-uttana-bandha, is when the wife, lying upon her back, raises with her hands both legs, drawing them as far back as her hair; the husband, then sitting close to her, places both hands upon her breasts and enjoys her.

"5. Smarachakrasana, or the position of the Kama's wheel, a mode very much enjoyed by the voluptuary. In this form, the husband sits between the legs of his wife, extends his arms on both sides of her as far as he can, and thus enjoys her.

"6. Avidarita is that position when the wife raises both her legs, so that they may touch the bosom of her husband, who, sitting between her thighs, embraces and enjoys her.

"7. Saumya-bandha is the name given by the old poets to a form of congress much in vogue amongst the artful students of the Kamashastra. The wife lies supine, and the husband, as usual, sits; he places both hands under her back, closely embracing her, which she returns by tightly grasping his neck.

"8. Jrimbhita-asana. In order to bend the wife's body in the form of a bow, the husband places little pillows or pads beneath her hips and head; he then raises the seat of pleasure and rises to it by kneeling upon a cushion. This is an admirable form of congress, and is greatly enjoyed by both.

"9. Veshita-asana, is when the wife lies upon her back

cross-legged, and raises her feet a little; this position is very well-fitted for those burning with desire.

"10. Venuvidarity is that in which the wife, lying upon her back, places one leg upon her husband's shoulder, and the other on the bed or carpet.

"11. Sphutma-uttana-bandha is when the husband, after insertion and penetration, raises the legs of his wife, who still lies upon her back, and joins her thighs close together.

"Here end the eleven forms of Uttana-bandha; we now proceed to the:—

"(B) Tiryak (i.e., aslant, awry posture) whose essence consists of the woman lying upon her side. Of this division, there are three subdivisions:

"1. Vinaka-tiryak-bandha is when the husband, placing himself alongside of his wife, raises one of his legs over her hip and leaves the other lying upon the bed or carpet. This asana is fitted only for practice upon a grown-up woman; in the case of a younger person, the result is by no means satisfactory.

"2. Samputa-tiryak-bandha is when both man and woman lie straight upon their sides, without any movement or change in the position of their limbs.

"3. Karkata-tiryak-bandha is when both being upon their sides, the husband lies between his wife's thighs, one under him, and the other being thrown over his flank, a little below the breast.

"Here end the three forms of the Tiryak-bandha; and, we now proceed to the:—

"(C) Upavishta (i.e., sitting) posture. Of this division there are ten subdivisions shown in the following figure:

"1. Padmasana. The husband in this favorite position sits crossed-legged upon the bed or carpet, and takes his wife upon his lap, placing his hands upon her shoulders.

"2. Upapad-asana. In this posture, whilst both are sitting, the woman slightly raises one leg by placing the hand under it, and the husband enjoys her.

"3. Vaidhurit-asana. The husband embraces his wife's neck very closely, and she does the same to him.

"4. Phanipash-asana. The husband holds his wife's feet, and the wife those of her husband.

"5. Sanyaman-asana. The husband passes both legs of his

wife under his arms at the elbow, and holds her neck with his hands.

"6. Kaurmak-asana (or the tortoise-posture). The husband must so sit that his mouth, arms, and legs touch the corresponding members of his wife.

"7. Parivartit-asana. In addition to the mutual contact of mouth, arms and legs, the husband must frequently pass both the legs of his wife under his arms at the elbow.

"8. Yugmapad-asana is a name given by the best poets to that position in which the husband sits with his legs wide apart, and, after insertion and penetration, presses the thighs of his wife together.

"9. Vinarditasana, a form possible only to a very strong man with a very light woman, he raises her by passing both her legs over his arms at the elbow, and moves her about from left to right, but not backward or forward, till the supreme moment arrives.

"10. Markatasana, is the same position as No. 9; in this, however, the husband moves the wife in a straight line away from his face, that is backward and forward, but not from side to side.

"Here end the forms of Upavishta, or sitting-posture. The next is:—

"(D) Utthita, or the standing posture which admits of three subdivisions:

"1. Janu-kuru-utthitha-bandha (that is, 'knee and elbow standing-form'), a posture which also requires great bodily strength in the man. Both stand opposite to each other; and the husband passes his two arms under his wife's knees, supporting her upon the *saignee,* or inner elbow; he then raises her as high as his waist, and enjoys her, whilst she must clasp his neck with both her hands.

"2. Hari-vikrama-utthita-bandha: in this form the husband raises only one leg of his wife, who with the other stands upon the ground. It is a position delightful to young women, who thereby soon find themselves *in gloria.*

"3. Kirti-utthita-bandha; this requires strength in the man, but not so much as is wanted for the first subdivision. The wife, clasping her hands and placing her legs round her husband's waist, hangs, as it were, to him, whilst he supports her by placing his forearms under her hips.

"Here end the forms of Utthita, or standing-posture; and we now come to the:—

"(E) Vyanta-bandha, which means congress with a woman when she is prone, that is, with the breast and stomach to the bed or carpet. Of this asana, there are only two well-known subdivisions:

"1. Dhenuka-vyanta-bandha (the cow-posture): in this position the wife places herself upon all fours, supported on her hands and feet (not her knees), and the husband, approaching from behind, falls upon her waist, and enjoys her as if he were a bull. There is much religious merit in this form.

"2. Aybha-vyanta-bandha (or Gajasawa, the elephant-posture). The wife lies down in such a position that her face, breast, stomach and thighs all touch the bed or carpet, and the husband, extending himself upon her, and bending himself like an elephant, with the small of the back much drawn in, works underneath her, and effects insertion.

"Purashayita-bandha is the reverse of what men usually practice. In this case the man lies upon his back, draws his wife upon him and enjoys her. It is especially useful when he, being exhausted, is no longer capable of muscular exertion, and when she is ungratified, being still full of the water of love. The wife must, therefore, place her husband supine upon the bed or carpet, mount upon his person, and satisfy her desires. Of this form of congress there are three subdivisions:

"1. Viparita-bandha, or 'contrary-position,' is when the wife lies straight upon the outstretched person of her husband, her breast being applied to his bosom, presses his waist with her hands, and moving her hips sharply in various directions, enjoys him.

"2. Purashayita-bhramara-bandha ('like the large bee'): in this, the wife, having placed her husband at full length upon the bed or carpet, sits at squat upon his thighs, closes her legs firmly after she has effected insertion; and, moving her waist in a circular form, churning, as it were, enjoys her husband, and thoroughly satisfies herself.

"3. Utthita-uttana-bandha. The wife, whose passion has not been gratified by previous copulation, should make her husband lie upon his back, and sitting cross-legged upon his thighs, should seize his Linga, effect insertion, and move her waist up and down, advancing and retiring; she will derive great comfort from this process.

"4. At all times of enjoying Purushayita the wife will remember that without an especial exertion of will on her part, the husband's pleasure will not be perfect. To this end she must ever strive to close and constrict the Yoni until it holds the Linga, as, with a finger,* opening and shutting at her pleasure, and finally, acting as the hand of the Gopala-girl, who milks the cow. This can be learned only by long practice, and especially by throwing the will† into the part to be affected, even as men endeavor to sharpen their hearing, and their sense of touch. While so doing, she will mentally repeat, 'Kamadeva! Kamadeva,' in order that a blessing may rest upon the undertaking. And she will be pleased to hear that the act once learned is never lost. Her husband will then value her above all women, nor would he exchange her for the most beautiful Pani (queen) in the three worlds. So lovely and pleasant to man is she who constricts."

Kalyana-Malla concludes his chapter on the internal enjoyments of love with:

"And now having duly concluded the chapter of internal enjoyments, it is good to know that if husband and wife live together in close agreement, as one soul in a single body, they shall be happy in this world, and in that to come. Their good and charitable actions will be an example to mankind, and their peace and harmony will effect their salvation. No one yet has written a book to prevent the separation of the married pair and to show them how they may pass through life in union. Seeing this, I felt compassion, and composed the treatise, offering it to the god Pandurang.

"The chief reason for the separation between the married

---

* Amongst some races the constrictor vaginae muscles are abnormally developed. In Abyssinia, for instance, a woman can so exert them as to cause pain to a man, and, when sitting upon his thighs, she can induce the orgasm without moving any other part of her person. Such an artist is called by the Arabs, "Kabbazah," literally meaning "a holder," and it is not surprising that the slave dealers pay large sums for her. All women have more or less the power, but they wholly neglect it; indeed, there are many races in Europe which have never even heard of it. To these the words of wisdom spoken by Kalyana-Malla, the poet, should be peculiarly acceptable.

† This concentration of will can be built and strengthened through the Hatha Yoga exercises previously described.

couple and the cause, which drives the husband to the embraces of strange women, and the wife to the arms of strange men, is the want of varied pleasures and the monotony which follows possession. There is no doubt about it. Monotony begets satiety, and satiety distaste for congress, especially in one or the other; malicious feelings are engendered, the husband or the wife yields to temptation, and the other follows, being driven by jealousy. For it seldom happens that the two love each other equally, and in exact proportion, therefore is the one more easily seduced by passion than the other. From such separations result polygamy, adulteries, abortions, and every manner of vice, and not only do the erring husband and wife fall into the pit, but they also drag down the names of their deceased ancestors from the place of beautified mortals, either to hell or back again upon this world. Fully understanding the way in which such quarrels arise, I have in this book shown how the husband, by varying the enjoyment of his wife, may live with her as with thirty-two different women, ever varying the enjoyment of her, and rendering satiety impossible. I have also taught all manner of useful arts and mysteries, by which she may render herself pure, beautiful and pleasing in his eyes. Let me, therefore, conclude with the verse of blessing:—

May this treatise, 'Ananga-ranga,' be beloved of man and woman, as long as the Holy River Ganges springeth from Shiva, with his wife Gauri on his left side; as long as Lakshmi loveth Vishnu; as long as Brahma is engaged in the study of the Vedas; and as long as the earth, the moon and the sun endure.

*Who are you? A dirty old man*
*I've always been since the day I began,*
*Mother and Father were dirty before me,*
*Hot or cold water has never come o'er me.*

Karma sex is little discussed in astrology books, but it bears mentioning here, we think. Briefly, the theory involved is this: in the law of Karma, the ancients state that natives of each sign will take on certain characteristics of the sign immediately preceding their Sun Sign These attributes are generally not positive ones, but weaknesses instilled in the individual which need to be overcome. Throughout life instances will arise giving one the opportunity to be rid of this Karma for good. Each experience which comes to us is something from which we can learn. Since sex is such a strong force in life, it too plays an important part in Karma. By the term Karma sex we refer to the sexual experiences one is able to have to best clear himself of negative tendencies; more specifically, it is sex involved with the type of individuals from whom we can gain the most for our total advancement. Gaining this attitude and understanding of this concept can help put any unpleasant sexual encounters we have had into a better perspective, remembering always that *you* are not your *experience.*

The Aries natives will come into life with some of the negative Karma of the preceding sign, Pisces, and to compensate for this weakness they know themselves to have, they create stubborn attitudes and in general are apt to be rebellious enough to fight windmills. To help headstrong Aries fit into a good Karma sex pattern, read the next chapter on complementary Sun Signs for positive cosmic sex expression.

The Taurus natives bring the Karma of Aries, and as a consequence may be unhappy and feel unsettled. Often they exhibit a lack of self-discipline, a self-indulgence which is the fruit of Aries' rebelliousness and self-will. To soothe the Taurus' bull-headedness, and achieve a good Karma sex pattern, read the next chapter.

Gemini people can be moody and irritable, changeable and unreliable, interested in self-gratification, which is a reflection of the Taurus Karma, brought about by the negative influence of Venus, the ruler of Taurus. To arrest these tendencies and bring about a better balance in Karma sex pattern read the next chapter.

Cancer people have inherited a moodiness and fear and an excessive emotionalism which comes from the preceding sign, Gemini's Karma. To enhance sensitive Cancer's self-esteem and balance negative feelings and achieve a good Karma sex pattern, read the next chapter.

Leo people, although strong individuals, when influenced by the negative Karma of Cancer, are apt to be subject, as are Cancer people, to the cycles of the moon. In addition they have inherited the Cancer tendency to self-pity and feelings of not being appreciated the way they think they should be. Leo has on the positive side inherited the Cancer propensity to being good with children and the Cancer aptitude for making money. For a fully developed sense of Karma sex, Leo should read the next chapter.

Virgo has grown cautious. As Leos are sunny people and thrive in the limelight, Virgos hide in the shadows, almost ashamed sometimes to show their faces, their true side to the world, as if they were repenting for the showiness and ostentation of the Leo sign's Karma. Virgo has kept the glibness of Leo and is a good talker, able to express himself well, but as Leo is an active and impetuous spender, Virgo has inherited the tendency to have monetary hang-ups. In addition, as a rebellion against the impulsiveness of Leo, Virgo has become exceedingly cautious and afraid of making necessary moves. It is for this reason most spinsters and bachelors in the world are of the sign Virgo. They are afraid of taking the risk, afraid of being shown up. In order to magnetize cool, chaste Virgo into a sexier way of life and a positive Karma sex, we suggest reading the next chapter on complementary Sun Signs for positive cosmic sex expression.

As a rebellion against the often cool qualities of Virgo, Libras have taken a step in the opposite direction and determined to have the best of everything, both in the home, and otherwise. Nothing is too good for them, and they demand the best sexual partners. But they can never quite escape the shadow of Virgo and as a result have trouble making up their minds, and try to weigh things too heavily and become vacillating individuals. To cancel out their redoubtable inheritance and establish a good Karma sex pattern, read the next chapter.

Scorpio, having been torn apart all too often under the Libra influence of weighing and balancing everything, tends to suffer from excessive emotionalism and feelings of not being oriented inwardly toward a clear concise goal. As a result they compensate by driving themselves to become very self-willed and self-determined. When they have lost their traditional Libra carry-over balance, they can collapse and end life tragically and inexplicably. They are apt to suffer acute depressions. To compensate and to establish a good Karma sex pattern, read the next chapter.

Sagittarius, revolting against the Scorpio Karma, is stubborn and determined, a fool rushing in where angels fear to tread. They like to believe they can do anything but often they overestimate their own abilities. They can take on things of which they are incapable and be caught holding the bag. To show a Sag where it's at and to establish a good Karma sex pattern, read the following chapter.

Although Capricorn is a natural businessman, he will, if influenced by the negative Karma of Sagittarius, run from responsibility and his life will come to naught. He will spend his lifetime dreaming, hallucinating and philosophizing, as is often the case with the lazy Sagittarian, and not use his Capricorn gifts for hard work. This is one of the most irreconcilable Karmas of all the signs, for it is so foreign to the true nature of the Capricorn to act thus, that he must (of needs be) suffer enormously from not realizing his true worth and capabilities. Generally these Capricorns are the ones most prone to melancholy and fits of deep depression. To offset negative propensities of Karma, and establish a good Karma sex pattern, read the next chapter.

If Aquarius has earned good Karma from Capricorn, the native will be endowed with the ability to make correct decisions, and will have wonderful intuitions and choose the correct sex partners as well as other types of associates. With negative Karma, he will carry over some Capricorn taciturnity and melancholy and seek isolation rather than using the natural Aquarian adaptability and ability to meet others graciously and well. For a good Karma sex pattern, read the next chapter.

Pisces is loaded with heavy Karma and has been called, as we said previously, the dust-bin of the Zodiac. Unfortunately they carry an excess of water, or emotion, from Aquarius, the water-bearer, which is apt to give the Pisces natives an imbalance, and to make them "two fishes swimming in opposite directions," always fighting against themselves, at war with their own natures. It is very difficult to be a developed Pisces, but when a higher type develops from this sign, they stand out as extraordinary. In order to make the most of yourself and establish a good Karma sex pattern, read the following chapter on complementary Sun Signs for positive cosmic sex expression.

*Jack Sprat*
*Could eat no fat*
*His wife could eat no lean;*
*And so, betwixt them both*
*They lick'd the platter clean.*

Complementary signs are another facet of astrology often neglected or passed over as inconsequential. Actually it is a very significant factor, as the sign directly opposite one's own sign is a polarity, and there is a reflex action formed between them. Therefore, this offers a great deal, much compensation and learning. With a native of the opposite sign we can often gain exactly what is needed and missing in our own nature, exactly what the doctor ordered to round out our development and understanding. It is a very high expression indeed when two complementary opposites blend harmoniously to form a completed whole. Sex under these conditions combines the ideal of cosmic forces, the rays being most beneficial to the natives (the rest of whose individual charts must, of course, also be compatible). To the extent that one can generalize regarding Sun Signs, the following is applicable. But may we advise you to seek a more thorough counsel by having your total chart, and that of your prospective sex partner, gone over by someone who can successfully interpret an astrological chart.

For the time being, let us content you with the following general knowledge regarding the Sun Signs and their complementary opposites, for cosmic sex:

ARIES-LIBRA: Aries lacks what Libra supplies, and vice versa. Libra is a very diplomatic and tolerant sign, seeing the best in people, encouraging them with patience. Aries on the other hand is quick to judge, impatient and intolerant. Libra devotes its artistic nature to the cultivation of the home, whereas Aries would rather be out in the world gaining adventures. Libra vacillates and has trouble making up his mind, whereas Aries always knows what he wants and is able to make wonderful snap decisions. His impulsiveness is good for Libra.

TAURUS-SCORPIO: These are both money signs but differ in their attitude of how to buy. Taurus wants to set everything just so and to be able to believe everything will continue in the same vein; he is a collector and a sedentary person. Scorpio likes to be on the move, dislikes retaining and wants to throw everything out. He desires change, and dislikes being burdened with the past. Whereas Taurus is conservative, Scorpio is extreme.

GEMINI-SAGITTARIUS: Both are mental signs and blend well together, their polarity being very beneficial and interesting together. There'll never be a dull moment, for Gemini is full of inventiveness and ideas, which Sagittarius is eager to grasp hold of and keep moving once the ball is in motion. Gemini is impersonal; Sagittarius is personal. Gemini is a critic of everyone and everything; Sagittarius is an inveterate accepter of things and people as they are.

CANCER-CAPRICORN: Cancer represents the home, Capricorn the office. Although Cancer's natural habitat is the home he is also good as a businessman and blends well with Capricorn in this respect. Capricorn is eager to acquire new things, materially speaking, and Cancer will cling to the old, never wishing to let go of the past. Capricorns have a great deal of self-sufficiency which Cancers lack; the latter always seek someone to take care of them and to lift the burdens from their shoulders while Capricorn has the ability to shoulder responsibility and can be of help to Cancer. Yet the softening influence of Cancer can help the hard-nosed Capricorn to be more humane and tolerant.

LEO-AQUARIUS: Here again we find a personal versus impersonal character meeting face to face. Leo is the personal,

Aquarius the impersonal. While Leo expresses his love for the individual, Aquarius is more prone to showing his on a humanitarian level, studying life through groups rather than learning from individuals. He has a love for ideals, whereas Leo is very specific in his emotional attachments, and demanding that he receive his due. Leo seeks fulfillment from individual contacts, and accepts things at face value, whereas Aquarius will analyze things to death. Leo never worries about the impression he is creating, Aquarius holds this as a sore spot, a bane of existence. That which is beyond his own immediate sphere of influence is of little concern to a Leo, but of vital importance to an Aquarius. Whereas Leo will pour out his affections liberally, Aquarius will often withhold and save his noble feelings for humanity.

VIRGO-PISCES: Virgo is a great detail man, but has trouble seeing the forest for the trees. Pisces on the other hand has the opposite problem: he is too immersed in the whole and unable to be practical. Virgo is always on time, Pisces is always late. Pisces people cannot be pinned down to such mundane things as a schedule since they have no sense of time. Virgo is expert in all the areas Pisces falls short. But Pisces is poetic and Virgo prosaic; therefore the Virgo has a lot to learn regarding self-expression, giving and opening up. This is often the most difficult thing for a Virgo to do, and Pisces can be of great help to him in this.

*I am a pretty wench,*
*And I come a great way hence,*
*And sweethearts I can get none:*
*But every dirty sow,*
*Can get sweethearts enow,*
*And I, pretty wench, can get never a one.*

Girls, just a few beauty tips to enhance your desirability so there'll be no question of your being able to pull in the man of your choice—and more important still, to hold him.

ARIES: You have noticeably lovely eyes, expressive and large. Being very active, you can sometimes run yourself ragged. It may seem you have inexhaustible energy but you're apt to push yourself beyond your capacity. Be sure you get enough rest—being high-strung, you need it. You burn up a lot of nervous energy and something's got to compensate for it.

TAURUS: Your hair is apt to be soft and you may have a tendency to put on weight if you're not careful. Try to add some body to your hair at the same time you're trying to lose some weight—might just be that you retain water and are apt to bloat. Still you'd best stay away from those sweets you crave so much. Try to lighten your outlook and attitudes. Beauty is as beauty does, you know.

GEMINI: You have delicate skin, prone to eruptions if you get lax with your diet. It will also freckle and wrinkle if you're not careful in the sun. Try to be more aware of your beauty, health and diet. You are certainly no gourmand, and often even underweight. You can afford generous helpings, and even desserts and snacks.

CANCER: Stay away from sweets, soft drinks, alcohol and nuts. (Bet you like to cook, too.) You are too sensitive to tolerate these things even though you crave them. Like Taurus, you too may have a tendency to retain water and to gain weight, particularly in the midsection. Your nervous stomach is another one of your weak areas, and there's no greater hindrance to beauty than nervous tension.

LEO: You are queenly, regal, and have innate dignity and presence. The sun may rule your sign, but it will ruin your fair sensitive skin, so watch out in the summertime. Make sure it's well-protected and only sunbathe at short intervals. You must also be careful of your heart since Leo rules that particular organ.

VIRGO: Your great mental capabilities give you a cool, intelligent look with a high forehead. You look best when your clothes are simple, basic and understated. You have no figure problem as a rule but you often have strange eating habits and should never indulge in food fads, fasts and crash diets, which you are prone to do.

LIBRA: Serene and poised, quiet and self-composed, you have to watch you don't spoil your naturally good skin by clogging the pores with makeup residual and/or overexposure to the elements. You were made for the fresh air; being an air sign you need the out-of-doors, but guard against too much of a good thing. For optimum health, you need to drink plenty of water. This will balance your tendency to airiness.

SCORPIO: You have an allure and magnetism, innate sex appeal, great bone structure. You must be careful of your intake of foods and alcohol. You are tempted to overindulgence in these as well as a lot of other things. For no sign can we stress moderation more than for yours, especially if you want to maintain that natural Scorpio beauty and sex appeal with which your cup runneth over.

SAGITTARIUS: You're a busy bee and thus your manifold activities may cause you to ignore or neglect beauty routines. Your health is good to begin with and usually improves with age, but you do have the tendency to be overweight, particularly in the middle, so gear your many sports and games to correct this situation. Your usual natural, wholesome, outdoorsy look usually surpasses any you could ever duplicate with makeup or plastic hairdos, so you're an inexpensive pet to keep in that respect.

CAPRICORN: You wear well and get younger every year, unless you indulge in alcohol. As a rule you are readily identifiable as a Capricorn by your triangular shaped face. You should have no major health bouts—yours is about the sturdiest and most-enduring sign in the Zodiac. You'll live long into old age with all your faculties intact, so cease worrying—one of your major problems, and there's absolutely no need for it. You must most of all be wary of nervous tension. You need lots of fresh air, being an earth sign. You'll always be able, agile, quick-witted and in possession of quick reflexes.

AQUARIUS: You have good clarity of features, skin and hair. You'll probably turn gray early but it will enhance your erudite, well-rounded personality. Your health is good and as a wife you'll prepare simple wholesome meals for your family. You might have a tendency to put on weight so try to stay involved in some kind of sporty outdoors activities. If you're a smoker, better stop. It's draining energy that's vital to your involved, always-on-the-go way of life.

PISCES: Pay attention to your hair and feet, also to your propensity toward acquiring a double chin. Take care of your health because you haven't as much strength or physical well-being as other people, due to your hypersensitivity. You should watch your diet. You have a propensity for exotic spicy foods which is the worst thing for you. This also applies to alcohol, another one of your weaknesses. You have the tendency to choose your mate unwisely, so be careful.

And now some general beauty tips that apply to all the signs, age-old, but we think useful for that "natural" look that's always in style. First of all, for daytime your makeup should conform to the outdoors, where you'll be seen under the naked light of day as well as indoors under artificial. So keep it subtle for everyday, unless it's a special occasion for which you're sprucing up. Then nothing is too bizarre for this day and age, A.M. or P.M.

We suggest you let your hair fall freely, in a natural style that fits the contour of your face. Always keep it clean and trimmed and have those split ends cleaned up too every now and then. To keep it really healthy, bend over forward from the waist and give it a brisk, vigorous brushing every day starting from the nape of the neck. Unless you're John L. Lewis, we suggest you leave the line of the eyebrow natural, with no tweezing. If you feel extra eyelashes are essential to enhance your beauty, use the short round kind that look as natural as possible. Follow whatever complexion care program your skin and/or dermatologist dictate.

Never neglect the hands and nails. They should be kept clean with nails manicured, and cream as often as is necessary each day. A little light polish is nice from time to time if it blends well with the skin's tone. The feet are important, too, and should receive a pedicure at least once a week. Always trim the cuticles and make the toenails short. A pale polish can be fun, especially in the summertime when barefoot sandals are so popular.

There are numerous exercises to keep the body in shape and we suggest for physical fitness a couple of dance or Hatha-Yoga classes every week. If you run around the house or out on errands in Swedish clogs you can help trim up the ankles and calves.

Of course, no matter what you do to the outside, the greatest beauty comes from within. Finding the right man to share her life is the most important function in every woman's life. Certainly one awaits each and every one of us somewhere, one who entered this particular cycle to accompany us on our path—it's just a matter of getting ourselves together, and then getting together with him. Maybe he's someone you already know. A lot of women today make the mistake of coming on too strong, scaring men away. It's still the gentle approach that appeals to most of them. Try to maintain a positive cheerful outlook and to develop that serene quality no man can resist. Relax, enjoy life and be optimistic about the future, despite everything the sociologists, ecologists and newscasters keep telling us. Remember, especially if you were one of the first ones to go out and buy a bomb shelter, that everyone has a bag, something he's trying to put across, and if you look hard enough, you'll probably find someone else with another game that contradicts or even voids out completely what the other has just frantically purported.

We've got a bag, too. We're women, finally getting it together and really declaring the equality that has always been innately ours. And in a world that often seems to be pulling apart at the seams, more than ever before it seems up to us to try to hold it together. The ability to do this will probably be the greatest attraction there is for frantic, hysterical twentieth-century man.

The astrologers tell us that only Libra and Taurus are ruled by Venus. We beg to differ with them here, if only in a figurative sense. It seems a woman's whole life always has been, still is and always will be dictated by this age-old Goddess of Love.

Although this is a book specifically pertaining to celestial mating, we have purposely not included a section on the arbitrary coupling of various Sun Signs since no accurate horoscope comparison can ever be based on the Sun Sign only. In synastry, or horoscope comparison, the complete horoscope of each person must be taken into consideration, the weighing of each factor in each chart against every other factor, before anything concrete can be arrived at.

Earlier we discussed each of the planets and the aspects they represent in your chart according to the time of your birth. Compatibility in the different areas represented by these aspects depends upon their relationship to the various placement of aspects in the other person's chart. For instance, if your Venus which applies to your affections and romantic inclinations is favorably related to another's Uranus which is the planet of impulsive and sometimes eruptive beginnings you two could really hit it off in a big, spontaneous way emotionally. On the other hand, should your Saturn be negatively aspected to someone's Venus, forget it. You'll never get to first base with him. If you're pursued by someone whose Jupiter, the planet of magnanimity and expansion, has contact with your Venus, you could have a materially abundant love affair; with Mercury hitting your Venus it'll be good communication; Mars against your Venus—well, that should be an earthshaking, mind-blowing sexual encounter, and so on. This also of necessity is a very mean description of chart comparison which gets much more involved when undertaken by a professional astrologer, whom we cannot urge you strongly enough to contact.

Studies are constantly being made by astrologers to determine which synchronicity of aspects is most determinant of a successful marriage. Some American astrologers say a man's ascendant conjunct the moon in a woman's horoscope makes for harmonious mating; or the woman's ascendant conjunct a man's natal Venus is a strong indication of potential conjugal longevity. Also moon conjunct sun, moon conjunct moon, or ascendant conjunct moon. It is not surprising that the influence of these three aspects—moon, sun and ascendant—are so closely linked with the determining of a successful marriage, for they are the trine of aspects which the astrologers say determine one's fate and character. In India astrologers have established thirty-six points in the chart which are analyzed and compared with the chart of the prospective mate. Out of these a minimum of eighteen should tally to merit any marriage at all, twenty-two synchronizing will mean a highly successful union, and if the couple finds that all thirty-six match, astrologers say that nothing can ever come between them.

Chart comparison can be a very valid and beneficial undertaking, whether the information sought be for upcoming business ventures, any kind of personal association or liaison, or pertaining to a romantic relationship. If the divorce statistics cited earlier in the book made any impression on you at all, and you're seriously considering the "trial marriage" before you get really hooked, how about giving this a try too?

In the meantime, on the following pages there's a brief rundown of what to expect in the romance/love area from each of the boys and girls in the Zodiac according to their Sun Signs.

*What are little girls made of?*
*What are little girls made of?*
  *Sugar and spice*
  *And all that's nice*
*That's what little girls are made of.*

Your Aries Girl: She is energetic, tireless and perceptive. Better be sure you're completely honest with her—she hates a four-flusher and will see right through phoniness. She may often take the initiative in sex, and will always respond with ardor, enthusiasm and passion as long as you are completely natural and aboveboard with her. You'll have to be on your toes to keep up with her adventurous and fiery nature.

Your Taurus Girl: Feminine, engaging and a good home-maker, she should put you at your ease immediately, for she's easygoing and friendly. She will be most receptive to your physical overtures and would prefer that you take the initiative in sex. You'll find her an excellent manager and business partner. She will make you a devoted wife.

Your Gemini Girl: She is interested in many things and talks intelligently on a variety of subjects. A born flirt, she can be very fickle. Extremely witty, she is ever in search of variety in her love affairs. She bores easily and it will take a lot from you to sustain her interest. She can become very moody if you're not satisfying all her needs. Not an easy woman to understand.

Your Cancer Girl: Sweet and docile, a homebody, who needs your affection and appreciation. She wants to rely on you to give her life meaning. She will be wonderful with the children. But she is sensitive and apt to crawl into her shell when hurt. Easily offended. Responsive and emotional about sex.

**Your Leo Girl:** Enterprising and fun-loving, with a flair for the dramatic. Sunny in disposition, she is a go-getter and gadabout with a storehouse of energy. She'll respond with ardor to your sexual overtures. Be careful she doesn't outshine you as she has the tendency to take center stage.

**Your Virgo Girl:** She is an excellent manager and cook. All is in order in her life and her environment. The most organized woman you can find. Unless her Venus, ascendant and moon are placed in a fire sign, she will be cool and not as eager as another woman you might find regarding lovemaking.

**Your Libra Girl:** A born homemaker who loves beauty and balance. She despises vulgarity and scenes, prefers men who show their appreciation of her charming and warm nature. She is not the best shopper as she overspends. Fond of luxury, her taste here carries over to sex, where she is warm and voluptuous.

**Your Scorpio Girl:** She is aggressive and demanding, responding with passion. She can be extremely jealous and possessive, overbearing and domineering. She needs a man to subdue her, and you will have to be quite a man to handle her difficult moods.

**Your Sagittarius Girl:** A joy to be with. Easygoing and fun-loving, she delights in chitchat and is always entertaining and amusing. In matters of sex, she first needs to feel your companionship, then will be eager to accommodate. She's a born flirt and doesn't settle down easily.

**Your Capricorn Girl:** She will provide you with the stimulus you need to succeed in life. Ambitious, practical and down-to-earth, she can spot a phony from a distance and will stand for no nonsense. Earthy and lusty, she'll be with you all the way if you have talent for lovemaking.

Your Aquarius Girl: Vital and interested in all areas of life. Well-balanced and wholesome, she is affectionate and kind, considerate and helpful. She will welcome your lovemaking, responding with the appreciation of her airy nature. Sex has to first be mental for her before it can move to other areas. Often it rests on the mental plane, as her emotions and physical nature sometimes lie buried.

Your Pisces Girl: She will need a great demonstration of devotion from you as she is insecure and often feels inadequate. She is romantic and sometimes gets very depressed. But when you make her feel good she will respond with a great depth of feeling and emotional display.

*What are little boys made of?*
*What are little boys made of?*
*Frogs and snails*
*And puppy dog tails*
*That's what little boys are made of.*

Your Aries Man: Dynamic, never a dull moment, enthusiastic, can be temperamental, he is honest, passionate, faithful with the right woman.

Your Taurus Man: Loves food, is both a gourmet and chef, can put on pounds if he's not careful. He is very possessive and protective, fond of giving advice; he is a home-lover and collector. Although he himself is possessive, he will not care for this quality in a woman.

Your Gemini Man: Great sense of humor, he's hard to pin down, very elusive. Once you land him, if you do, it will be hard to keep him. He has a dual nature, loves to be on the go and moving. He likes variety, can't stand boredom. He despises possessiveness and jealousy in a woman. He is not always truthful.

Your Cancer Man: Home-loving, a success at business, good wage earner, very sensitive, sympathetic, understanding, but moody and is affected by the four phases of the moon. He is emotional, hypercritical, fussy, has great need of affection.

Your Leo Man: He is passionate, romantic, likes to dominate and be in control; good money earner, possessive, jealous,

243

warm, entertaining, loses his temper easily, generous, adventurous.

Your Virgo Man: He is a perfectionist, apt to be fussy and critical, a born bachelor even when married, will not be easy to land but the best way to try is by appealing to his mind.

Your Libra Man: Prone to marriage and to remarriage. He is practical, charming, whimsical, lacks common sense, a dreamer with many schemes in his head that never materialize. He's a good lover, loves luxury and the fine things of life. He is generous, easily bored, diplomatic, hates scenes— he is sensual.

Your Scorpio Man: Secretive, passionate, sexy, strong, restless, elegant, self-willed, exciting, jealous, suspicious and sensuous.

Your Sagittarius Man: Idealistic, enjoys being a bachelor, likes freedom, many women instead of one, loves travel, sports, the out-of-doors, politics, gambling, horses and cards. He loves to philosophize and has one of the great roving eyes of the Zodiac. One thing he is without is jealousy, which is maddening to many women. His motto is live and let live.

Your Capricorn Man: He is practical, orderly, conservative, dignified, critical, hard-working—has no weight problems, hates to be pursued.

Your Aquarius Man: Not greatly prone to marriage but a good friend, a free soul, unpredictable, moody, a man of worldly interests, a mental type, kind and generous, not overly passionate but warm and giving, considerate, unpossessive and not jealous. Liberal, fair-minded.

Your Pisces Man: Sensual, idealistic, spiritual, empathetic, apt to be lazy at times. He procrastinates; he is sympathetic, kind, might have trouble bringing home the bread because his sensitive nature makes him frightened of the outside world at times, besides which he can be lazy.

*As your bright and tiny spark,*
*Lights the traveler in the dark,—*
*Though I know not what you are,*
*Twinkle, Twinkle, Little Star.*

In conclusion we would like to say we hope we've been able to somehow enrich your life with this book and bring you a little closer to that special dream your particular pattern of the astral bodies has outlined for you. There will be those who will scoff at you as you seek, especially into the world of the esoteric and occult. However, suffice it to assume that many of these same people who are putting you down, in your quest, hope to attain much of the happiness you're after, but perhaps dare not even think of having it now, and are saving it for the hereafter. Others who will discourage you are already realizing and enjoying a lot of the things of which you now dream. And so at every turn the sign will say, "From here on, you must proceed alone."

As you look back longingly at those you leave behind in your venture, remember Gibran's words: "For life goes not backward, nor tarries with yesterday." Hopefully you will one day meet on your Journey your heart's fulfillment, your divinely ascribed soulmate, whose pleasure it will be to pursue that similar goal with you, hand in hand. Before that time, you may stumble and falter many times as so many have before you. But it's out there and if you keep looking you're certain to find it. We were all put here for a purpose, no matter how many excuses and cop-outs we may find to ever begin to try to discern what it is.

"Know thyself," Socrates counseled, and yet we find ourselves surrounded by people who in their quest choose degradation, deprivation and self-destruction in an effort to avoid confronting the glorious truth of who they really are. So afraid are we, it seems, of the glory and grandeur of our destinies—almost as frightened as we are of love itself. Still, we must try to remember that what it is we are looking for, we are looking with.

For the rest of you, the ones who have already accepted that you have not made this trip for naught, go out and find your reason and purpose for living, your Karma for this incarnation, the meaning behind your life's function. When you do, look at it face to face, and say, "I'm going to get you!" and then go after it and don't stop until you do!

## *Invest $6.95 in a better marriage.*

Every year, one half million American marriages break up. Very often because of sexual ignorance, frustration, boredom, and apathy.

It doesn't have to happen. Not to you.

You can enjoy more sexual satisfaction. You can know the secret of woman's "cycle of desire."

You can enjoy more sexual freedom.

A Marriage Manual is a tactful, illustrated guide that delves into every aspect of the art of marriage from the first sex act to Vatsyayana's Kama Sutra. It has already sold three-quarters of a million copies.